The Imagination in Hume's Philosophy

Edinburgh Studies in Scottish Philosophy

Series Editor: Gordon Graham
Center for the Study of Scottish Philosophy, Princeton Theological Seminary

Scottish Philosophy Through the Ages

This new series will cover the full range of Scottish philosophy over five centuries – from the medieval period through the Reformation and Enlightenment periods, to the nineteenth and early twentieth centuries.

The series will publish innovative studies on major figures and themes. It also aims to stimulate new work in less intensively studied areas, by a new generation of philosophers and intellectual historians. The books will combine historical sensitivity and philosophical substance which will serve to cast new light on the rich intellectual inheritance of Scottish philosophy.

Editorial Advisory Board

Angela Coventry, University of Portland, Oregon
Fonna Forman, University of San Diego
Alison McIntyre, Wellesley College
Alexander Broadie, University of Glasgow
Remy Debes, University of Memphis
John Haldane, University of St Andrews and Baylor University, Texas

Books available
Adam Smith and Rousseau: Ethics, Politics, Economics edited by Maria Pia
    Paganelli, Dennis C. Rasmussen and Craig Smith
Thomas Reid and the Problem of Secondary Qualities by Christopher A. Shrock
Hume's Sceptical Enlightenment by Ryu Susato
The Imagination in Hume's Philosophy: The Canvas of the Mind by Timothy
    M. Costelloe

Books forthcoming
*Adam Ferguson and the Idea of Civil Society: Moral Science in the Scottish
    Enlightenment* by Craig Smith
Essays on Hume, Smith and the Scottish Enlightenment by Christopher Berry
Eighteenth-Century Scottish Aesthetics: Not Just a Matter of Taste by Rachel
    Zuckert

www.edinburghuniversitypress.com/series/essp

The Imagination in Hume's Philosophy

The Canvas of the Mind

Timothy M. Costelloe

EDINBURGH
University Press

For Amy, whose fancy sometimes roams

Edinburgh University Press is one of the leading university presses in the UK. We publish academic books and journals in our selected subject areas across the humanities and social sciences, combining cutting-edge scholarship with high editorial and production values to produce academic works of lasting importance. For more information visit our website: edinburghuniversitypress.com

© Timothy M. Costelloe, 2018

Edinburgh University Press Ltd
The Tun – Holyrood Road
12(2f) Jackson's Entry
Edinburgh EH8 8PJ

Typeset in 11/13 Adobe Sabon by
Servis Filmsetting Ltd, Stockport, Cheshire

A CIP record for this book is available from the British Library

ISBN 978 1 4744 3639 7 (hardback)
ISBN 978 1 4744 3641 0 (webready PDF)
ISBN 978 1 4744 3642 7 (epub)

The right of Timothy M. Costelloe to be identified as the author of this work has been asserted in accordance with the Copyright, Designs and Patents Act 1988, and the Copyright and Related Rights Regulations 2003 (SI No. 2498).

Contents

Acknowledgements

This book has been a long time in the writing. The ideas at the heart of it were first aired, in rudimentary and tentative form, at a colloquium in the Department of Philosophy at the College of William & Mary in the autumn of 2005, and presented later in St Andrews, Scotland, in the summer of 2007 as part of an NEH seminar, 'Aesthetics of the Scottish Enlightenment and Beyond', organised by Paul Guyer and Rachel Zuckert; they also received an initial formulation in a published article ('Hume's Phenomenology of the Imagination', *Journal of Scottish Philosophy*, 5: 1 (2007), pp. 31–45). I would like to thank both Miriam McCormick, who responded to the paper at William & Mary, and the general audiences on both occasions for their thoughtful questions and useful comments. I first wrote portions of the book while an Alexander von Humboldt Research Fellow in the Department der Philosophie at Maximilians-Universität München in 2006 and as a visiting scholar at Northwestern University in 2008–9. My thanks to Günter Zöller in Munich and Rachel Zuckert in Evanston for helping to arrange my visits and for being such gracious hosts, and to the Humboldt Stiftung for their financial and institutional support. I am grateful to the College of William & Mary for releasing me from my usual teaching and administrative duties so that I might take up the Humboldt Fellowship, and for their support in the form of scheduled semester research leaves both in 2008–9, when I visited Northwestern, and again in 2015–16, under the aegis of which I was able largely to complete my work on the manuscript. The criticisms, comments and suggestions of the anonymous reviewers who read the manuscript have proved invaluable. Not only did they save me from committing a number of embarrassing errors, but their remarks also enabled me to make many improvements, both large and small, to the book as a whole.

Any remaining errors, embarrassing or otherwise, are my responsibility alone.

Some of the material in Chapters 4 and 5 has appeared in contributions I made to two collections of papers on Hume: 'Fact and Fiction: Memory and Imagination in Hume's Approach to History and Literature', in Mark G. Spencer (ed.), *David Hume: Historical Thinker, Historical Writer* (University Park, Pennsylvania: The Pennsylvania State University Press, 2013), pp. 181–99, and 'Hume as Historian', in Alan Bailey and Dan O'Brien (eds), *The Continuum Companion to Hume* (London: Continuum Publishing, 2012), pp. 364–76. I would like to thank Bloomsbury Continuum, an imprint of Bloomsbury Publishing, and The Pennsylvania State University Press for permission to reproduce the relevant material.

Preface

There is scarcely any subject broached by David Hume in the course of his philosophical writings that is not touched in some way by the faculty he calls 'the imagination' and the principles that he takes to govern it. The imagination makes its appearance early in the *Treatise*, when Hume is expounding his theory of ideas, and remains his constant companion to the last, where, in a final act of recognition, he acknowledges that all his anatomical labours might be for naught should the 'hideous' details he has uncovered not be smoothed over and made 'engaging to the eye and the imagination'. It falls to the painter – that master of representation, trader in images and purveyor of effect – to 'set [objects] more at a distance' by shifting the focus of the philosophical eye from the 'minute views of things' to one of general outlines and surfaces across which eye and imagination might move more easily (T 3.3.6.6/SBN 621). In the reflections that make up his Appendix, moreover, recognition turns to capitulation: here, Hume admits defeat in rendering intelligible the mysteries of 'self' and 'substance', ideas in which the intrigues of the imagination are so deeply implicated that even Hume's considerable genius (or so he claims) cannot root them out. He pleads the 'privilege of a sceptic' in the face of a 'difficulty ... too hard for [his] understanding' (T. App.21/SBN 636). One is reminded here of Hume's memorable battle earlier with the demon of 'total scepticism' at the end of Book 1, with the philosopher, in the famous image, on his weather-beaten vessel heading into the immense depths of philosophy with only the strangest and most unexpected of bedfellows for company: the imagination, the bottom upon which Hume's line (to borrow from John Locke's earlier nautical metaphor) sounds. The imagination provides Hume with the fundamental principle upon which philosophy and common life rest (the 'quality', 'seemingly so trivial', through which the 'mind enlivens some ideas beyond others' [T 1.4.7.3/SBN 265]), and offers the sole hope of escaping his apparently crippling doubts (we are saved from total scepticism only by a 'singular and seemingly trivial property of the fancy' [1.4.7.7/SBN 268]).

The prominence of the imagination in Hume's philosophy has not been lost on his readers, who have effectively agreed with E. J. Furlong's remark, made in 1961, that Hume is 'constantly referring to imagination', so often, in fact, that it becomes his 'universal remedy', for which he reaches to treat problems that other philosophers solve 'by recourse to reason or intellect'. Hume, Furlong observes, assigns to the faculty 'unprecedented functions' and gives it a 'star role' to play (Furlong, *Imagination* [London: Allen and Unwin, 1961], p. 96). Subsequent writers might take issue with the sweep of this assessment, but few would dispute either the extent to which Hume relies on the imagination or the demands he makes on it compared with his predecessors and contemporaries. The prominent place the imagination occupies in Hume's philosophy is certainly striking enough to have aroused interest in and demanded comment from generations of readers, and recent years in particular have witnessed a gradual but steady accumulation of a substantial body of commentary, both on his view of the faculty and the ways it is manifested in various aspects of his thinking.

Interest in the subject notwithstanding, articles, papers or chapters devoted specifically to Hume's concept of imagination are rare gems, and book-length studies priceless jewels. Of the former, earlier (and not all necessarily sympathetic) treatments by Charles Hendel (1925), H. H. Price (1940), Norman Kemp Smith (1941), J. A. Passmore (1952), Furlong (1961) and Robert Sokolowski (1968) stand out, along with more recent contributions by Gerhard Streminger (1980), Eva Brann (1991), Beryl Logan (1993) and Douglas Long (1998). The imagination has also received close attention in the course of studies that focus on other aspects of Hume's thought, notably the contributions made by Don Garrett (2015 and 1997), Peter Kail (2007) and David Owen (1999), and it has been given a prominent place in the studies by Ryu Susato (2015) and Wayne Waxman (1994). Donald Ainslie (2015) provides perhaps the most detailed and extensive treatment of the role of imagination in recent scholarship by focusing on the infamously difficult sections of Book 1 of the *Treatise*, where

Hume broaches the issues of, inter alia, time and space, identity and continued existence. Of the book-length studies devoted specifically to the subject, there are only three monographs to date: W. C. Gore's *The Imagination in Spinoza and Hume: A Comparative Study in the Light of Some Recent Contributions to Psychology* (1902); Jan Wilbanks' *Hume's Theory of Imagination* (1968); and Mary Banwart's *Hume's Imagination* (1994). Of these, Wilbanks' study is by far the most systematic and penetrating, and despite being some five decades old and thus oblivious to any interpretive advances made in the interim, it remains a valuable resource and required reading for anybody interested in the subject.

It would be an exaggeration and potentially misleading, however, to conclude from the commentary that Hume has a 'theory' of imagination, if by that one means a complete and formal classification of the faculty and its powers along with a conscious and systematic application of them; one would search Hume's work in vain for such an animal. This might explain, at least in part, why the literature has tended to treat Hume's imagination in a piecemeal way, commentators being content mostly to rouse it from slumber for purposes of completing some specific task of interpretation: to elucidate the theory of ideas, reconstruct Hume's account of the self, explain his view of sympathy, untangle his difficult views on religion, or disambiguate mitigated scepticism from its conceptual kin, to cite a few examples of oft-discussed areas where the imagination looms large. While acknowledging that attention has been paid to the subject, it is not inaccurate, then, to describe the secondary literature as offering a collection of partial treatments, pieces of a whole, elements of a story still to be told; nowhere does one find a sustained attempt to elucidate the powers and principles Hume assigns the imagination, and to explore the various way he applies them in the course of his various inquiries.

From this lack in the literature the current study takes its inspiration, in pursuit of a threefold aim: to demonstrate that Hume has a coherent concept of the imagination; to formulate the principles he consistently cites that give the faculty its motion and distinctive character; and to demonstrate, by turns, how it finds its way, more or less explicitly, into his treatment of everything into which his philosophical spirit passes: metaphysics, morals and politics, aesthetics, history, religion and the nature and practice of philosophy itself. I take this to be a relatively modest undertaking (though neither small nor insubstantial) and clearly circumscribed at its limits: it is not primarily an attempt to employ the imagination thus understood in some strategic offensive decisively to clear away stubborn contradictions or to solve puzzles that continue to occupy some of Hume's interpreters. Campaigns of this sort rarely, if ever, have their desired effect, and anything that claims to be the last word on a subject is always taken as an invitation for more to be said. That is not to say that the current study does not offer any new illumination of the issues it touches, and my hope is that focusing on the imagination does open a door to Hume's thought that might otherwise remain closed. Readers, however, who seek ultimate explanations in what follows will meet with frustration and disappointment, although I do hope that they will find instead something close to Hume's own way of philosophising, namely, a genuine effort to reveal and articulate the complicated and not altogether coherent picture of the imagination that Hume paints, from his own imagination no less, for those who engage his work and thought.

To capture the picture of the imagination that emerges, the metaphor of a canvas seems most apt. Hume himself does not describe the imagination in this way, though it is well known that he appeals in various contexts to the metaphors of painting, gilding, staining and the like. For the imagination, he chooses instead the image of an 'empire' in which the imagination has 'great authority over our ideas' (T Abs. 35/SBN 662); a 'universe' within ourselves that sets the limits of our world (T 1.2.6.8/SBN 67–8); and part of the mental scenery of the mind, which is a 'kind of theatre, where several perceptions successively make their appearance; pass, re-pass, glide away and mingle in an infinite variety of postures and situations' (T 1.4.6.4/SBN 253). These metaphors of political power, space and performance serve their purposes well, but they are confined to the specific contexts in which Hume deploys them: to underline the importance of the 'principles of association' that unite ideas (T Abs. 35/SBN 662); to emphasise that all our ideas are ultimately formed from perceptions we have 'within ourselves' (T 1.2.6.8/SBN 67); and to characterise how, in the context of personal identity, 'successive perceptions only . . . constitute the mind' (T 1.4.6.4/SBN 253). None of these, however, captures the fundamentally creative element that lies at the heart of the imagination and – what is included in that concept – the curious mix of order and disorder, calculation and spontaneity, careful study and inexplicable genius that accompanies any great artistic endeavour.

The image of a canvas, by contrast, and the implied presence of a painter who works upon it, reflects nicely the inventiveness of the faculty and the simultaneously active and passive elements that Hume discovers in it.

Indeed, we can observe that, generally, Hume's imagination is a Janus-faced creature, and that he comes to know it as such goes a good way towards explaining the many guises it adopts as Hume puts it to work, as a Prospero to his Ariel, in the science of man: it is variously hedonistic, frivolous, beguiling, lazy, duplicitous, unreliable, self-contradictory, ubiquitous, elusive and inspiring, but always, if it can be said to have an underlying character, the canvas of the mind where one finds displayed in brilliant colours the complex of impressions and ideas that fill our waking and sleeping hours. Throughout Hume's writing, the imagination appears as both friend and foe, supporter and detractor, creator and destroyer, untrustworthy yet indispensable, a thing so common, commonplace, ordinary or everyday – 'trivial', to use again one of Hume's favourite epithets – that it is hardly credible, embarrassing even, to admit it as the basis of our most deeply held beliefs, existential categories, revered political institutions and cherished social practices.

If I could choose one thing that the reader might take from what follows, it would be this: that, for Hume, the imagination is a condition of all we hold dear, and, shocking as it might be to learn, the solidity of our lives, the sanity of our conceptions, and our general faith in the order of the world follow not primarily the cool dictates of reason but from the fancy, which, once warmed, is inclined to wander the paths of pleasure, wherever they may lead. Whatever route it takes, however, this faculty works ceaselessly – sometimes overtly, often secretly, but ever presently – and, on balance, Hume teaches us, this is a fact for which we should all be immensely grateful.

T. M. C.
Williamsburg, VA

List of Abbreviations

DNR *Dialogues Concerning Natural Religion*. In *Dialogues Concerning Natural Religion and Other Writings on Religion*, ed. Dorothy Coleman (Cambridge: Cambridge University Press, 2007). Citations are given according to part and paragraph.

E *Essays: Moral, Political, and Literary*, ed. Eugene F. Miller (Indianapolis, IN: Liberty Fund, 1985).

EHU *Enquiry Concerning Human Understanding*, ed. Tom L. Beauchamp (Oxford: Oxford University Press, 1999). Citations are given according to section and paragraph, followed by page numbers to *Enquiries Concerning Human Understanding and Concerning the Principles of Morals, Reprinted from the 1777 Edition with Introduction and Analytical Index by L. A. Selby-Bigge* (Oxford: Clarendon Press, [1888] 1974) (SBN).

EPM *Enquiry Concerning the Principles of Morals*, ed. Tom L. Beauchamp (Oxford: Oxford University Press, 1998). Citations are given according to section and paragraph, followed by page numbers to *Enquiries Concerning Human Understanding and Concerning the Principles of Morals, Reprinted from the 1777 Edition with Introduction and Analytical Index by L. A. Selby-Bigge* (Oxford: Clarendon Press, [1888] 1974) (SBN).

H *The History of England, From the Invasion of Julius Caesar to the Revolution in 1688*, based on the edition of 1778, with the author's last corrections and improvements, 6 vols, ed. William B. Todd (Indianapolis, IN: Liberty Fund, 1983).

L *The Letters of David Hume*, ed. J. Y. T. Greig, 2 vols (Oxford: Oxford University Press, 1969). Citations are given according to volume and page number.

NHR   *The Natural History of Religion.* In *A Dissertation on the Passions; The Natural History of Religion: A Critical Edition*, ed. Tom L. Beauchamp (Oxford: Clarendon Press, 2007). Citations are given according to part and paragraph.

T   *A Treatise of Human Nature*, ed. David Fate Norton and Mary Norton (Oxford: Oxford University Press, 2001). Citations are given according to book, part, section and paragraph, followed by page numbers to *A Treatise of Human Nature, with an Analytical Index by L. A. Selby-Bigge,* 2nd edn with text revised and notes by P. H. Nidditch (Oxford: Clarendon Press, [1888] 1978) (SBN).

Series Editor's Introduction

It is widely acknowledged that the Scottish Enlightenment of the eighteenth century was one of the most fertile periods in British intellectual history, and that philosophy was the jewel in its crown. Yet, vibrant though this period was, it occurred within a long history that began with the creation of the Scottish universities in the fifteenth century. It also stretched into the nineteenth and twentieth centuries, as those universities continued to be a culturally distinctive and socially connected system of education and inquiry.

While the Scottish Enlightenment remains fertile ground for philosophical and historical investigation, these other four centuries of philosophy also warrant intellectual exploration. The purpose of this series is to maintain outstanding scholarly study of great thinkers like David Hume, Adam Smith and Thomas Reid, alongside sustained exploration of the less familiar figures who preceded them and the impressive company of Scottish philosophers, once celebrated, now neglected, who followed them.

Gordon Graham

Ever let the Fancy roam,
Pleasure never is at home:
At a touch sweet Pleasure melteth,
Like to bubbles when rain pelteth;
Then let wingèd Fancy wander
Through the thought still spread beyond her:
Open wide the mind's cage-door,
She'll dart forth, and cloudward soar.

John Keats, 'Fancy' (written 1818–19, published 1820)

The *imagination* of man is naturally sublime, delighted with whatever is remote and extraordinary, and running, without controul, into the most distant parts of space and time, in order to avoid the objects, which custom has rendered too familiar to it.

David Hume, *An Enquiry Concerning Human Understanding* (1751)

Hume's Imagination

Hume's view of the imagination and its powers is an amalgam of elements that can be traced back from the systems of the late seventeenth and early eighteenth centuries, through Renaissance and medieval philosophy to the Ancients, primarily to Plato's *Symposium* and *Republic* and to Aristotle's *Poetics* and *De Anima*. Hume's originality in this area lies less in the contributions he makes to the philosophical concept of the imagination per se than in the use he makes of it for his own purposes, employing it as a resource when developing positions on various explananda that compose the body of his philosophical system. As I noted in the preface, however, Hume cannot be said to have any theory or clearly articulated model of the imagination and, for that reason, one has to form some picture of it by extracting the powers he attributes to it from the various contexts in which he applies them. To form such a picture and a terminology to go with it is the aim of this first chapter.

We begin by considering Hume's own use of the term 'imagination', before delineating its main principles or powers (terms I use interchangeably) and situating them in the context of Hume's contemporaries and immediate forbears in the early-modern period: its 'mimetic' power to copy or represent and its 'productive' power to combine ideas and create new ones. At the heart of this latter power, moreover, Hume identifies a hedonistic tendency that inclines the imagination always to seek and make an easy and smooth transition among ideas in order to form a union or complete a whole, from which it derives pleasure. Having delineated its powers, we turn to the errors the imagination is liable to make and to the belief-like states (or lack thereof) that accompany them: 'mistakes' under its mimetic power and 'fictions' under its productive. In subsequent chapters we will draw on this schema in order to show that, and how Hume's view of the imagination plays a central role in his approach to metaphysics, morals and politics, aesthetics, history, religion and the practice of philosophy.

Hume's Use of the Term 'Imagination'

While Hume appeals to the imagination a great deal, he spends scant time explaining what he means by the term, the only formal definition he provides being brief and by way of a contrast with memory: it is the faculty by which we 'repeat our impressions' in such a way that they lose their 'first vivacity' (T 1.1.3.1/SBN 8). Hume's brevity in explaining how he uses 'imagination' is complicated by the fact that he associates the attendant faculty closely with 'reason', 'understanding' and 'memory', terms that have themselves been the occasion of long-standing and ongoing interpretive debate. In the case of 'imagination', some have solved Hume's apparent inconsistencies by insisting that he is committed to certain views (such as equating thinking and imagining) even if he does not always acknowledge it, while others are willing to put it down to simple terminologically infelicity.[1] Another possibility is that Hume represents a break in the tradition, insofar as he criticises and rejects the model of early-modern logic and faculty psychology but lacks a fully formed alternative vocabulary to replace it. What appears as inconsistency and contradiction is, then, really a side effect of trying to address familiar philosophical issues while resisting the parameters traditionally used to do so, especially – as David Owen has argued persuasively – the tendency to treat 'reason' as a special, independent, master category under which the other faculties are dutifully arraigned. While Hume needs 'substantive concepts' or 'faculty terms' such as imagination, memory and reason for 'ease of exposition', Owen observes, they actually 'carry baggage that is against the whole spirit of his theory', namely, that, in the final analysis, there are simply 'ideas and impressions that can be classified in various ways'.[2] If John Laird's much less recent assessment of the tradition and Hume's place in it is accurate, Owen's proposal should come as no great surprise. Laird observes how Thomas Hobbes, René Descartes and Nicolas Malebranche also 'regarded the "imagination" as a very extensive faculty', so that Hume's 'use of the term imagination, including its alliance with fancy, memory, and prudential "understanding", was in accordance with tradition' and the 'general literature' of the time. Given that Pico della Mirandola used reason as an 'intermediary between phatansia and intellectus . . . Hume's inclusion of the "understanding" and of a sort of "reasoning" in the scope of "imagination" need not be regarded as an utter innovation'.[3] Hume certainly continues to employ the language of faculty talk quite unselfconsciously, and he often seems more interested in the origin and employment of terms than in rejecting the use of them per se, as in his observation of 'faculty' (along with 'occult quality') as an 'invention' of ancient philosophers, really an 'illusion' that at bottom signifies nothing. Such corruptions, moreover, still trade on a prior meaning that is 'really significant and intelligible' (T 1.4.3.10/SBN 224). Hume appears untroubled by faculty talk in this latter sense, and I shall follow his lead.

In the case of the imagination, at least, Hume offers his readers some direction in a well-known and much-discussed footnote in the *Treatise*. The final version appears to have been something of an afterthought, and one wonders why he relegated such an important point of terminological and conceptual clarification to such a relatively obscure place at the outset. The note originally appeared fairly late in the work, at T 2.2.7.6 (the end of the section entitled 'Of compassion'), and, one assumes, being unhappy with its form and placement, he took the trouble to remove it and incorporate a revised version into a longer note inserted in Book I (T 1.3.9.18n22, 'Of the effects of other relations and other habits') after the work had already gone to print. It was added to the text by replacing the original leaf with a new one (called a 'cancel'), which, even by Hume's standard of excessive revision, seems like a good deal of trouble to go to.[4] The original note reads as follows:

> To prevent all ambiguity, I must observe, that where I oppose imagination to the memory, I mean in general the faculty that presents our fainter ideas. In all other places, and particularly when it is oppos'd to the understanding, I understand the same faculty, excluding only our demonstrative and probable reasonings. (SBN 371n)[5]

The revised version deletes the reference to the understanding and adds language concerning imagination in a 'larger or more limited sense'. Hume obviously intended this as an elaboration and a clarification of the earlier note, but the substance of the distinction appears unchanged:

> In general we may observe, that as our assent to all probable reasonings is founded on the vivacity of ideas, it resembles many of those whimsies and prejudices, which are rejected under the opprobrious character of being the offspring of the imagination. By this expression it appears that the word, *imagination*, is commonly us'd in two different senses; and tho' nothing be more contrary to true philosophy, than this inaccuracy, yet in the following reasonings I have often been oblig'd to fall into it. When I oppose the imagination to the memory, I mean the faculty, by which we form our fainter ideas. When I oppose it to reason, I mean the same faculty, excluding only our demonstrative and probable reasonings. When I oppose it to neither, 'tis indifferent whether it be taken in the larger or more limited sense, or at least the context will sufficiently explain the meaning. (T 1.3.9.18n22/SBN 118–19n1)

'Imagination', in the 'larger' or wider sense, refers to the faculty 'by which we form our fainter ideas', that is to say, how we come by *all* our ideas except those that originate with the faculty of memory. The latter, non-memory ideas, are distinguished by being better-preserved versions of the originals they copy and by having greater force and vivacity than those of imagination. Given its width (all ideas except those concerning memory), this sense of imagination must include, in some way, both the inferential faculty of 'reason' (concerned with 'demonstrable and probable reasonings') and 'understanding', the faculty concerned with 'ways of conceiving our objects' (T 1.3.7n20/SBN 97n). As Don Garrett argues persuasively, since understanding 'itself turns out to be a set of operations of the imagination' and reason 'itself a particular *manner* of having ideas of the imagination', both faculties are features or aspects of the 'representational faculty of imagination', and thus identified with the imagination in the wider sense.[6] When Hume elsewhere describes 'understanding' as the 'general and more establish'd properties of the imagination' (T 1.4.7.7/SBN 267), he presumably has this sense in mind; the same goes for the identification of imagination with the 'more frivolous properties of our thought and conception' (T 3.2.3n71.1/SBN 504n1); the otherwise baffling reference to 'imagination or understanding, call it which you please' (T 2.3.9.10/SBN 440); and the proposition, made without further comment, that the 'memory, senses, and understanding are . . . all of them founded on the imagination, or the vivacity of our ideas' (T 1.4.7.3/SBN 265). In the latter case, Hume does seem to treat the options, as Thomas Holden observes, as 'really a distinction without a difference',[7] an observation cemented by Hume's comment that we do not have 'any idea but what is ... produc'd' in the 'universe of the imagination' (T 1.2.6.8/SBN 68).

Imagination, in Hume's more limited or narrower sense, on the other hand, refers to the same faculty – the one that forms non-memory ideas – but is intended to exclude these ideas that are obtained through the inferential faculty of 'reason' that discovers 'relations ... which two or more objects bear to each other' (T 1.3.2.2/SBN 73), be they a priori (demonstrative reasoning) or on the basis of matter of fact (probable reasoning). Reason is included in the wider sense of imagination because it is one way in which we form our non-memory ideas, but it is excluded from the narrower sense where Hume is emphasising other various non-inferential ways in which the imagination forms ideas. Needless to say, so far as understanding is identified with reason in terms of the 'general and more establish'd properties of the imagination', it too will fall outside Hume's narrower sense.[8]

Two observations are in order at this point. First, assuming that this is an accurate account of the senses of 'imagination' Hume had in mind, it remains unclear how seriously he takes it (or intends it to be taken) as reflecting his actual use of terminology in the *Treatise*. Even in its revised form, the footnote is hardly a model of perspicuous exposition, and carries with it the sense of being a somewhat rushed affair, a sense heightened by knowing the circumstances of its final composition and inclusion in the work. What force it contains, moreover, is enervated further by Hume's parting and remarkably casual invitation to the reader to take the term in either sense when it is opposed explicitly to neither, and otherwise simply to rely on context 'sufficiently [to] explain the meaning'. Neither option bodes well in using the footnote as a reliable guide to Hume's terminology.

This has not prevented some readers, however, from seeking and finding a principled use of 'imagination' and distinguishing it from its close kin, 'fancy'. This appears to originate with Norman Kemp Smith's proposal to read Hume as using fancy to refer to the 'faculty of "feigning"' and imagination for 'signifying "vivacity of conception"', what Kemp Smith later calls Hume's 'very special' use of the term as opposed to 'imagination' as 'ordinarily understood'.[9] Others have followed Kemp Smith's lead[10] and have even equated the 'trivial' workings of the imagination with the 'essential',[11] as if Hume considered the former 'trifling, inconsiderable, unimportant, or slight' rather than 'common, commonplace, ordinary, or everyday' (to quote the Oxford English Dictionary), the emphasis he intends when stressing the profound importance and necessity of the imagination and its principles without which, as Barry Stroud puts it, 'we could not think at all'.[12] If there is a clear line to be drawn between imagination and fancy, it is much closer to David Miller's more tentative observation that Hume 'sometimes' refers to 'fancy' as a way to distinguish the 'arbitrary' from the 'rule-governed', 'imagination' being the 'faculty whereby we form judgements according to the principles of association of ideas'.[13] These terms do not come to have a settled meaning until well into the nineteenth century, for which reason it is not surprising to find Hume using them interchangeably, in both nominal and verbal form, and connecting both with a variety of related terms – not only 'trivial 'but also 'slight', 'invention', 'disguising', 'feigning', 'propensity' and 'deception' – with little apparent discrimination. There are also areas of Hume's thought where he clearly draws on the concept of the imagination, even though he does not employ terms such as imagination and fancy at all.

Second, Hume's way of presenting the two senses of imagination puts a good deal of emphasis on its representational nature, that is to say, its function (along with memory) of copying impressions to form (fainter ideas) and providing the faculties of reason (inference) and understanding (conception) with material upon which to work. This is obviously an important part of Hume's view of the faculty (and I shall have a good deal to say about it in what follows), but focusing on that aspect of the imagination tends to downplay the other role he ascribes to it as a creative power. In addition to being a copyist, that is, the imagination rearranges ideas and combines them in new and extraordinary ways to form new ones, including fictions of various sorts. As such, the creative side of the imagination deserves to be distinguished from its representational side, not only because this is an equally important part of its nature but also because doing so opens a vista to ways in which Hume draws on the faculty. With these two observations in mind, then – that Hume's terminology does not track his concept of imagination and that his definition of imagination tends to emphasise its representational over its creative aspect – my proposal (as already signalled above) is to treat the imagination as a single faculty with two fundamental powers or functions – the 'mimetic' and the 'productive'. This division is intended to capture Hume's view of the faculty in a way that his own distinction between a 'larger or more limited sense' alone cannot. We begin with the mimetic power.[14]

The Mimetic Power of Imagination

The first power Hume attributes to the imagination is that of copy, or representation, the aspect of the imagination that, as already noted, has received considerable attention in the literature. The faculty has this function insofar as it is the source of images derived from experience, either from the senses or through reflection; it represents, by reproducing in the form of an idea, the original it confronts, not as the latter appears uninterpreted – sense and reflection have already done their work – but as an artist might reproduce in his own hand a painting done in that of another, although the copy will never and can never be exact. This mimetic power recalls Hume's wider sense of imagination as the 'faculty, by which we form our fainter ideas' or ideas not related to memory. This notion of the imagination as 'mimetic' is buried deep in the etymology of terms for the faculty and is reflected in the philosophical systems of Plato, Aristotle and the schools that followed them.[15] It is apparent early on in the Greek noun *eikasia* (literally 'picture-thinking'), in popular if not philosophical use in the pre-Socratic era, and employed later by Plato (most dramatically in the allegories of the line and the cave) to denote the inability of the soul to distinguish reality from its representations in the shape of images, dreams and memories, and give rise to the lowest order of knowing.[16] The term is derived in turn from the verb *eiko*, 'to be like' or 'capable of being compared', itself the source of another verb *eikazo*, 'to make like', 'to copy', 'to imitate' or 'to portray'. The mimetic power of the faculty is more pronounced still in the term 'imagination', derived from the Latin *imaginatio*, itself formed from *imaginem*, the accusative form of *imago* (image or picture), and cognate with *imitatio* (imitation), denoting (with the suffix '–ion') a psychic power or faculty that forms internal images of external objects mimetically, that is, through copy or representation. By extension, the same faculty employs these images to shape perception of the external world.

A whole semantic domain follows in English (with cognates in other languages, of course) to denote variously a faculty, its activity and the products to which it gives rise: *image* (the individual representational product of the imagination); *imagery* (the representational contents of the mind taken collectively); *imagining* (the activity of forming complexes of images); *imaginable* (capable of being formed as an image); *imaging* (the production of real image-products in inner and outer space); *imaginative* (the creative mode of informing or rectifying the external world and a source of charm and pleasure); and *imaginary* (images of unreal or fictional objects). This linguistic history is complicated further by the fact that the Latin *imaginatio* was a translation of the older Greek *phantasia*, a verbal noun derived from *phainesthai* ('to bring to light', 'to make shine out', 'to appear') and, more immediately, *phantazesthai*, employed typically to denote the having of memories, dreams and hallucinations, and used synonymously with *phainomenon* (appearance). The use of *imaginatio* to render the Greek *phantasia* was not established until relatively late in the western tradition – it does not appear before Augustine, it seems – and before that time *visum* (thing seen) or *visio* (sight) was the preferred translation.[17]

Many writers in the early-modern period use 'imagination' and 'fancy' as cognate terms, as does Hume, although, as noted above, some interpreters emphasise passages where Hume appears to use 'fancy' with his narrower sense of imagination in mind, excluding understanding and isolating our tendency to connect ideas haphazardly. This contrasts with the wider sense of imagination that includes understanding and emphasises the general and established properties by which we produce all non-memory ideas. To the extent that Hume's terminology does track his meaning in this way, he anticipates the fate of the English 'fancy' to preserve the original Greek, and, over time, to denote (as a noun) a whimsical notion or the faculty responsible for such a notion; to describe (adjectivally) things pretentiously as fine or excellent; and to mark (as a verb) the pursuit of some frivolous preference. In contrast to imagination, fancy thus refers variously to a faculty or its products that involve illusion and mistake ('fantasy'), hallucination ('phantasm'), and artistic products of no fixed form (as in a musical 'fantasia'). Ironically, this sedimentation of meaning involves a partial reversal of the ancient tradition where creativity was awarded not to *imaginatio*, the mimetic faculty limited to the mechanical task of copying, but to *phantasia*, disordered in its operations but at the same time and, crucially for the artist, free, and thus signifying a realm of liberty where – as late as the opening lines of John Keats' eponymous poem (written 1818–19 and published in 1820) – the mind can 'roam', 'wander', 'dart forth, and cloudward soar'.[18] The older meanings find formal expression at around the same time in William Taylor's entry 'Imagination, Fancy' in his *British Synonyms Discriminated* (1813).[19] The later, quite modern reversal, which renders the imagination creative and fancy whimsical, is adumbrated in William Duff's *An Essay on Original Genius* (1767), although it is not explicit until 1815 when, in the Preface to his *Poems*, William Wordsworth takes Taylor to task for being 'enthralled by Etymology', and relegates 'fancy' instead to an aggregative mode of memory, leaving 'imagination' to stand for 'a sublime consciousness of the soul in her own mighty and almost divine powers'. Shortly thereafter, in his *Biographia Literaria*, Samuel Taylor Coleridge affirms and articulates Wordsworth's division and effectively settles the matter once and for all.[20]

More immediately for Hume and the present study, the mimetic power of imagination – meaning the power to copy ideas – is apparent in the systems of late seventeenth- and early eighteenth-century philosophy. René Descartes (1596–1650) captures it in his use of *imaginatio* to denote a 'special mode of thinking' (AT 7:78/CSM 2:54),[21] which either 'assists' or, as he comes to hold after 1630, hinders the intellect in its search for truth and the indubitable species of knowledge he terms *scientia*. This power of imagination is distinct from another he calls *phantasia* or the 'corporeal imagination', the standard translation that captures Descartes' use of the term in his corpuscular theory to denote that part of the brain where the physical processes associated with imagining occur: the 'membrane' of the senses takes on the shape of external objects that are then conveyed to the 'common sense' (*sensus communis*), which fashions them as images in the corporeal imagination, the latter faculty subsequently affecting the nervous system of the body.

While this notion of *phantasia* occurs consistently throughout Descartes' writings, his view of *imaginatio* undergoes revision, and by the time of *Meditationes de Prima Philosophiae* (*Meditations on First Philosophy*) (1641), its role as villain is solidified into a firm principle of character: *imaginatio* no longer assists the intellect in the search for truth but hinders and undermines it. In the second meditation, for example, Descartes limits it to 'contemplating the shape or image of a corporeal thing' and makes it the source of 'fictitious invention' when employed in understanding the nature of self (AT 7:27–8; CSM 2:18–19). Its impotence is nowhere more evident than in the famous passage where Descartes declares the essence of the wax 'in no way revealed by . . . imagination, but . . . perceived by the mind alone' in an act of *inspectio mentis*, 'purely mental scrutiny' (AT 7:31/CSM 2:21). Much the same picture dominates in the sixth meditation, where the imagination gives but a 'confused representation' of a thousand-sided shape that is grasped clearly by the intellect (AT 7:72/CSM 2:50–1) and yields only 'probable conjecture' when called to aid in proving the existence of external objects. While understanding 'turns towards itself' and inspects its ideas, imagination turns to external bodies for features that conform to an idea understood by intellect or given by sense. Imagination is expendable, and, as a final nail in the coffin, not even a 'necessary part of my own essence', for 'if I lacked it', Descartes writes, 'I should undoubtedly remain the same individual as I now am' (AT 7:73/CSM 2:51).[22]

The low view of the imagination held by Descartes is adopted and affirmed by Baruch Spinoza (1632–77), who assigns it a similar role, both in the early *Tractatus de Intellectus Emendatione* (*Treatise on the Emendation of the Intellect*) and later in the *Ethica ordine geometrica demonstrata* (*Ethics Demonstrated in Geometrical Order*).[23] The former reflects Spinoza's search for a method to 'amend' or 'purify' the intellect in its pursuit of the 'true good' (perfecting our nature) and the 'Supreme good' (attaining knowledge of the mind's union with the whole of Nature) (TIE 13 and 16). For Spinoza, realising these ends is tantamount to achieving a certain kind of knowledge, which he captures in the notion of an idea that is true 'intrinsically' because conforming with itself and without reference to other thoughts, and arising only from the power of intellect that can deduce things independent of external objects. In the acquisition of 'true ideas', the imagination is implicated as the source of errors, supplying as it does only images from the sensations that arise from external causes and motions of the body: the ideas of imagination are 'fictitious' (in some way made up) (TIE 52), 'false' (involve unjustified assent) (TIE 67) or are cases of 'doubtful perception' (from a lack of clarity and distinctness) (TIE 77–8). In the *Ethics*, Spinoza distinguishes further between a 'true' idea that involves 'agreement with that of which it is an idea' (E1A6) and an 'adequate' idea, what is 'considered in itself without reference to anything intrinsic' (E11D4). Spinoza associates the latter with knowledge of the 'second' kind, which is based on reason and understanding (of common notions and science), and of the 'third' kind, the intuitive (and infamously obscure) knowledge that 'proceeds from an adequate idea of the formal essence of certain attributes of God to an adequate knowledge of the essence of finite things' (EIIP40Cor.2). Imagination, by contrast, operates at the lowest level, knowledge of the 'first' kind, the confused acquaintance we have with the moment-to-moment state of our body (warmth, cold, hunger, thirst and desire) and the sensed properties of external bodies. Such knowledge is always partial and inadequate and, therefore, a source of falsehood.

In the empiricist tradition, there are hints of the mimetic power of imagination in the writings of John Locke (1632–1704), notably in *An Essay Concerning Human Understanding* (1690) where one reads of the 'vast store' of ideas being 'painted' on the mind by the 'busy and boundless Fancy of Man' (*Essay* 2.1.2, 104).[24] The most important treatment prior to Hume, however, is given by Thomas Hobbes (1588–1679) who, in *Leviathan*, refers to the term's etymological roots and thus emphasises the representational power of the faculty: it is what 'the Latines call *Imagination*, from the image made in seeing'. 'For after an image is removed, or the eye shut', he continues, 'wee still retain an image of the thing seen, though more obscure than when we see it'. Hobbes treats imagination in this sense as synonymous with *phantasia*, what 'the Greeks call . . . *Fancy*; which signifies *apparence*', the only difference being that *imaginatio* is applied 'though improperly' to the other senses, as when one speaks of an image made in hearing or tasting, whereas *fancy* or *appearance* 'is as proper to one sense, as to another' (2:5/15).[25] Hobbes thus conflates the terms, using 'fancy' and 'imagination' to refer to the same faculty, and speaks promiscuously of 'imaginations', 'images', 'fancies' and 'seemings', all manners of appearance of the object itself.

This picture is complicated, however, by the fact that Hobbes uses the same terminology in his corpuscular theory of perception for the physical processes whereby imagining occurs, but does so without the terminological felicity of Descartes. He distinguishes, at least implicitly, between the mimetic imagination in the form of the retained image of a thing seen (*imaginatio/phantasia*) and the corporeal faculty that stores the internal representation of some object that is produced through the workings of external sense, in combination with the internal 'motion' in the heart and brain.

The division is clear from Hobbes' famous characterisation of imagination as 'nothing but *decaying sense*' (2:5/16), which, as he goes on to explain, refers to the process whereby the 'original motion made in sense' is 'obscured' by subsequent stronger ones and effectively fades from view like the stars when their twinkling is overpowered by the stronger light of the sun. The longer the span of time after an object is seen, the weaker the imagination becomes or, what amounts to the same thing, the more obscure the image grows. For this reason, Hobbes concludes, imagination and memory are really two sides of the same coin: when we emphasise the faculty responsible for the copy and storage of images, we speak of 'imagination' or '*fancy* it selfe', but when we 'would express the *decay*, and signifie the Sense is fading, old, and past, it is called *Memory*. So that *Imagination* and *Memory*, are but one thing, which for divers considerations hath divers names' (2:5/16).

Hume's appreciation of the mimetic power of imagination appears against the backdrop of these earlier treatments. He follows Locke in employing (generally) the English terms interchangeably, but departs from Hobbes and Descartes in offering no principled distinction between *imaginatio* and *phantasia* except insofar as they are reflected in the wider and narrower senses of imagination discussed above. Indeed, we should expect as much, given Hume's declared lack of interest in discovering the 'causes' of sensations (or 'original impressions'), which he considers 'unknown' and the examination of which 'belongs more to anatomists and natural philosophers than to moral' (T 1.1.2.1/SBN 8). Hume does refer to the 'constitution of the body' and 'the 'application of objects to the external organs' as candidate explanations (T 2.1.1.1/SBN 329), and he occasionally employs the language of 'spirits' and 'nerves' to explain certain phenomena, including mistakes that can attend the principles of association (T 1.2.5.20/SBN 60), the effect of pressing on the eye with one's finger (T 1.4.2.45/SBN 210–11) and the sensation of resistance that arises when we touch an object (T 1.4.5.13/SBN 211). Some commentators have also identified the influence of Malebranche in Hume's discussion of resemblance.[26] Hume's appeal to physiology is *en passant*, or 'carefully left in the background' as Marina Frasca-Spada observes, and even when he does employ that language, it is tangential to his main discussion; he remains true to his official position of being sceptical of and largely uninterested in the physiological processes that seventeenth-century philosophers made part of their philosophy of mind.[27] On balance, it is fair to conclude that Hume has no serious psychophysical theory comparable to anything found in earlier writers, and the fact that he uses 'imagination' and 'fancy' for one and the same faculty strongly suggests that he simply had no need for the 'corporeal imagination' or any equivalent to it.

Hume, moreover, integrates the established view of imagination as a mimetic power easily into the various parts of his copy principle. All 'perceptions' – the immediate objects of thought – are either 'impressions' or 'ideas', Hume argues;[28] impressions of sensation or 'original' impressions (T 2.1.1.1/SBN 275) have their source in external objects, while impressions of reflection or 'secondary impressions' arise from ideas and, when recalled or otherwise conceived by the mind, give rise to pleasure or pain, a new impression that is the basis for further ideas of passions and emotions. All impressions are 'antecedent to their correspondent ideas; but posterior to those of sensation, and deriv'd from them' (T 1.1.3.1/SBN 8). In contrast to impressions, ideas are fainter copies, representations or images in 'thinking and reasoning' (T 1.1.1.1/SBN 1) of impressions of sensation or reflection. Ideas can, in principle, be traced back to the impressions they resemble, are subsequent to and caused by them, and differ from them quantitatively, not qualitatively, that is, in terms of the degree of liveliness, violence or force and vivacity they contain. Since force and vivacity are the only way to distinguish perceptions from one another, lively ideas can come close to or be 'converted' into impressions and faint impressions can approach ideas. While in particular instances they might blend into one another, as in a fever or madness, Hume insists that they are 'in general so different' that we can 'assign to each a peculiar name to mark the difference' (T 1.1.1.1/SBN 2).[29] Further, ideas and impressions are 'simple' if they 'admit of no distinction or separation, and so cannot be analysed into any component parts' (T 1.1.1.2/SBN 2). Alternatively, ideas and impressions are 'complex' when they are compounds of qualities that can, on reflection, be separated into their component parts and thus be reduced to the simple impressions and corresponding ideas that compose them. The idea of 'apple' is of this sort, Hume urges, since it can be broken down into the distinct ideas of colour, taste and smell (T 1.1.1.2/SBN 2). In perception, however, these parts are experienced not separately as atoms of raw data, but together as compounds; the complex impression is copied and represented as an idea that, like its simple counterpart, can be traced back to an impression, is subsequent to and caused by it, and differs quantitatively in terms of the degree of force and vivacity it contains. Again, complex ideas will have less force and vivacity than the impression to which they correspond.

In this picture, the mimetic imagination appears as a 'faithful mirror' (EHU 2.2/SBN 18) that reflects original impressions or, strictly speaking, re-presents them in such a way that they make a 'new appearance' as ideas (T 1.1.3.1/SBN 8). Impressions appear in the form of ideas, as images copied from the original (again, as a painter might copy the work of another). Since these images are necessarily painted in colours 'faint and dull, in comparison of those in which our original perceptions were clothed' (EHU 2.2/SBN 18), an idea is unlikely to capture fully or replicate completely the details of the original. Representations are still 'exact' or 'adequate', however, insofar as they can be traced back to impressions they resemble, in which case the 'relations, contradictions and agreements of the ideas are all applicable to the objects' (T 1.2.2.1/SBN 29).[30] As such, when the imagination copies an impression, the resulting idea loses the vivacity of the original and becomes what Hume calls 'perfect' (T 1.1.3.1/SBN 8), a characteristic that puts it in stark contrast to memory, the other faculty of mind that Hume credits with mimetic power. Hume here follows those in the early-modern tradition in seeing memory and imagination as different ways of describing the same faculty (or power of mind), although he marks the difference in terms of the degree to which each retains the original force and vivacity of the impression they copy.[31] Both 'borrow their simple ideas from the impressions, and can never go beyond these original perceptions' (T 1.3.5.3/SBN 85), but memory retains in its ideas a 'considerable degree' of the 'first vivacity' of the original impression and 'paints its objects in more distinct colours, than any which are employ'd by the [imagination]' (T 1.1.3.1/SBN 9). It also 'preserves the original form, in which its objects were presented' (T 1.1.3.3/SBN 9), and thus generates ideas that are repetitions of impressions or 'equivalent' to them (T 1.3.4.1/SBN 82). To have a 'good' memory means, in Humean terms, that one's ideas accurately and adequately reiterate the order of past matters of fact and 'wherever we depart from it in recollecting any thing, it proceeds from some defect or imperfection in that faculty' (T 1.1.3.3/SBN 9).

The Productive Power of Imagination

The second power Hume attributes to the imagination recalls his 'more limited sense' of 'imagination', which, in excluding demonstrative and probable reasoning, points to ways other than inference whereby ideas are imbued with force and vivacity. Calling the imagination 'productive', however, emphasises its function of combining ideas it already possesses to create new ones. Jan Wilbanks has emphasised the combinatory side of imagination, pointing out that Hume considers it a 'faculty of forming, uniting and separating ideas'; Wilbanks regards it as so prominent that he calls it Hume's 'general conception of imagination'.[32] The use of 'general' certainly reflects the importance Hume bestows on this feature of the imagination, but it at once obscures the creative side of the faculty to which he gives at least equal weight. In calling the faculty 'productive', I aim to reflect both elements: that it is both combinatory *and* creative.[33]

Combinatory Power

The notion of the imagination as a combinatory power can be traced back, in the form of 'free play', to Aristotle and his Stoic and Neo-platonic commentators. The 'materials are present in Aristotle for a recognition of . . . "free phantasy", the free play of imagination', as Murray Wright Bundy observes in his seminal study, 'but in him there is no statement so explicit as this. This recognition of the power of phantasy to conceive of hippocentaurs, chimaeras, and castles in Spain was to become a commonplace of mediaeval views.'[34] The more immediate source for Hume, however, is the early-modern period in the shape of Locke. Locke devotes little time in his *Essay* to imagination or fancy per se (he, too, uses the terms interchangeably), and when he does so it is primarily to explain and deride the unfortunate tendency of the mind towards untruth and unreality in the form of 'Extravagant . . . Opinions, Reasonings, and Actions' (*Essay* 2.33.1, 394) caused by 'wrong and unnatural combinations of *Ideas*' arising from custom, prejudice and education (*Essay* 2.33.18, 400).[35] At the extreme, Locke equates this process with madness, a malady where reason remains as strong as ever (he calls its outright loss 'idiocy') but at once mistakes falsehood for truth, an error of judgement rather than imagination (*Essay* 2.11.13, 161). Interpreters have long noted, however, that at least some of the 'powers' Locke discusses under the auspices of 'Understanding' and 'Operations of the Mind' actually constitute a distinct and separate faculty, which he could and, in the view of some, should have called the imagination, namely the 'power' of the mind, as he characterises it at one point, 'to repeat, compare, and unite them [Ideas] even to an almost infinite Variety, and so . . . make at Pleasure new complex *Ideas*' (*Essay* 2.2.2, 117).[36] Chief among these 'Acts of Mind', as Locke goes on to detail them, are combination, relation and abstraction (*Essay* 2.12.1, 163–4), the very features identified by later writers (including Hume) as the purview of imagination. Indeed, this seems to be a lesson that George Berkeley (1685–1753) learned from his reading of Locke, and in *The Principles of Human Knowledge* (1710) – published only some two decades after the *Essay* – he credits the imagination explicitly with the various operations that Locke had granted more liberally to understanding or the mind generally.[37]

Hume's inheritance of this combinatory power emerges in his discussion of the mimetic power of imagination and its relation to memory. The latter, as we have seen, is able to reproduce past impressions with accuracy, but that advantage is won only at the expense of a corresponding constraint on its freedom, memory being 'in a manner ty'd down . . . without any power of variation' (T 1.1.3.2/SBN 9). The imagination, conversely, might be unable to preserve objects in their original form but finds compensation in not being 'restrain'd to the same order and form with the original impressions' (T 1.1.3.2/SBN 9), enjoying instead a *'liberty . . . to transpose and change its ideas*' at will (T 1.1.3.4/SBN 10). 'Nothing is more free than the imagination of man', Hume declares expansively, 'and though it cannot exceed that original stock of ideas, furnished by the internal and external senses, it has an unlimited power of mixing, compounding, separating, and dividing these ideas, in all the varieties of fiction and vision' (EHU 5.10/SBN 47). The imagination 'has the command over all its ideas, and can join and mix and vary them, in all the ways possible' (EHU 5.12/SBN 49), distinguishing and separating ideas into their simplest components and rearranging them to produce new ideas that might, in the shape of 'winged horses, fiery dragons, and monstrous giants', even 'confound nature' (T 1.1.3.4/SBN 10). At one point, recalling his image of 'chac[ing] our imagination to the heavens' and its domain as a 'universe' (T 1.2.6.8/SBN 68), he describes the faculty as 'naturally sublime, delighted with what-ever is remote and extraordinary, and running, without controul, into the most distant parts of space and time, in order to avoid the objects, which custom has rendered too familiar to it' (EHU 12.25/SBN 162).

Hume emphasises at once, however, that, in its use of the combinatory power, the productive imagination does not have *completely* free reign – a point emphasised in an early treatment of the subject by Charles Hendel[38] – it being guided by certain rules or 'principles' manifest in the orderly and regular ways in which it forms its new ideas. Not only in our waking lives, in fact, but 'even in our wildest and most wandering reveries, nay in our very dreams', Hume cautions, 'we shall find, if we reflect, the imagina-tion ran not altogether at adventures, but that there was still a connexion upheld among the different ideas, which succeeded each other' (EHU 3.1/SBN 23). Many ideas are simply ruled out as nonsensical by the laws of logic: ideas can be extravagant but still conceivable, while others are simply impossible.[39] 'What never was seen, or heard of, may yet be conceived', Hume insists, but whatever 'implies an absolute contradiction' is beyond the powers of thought (EHU 2.4/SBN 18). Thus we can form the idea of a 'gold mountain' but not the 'idea of a mountain without a valley', which we 'therefore regard ... as impossible' (T 1.2.2.8/SBN 32). The imagination can do extraordinary things but it cannot perform miracles.

More fundamentally, however, Hume regards the imagination as being governed by certain internal principles by which ideas come to be connected in regular and orderly ways that work, in Gerhard Streminger's phrase, to '*structure* the stream of percep-tions'.[40] As Hume observes:

> As all simple ideas may be separated by the imagination, and may be united again in what form it pleases, nothing wou'd be more unac-countable than the operations of that faculty, were it not guided by some universal principles, which render it, in some measure, uniform with itself in all times and places. Were ideas entirely loose and uncon-nected, chance alone wou'd join them; and 'tis impossible the same simple ideas shou'd fall regularly into complex ones (as they regularly do) without some bond of union among them, some associating quality, by which one idea naturally introduces the other. (T 1.1.4.1/SBN 10; see also T 2.2.8.20/SBN 380)

Hume discovers this 'bond or union' in certain qualities of our perceptions 'by which the mind is . . . convey'd from one idea to another', those principles of association that he reduces to resemblance, contiguity in time or space, and cause and effect: a picture 'naturally leads our thought to the original'; the idea of an apartment 'naturally induces' the idea of others adjacent; and the idea of a wound cannot but lead to the idea of pain that it causes (EHU 3.3/SBN 24). The imagination is here a 'natural instinct' or 'propensity of human nature', a 'gentle force' (T 1.1.4.1/SBN 10), its operations going unnoticed because the 'passage from one moment to another is scarce felt' (T 1.4.2.33/SBN 203). Hume's language is haunted by the ghost of Locke's famous images in the *Essay* of the mind as both passive and active, an empty cabinet (*Essay* 1.2.15, 55), white paper void of characters (*Essay* 2.1.2, 104), or a dark room (*Essay* 2.11.17, 163) that comes to be furnished or lit by ideas, but also with powers enabling it to rearrange the furniture and pictures once they have moved in. Thus, as Hume variously describes it, the imagination is passive insofar as it is guided, conveyed, seduced, placed, runs easily, displays propensities and tendencies, and takes objects 'as they lie' (T 1.1.4.2/SBN 11), and active in that it confuses, confounds, supposes, attributes, associates, bestows, justifies, avoids and seeks relief. The imagination is at once affected by the ideas it confronts and it feels the natural attraction they exhibit, but it must recognise this attraction and actively provide the connecting or uniting principle that relates them in orderly and predicable ways.[41] As Hume characterises the imagination in the Abstract of the *Treatise*, the faculty is both an 'empire' with independence and legislative authority, and also influenced causally by some 'secret union' among the materials over which it has jurisdiction:

> Our imagination has great authority over our ideas; and there are no ideas that are different from each other, which it cannot separate, and join, and compose into all the varieties of fiction. But notwithstanding the empire of the imagination, there is a secret tie or union among particular ideas, which causes the mind to conjoin them more frequently together, and makes the one, upon its appearance, introduce the other. (T Abs. 35/SBN 662)

Ideas thus lead the imagination when they display qualities that provide a 'sufficient bond and association' (T 1.1.4.2/SBN 11) that the imagination cannot resist. At the same time, the natural attraction and bond between ideas does not constitute a connection, which the imagination has to make itself; it supplies or provides the active power through which one perception, though naturally attracted to another, is related in thought. Like the natural attraction between objects, this power of the imagination is largely mysterious; it is one of the 'original qualities of human nature' (T 1.1.4.6/SBN 13), known by its effects, whose principles can be delineated and explained.

Creative Power

While the combinatory element of the productive imagination has a long pedigree, its creative counterpart is of more recent stock. This might account for the fact that Hume commentators have not tended to single it out as a distinguishing element in his approach, even though it is signalled early in the *Treatise* when Hume appeals to the imagination to explain how someone can 'raise up to himself' the idea of a shade of blue 'tho' it had never been convey'd to him by his senses' (T 1.1.1.10/SBN 6). Notable exceptions are Donald Ainslie's appreciation of the central role of imagination in understanding Hume's scepticism[42] and Paul Guyer's interpretation of Hume as a central figure in the 'development of the theory of aesthetic response of mental play', in which the imagination looms large, especially in his aesthetics, where Hume emphasises how 'our pleasure arises from the imagination's play with the appearance of utility of objects, itself not a formal property of their structure'.[43] This creative element of the imagination is also reflected in Streminger's earlier choice of the term 'artistic faculty' to describe Hume's interest in the inventiveness of the imagination, but he uses the phrase to denote what we have called its combinatory power, namely the 'ability to place known impressions into new relationships with one another' and thus 'to *reorganise* past impressions, which serve as elements or building-blocks'.[44] What is now thought of as the 'creative imagination' is generally traced to developments after Hume, and more specifically to views expressed in the latter part of the eighteenth century, such as those found in Sir Joshua Reynolds' lectures to the Royal Academy, Duff's aforementioned *An Essay on Original Genius*, and especially the associationist aesthetics of Alexander Gerard and Archibald Alison, which, with various twists and turns, found expression in the high Romanticism of Wordsworth and the subsequent tradition of Victorian criticism that reached a conclusion in the voluminous writings of John Ruskin.[45] In this tradition, the place of imagination reflects a guiding faith in the existence of a power from which works of original artistic genius arise in spontaneous, mysterious and even quasi-divine ways. In the early-modern tradition there are obvious adumbrations of this creative power as early as Hobbes' *Leviathan,* where one finds the notion of a '*Seeking,* or the faculty of Invention' that hunts out relations of causes and effects among a 'regulated' 'Trayne of Thoughts' or 'Trayne of Imaginations' (3:9–10/21–2). The first decisive fusion of the imagination with creativity and artistic production, however, comes early in the eighteenth century with 'The Pleasures of the Imagination' (1711), the influential series of papers written by Joseph Addison (1672–1719) for *The Spectator,* the periodical he edited and published with Richard Steele.[46] Addison writes in the language of Locke, and he follows Berkeley in explicitly naming the imagination or fancy (terms he also uses interchangeably) as the seat of the power 'to enlarge, compound, and vary' at will the 'particular Ideas' with which it is 'Stocked' primarily through the sense of sight (No. 416, 558).[47] He goes further, however, in identifying the imagination as a hedonistic or pleasure-seeking faculty: its pleasures are 'primary' when they 'entirely proceed from such Objects as are before our Eyes', and 'secondary' if they 'flow from the Ideas of visible Objects, when the Objects are not actually before the Eye, but are called up into our Memories, or form'd into agreeable Visions of Things that are either Absent or Fictitious' (No. 411, 537). Artistic creations fall squarely into this latter category: the ideas conveyed by a statute, picture or literary description are compared to the ideas of the objects they represent, and the greater the resemblance of copy to original, the more intense is the pleasure that results.

In addition to equating the imagination with pleasure, Addison identifies features that mark it with a specific character and explain how it works: the imagination involves a 'gentle Exercise' and easy 'Bent of Thought', in contrast to the 'Labour or Difficulty' associated with reason and understanding (No. 411, 539); it hates restraint and confinement but 'loves to be filled with an Object or graspe at any thing that is too big for its Capacity', the source of that 'pleasing Astonishment' that defines the sublime (No. 412, 541). It is also curious and gratified by what is novel (No. 412,

541) and feels an 'inward Joy' in beauty (No. 412, 542), a quality it recognises immediately, whether as the fondness aroused by members of our own species or in colours, symmetry and the arrangement of forms. In general, Addison finds in imagination a magical power to transform otherwise ordinary or even ugly objects in ways that make them a source of entertainment, rendering 'the whole Creation more gay and delightful' by representing them aesthetically as a 'pleasing Delusion' (No. 413, 546): imagination 'bestows charms on a Monster' (3:541, no. 412) and through it 'a Man in a Dungeon is capable of entertaining himself with Scenes and Landskips more beautiful than any that can be found in the whole Compass of Nature' (3:537, no. 411). Its boundless capacity to vary ideas and enhance the world makes the imagination an almost inexhaustible treasure, its riches depleted only by the failure to perfect it, when doing so might place one in a state – as Keats would express the insight more than a century later – of 'Negative Capability', as when 'a man is capable of being in uncertainties, mysteries, doubts, without any irritable reaching after fact or reason' and might glimpse into the 'Penetralium of mystery' where 'the sense of Beauty overcomes every other consideration, or rather obliterates all consideration'.[48]

It would be anachronistic, of course, to read the mature Romantic view of the creative imagination into either Addison or Hume – although there are clear intimations of it in both[49] – but in the present context, the term 'creative' effectively captures Hume's emphasis on the power of a faculty to produce original ideas formed either through its combinatory power when it works on ideas already at its disposal or, as we shall see below and in the next chapter, when it generates a class of ideas – 'fictions' of a certain sort – independent of experience and according to its own inner logic.

The Principle of Easy Transition

One notable way in which 'The Pleasures of the Imagination' find their way into Hume's thought is through his observation that the productive power of the imagination is guided by a 'principle of easy transition', which Hume introduces when he writes, in what has become a famous and oft-quoted passage, 'that the imagination, when set in any train of thinking, is apt to continue, even when its object fails it, and like a galley put in motion by the oars, carries on its course without any new impulse', and that 'as the mind is once in the train of observing an uniformity among its objects, it naturally continues, till it renders the uniformity as compleat as possible' (T 1.4.2.22/SBN 198). Hume's metaphor effectively rephrases Newton's first law of motion – 'Every body persists in its state of being at rest or of moving uniformly straight forward, except insofar as it is compelled to change its state by force impressed' – which is echoed in the way some commentators have described the principle Hume has in mind. H. H. Price speaks of the '*inertia* of the imagination' and Hume's 'Inertia Principle', for example, and Douglas Long more recently of the imagination involving a 'sort of cognitive momentum'.[50] The concepts of 'inertia' and 'momentum' are certainly close to what Hume has in mind, though it is better conceived in terms of 'conatus', an endeavour, intrinsic impulse, tendency, inclination or striving on the part of imagination to work out and fulfil the dominant structure of its inherent nature. This is not intended to reify the faculty in any sense, only to capture a fundamental feature of it that Hume appears to isolate; it is also an idea with which he would have been familiar from his reading of early-modern writers. Hobbes connects the idea of such motion – what he calls 'endeavour' – with the imagination itself, characterising the faculty as the 'first internall beginning of all Voluntary Motion' (6:23/38).

Some have explained the principle in terms of the psycho-physiological model noted above, and in that vein traced its origins to Locke and Malebranche, although the sparse evidence for Hume's commitment to 'animal spirits' inevitably weakens any claim for the proposed connection and thereby undermines any significance it might have.[51] Candidate historical sources notwithstanding, there are better reasons, and philosophical ones at that, to treat it as reflecting the view that, at bottom, the faculty of imagination is fundamentally hedonistic, an insight that effectively unifies under a single principle a wide range of different tendencies that might otherwise appear as ad hoc and unrelated. Historically speaking, one finds this view adumbrated already in Addison – indisputably Hume's model for his early attempts at the essay style[52] – for whom, to recall, the pleasures of the imagination are found in the faculty's capacity to transform what is ordinary into something extraordinary, and in its natural love of ideas of objects that stretch it (sublimity), gratify its curiosity (novelty), or strike it with an immediate satisfaction (beauty). Whether or not this was an explicit source for Hume it is impossible to say, but he clearly develops a similar view, albeit with the important addition of identifying the source of pleasure with the satisfaction of the imagination's desire to create a union or form a whole. We feel pain, correspondingly, when the faculty is stretched beyond its capacity or when confronted with a break, interruption or contradiction among its ideas, a condition from which it will always 'seek relief' (T 1.4.2.37/SBN 206).[53] As a result, Hume treats the imagination as an indolent faculty, ready to gloss differences and confuse ideas that appear – from its tendency to give only cursory inspection – much the same as one another. 'Nothing is more apt to make us mistake one idea for another', Hume observes, 'than any relation betwixt them [ideas], which associates them together in the imagination, and makes us pass with facility from one to the other'. It is a maxim, moreover, Hume continues in the same vein, 'that whatever strikes the mind in the same disposition or in similar ones, are very apt to be confounded. The mind readily passes from one to the other, and perceives not the change without a strict attention, of which, generally speaking, 'tis wholly incapable' (T 1.4.2.32/SBN 203).

In pursuit of its end of totality and satisfaction, the imagination displays a 'natural propensity' to take the path of least resistance, searching for the easiest way possible to move among its ideas and reach the pleasure of resolution while avoiding the pain of interruption. The fundamental maxim guiding the imagination in this regard is that 'Whatever has the greatest influence is most taken notice of; and whatever is most taken notice of, presents itself most readily to the imagination' (T 2.2.2.20/SBN 342). As such, it moves from the lesser to the greater and 'passes easily from obscure to lively ideas, but with difficulty from lively to obscure' (T 2.2.2.15/SBN 339). For '. . . men are mightily govern'd by the imagination', Hume writes, in an important observation worth quoting at length:

and proportion their affections more to the light, under which any object appears to them, than to its real and intrinsic value. What strikes upon them with a strong and lively idea commonly prevails above what lies in a more obscure light; and it must be a great superiority of value, that is able to compensate this advantage. Now as every thing, that is contiguous to us, either in space or time, strikes upon us with such an idea, it has a proportional effect on the will and passions, and commonly operates with more force than any object, that lies in a more distant and obscure light. Tho' we may be fully convinc'd, that the latter object excels the former, we are not able to regulate our actions by this judgement; but yield to the sollicitations of our passions, which always plead in favour of what is near and contiguous. (T 3.2.7.2/SBN 534–5)

The imagination is thus warmed and entertained by what is novel and wonderful, and cooled and bored by the familiar and dull, and it progresses 'with greater facility' when influenced by what is large, superior, important, high and contiguous than by what is small, inferior, trivial, low and remote. The 'imagination naturally turns to whatever is important and considerable', as Hume expresses the same thought elsewhere, 'and where two objects are presented to it, a small and a great one, usually leaves the former, and dwells entirely on the latter' (T 2.1.9.13/SBN 308), as it moves from the idea of the moons of Jupiter to the planet itself, for example, or from the provinces of a country to the idea of its capital, the great size of Jupiter and the importance of the capital holding more appeal than the relative smallness and insignificance of the moons and the provinces (T 2.2.2.20/SBN 342). The same holds for 'present motives and inclination', which strike the imagination with more force than those that are distant and obscure (T 3.2.6.9/SBN 531). When the objects of our affections 'approach nearer to us or acquire the advantages of favourable lights and positions, which catch the heart or imagination; our general resolutions are frequently confounded, a small enjoyment preferred, and lasting shame and sorrow entailed upon us' (EPM 6.15/SBN 239). As we shall see in Chapter 3, this tendency of the imagination looms large in Hume's treatment of morals, the founding of political society and the formation of rules governing the establishment and ownership of property.

A major consequence of the tendency of the imagination to seek an easy transition is that it moves easily from experience to what Hume sometimes refers to as 'suppositions'. Hume uses this term many times, often in the sense of assumption, surmise or conjecture for the sake of argument, but also as a way of characterising occasions where something is taken to be the case even when not perceived, as in his discussions of the 'supposition of . . . continued existence' (T 1.4.2.22/SBN 198) or the 'supposition of a difference [between objects and perceptions], that is unknown and incomprehensible' (T 1.4.5.23/SBN 244). On occasion, Hume adds the qualifier 'false' or 'falsehood' to emphasise the lack of justification that accompanies the idea (see T.1.4.2.56/SBN 217, and T 2.3.3.7/SBN 416). Again, commentators have drawn attention to this aspect of Hume's view of imagination and called it by various names. Willard Clark Gore, writing as early as 1902, notes the *'carrying or propensive quality of the imagination'* to pass *'from a present object to absent attendant'*; Price uses the term 'postulation' to describe the imagination's capacity to fill gaps in experience, to 'supplement our exiguous sense-impressions with a vast multitude of unsensed sensibilia'; and Wilbanks later captures the same through the rubric of Hume's '"special" usage of "imagination"' (in contrast to the aforementioned 'general conception of imagination'), namely that Hume 'recognises a *supposing* activity of this faculty', in which 'no idea . . . of the entity supposed or imagined to exist is possible'. More recently, Streminger draws attention to the same principle in discussing the 'metaphysical faculty of the imagination', which he finds in its ability 'to construct concepts (propositions, objects, systems) *transcending* the empirical realm', and Barry Stroud seems to have the same point in mind when he speaks of the 'mental operation' of 'projection', that we 'put on to objects in our thoughts about them certain features that they do not really possess'.[54] Whichever term one chooses, the result is much the same: the imagination is free to conceive objects that cannot be traced directly to an impression, and seeks the pleasure it receives from creating a union while avoiding the pain it feels when stretched or faced with a break, interruption or contradiction among its ideas. In seeking this end, moreover, the imagination will take the path of least resistance, even if that means moving from what is experienced to postulating the existence of things that have never been (and in some cases could never be) experienced, and in the process committing errors: ideas, that is, formed through its mimetic power that are taken for those of memory, and others formed through its productive power that do not correspond to any real existence or matter of fact at all. The former are what we can call mistakes, while the latter are fictions, and it is to the nature of these that we now turn.

Table 1.1

Power of Imagination	Error	Belief-like state	Correctable
Mimetic	Mistake	False	Yes
Productive	Fictions—Artificial 1. Poetic 2. Religious (polytheism) 3. Philosophical	None, only persuasion	N/A
	Fictions—Vulgar 1. Of Metaphysics	Natural (first order)	No
	2. Rules of Property	Natural (first order)	No
	3. Religious (popular theism)	Natural (second order)	Yes

Errors and Belief-like States

I now want to propose a terminology for classifying the powers of the imagination and the effects Hume associates with them; this will guide the discussion in subsequent chapters when deciphering how Hume draws on the imagination in the course of his investigation of various subjects. The Table 1.1 summarises in advance what I have in mind. While the principles of the imagination account for and explain the representational and creative capacities of human beings, these depend at once on the fact that the imagination departs from and effectively subverts experience, a feature revealed in its tendency to commit what, in most general terms, we can call errors. These are ideas that depart from experience and matter of fact, but their character depends on the power of the imagination involved, as do the belief-like states that correspond to them. Belief, as Hume understands it, is based on any present impression – of sense, memory or passion – that carries the mind to a related idea through the natural principles of association – contiguity, resemblance and cause and effect – and in so doing imparts to it force and vivacity from the original impression (see T.1.3.8.2/SBN 98–9 and T 1.3.8.8/SBN 101–2). Belief thus involves a *stronger and lively idea deriv'd from a present impression related to it* (T 1.3.8.15/SBN 105) where 'stronger and lively' means that the idea produces the 'same effect with those impressions, which are immediately present to the senses and perception' (T 1.3.10.3/SBN 119). It is not then anything above and beyond or in addition to any present impression, but a feeling, conception, quality or 'manner of appearance' that works 'to enliven and infix any idea in the imagination' (T 2.3.10.12/SBN 453). As Hume puts it succinctly in the first *Enquiry*, 'the sentiment of belief is nothing but a conception more intense and steady than what attends the mere fictions of the imagination, and ... this *manner* of conception arises from a customary conjunction of the object with something present to the memory or senses' (EHU 5.13/SBN 50).[55]

As such statements make clear, belief proper, what we think of as true or genuine belief, requires at bottom some matter of fact, an impression that gives it content and imparts a considerable degree of its force and vivacity to the idea that copies it. Ideas of the mimetic imagination do not, like ideas of memory, reach this level. At the same time, Hume entertains the possibility that ideas of the imagination might exhibit and strike with sufficient force and vivacity to inspire some state that is belief-like, that resembles true belief in terms of force and vivacity but lacks the content derived from experience: there is no real existence to which the idea corresponds. People might hold such beliefs – or at least profess to do so – and they give assent to the existence of an object to which the idea putatively refers, even though the conviction is 'diminished' and the belief not 'entire' (T 1.4.1.11/SBN 186). This possibility is built into the imagination and the way it works: it is hedonistic, lazy, easily influenced and willing to take the path of least resistance even if that involves error and confusion. Hume writes in this vein that:

> a lively imagination very often degenerates into madness or folly, so they [the operations of the imagination] influence the judgement after the same manner, and produce belief from the very same principle. When the imagination, from any extraordinary ferment of the blood and spirits, acquires such a vivacity as disorders all its powers and faculties, there is no means of distinguishing betwixt truth and falsehood. (T 1.3.10.9/SBN 123)

Or, as he expresses the same thought elsewhere:

> assistance is mutual betwixt the judgement and fancy, as well as betwixt the judgement and passion; and that belief not only gives vigour to the imagination, but that a vigorous and strong imagination is of all

talents the most proper to secure belief and authority; [sometimes the] vivacity produc'd by the fancy is ... greater than that which arises from custom and experience. (T 1.3.10.8/SBN 123)

Mimetic Power, Mistakes and False Beliefs

Not all errors that accompany the ideas of imagination are the same, but depend upon whether they can be traced to the mimetic or productive power of imagination. In the mimetic power of imagination, the faculty is liable to form ideas that might be confused with those of memory; since there is always some matter of fact the imagination copies, this sort of error can be recognised as such and corrected. For that reason, the error in question is a mistake and the belief-like state it inspires correspondingly false.[56] This eventuality is analogous to the case of the copy principle, where the force and vivacity of ideas might approach that of the impressions they copy. Thus, as Hume acknowledges:

> Wherever we can make an idea approach the impressions in force and vivacity, it will likewise imitate them in its influence on the mind; and *vice versa*, where it imitates them in that influence ... this must proceed from its approaching them in force and vivacity. (T 1.3.10.3/SBN 119)

There is no doubt that 'the ideas of the memory are more *strong* and *lively* than those of the fancy', but still we are

> frequently in doubt concerning the ideas of the memory, as they become very weak and feeble; and are at a loss to determine whether any image proceeds from the fancy or the memory, when it is not drawn in such lively colours as distinguish that latter faculty. (T 1.3.5.5/SBN 628 and 85)

Hume seems to think that, for the most part, we have little difficulty in distinguishing ideas of the imagination from those of memory, and even if mistakes do arise they can be corrected.[57] The case is again analogous to the relation between ideas and impressions, where the feeling in each case is 'in general so different' that Hume finds warrant for assigning a 'peculiar name' to each. An idea of memory retains a 'considerable degree of its first vivacity' (T 1.1.3.1/SBN 8) and for that reason will be attended by a 'different *feeling*' than one formed by the mimetic power of imagination. Even when one forgets – when the idea has grown vague – memory can be jogged (as we say) in such a way as to revive it: 'as soon as the circumstance is mention'd, that touches the memory', Hume observes, ' ... ideas now appear in a new light, and have, in a manner, a different feeling from what they had before. Without any other alteration, beside that of the feeling, they become immediately ideas of the memory, and are assented to' (T 1.3.5.4/SBN 628). Ideas copied from impressions by imagination are by their nature faint and languid, and inspire neither the same feeling nor assent to the existence of its object. Ideas formed through memory and imagination are thus rarely confused with each other and, even when a mistake of this sort does arise, the belief-like state involves falsehood, can be revealed as such, and is amenable to correction by reference to matter of fact, of which each idea – that of memory or imagination – is a more or less accurate copy.

Productive Power and Fictions

The second class of errors committed by the imagination follows on the endless possibilities the faculty has under its productive power for combining ideas and creating new ones. This results, to use Hume's phrase from the Abstract, in different 'varieties of fiction', though it is important to note that he does not always use the term 'fiction' even when he has the concept in mind. As the discussion in subsequent chapters aims to show, the same principles of imagination are at work – albeit in various ways and with respect to a different fictions – whether Hume is discussing phenomena as diverse as justice or continued existence.[58] In everyday language, a 'fiction', as its origin in the Latin *fingere* (to fashion or form) suggests, is something fabricated, created or invented, and it carries the implication of deceit, dissimulation, pretence and thus outright falsehood.[59] The central feature of fictions, as I take the term in the present context, is that they are errors arising specifically from what we characterised above as the propensity of the productive imagination to suppose, posit or hypothesise something that cannot be traced directly to a corresponding impression, but that go beyond the evidence of sense and experience and transcend the human power of comprehension; some fictions, moreover, have the added character of being unverifiable (of which more below). A fiction should be distinguished clearly from 'illusion', a term that has a very different origin, coming as it does via *illusionem* (mocking, jesting, ironic) from *illudere* (to mock at or play with). Some commentators have used this term in connection to Hume who does, admittedly, use it (at T 1.4.5.11/SBN 237, 1.4.7.6/SBN 267, and 2.1.10.9/SBN 314, for example), though as a synonym for 'fiction' and not in the sense of mock, jest or irony.[60] It is difficult to see why Hume would appeal to the imagination in the ways that he does if he had decided from the outset that the ideas to which it gives rise are merely illusions in this sense.

Hume appears to have this general concept of fiction in mind when he writes that 'Ideas always represent the objects or impressions, from which they are deriv'd, and can never without a fiction represent or be apply'd to any other' (T 1.2.3.11/SBN 37); he refers readers, by way of example, to the later discussion of how we apply the idea of time to what is unchangeable and 'suppose' duration to be a measure of rest as well as motion, suggesting that there is some confusion or error involved rather than a simple substitution of one idea for another.[61] A fiction might be contrasted to genuine ideas, namely those that can be traced to real existence and matter of fact via the copy principle. A fiction then, as Saul Traiger characterises it, is 'an idea applied to something from which it cannot be derived'; an idea 'not directly derived from the impressions that the idea copies', as Ainslie puts it, or as Henry Allison writes, emphasising the evidentiary over the representational aspect of a fiction, an idea or judgement 'for which there is no sufficient evidentiary basis'.[62] It follows that when this lack of evidence becomes apparent, fictions will be revealed as false, and the belief-like state they inspire will be corrected. Hume writes:

> Truth or falsehood consists in an agreement or disagreement either to the *real* relations of ideas, or to *real* existence and matter of fact. Whatever, therefore, is not susceptible of this agreement or disagreement, is incapable of being true or false, and can never be an object of our reason. (T 3.1.1.9/SBN 458)

Within the class of 'fictions', we can distinguish further between those that are 'artificial' and others that are 'natural', a distinction I take from Hume's own observation about the 'word *relation*', which

> is commonly us'd in two senses considerably different from each other. Either for that quality, by which two ideas are connected together in

the imagination, and the one naturally introduces the other . . .; or for that particular circumstance, in which, even upon the arbitrary union of two ideas in the fancy, we may think proper to compare them. In common language the former is always the sense, in which we use the word, *relation*; and 'tis only in philosophy, that we extend it to mean any particular subject of comparison, without a connecting principle. (T 1.1.5.1/SBN 13–14)

There is no prior force or natural attraction that excites the imagination to relate one idea to another, philosophical relations being principles – tools or instruments, even – that philosophers employ in order to elucidate the phenomena they investigate. Since the fictions that originate from them are artificial constructions, there is no matter of fact to which the ideas refer, although they often contain such force and vivacity as to persuade practitioners into professing belief in their existence.

Productive Power, Artificial Fictions and Persuasion

The first class of fictions are 'artificial' and result from the voluntary act of imagination to combine ideas to create new ones that do not correspond directly to anything in experience. These fictions hardly produce any belief-like state but, to borrow a phrase from Hume's observation about the 'fervours of poetry and eloquence', are the 'mere *phantom of belief or perswasion*' (T 1.3.10.10/SBN 630). Hume thinks that, for the most part, artificial fictions are rarely taken actually to refer to objects with real existence and that any professed belief is really a matter of people being persuaded of something and taking the ideas in question as having real referents, thus only lending themselves to their existence for one reason or another. Even if one is ostensibly convinced that a putative object is real, the feeling on which the claim is based is only short-lived. For this reason, the states produced by artificial fictions do not even count as belief-like. When the idea of imagination gains sufficient force and vivacity, it 'counterfeit[s] its effects on the belief and judgement' (T 1.3.5.6/SBN 86), as Hume describes them, and in such cases the imagination can

feign a train of events, with all the appearance of reality, ascribe to them a particular time and place, conceive them as existent, and paint them out to itself with every circumstance, that belongs to any historical fact, which it believes with the greatest certainty . . . we can, in our conception, join the head of a man to the body of a horse; but it is not in our power to believe, that such an animal has really existed. (EHU 5.10/SBN 47–8)

'It follows, therefore', he concludes, 'that the difference between *fiction* and *belief* lies in some sentiment or feeling, which is annexed to the latter, not to the former, and which depends not on the will, nor can be commanded at pleasure' (EHU 5.11/SBN 48). Imagination 'has the command over all its ideas, and can join and mix and vary them, in all ways possible', Hume declares.

It may conceive fictitious objects with all the circumstances of place and time. It may set them, in a manner, before our eyes, in their true colours, just as they might have existed. But . . . it is impossible that this faculty of imagination can ever, of itself, reach belief. (EHU 5.12/SBN 49)

Imagination, to recall Addison's remark, bestows charms on a monster and entertains the poor soul in a dungeon, but neither fabulous creatures nor beautiful landscapes are thus made real or believed to be so.

Fictions of this kind are found wherever the imagination combines ideas, deliberately and voluntarily, to create new ones that have no direct correspondence to anything in experience, and there are three areas in which he takes them to be manifest. The first (and the subject of Chapter 2) is the class of what we can call 'poetic fictions', the creations found in the works of poetry and literature. Hume at once respects and admires the imagination insofar as it is the source of poetic genius, but he also recognises that poets are 'liars by profession' since they 'always endeavour to give an air of truth to their fictions' (T 1.3.10.5/SBN 121); even the considerable powers of persuasion at the command of the poet, however, 'can never cause a passion, like one in real life' (T Abstract, 22/SBN 654). The second concerns the 'invisible powers' (considered in Chapter 6), which populate the systems of polytheistic religions and that Hume ultimately explains as self-delusion and wishful thinking in the face of an unpredictable and threatening world. The third kind of artificial fiction to which Hume draws attention (and the subject of Chapter 7) is 'philosophical fictions'. These are artificial because, like winged horses and fiery dragons, the ideas involved arise from a voluntary and deliberate act of imagination to combine ideas and create new ones, but they are the peculiar purview of philosophers who compare ideas in order to discover connections that would not otherwise be perspicuous. These originate in what Hume calls 'philosophical relations' (resemblance, identity, space and time, quantity or number, degrees of a particular quality, contrariety and cause and effect), not themselves fictions but instances where philosophers risk drawing connections where none are to be found.[63] We should note that, in the case of philosophy and polytheism, Hume thinks that while the fictions are artificial and only persuade those who profess them, they still exert a powerful influence on the mind, and that makes them difficult to eradicate.

Productive Power, Vulgar Fictions and Natural Beliefs

The second class of fictions are 'natural' or what, to distinguish them clearly from the belief-like states they inspire, we can call 'vulgar' or 'natural fictions of vulgar reason'. I shall use these terms interchangeably to reflect the fact that the ideas in question arise in the rounds of common life from the 'secret tie or union' that Hume finds in the principles of association, the 'natural relations' that cause the mind to join ideas such that the appearance of one naturally introduces the other. The imagination forms them automatically and without reflection and corresponds to what writers in the phenomenological tradition have called part of a natural attitude or world taken for granted, what Ainslie has characterised as an 'immersion in the world', a 'vulgar sense' that consists of an 'unstated set of attitudes toward and commitments about what we perceive'.[64] These fictions inspire correspondingly 'natural beliefs', which (as we shall see below) are either first or second order, depending on the 'propensity' that gives rise to them.

One notable characteristic of vulgar fictions, which distinguishes them from their artificial counterparts, is that they are not falsifiable.[65] They lack the sort of evidence that, once made apparent, would show them to be either true *or* false; they are, to borrow a phrase from Annette Baier, 'unverifiable, and so unverified'.[66] According to Hume's theory of ideas, this means that, strictly speaking, such a fiction is not genuine but unintelligible because it lacks any content derived from impressions.[67] That does not make it incoherent: a fiction is *supposed* to refer to some phenomenon (even if that phenomenon cannot be understood) and will have suppositional content that is provided by the imagination and immune from truth-value.[68] They are neither true nor false because they refer to objects without any demonstrable real existence; they are unintelligible according to the theory of ideas but coherent insofar as they are suppositional. Unlike artificial fictions, where Hume considers the beliefs in question to be 'counterfeit' and thus a matter of persuasion, natural fictions inspire belief-like states that people profess to hold. These are not false beliefs because they cannot be corrected, and yet they have intentional content: they are about something.

Given their origin in natural relations, we can call the beliefs that vulgar fictions inspire 'natural'. By 'natural' in this context I have in mind the view that for Hume there are certain beliefs that, as Kemp Smith described it in 1905, are 'due to ultimate instincts or properties that constitute our human nature'.[69] Following G. C. A. Gaskin, we can think of such beliefs as exhibiting four main characteristics that, as he puts it, make them 'beliefs of naïve common sense':[70] they arise pre-reflectively and prior to any education and thus no argumentation is required to reach them; they are unavoidable, necessary, or required as a precondition for action since it would be impossible to act in the world without them; they are 'universally, if inarticulately held'; and, finally, non-rational because there is 'no rational justification for holding them'. Further, we can draw on a distinction Hume draws between an 'original instinct or primary impression of nature' and a 'secondary' one that 'may be easily perverted by various accidents and causes' or 'may, by an extraordinary concurrence of circumstances, be altogether prevented' (NHR Intro. 1). Under the first, Hume includes self-love, sexual attraction, love of one's children, gratitude and resentment, all of which are marked by being universal, having specific objects, and being pursued inflexibly across a range of social and historical circumstances. Under the latter, in the context of the *Natural History*, he places religion, but we can extend that to include other principles that are established and followed only contingently. Keith Yandell provides a useful way of sharpening this distinction. A first-order or 'primary' instinct, as Yandell calls it, is 'possessed by all, is efficacious in all, and yields the same results in all', whereas a 'secondary' or second-order one is 'possessed by all, but is not efficacious in all, and does not yield the same results in all'. Both primary and secondary instincts can be 'original', however, insofar as they are both part of human nature.[71] Further, a propensity can be thought of as 'basic' if it is a condition for another arising such that the latter depends upon it. 'A propensity A is basic relative to property B', Yandell writes, 'if one's having A does not presuppose that one has B, but that one has B does presuppose that one has A'.[72] First-order propensities (possessed by, efficacious and effective in all) are thus original (part of human nature) and basic (not dependent on more fundamental propensities); second-order ones (possessed by all but neither efficacious nor effective in every individual) are original (part of human nature) but non-basic (dependent on other more fundamental propensities).

Following Gaskin, Yandell and Hume himself, then, we can thus distinguish first-order natural beliefs from second-order natural beliefs that connect to vulgar fictions and identify them with specific areas in which Hume thinks they arise. First-order natural beliefs are obstinate, intractable and unavoidable; they might be thought of as instinctive or, as Terence Penelhum suggests, 'Darwinian' because they are 'indispensable for our survival, and it is our good fortune that nature supplies them'.[73] They follow from the 'permanent, irresistible and universal' principles of the imagination and explain the existence and persistence of certain fictions; people hold beliefs about the objects to which these ideas refer even though there is no matter of fact to which they correspond. They are ideas that are not falsifiable and cannot therefore be corrected.[74] Second-order natural beliefs are still natural in being part of human nature, but in the way of a disease: a 'malady is said to be natural', Hume remarks in an echo of Locke, 'as arising from natural causes, tho' it be contrary to health, the most agreeable and most natural situation of man' (T 1.4.4.1/SBN 225). Like a malady, these second-order natural beliefs can and should be corrected and, instead of threatening the order of common life, doing so might actually enhance it.

There are three areas where this division can be applied to help elucidate Hume's view of the productive imagination and the fictions it creates: in metaphysics, where Hume identifies the fictions and first-order natural beliefs (that cannot be corrected) in external existence and the self; in the sphere of politics, where Hume discovers the fictions and first-order beliefs (that cannot be corrected) that underlie and gives rise to the ideas and rules governing property; and in popular theism, which consists of fictions that give rise to second-order beliefs (that can be corrected). As in the case of the artificial fictions of polytheism and philosophy, Hume thinks that the religious fictions of popular theism, even though second order, are powerful and difficult to root out. In both cases (as we shall see in Chapters 6 and 7, respectively) Hume identifies an alternative to the natural fictions of both – 'true' religion and 'true' philosophy that he juxtaposes to their 'false' counterparts – and thus a way to resist the temptations the imagination offers to take ideas as referring to objects with real existence.

As emphasised at the outset, while Hume appeals to the imagination routinely and as a matter of course in his writings, nowhere does he undertake any systematic treatment of the main features he associates with it. This does not mean, however, that he did not conceive of it as displaying a set of powers and orderly principles that compose its operations, nor that his frequent appeal to it is arbitrary. The aim of this first chapter has been to support the first of these contentions; defending the latter claim will occupy us in the chapters that follow. As we have seen, it is possible to isolate and classify the main functions Hume attributes to the faculty in terms of two fundamental powers and a dominant principle. First, the imagination is a mimetic faculty, which, in conjunction with memory, copies and represents impressions and supplies the mind with ideas. When ideas of imagination are confused with those of memory, the results are mistakes and the beliefs it inspires are false. It also has, second, a productive power with the ability to transpose and change the material on which it works to create new ideas; these are fictions, because there is no object to which the idea corresponds and the beliefs to which they give rise are phantom beliefs in objects with no real existence (or none that can be demonstrated). These fictions are artificial, with the outcome of combining ideas deliberately and voluntarily, and are rarely taken to refer to real objects; at best, professed belief in them is a matter of being temporarily persuaded. The fictions are natural, on the other hand, when they spring from the natural attraction ideas have for one another according to the relations of resemblance, contiguity and cause and effect. Some of these fictions are instinctual and inspire first-order natural beliefs, which are pre-reflective, necessary and universal; others do not qualify as natural in this sense but arise from a propensity of human nature and for that reason the beliefs they inspire are second order.

The classification developed in this first chapter is done with a view to identifying and organising the various functions Hume gives the imagination, and is also intended to reflect its Janus-faced character. Hume recognises the imagination as an extraordinary power, the source of ideas and the condition for the possibility of experience, capable even, in its productive capacity, of raising ideas when impressions of sense and reflection are lacking. At the same time, he acknowledges its sinister side. The imagination is an unnerving presence and an unpredictable companion, with the power to confuse, beguile and convince its victims that the images it paints on the canvas of the mind are indubitably and clearly connected with real existence and matter of fact. The imagination thus enters Hume's philosophical system as both friend and foe, an ally whose assistance is indispensable for anatomising the body of common life, but always threatening to tear apart good work already done. This is reflected in a deep ambivalence on Hume's part towards the faculty, which he both admires as the origin of creativity but often criticises as the source of corruption. This will become clear as we examine the role the imagination plays in Hume's approach in the various parts of his philosophical system. It is to the first of these – metaphysics – that we now turn.

Notes

1. See, for example, E. J. Furlong, *Imagination* (London: Allen & Unwin, 1961), pp. 96–7; Jan Wilbanks, *Hume's Theory of Imagination* (The Hague: Martinus Nijhoff, 1968), pp. 62–3; Mary Warnock, *Imagination* (Berkeley: University of California Press, 1976), p. 15; Alan R. White, *The Language of Imagination* (Oxford: Basil Blackwell, 1990), p. 38; and Eva Brann, *The World of the Imagination: Sum and Substance* (Savage, MD: Rowman & Littlefield, 1991), pp. 83–4.

2. See David Owen, *Hume's Reason* (Oxford: Oxford University Press, 1999), p. 76, and his discussion in Chapters 1–2 generally. For historically informed discussions of the issue, see Charles Echelbarger, 'Hume and the Logicians', in *Logic and the Workings of the Mind: The Logic of Ideas and Faculty Psychology in Early Modern Philosophy*, North American Kant Society Studies in Philosophy, vol 5, ed. Patricia A. Easton (Atascadero, CA: Ridgeview Publishing Company, 1997), pp. 137–52, and Don Garrett, *Cognition and*

Commitment in Hume's Philosophy (Oxford: Oxford University Press, 1997), Ch. 1, esp. pp. 14–21.

3. See John Laird, *Hume's Philosophy of Human Nature* (London: Methuen, 1932), pp. 37–46; the quotations are from pp. 45 and 46. Garrett, *Cognition and Commitment*, pp. 14–25, emphasises Hume's departure from the early-modern tradition both in rejecting a higher intellectual faculty and in his treatment of imagination and memory: 'he follows his predecessors in regarding the imagination as a representational faculty' but 'differs from their common usage only in explicitly distinguishing memory of past events as a separate representational faculty, rather than subsuming it as a function of the imagination' (p. 20). Charles W. Hendel, *Studies in the Philosophy of David Hume*, 2nd ed. (Indianapolis: Bobbs Merrill, [1925] 1963), pp. 74–45, suggests Montaigne as an important precursor along with Malebranche and Locke. Wayne Waxman, *Hume's Theory of Consciousness* (Cambridge: Cambridge University Press, 1994), probably overstates the case when he writes of Hume being 'prompted radically to recast the relations between imagination and the other faculties' (p. 62).

4. For a brief account of the note and circumstances of its revision, see Norton's edition of the *Treatise* (p. 458, n.19) and, for the details of the change, note 2 in the *apparatus criticus* of Selby-Bigge/Nidditch (SBN 664), which reports this change as accounting for two of only a few 'cancels' that Hume made. That Hume was rather obsessively involved in overseeing the work as it was in press is borne out historically. Hume appears to have left France in August 1737 with what would become the first two books of the *Treatise*, and remained in London overseeing the process until they were published early in 1737. See James A. Harris, *Hume: An Intellectual Biography* (Cambridge: Cambridge University Press, 2015), pp. 80–1. In one of the few surviving letters from this period – to Henry Home, dated 2 December 1737 – Hume reports having been in London 'near three months, always within a week of agreeing with my printers' (L 1.24).

5. In Norton's edition the original note is omitted from the main text and placed in the annotations to the section (see p. 515).

6. Garrett, *Cognition and Commitment*, pp. 27–9. Garrett characterises reason as the 'faculty of reasoning: of making inferences, or providing, appreciating, and being moved by arguments' (p. 25), and understanding as a 'general faculty of performing cognitive acts' (p. 28). To say that all ideas except memory come from imagination thus amounts to a 'classification of representational faculties'

and a rejection of any 'higher, non-imagistic faculty of intellect' (p. 26). The thesis that reason or understanding is a 'sub-class of the imagination' is proposed and defended by Owen, *Hume's Reason*, pp. 73–6 *passim*. Owen contends that there is no 'separate "faculty" of the understanding . . . only characteristic activities that require explanation', which Hume provides 'in terms of broader principles of the imagination' (p. 74). More recently, Garrett has departed somewhat from Hume's terminology and emphasised the connections among imagination, reason and understanding by referring to the wider and narrower senses of imagination as the 'inclusive imagination' and 'unreasoning imagination', respectively. See Don Garrett, *Hume* (London: Routledge, 2015), pp. 86–8. Cf. Harold W. Noonan, *Hume On Knowledge* (New York: Routledge, 1999), pp. 123–31, who speaks of imagination in the 'broad sense' and 'narrow sense', connecting the former with 'good reasoning' and the latter with 'bad reasoning', the latter so called because it 'compares unfavourably' with judgement or reason.

7. Thomas Holden, *Spectres of False Divinity: Hume's Moral Atheism*. (Oxford: Oxford University Press, 2010), p. 66. A similar emphasis is given by Waxman, *Hume's Theory of Consciousness*, Ch. 2, who reads Hume's account of the imagination as developmental, the faculty undergoing 'various metamorphoses . . . over the course of *Treatise* I, so that what is initially a marginal faculty conventionally conceived becomes, by the end, the foundation of all our knowledge' (p. 63): a 'reduction' of memory, the senses, and understanding to the imagination (p. 77). John B. Stewart, *The Moral and Political Philosophy of David Hume* (New York: Columbia University Press, 1963), who writes of a 'kind of imagining involved when we engage "demonstrative reasoning"' involving 'our knowledge of certain standardized relations, such as the relations among the angles of an isosceles triangle, or between "two and six"' (p. 39). Cf. Jerry A. Fodor, *Hume Variations* (Oxford: Clarendon Press, 2003), Ch. 5, who distinguishes between the 'narrow' and 'broad construal' of imagination, though these have nothing to do with Hume's footnote, which Fodor describes as 'pretty enigmatic' (p. 125). Fodor's distinction is supposed to track the imagination as it 'supplements' and 'implements' the principles of association, respectively.

8. I here follow Garrett and others and take Hume to have a univocal sense of 'reason'. The school of thought that sees him as using 'reason' equivocally goes back to Barbara Winters, 'Hume on Reason', *Hume Studies*, 5: 1 (1979), pp. 20–35. It is worth noting

that Hume extends both senses of imagination to animals: they, too, sense, infer and cognise (wider sense) and come by ideas in ways other than through reasoning (narrow sense), and have the capacity to sympathise (see T 2.2.12.6/SBN 398), which depends in turn on the imagination. Hume does consider animals 'less susceptible either of the pleasures or pains of the imagination' (T 2.2.12.3/SBN 397), however, and less inclined to feel pity, the latter requiring more 'effort and thought of imagination' than envy and malice, both passions that are 'very remarkable in animals' (T 2.2.12.8/SBN 398).

9. Norman Kemp Smith, *The Philosophy of David Hume: A Critical Study of its Origins and Central Doctrines* (London: Macmillan, 1941), pp. 137 and 459 (see below, n. 32).

10. See, for example, Stewart, *The Moral and Political Philosophy of David Hume*, who takes 'fancying' as the kind of imagining involved when we 'take simple ideas and assemble them into all sorts of complex ideas' (p. 38); Holden, *Spectres of False Divinity*, who identifies the wider sense with the 'settled and regular associative mechanisms by which we produce our non-memory ideas', which he juxtaposes to the 'more haphazard associative operations that constitute the 'fancy', i.e. imagination in the narrower sense' (pp. 66–7); and, most recently, Ryu Susato, *Hume's Sceptical Enlightenment* (Edinburgh: Edinburgh University Press, 2015), who writes of Hume recognising 'two levels of imagination: one is more fundamental and indispensible, while the other is capricious and whimsical' (p. 38). Cf. Garrett, *Cognition and Commitment*, p. 12, who notes Kemp Smith's mistake in taking Hume's two senses as being 'almost directly opposite [in] meaning' when they are clearly not.

11. See Susato, *Hume's Sceptical Enlightenment*, who claims that Hume was 'sceptical about the possibility of demarcating the workings of the two (trivial and essential) levels of imagination, . . . [which] gives his overall arguments a *tone* of moral and cultural relativism' (p. 54). Cf. Susato's (to my mind) accurate observation that the '"slight" nature of the imagination does not indicate its weakness; rather, according to Hume, it provides scope for contingency in uncertain situations such as the glorious revolution' (p. 69).

12. Barry Stroud, 'Hume's Scepticism: Natural Instincts and Philosophical Reflection', *Philosophical Topics*, 19: 1 (1991), pp. 271–91; reprinted in Barry Stroud, *Philosophers Past and Present* (Oxford: Oxford University Press, 2011), pp. 144–66. Stroud writes: 'In calling them "trivial" Hume does not mean that the properties of imagination are trivial in their effects. Without the operations of the

imagination which he is interested in, we could not think at all. . . .
So the principles of imagination are not trivial for human nature;
they make it what it is' (p. 46). The same point is made explicitly by
Streminger, 'Hume's Theory of Imagination', p. 104.

13. David Miller, *Philosophy and Ideology in Hume's Political Thought*
(Oxford: Clarendon Press, 1981), pp. 26–7.

14. Cf. Richard Kearney, *The Wake of Imagination: Ideas of Creativity in
Western Culture* (London: Hutchinson, 1988), pp. 16–18, who uses
similar terminology but in quite a different way to refer to 'historical
paradigms', each of which 'privileges some metaphor characterising
the domination function of imagination at a given time'. Thus the
'mimetic paradigm' (biblical, classical and medieval) privileges the
'referential figure of the *mirror*'; the 'productive paradigm' (modern
period) that of the 'expressive figure of the *lamp*'; and the 'parodic
paradigm' (the postmodern) the 'reflexive figure of a *labyrinth of
looking-glasses*' (p. 17). Cf. Fodor, *Hume Variations*, who claims
that Hume does not 'set out the principles according to which imagination operates to compose novel concepts' (p. 118), nor does he
'know how the imagination synthesises ideas; or if he does know, he
isn't telling' (p. 122). I should also note that the following discussion
represents a significant departure from my earlier (and, as I now see
it, flawed) attempt to find a rubric for discussing Hume's concept of
imagination in 'Hume's Phenomenology of the Imagination', *Journal
of Scottish Philosophy*, 5: 1 (2007), pp. 31–45.

15. For historical treatments of the imagination in the western tradition,
see Murray Wright Bundy, *The Theory of Imagination in Classical
and Medieval Thought, University of Illinois Studies in Language
and Literature*, 12: 2–3, May–August 1927 (Urbana: University of
Illinois Press), and Brann, *The World of the Imagination*.

16. Plato's orders of knowing (in ascending order) are *eikasia* (picture-thinking), *pistis* (knowledge from sense experience), *dianoia*
(knowledge from first principles) and *noesis* (apprehension of time-
less and unchangeable entities). See *Republic* VI, 509d-511e, trans.
G. M. A. Grube, rev. C. D. C. Reeve, in *The Complete Works of
Plato*, ed. John M. Cooper (Indianapolis: Hackett, 1997). For the
etymology that follows, I am indebted to Bundy, *The Theory of
Imagination*, pp. 11–13, and Brann, *The World of the Imagination*,
pp. 17–23.

17. See Bundy, *The Theory of Imagination*, pp. 157–9, who writes of
there being 'no conclusive evidence . . . that *imaginatio* was employed
before the time of Augustine'. Augustine deliberately breaks with

the Neo-platonic association of *phantasia* 'with the concrete image resulting from sensation', and thus 'had a profound influence upon the terminology of the Middle Ages' (p. 158). Brann repeats Bundy's observation.

18. See John Keats, 'Fancy', lines 1–18, in *The Poetical and Other Writings of John Keats, Hampstead Edition*, ed. H. Buxton Forman, rev. Maurice Buxton Forman, 8 vols (New York: Phaeton Press, 1970), 3: p. 164.

19. William Taylor, '*Imagination, Fancy*', in William Taylor (ed.), *British Synonyms Discriminated* (London: W. Pople, 1813), p. 242.

20. See William Duff, *An Essay on Original Genius; and Its Various Modes of Exertion in Philosophy and the Fine Arts, Particularly in Poetry* (London: Edward & Charles Dilly, 1767), especially pp. 7 and 70–1; William Wordsworth, 'Preface to the Edition of 1815', in *The Prose Works of William Wordsworth*, ed. W. J. B. Owen and Jane Washington Smyser, 3 vols (Oxford: Clarendon Press, 1974), 3: pp. 26–39; and Samuel Taylor Coleridge, *Biographia Literaria or Biographical Sketches of My Literary Life and Opinions*, in *The Collected Works of Samuel Taylor Coleridge*, 16 vols (Princeton: Princeton University Press, 1983), vol. 7 (two parts), ed. James Engell and W. Jackson Bate, esp. pp. 82, 124, 168, and 305. For a discussion of Wordsworth, Coleridge and their predecessors on imagination and fancy, see Timothy M. Costelloe, *The British Aesthetic Tradition: From Shaftesbury to Wittgenstein* (Cambridge: Cambridge University Press, 2013), Ch. 5.

21. All references are to volume and page of *Ouvres de Descartes*, ed. C. Adam and P. Tannery, new ed., 11 vols (Paris: J. Vrin, 1964–74) (AT), and the corresponding volume (1 or 2) and page numbers of translation from *The Philosophical Writings of Descartes*, trans. John Cottingham, Robert Stoothoff and Dugald Murdoch (Cambridge: Cambridge University Press, 1984) (CSM).

22. For discussion of Descartes' changing view of the imagination, including the continuity between the earlier and later work, see Véronique M. Fóti, 'The Cartesian Imagination', *Philosophy and Phenomenological Research*, 46:4 (1986), pp. 631–42, and the book-length study by Dennis L. Sepper, *Descartes' Imagination: Proportion, Images, and the Activity of Thinking* (Berkeley: University of California Press, 1996).

23. Baruch Spinoza, *Tractatus de Intellectus Emendatione* (*Treatise on the Emendation of the Intellect*) (TIE) and *Ethica ordine geometrica demonstrata* (*Ethics Demonstrated in Geometrical Order*), in *The*

Collected Works of Spinoza, ed. and trans. Edwin Curley (Princeton: Princeton University Press, 1985), vol. 1. References to TIE are to paragraph numbers as supplied by Curley; those to the *Ethics* follow the standard reference of 'E' followed by book number, axiom, proposition, corollary and so forth, as the case may be.

24. John Locke, *An Essay Concerning Human Understanding*, ed. P. H. Nidditch (Oxford: Oxford University Press, [1690] 1975). Here and elsewhere, all references are to book, chapter, paragraph and page number of the Nidditch edition.

25. Thomas Hobbes, *Leviathan, or the Matter, Forme, and Power of a Common-wealth Ecclesiasticall and Civill*, ed. Richard Tuck (Cambridge: Cambridge University Press, [1651] 1991), 2: 5/15. All references are to chapter and pagination of Hobbes' original text (the '*Syn*' edition in the Cambridge University Library used by Tuck) followed by page numbers of Tuck's edition.

26. See, for example, P. J. E. Kail, *Projection and Realism in Hume's Philosophy* (Oxford: Oxford University Press, 2007), pp. 52–3. Kail describes Hume as appealing 'somewhat more reticently' than Malebranche 'to the quasi-physiological understanding of the imagination to explain the operations of resemblance' (p. 53). See also Donald C. Ainslie, *Hume's True Scepticism* (Oxford: Oxford University Press, 2015), pp. 79–80 (who describes it anachronistically as the 'neuroscience of his [Hume's] day'); Garrett, *Hume*, pp. 84–5; Hendel, *Studies in the Philosophy of David Hume*, pp. 77–85; Susato, *Hume's Sceptical Enlightenment*, pp. 34–5; John P. Wright, *The Sceptical Realism of David Hume* (Minneapolis: University of Minnesota Press, 1983), pp. 68–70; and John Bricke, *Hume's Philosophy of Mind* (Edinburgh: Edinburgh University Press, 1980), *passim*, and below, n.51. Cf. Harris, *Hume*, pp. 83–4 and 491 n.27; Beryl Logan, *A Religion without Talking: Religious Belief and Natural Belief in Hume's Philosophy of Religion* (Dordrecht: Nijhoff, 1993), pp. 27–8, and Laird, *Hume's Philosophy of Human Nature*, pp. 40–1, who juxtaposes Malebranche's psychophysiology with Hume's approach and notes that 'Despite one marked exception . . . – which, in its way, was a curiosity because of its doctrine of "proper traces" and "rummaging" of some individual cell – Hume, in general, renounced physiological explanations'.

27. Marina Frasca-Spada, 'Belief and Animal Spirits in Hume's *Treatise*', *Eighteenth-Century Thought*, 1 (2003): 151–69, p. 163. In something of an interpretive stretch, Frasca-Spada does claim that 'Hume

still cast his attempted phenomenological descriptions of experience in the idiom of the animal spirits and brain traces physiology, transposing the theory into his own explorations of experience' (p. 163).

28. This doctrine separates Hume squarely from the rationalist tradition, which assumed an intellectual capacity to form non-imagistic ideas. This point has been made forcefully by Garrett, *Cognition and Commitment*, pp. 25–6, and more recently by Kail, *Projection and Realism in Hume's Philosophy*, p. 48. See also Douglas Long, 'Hume's "Imagination" Revisited', *Lumen: Selected Proceedings from the Canadian Society for Eighteenth-Century Studies*, 17 (1998), pp. 127–49, who considers the imagination in relation to Hume's 'mitigated' scepticism and situates his view in the context of a developing commercial society in the early-modern period.

29. On this point, see Colin McGinn, *Mindsight: Image, Dream, Meaning* (Cambridge, MA: Harvard University Press, 2004), pp. 8–11, and David Pears, *Hume's System: An Examination of the First Book of his 'Treatise'* (Oxford: Oxford University Press, 1990), pp. 40–1, who takes the criterion of 'strength and liveliness' to be insufficient for distinguishing imagination from memory. Cf. R. J Collingwood, *The Principles of Art* (Oxford: Clarendon Press, 1938), pp. 184–5. In general, Collingwood credits Hume with solving the long-standing 'problem of distinguishing real sensation from imagination' (p. 175) via the doctrine of the force and vivacity of impressions and ideas through which 'the distinction between real sensation and imagination is resolved into a distinction between our inability and ability of set purpose to control, excite, suppress, or modify our sensory experiences' (p. 184). For a critical evaluation of Collingwood's reading and appropriation of Hume, see S. K. Wertz, 'Collingwood's Understanding of Hume', *Hume Studies*, 20: 2 (1994), pp. 261–87, especially pp. 262–8.

30. Cf. Locke, who writes in the *Essay* that 'adequate ideas' are those 'which perfectly represent those Archetypes, which the Mind supposes them taken from; which it intends them to stand for, and to which it refers them' (*Essay* 2.31.1–4).

31. It is also worth noting that Hume has been roundly criticised for the apparent inadequacy of this view for distinguishing memory from imagination, or correct memories from false ones. J. A. Passmore, *Hume's Intentions* (Cambridge: Cambridge University Press, 1952) goes so far as to find in it 'inconsistencies' of 'epic proportions' (p. 94). For a recent (and more sympathetic) discussion, see Saul Traiger, 'Hume on Memory and Imagination', in *A Companion*

to *Hume*, ed. Elizabeth S. Radcliffe (Oxford: Blackwell, 2008), pp. 58–71. Traiger himself emphasises the 'specificity' of ideas of memory as opposed to those of sense, although, as he acknowledges, this is not a point Hume himself makes explicitly.

32. Wilbanks, *Hume's Theory of Imagination*, p. 72. Cf. Kemp Smith, *The Philosophy of David Hume*, pp. 459–63, who considers this Hume's use of 'imagination' as 'ordinarily understood': the 'faculty which deals with those "perceptions" which allow of being distinguished from impressions, and which in proportion as they become "perfect ideas" . . . can be freely conjoined and separated'. As already noted above, he distinguishes this from the 'very special' sense in which Hume uses it to signify 'vivacity of conception' (p. 459). Wilbanks, *Hume's Theory of Imagination*, pp. 22–30, also offers an extended and trenchant critique of Smith's discussion, especially his extraordinary conclusion that 'Hume's ascription of primacy to the imagination has no greater importance in the philosophy of the *Treatise* than that of being merely a corollary to his early doctrine of belief' (pp. 462–3). What I am calling the combinatory power is also the focus of the discussion in Miller, *Philosophy and Ideology in Hume's Political Thought*, Ch. 1, and figures prominently in Susato, *Hume's Sceptical Enlightenment*, Ch. 2, although the emphasis there is exclusively on the imagination's role in the association of ideas.

33. The meaning of the term 'productive' to capture Hume's position should not be conflated with Kant's use of the same to denote the faculty that produces original representations of objects that precede experience (*exhibitio originaria*), a power that Kant contrasts with the empirical or reproductive imagination, the faculty of derived representation (*exhibito derivativa*) that recalls to mind previous empirical perceptions. See Immanuel Kant, *Kritik der reinen Vernunft* (KrV), in *Kants gesammelte Schriften, herausgegeben von der Deutschen (formerly Königlich Preussischen) Akademie der Wissenschaften*, 29 vols (Berlin: Walter de Gruyter [and predecessors], 1902), vols 3 and 4: A118 and A140–42/B179–181. This is not to deny any connections between Hume and Kant on this and related issues, interest in which is long-standing. See, for example, H. H. Price, *Hume's Theory of the External World* (Oxford: Clarendon Press, 1940), pp. 15–17 *passim*; Furlong, *Imagination*, Ch. 11; Wilbanks, *Hume's Theory of Imagination*, p. 82; P. F. Strawson, 'Imagination and Perception', in *Experience and Theory*, ed. Lawrence Foster and J. W. Swanson (Cambridge, MA: MIT Press, 1970), pp. 31–54; Philip P. Wiener, 'Kant and Hume on Reason and Experience in Ethics', in

Hume and the Enlightenment: Essays Presented to Ernest Campbell Mossner, ed. William B. Todd (Edinburgh: Edinburgh University Press, 1974), pp. 45–51; and S. C. Daniel, 'The Nature and Function of Imagination in Hume and Kant', *Indian Philosophical Quarterly*, 15: 1 (1988), pp. 85–97.

34. See Bundy, *The Theory of Imagination*, pp. 85–6 n.11.

35. On this point, see Roland Hall, 'Some Uses of Imagination in the British Empiricists: A Preliminary Investigation of Locke, as Contrasted with Hume', *The Locke Newsletter: An Annual Journal of Locke Research*, 20 (1989), pp. 47–62, esp. p. 56. Hall (pp. 54–5) usefully collects and categorises the various occurrences of 'imagination' and 'fancy' as they appear in the *Essay*.

36. This observation goes back at least to D. G. James, *The Life of Reason: Hobbes, Locke, Bolingbroke* (London: Longmans, 1949), p. 120. Hall, 'Some Uses of Imagination in the British Empiricists', pp. 51–3, follows James explicitly. See also James Engell, *The Creative Imagination: Enlightenment to Romanticism* (Cambridge, MA: Harvard University Press, 1981), pp. 18–19, who identifies Locke as the decisive break with the rationalists' emphasis on reason, and credits him with first distinguishing (albeit tentatively) different functions of imagination.

37. See, for example, George Berkeley, *A Treatise Concerning the Principles of Human Knowledge*, ed. Jonathan Dancy (Oxford: Oxford University Press, 1998), Introduction, sects. 8–10 and Part 1, sects. 1–2. It is also worth noting that, after Berkeley but before Hume (Books 1 and 2 of the *Treatise* appeared in 1739), Francis Hutcheson employed Locke's terminology in his treatment of beauty and morals, albeit without any systematic appeal to the faculty of imagination. Joseph Addison had already published his essays on 'The pleasures of the imagination' in 1711. See Francis Hutcheson, *An Inquiry into the Original of Our Ideas of Beauty and Virtue in Two Treatises*, 2nd edn (Indianapolis: Liberty Fund, [1726; 1st ed. 1725] 2004), I.I–IX. (I consider the philosophical connection between Addison and Hume in the next section.) In this context, see Furlong, *Imagination*, pp. 95–6, who suggests that the main difference between Hume and Berkeley is the distinction 'between ideas of memory and ideas of imagination', which the latter does not have at all. For Berkeley, imagination is primarily the active principle that explains the agency of spirits, something that Hume obviously rejects.

38. Hendel writes: 'What . . . inferences from cause to effect and effect to cause reveal is that our imagination, though seeming to be free to

combine, take apart, and produce ideas in any order at all, is actually determined by our very human nature to operate in certain regular ways'. See *Studies in the Philosophy of David Hume*, p. 73.

39. See Robert Sokolowski, 'Fiction and Illusion in David Hume's Philosophy', *Modern Schoolman*, 45: 3 (1968), p. 195, who cites non-contradiction and matter of fact as Hume's criteria for 'distinguishing reality from illusion'.

40. Gerhard Streminger, 'Hume's Theory of Imagination', *Hume Studies*, 6: 2 (1980), pp. 91–118, identifies what he calls the 'scientific faculty of the imagination' with its ability 'neither to transcend the empirical world nor to impose a new order upon the sense impressions, but rather to *structure* the stream of perceptions' (p. 98).

41. See Logan, *A Religion without Talking*, Ch. 2, who emphasises this dual aspect of the way the imagination functions.

42. See Ainslie, *Hume's True Scepticism*, esp. pp. 64–9 and Ch. 3. Ainslie notes that Hume's response to the problem ostensibly posed by the missing shade of blue reveals how 'right from the start, his empiricism allows that the imagination has a capacity to generate novel content' (p. 64).

43. See Paul Guyer, *A History of Modern Aesthetics*, Vol. 1, *The Eighteenth Century* (Cambridge: Cambridge University Press, 2014), pp. 124–39. The quotations are from pp. 129 and 133, respectively.

44. See Streminger, 'Hume's Theory of Imagination', pp. 95 and 108–10. The same emphasis is found in James Farr, 'Hume, Hermeneutics, and History: A "Sympathetic" Account', *History and Theory*, 17: 3 (1978), pp. 285–310, who writes that in Hume's account, imagination functions as an active, creative and regulative propensity or faculty of mind which 'has command over all its ideas and can join and mix and vary them in every possible way' (ICHU 62 [EHU 5.12])' (p. 296).

45. See Sir Joshua Reynolds, *Discourses on Art*, ed. Robert R. Wark (New Haven: Yale University Press, [1797] 1997); Alexander Gerard, *An Essay on Taste. To Which Is Now Added Part Fourth, Of the Standard of Taste; with Observations Concerning the Imitative Nature of Poetry*, 3rd edn (Edinburgh: J. Bell & W. Creech; London: T. Cadell, [1759] 1780); Alexander Gerard, *An Essay on Genius* (London: W. Strahan; Edinburgh: W. Creech, 1774); Archibald Alison, *Essays on the Nature and Principles of Taste* (Dublin: Byrne, Moore, Grueber, McAllister, Jones & White, 1790); and John Ruskin, *The Complete Works of John Ruskin (Library Edition)*, ed. E. T. Cook and Alexander Wedderburn, 39 vols (London:

George Allen, 1903–12). For a discussion of these developments, see Costelloe, *The British Aesthetic Tradition*, part 2, and Paul Guyer, *A History of Modern Aesthetics,* vol. 1, Ch. 4, and *A History of Modern Aesthetics*, vol. 2, *The Nineteenth Century* (Cambridge: Cambridge University Press, 2014), Ch. 5.

46. Joseph Addison, 'The Pleasures of the Imagination', in *The Spectator*, ed. Donald F. Bond, 5 vols (Oxford: Clarendon Press, 1965), Nos. 411–21, 21 June–3 July 1712, 3: 535–82. Here and elsewhere, all references are to this volume with essay number followed by the pagination of Bond's edition.

47. See in this context Sébastien Charles, 'Fictions in Berkeley: From Epistemology to Morality', *Berkeley Studies*, 20 (2009), pp. 13–21, who argues that 'Berkeley appeals to the imaginative aspects of reason itself' (p. 13), and 'opens up a space for both a representative and a creative, constitutive function for imagination in reasoning' (p. 21).

48. See Keats, *Writings*, 6: pp. 103–4.

49. For one view of this history, see Engell, *The Creative Imagination*, Chaps 4 and 5.

50. See Price, *Hume's Theory of the External World*, pp. 54–9, and Long, 'Hume's "Imagination" Revisited', p. 134. Price calls the principle 'curious and questionable' (p. 55). A similar emphasis is found in Frederick G. Whelan, *Order and Artifice in Hume's Political Philosophy* (Princeton: Princeton University Press, 1985), pp. 57–8, and Ainslie, *Hume's True Scepticism*, who uses the same term: the 'imagination's inertia leads it to posit a kind of structure in the world that outstrips what we directly experience' (p. 73 n.2).

51. See Duncan Forbes, *Hume's Philosophical Politics* (Cambridge: Cambridge University Press, 1975), p. 10 n. 2, and Wright, *The Sceptical Realism of David Hume*, pp. 69–70. Locke writes of 'Trains of Motions in the Animal Spirits, which once set a going continue on in the same steps they have been used to, which by often treading are worn into a smooth path, and the Motion in it becomes easy and as it were Natural' (*Essay* 2.33.6), and Malebranche of how '. . .l'attention fatigue beaucoup l'esprit . . . l'esprit suppose donc des resemblances imaginaires où il ne remarque pas les différences positives et réelles' (attention greatly wearies the spirit . . . the spirit thus assumes imaginary resemblances where it does not notice the positive and real differences) (translation mine). See Nicolas Malebranche, *De la recherche de la vérité. Où l'on traite de la Nature de l'Esprit de l'homme, et de l'usage qu'il en doit faire pour éviter l'erreur dans*

les Sciences, in *Oeuvres complétes de Malebranche*, 20 vols, ed. A. Robinet (Paris: J. Vrin, 1958–84), 1:3.2.10. Quoted in Forbes, *Hume's Philosophical Politics*, p. 10 n. 2.

52. For a discussion of Hume's engagement with Addison's 'polite' style, see Harris, *Hume*, Ch. 3. A similar emphasis is evident in some of Adam Smith's writing. See Andrew S. Skinner, 'Adam Smith, Science and the Role of the Imagination', in *Hume and the Enlightenment: Essays Presented to Ernest Campbell Mossner*, ed. William B. Todd (Edinburgh: Edinburgh University Press, 1974), pp. 164–88. Skinner focuses on the role Smith assigned to the imagination in scientific discourse (he focuses on the essay on astronomy) through principles taken over from Hume, including (in Smith's words) that the faculty seeks the pleasure of 'sedateness, tranquility, and composure' while avoiding the pain of 'uncertainty and anxious curiosity' and 'giddiness and confusion' (see pp. 166–7).

53. Guyer, *A History of Modern Aesthetics*. vol. 1, emphasises the importance of Addison for effectively introducing into aesthetics the 'new and fundamental' idea of free play and the pleasure it brings (p. 64). Guyer, as already noted, highlights Hume's role in the development of this idea, although he does not draw a specific connection between him and Addison.

54. See Willard Clark Gore, *The Imagination in Spinoza and Hume: A Comparative Study in the Light of Some Recent Contributions to Psychology. The University of Chicago Contributions to Philosophy* 2, 4 (Chicago: The University of Chicago Press, 1902), pp. 42–3; Price, *Hume's Theory of the External World*, p. 43; Wilbanks, *Hume's Theory of Imagination*, pp. 80–2; Streminger, 'Hume's Theory of Imagination', p. 94; and Barry Stroud, '"Gilding and Staining" the World with "Sentiments" and "Phantasms"', *Hume Studies*, 19: 2 (1993), pp. 253–72, 260. Stroud makes the same claim earlier in *Hume* (London: Routledge, 1977), pp. 86–7 *passim*. See also Logan, *A Religion without Talking*, Ch. 4, esp. pp. 80–7, and Miller, *Philosophy and Ideology in Hume's Political Thought*, who equates the 'propensity to *project* impressions in the mind on to the objects which produce them' with the 'tendency [of the imagination] to *perfect* its ideas by conceiving of perfect instances of some property X, even though experience has only furnished us with imperfect instances of X' (p. 33). Cf. Galen Strawson, *The Secret Connexion: Causation, Realism, and David Hume*, 2nd edn (Oxford: Oxford University Press, [1989] 2014), who uses 'Hume's special use of the imagination' – or simply 'the Imagination' – to refer to 'very basic

features of our cognitive apparatus ... in virtue of which we automatically come to conceptualise the world in certain fundamental
ways ... on the basis of our sensory experience' (p. 47).

55. Hume is here clearly not concerned with imagination insofar as it is
the source of 'whimsies and prejudices', but is using 'imagination' in
the 'more limited' sense discussed earlier, namely 'excluding only our
demonstrative and probable reasonings' but including the species of
reasoning that accounts for the inferential processes involved in the
association of ideas. The importance of imagination for the copy
principle and in belief formation has been emphasised by Logan, *A
Religion without Talking*, Ch. 1.

56. Distinguishing a mistake as one kind of error makes it clear that
not all 'errors' are the same and helps avoid ambiguity of the sort
Ainslie, *Hume's True Scepticism*, struggles to avoid: he writes that
the vulgar's beliefs 'are not as such in error, even if they do embody a
philosophical error in their unarticulated assumption of direct access
to objects' (p. 71), that fictional thoughts 'are not ipso facto errors'
(p. 83), and that the vulgar are 'not always in error' about their
sensory beliefs or at least 'not in error in any straightforward way'
(p. 106).

57. This point has been emphasised by Waxman in particular. See
Hume's Theory of Consciousness, pp. 67–8.

58. This wider application of 'fiction' to the products of imagination is
to be found in Sokolowski, 'Fiction and Illusion in David Hume's
Philosophy', pp. 200–1, and Miller, *Philosophy and Ideology in
Hume's Political Thought*, pp. 71–2, who applies the notion of fiction
and illusion in his discussions of Hume's political philosophy. Cf.
Annette C. Baier, *The Commons of the Mind* (Chicago: Open Court,
1997), who similarly (albeit *en passant*) emphasises what she calls
Hume's use of a 'very gross fallacy' (T 3.2.2.11) in connection with
the origin of the ideas of 'property', 'right' and 'obligation' (p. 38).

59. Hume's concept of a fiction has received relatively little attention in
the secondary literature, although helpful discussions are to be found
in Strawson, *The Secret Connexion*, 1st edn (1989), pp. 55–6 n. 36
and 2nd edn (2014), pp. 46–8; Saul Traiger, 'Impressions, Ideas, and
Fictions', *Hume Studies*, 13: 2 (1987), pp. 381–99; Baier, *A Progress
of Sentiments*, p. 103; and Henry E. Allison, *Custom and Reason in
Hume: A Kantian Reading of the First Book of the* Treatise (Oxford:
Oxford University Press, 2008), pp. 280–7.

60. See Sokolowski, 'Fiction and Illusion in David Hume's Philosophy',
esp. pp. 196–202, who equates fictions with 'speculative illusions'. An

explicit (and quite erroneous) claim that this is Hume's settled view of imagination is to be found in Kearney, *The Wake of Imagination*, pp. 163–7. Kearney writes, for example, that 'for Hume, as for Plato in his allegory of the cave, the imaginary world is one of comfortable illusion' (p. 166). It is worth noting that Kant describes fictions in the same way when discussing the 'dialectical inferences of pure reason': 'In light of their results, these conclusions are really to be called pseudo-rational [*vernünftelnde*] rather than rational [*Vernunftschlüsse*], although in view of their origin they may well fall under the latter title, since they are not fictitious [*nicht erdichtet*] and have not arisen fortuitously [*zufällig*], but have sprung from the nature of reason itself' (KrV A339/B397) (translation mine).

61. See Ainslie, *Hume's True Scepticsim*, pp. 66–7, who uses Hume's discussion of general or abstract ideas as a paradigm for understanding all fictions as cases of 'idea substitution' and a 'model' involving the 'four elements' of 'proximate content', a 'revival set', 'linguistic label' and an 'intended object'. See also Garrett, *Cognition and Commitment*, pp. 24–5, and *Hume*, pp. 55–7. I offer some comments on Ainslie's suggestion below (see pp. 57–8) but, in general, it tends to narrow the concept of a fiction and cannot accommodate those that are cases of invention rather than confusion. For that reason alone, the current schema I am suggesting seems more suitable.

62. Traiger, 'Impressions, Ideas, and Fictions', p. 386, Ainslie, *Hume's True Scepticism*, p. 66, and Allison, *Custom and Reason in Hume*, p. 281.

63. See Stewart, *The Moral and Political Philosophy of David Hume*, p. 41, who refers to this as the 'natural imagination': by 'its natural constitution, the human mind tends to move on restlessly from one perception to another, but not erratically or at random'.

64. Ainslie, *Hume's True Scepticism*, p. 43.

65. The latter point is emphasised by Traiger, 'Impressions, Ideas, and Fictions', pp. 393–4, which he takes to be a significant difference between himself and Robert McRae, who, in 'The Import of Hume's Theory of Time', *Hume Studies*, 6: 2 (1980), pp. 119–32, gives primacy of place to 'fictional duration' (that an object can be unchangeable yet enduring) as *the* fiction from which 'are generated in a logically ordered series the basic metaphysical categories in terms of which the mind thinks, and all of them are fictitious' (p. 124). McRae also distinguishes duration, in the 'philosophical and vulgar' sense, from 'Humean time and succession'. The former,

McRae argues, is 'for Hume, a "fiction", something falsely attributed to objects' (p. 120).

66. Baier, *A Progress of Sentiments*, p. 103. See also Wright, *The Sceptical Realism of David Hume*, pp. 72 and 126; Strawson, *The Secret Connexion*, p. 50, and *The Evident Connexion: Hume on Personal Identity* (Oxford: Oxford University Press, 2011), p. 51; and Don Garrett, 'Hume's Naturalistic Theory of Representation', *Synthese*, 152: 3 (2006), pp. 301–19, esp. p. 306

67. See Strawson, *The Secret Connexion*, who writes that 'we can't form any idea of or term for X which has any positive content, in the special restricted sense of content specified by the theory of ideas' (p. 46).

68. In what follows, I will use the term 'idea' both for fictions of the productive imagination (fictions) and for images of the mimetic imagination that can be traced to impressions (ideas, in Hume's technical sense). Context and appropriate qualification will prevent any ambiguity or confusion.

69. See Norman Kemp Smith, 'The Naturalism of David Hume (I.)' and 'The Naturalism of David Hume (II.)', *Mind*, 14: 54 and 55 (1905), pp. 149–73 and 335–47, respectively (the quotation is from p. 151).

70. J. C. A. Gaskin, *Hume's Philosophy of Religion*, 2nd edn (London: Macmillan Press, [1978] 1988), p. 187. Gaskin formulates these characteristics in opposition to the claim that Hume thinks of religious belief in these terms. His principal target is R. J. Butler, 'Natural Belief and the Enigma of David Hume', *Archiv für Geschichte der Philosophie*, 42: 1 (1960), pp. 73–100. Cf. A. E. Pitson, 'Sympathy and Other Selves', *Hume Studies*, 22: 2 (1996), pp. 255–71, who argues that Hume presupposes the 'existence of others' and for that reason such a belief should be classified as 'natural'.

71. Keith E. Yandell, *Hume's 'Inexplicable Mystery': His Views on Religion* (Philadelphia: Temple University Press, 1990), p. 24. One might note an ambiguity in Yandell's presentation since he also identifies primary propensities as original, which would exclude secondary ones from displaying that characteristic. However, this does not affect the usefulness of the distinctions he draws.

72. Yandell, *Hume's 'Inexplicable Mystery'*, p. 77.

73. Terence Penelhum, *God and Skepticism. A Study in Skepticism and Fideism* (Dordrecht, Holland: Reidel Publishing Company, 1987), p. 132. See also Donald W. Livingston, *Hume's Philosophy of Common Life* (Chicago: Chicago University Press, 1984), pp. 172–7, and Yandell, *Hume's 'Inexplicable Mystery'*, pp. 71–7.

74. This corresponds in large part to Kemp Smith's view of natural belief, under which he puts ideas of existence of body and the external world, causal action, and identity and unity of the self. See also *The Philosophy of David Hume*, where he reformulates this in terms of 'twin beliefs', namely that 'objects have a continuing, independent existence' and that 'in the public worlds thus constituted bodies (some of which are also selves) are causally operative upon one another' (p. 455)

2

Metaphysics

In this chapter we begin our exploration of how Hume's view of the imagination informs his philosophical system by considering his approach to subjects that fall under the heading of metaphysics. Hume himself often uses this term in a positive, or at least neutral, sense to distinguish 'profound reasonings' (EHU 1.7/SBN 9) of philosophy that are 'accurate and abstruse' rather than 'easy and obvious' (EHU 1.1/SBN 5). In so doing, he includes within it subjects that, to contemporary ears at least, might have the ring of matters more appropriately classified as epistemological or relating to human cognition. At the same time, the term 'metaphysics' has its own natural history and, even today, its precise meaning and parameters remain a matter of some debate.[1] With this in mind, and following Hume, I propose to take 'metaphysics' as referring to a number of issues that fall traditionally under that heading and involve ideas, which, being created by the propensive quality of the productive imagination, refer to objects that transcend possible experience.[2] I exclude from the present discussion those fictions that underlie the formation of property and compose the body of popular theism; these, too, are natural fictions of vulgar reason that arise from the propensive quality of the imagination and might also be included under the title of 'metaphysics', but they require a separate treatment, which I will pursue in Chapters 3 and 6, respectively.

Hume identifies a number of fictions that fall under the heading of metaphysics, and these can be divided according to the schema elaborated in Chapter 1. Vulgar fictions of metaphysics are part of the immersion in a world taken for granted and can be neither avoided nor corrected; correspondingly, they inspire natural first-order beliefs that are pre-reflective, universal and necessary. Philosophical fictions, by contrast, are artificial, the result of phi-

54

losophers drawing connections where none otherwise exist, and they only persuade practitioners that the ideas contained in the doctrines to which they are committed refer to some real object or state of affairs. Two factors rather complicate this picture, however. First, Hume suggests that some philosophical doctrines involve more than the temporary persuasion that accompanies artificial fictions; some people, stained with a 'tincture of philosophy' (EPM 9.25/SBN 283; E 217) – such as Hume – feel an irresistible pull towards engaging in philosophical inquiry and, despite the strange and sometimes dangerous world into which it can lead, they are inspired to return to it again and again (Hume, famously, suffered a mental breakdown in 1729 as a result of the intensity of his endeavours). This does not change the artificial character of philosophical fictions, but it does suggest that sometimes the artifice of philosophy crosses over to become a propensity and inspires belief-like states (albeit second order) that ordinarily attach to natural fictions. Hume identifies a similar phenomenon in the case of polytheism. We shall postpone discussion of these matters to the final and penultimate chapter, respectively.

Second, Hume's discussions of metaphysical matters do not fall easily under the headings of 'vulgar' and 'artificial' fictions. This is not, of course, a division that Hume makes explicitly, so it is hardly surprising that he does not observe its boundaries in any systematic way; indeed, he moves freely between them and sometimes in the course of considering a single subject. For example, Hume treats a vacuum and an unchanging temporal object as fictions arising from the same principles of the imagination, but treats the former as the purview of philosophers and the latter as part of everyday experience. In other cases, such as the substratum view of substance, where qualities are taken to inhere in some underlying matter, or the tendency to give spatial location to intangible objects, Hume first identifies a vulgar fiction that inspires natural beliefs and then turns to doctrines that philosophers have devised by unwittingly following the imagination beyond its natural habitat into the more rarified domains of artifice and persuasion. In the case of personal identity, moreover, it is difficult to identify unequivocally whether Hume is identifying a fiction to which we all succumb or speaking only to philosophical doctrines that have been proposed to explain it. In other words, Hume's own treatment of metaphysical subjects makes it nigh impossible to organise the discussion in a way that at once reflects his own order of presentation and preserves the distinction between vulgar and artificial fictions and the beliefs that attend them.

In order to fashion a coherent narrative, then, in what follows I shall focus on the *way* the imagination forms its fictions, which I take to reflect the spirit of Hume's own discussions, where his primary goal is to expose the process or activity through which the imagination does its work. With this mind, I shall adopt a distinction proposed by Robert McCrae to identify cases where the imagination either confuses, confounds or combines ideas it already possesses to create a new one, or where it invents an idea to reconcile contradictory and irreconcilable propositions that otherwise cause pain and bewilderment. These correspond to what McRae calls fictions of 'misapplication' and fictions of 'invention', respectively, and I shall follow his lead by employing these terms. McRae writes:

> The first is a particular kind of 'mistake', 'confusion', 'deception', or 'illusion', consisting in the *misapplication* of an idea derived from some original impression to something other than its proper object. . . . The other kind of fiction is not derived from some original impression, nor is it a mistake, it is a pure *invention* of the imagination to resolve a contradiction.[3]

Fictions of misapplication thus conform closely to Hume's 'general maxim' that 'wherever there is a close relation betwixt two ideas, the mind is very apt to mistake them, and in all its discourse and reasonings to use the one for the other' (T 1.2.5.19/SBN 60). In these cases, Hume's tactic is to identify ideas that can be explained by reference to matter of fact, and then show how, through its productive power to compound, transpose, augment and diminish materials of sense and experience, the imagination finds – as he describes it in the course of explaining the idea of continued existence – a 'medium betwixt' them (T 1.4.2.29/SBN 201) to produce a third term that forms their fictional counterpart. Fictions of misapplication include a vacuum and a temporal object without change, the philosophical doctrines that compose debates over liberty and necessity, the idea of self or personal identity, and the species of general rules that Hume associates with the imagination. Hume also treats 'identity' (of which personal identity is a particular case) as a fiction of misapplication, but since this is part of his discussion of continued and distinct existence and too closely tied to fictions of invention to discuss in isolation without distorting the development of his argument, I discuss it below (see 'Substance as a Substratum').

It is worth noting at this juncture a point of departure with a recent proposal by Ainslie that Hume's discussion of general or abstract ideas yields not only an example of a fiction but a paradigm case of what Hume means by the term, and thus a 'model' for the other fictions he discusses. In T 1.1.7 ('Of abstract ideas'), Hume's general thesis is that some ideas – those called 'general' or 'abstract' by philosophers – have the peculiar character of being 'particular in their nature, but general in their representation' (T 1.1.7.10/SBN 22) or, as Ainslie expresses it, that an 'idea of a particular is used not to represent the content of the impression from which it is derived, but rather to represent a class'. He takes this in turn to be a fiction that follows from an 'idea-substitution mechanism' provided by the imagination, so called because the 'imagination inserts one idea in the place of another without our realizing it'.[4] Ainslie uses this to examine other fictions Hume discusses, including a vacuum and the vulgar belief in independently existing objects.

The main problem with this suggestion is that Hume does not appeal to the concept of a fiction to explain how we apply ideas 'beyond their nature', that is, when we use a particular idea derived from a particular impression for a whole class of objects (T 1.1.7.7/SBN 20). He does not 'apply the label "fiction"' to it, as Ainslie acknowledges, although this is hardly decisive given other cases of ideas that Hume does treat as fictions without using the term or its cognates. More to the point, however, is that Hume explains general ideas by appealing to the basic principles of his philosophy and without identifying any confusion or invention on the part of the imagination, something he does when considering other cases of fictions. In the case of general ideas, he maintains, we find a 'resemblance among several objects', then 'apply the same name to all of them', and subsequently form a habit or develop a 'custom' of thinking in this manner so that hearing the name 'revives the idea of one of these objects, and makes the imagination conceal it with all its particular circumstances and proportions' (T 1.1.7.7/SBN 20). General ideas are thus explicable as both particular (in their nature) and general (in their representation). Ainslie is surely justified in seeing this as a case of substituting one idea for another, but that is not sufficient for it to qualify as a fiction.[5] Moreover, even if the case of general ideas is a case from which a more general model can be inferred, it has the effect, as I noted in Chapter 1 (note 61), of narrowing Hume's concept of fiction in such a way that it cannot accommodate cases that are something other than substituting one idea for another, namely cases of invention.

Like those of misapplication, fictions of invention have their origin in the imagination but, rather than arising from confusing and compounding ideas, they are inventions the faculty creates to resolve a contradiction. This is not a formal contradiction but an inconsistency or gap between an idea that we possess (sometimes itself a fiction) and experience. The imagination seeks relief from the pain caused by these competing propositions by finding an idea that reconciles the contradiction and, being unrestrained by real existence or matter of fact, the faculty is at liberty to do so by way of fictions that are independent of matter of fact or experience. From its desire for completion, the imagination fills the gap, which becomes a 'habit', as Hume remarks at one point, 'acquir'd by what was never present to the mind' (T 1.4.2.21/SBN 197). While there might well be a way of reconciling or correcting the two, the contradiction is really an antinomy, opposing propositions born of fundamental and intractable features of human nature that, while they can be reconciled, are destined to appear as a recurrent feature of experience. These include continued and distinct existence, substance as a substratum, objective causal power, cases of reification, and primary and secondary qualities.

Fictions of Misapplication

A Vacuum and Time without Change

The first cases of metaphysical fictions we consider are the ideas of a vacuum (empty space) and time without change, or of an unchanging or 'stedfast' object in time' (T 1.2.3.11/SBN 37 passim). These are fictions of misapplication, where the imagination confuses ideas it possesses to produce a new one and fall within the domain of philosophers who, under its sway, follow the imagination and draw connections where none otherwise exist.[6] In order to understand what Hume has in mind, we need to consider, first, how we come by our genuine ideas of space or extension and time or duration (Hume uses the terms interchangeably) in T 1.2.3.[7] In an instructive discussion of the issue, Lorne Falkenstein points out that there are four possibilities open to Hume in this regard: ideas of space and time might be drawn from impressions of sense, from impressions of reflection, arise as 'distinctions of reason', or qualify as fictions of the imagination.[8] Falkenstein rejects the first possibility on Hume's behalf, given that ideas of time and space cannot be traced directly to corresponding impressions of sense but arise, as Hume puts it, from the 'manner, in which impressions appear to the mind' (T 1.2.3.4/SBN 34). Hume clearly dismisses the second possibility as well – that they might be impressions of reflection – remarking that 'Our internal impressions are our passions, emotions, desires and aversions; none of which, I believe, will ever be asserted to be the model, from which the idea of space is deriv'd' (T 1.2.3.3/SBN 33).[9] Falkenstein also denies that ideas of space and time can be fictions, since these are 'invented *subsequently* to experience by comparison, association, or other cognitive operations' and thus presuppose that the ideas of time and place have arisen in the first place.[10] As we shall see, although genuine ideas of space and time are not fictions, their fictitious counterparts – a vacuum and time without change – are to be characterised in just this way and their origin explained through the workings of the imagination.

Rejecting the possibility that ideas arise as a distinction of reason is less straightforward. Falkenstein argues against this option on the grounds that distinctions of reason require other ideas first: one would have to experience a block of *black* marble, to use Hume's example, before one could 'separate and distinguish the colour from the form' in the previously experienced block of *white* marble (T 1.1.7.18/SBN 25). It is worth noting that distinctions of reason are not, as Falkenstein apparently assumes, identical with the power of abstraction itself.[11] Hume treats the former as a particular application of the latter, shown clearly in the fact that he employs the discussion of general abstract ideas to clarify how a distinction of reason is possible and intelligible (T 1.1.7.17–18/SBN 24–5). A distinction of reason involves considering 'figure and colour together' but viewing them 'in different *aspects*, according to the resemblances, of which they are susceptible' (T 1.1.7.18/SBN 25, emphasis added). Abstraction is a more general act of mind and involves selecting a single idea from resembling ones. This elision of distinctions of reason and abstraction notwithstanding, Falkenstein's point is well taken: if ideas of space and time arise originally as the product of abstraction, there must be some other idea of a spatial object to form a point of comparison. In other words, the abstract ideas of space and time – that is, 'ideas of space and time considered apart from the objects in space and time' – presuppose that we already have the 'idea of a particular space and time'.[12] It is for this reason, Falkenstein emphasises, that, in Hume's view, the simple fact of an object before me (Hume's example is a table) 'is *alone sufficient* to give me the idea of extension' (T 1.2.3.4/SBN, 34 emphasis added).

Other commentators, by contrast, have argued that Hume's discussion in T.1.2.3 makes sense precisely as a direct application of the doctrine of general abstract ideas; while it might be correct to say that Hume does 'apply' (as Michael Costa puts it)[13] the latter doctrine in his discussion of the former, it is inaccurate to say that he does so to explain the origin of our ideas of space and time. Hume unequivocally speaks of abstract ideas of space and time arising subsequent to particular ones, to which they always refer. Consider his description of how the abstract idea of space is derived:

> Suppose that in the extended object, or composition of colour'd points, *from which we first receiv'd the idea of extension*, the points were of a purple colour; . . . *afterwards* having experience of the other colours of violet, green, red, white, black, and all of the different compositions of these, and finding a *resemblance* in the disposition of colour'd points, of which they are compos'd, we omit the peculiarities of colour, as far as is possible, and found an *abstract idea* merely on that disposition of points, or manner of appearance, in which they agree. (T 1.2.3.5/SBN 34, emphases added)

Hume immediately makes the same observation with respect to the abstract idea of time:

> The idea of time, *being deriv'd from the succession of our perceptions of every kind* . . . will afford us an instance of an abstract idea, which comprehends a still greater variety than that of space, and yet is represented in the fancy by some particular individual idea of a determinate quantity and quality. (T 1.2.3.6/SBN 34–5, emphasis added)

In both cases, the process of abstraction assumes that various particular ideas of space and time are already before the mind, on the basis of which some mark of resemblance or similarity can be isolated and form the abstract idea in question. As the latter quote makes clear, and as the general tenor of the discussion in T 1.1.7 indicates, Hume's aim is not to seek the origin of the ideas of space and time in the power of abstraction, but effectively to emphasise and support Berkeley's position against Locke that all abstract ideas refer to some 'particular individual idea' (see also EHU 12.15/SBN 156–7).[14]

If space and time are neither copies of impressions per se (of either sense or reflection) nor abstractions or fictions, how then, in Hume's view, do they arise? Hume is adamant that space and time are not copies or representations of any particular impression; space is not added to the impressions of 'color'd points' that compose the impressions of the table, just as time is not a 'sixth impression' above and beyond the 'five notes play'd on a flute' (T 1.2.3.10/SBN 36). As ideas, however, they are copies or representations of a collection of impressions: for space, the adjacent impressions that form the 'composition of color'd points' of an object (T 1.2.3.5/SBN 34), and for time the series of impressions given in the 'succession of our perceptions of every kind' (T 1.2.3.6/SBN 34–5). Thus ideas of space and time arise from a corresponding complex impression, an 'arrangement of content', as Costa puts it,[15] or, as Falkenstein emphasises, they are '*compound* impressions, where compound impressions are understood to be not just collections of simple impressions, but ordered arrangements of simple impressions'.[16] This ordered arrangement is what Hume refers to when he says that the idea of space is 'borrow'd from, and represents some [compound] impression, which this moment appears to the senses' (T 1.2.3.4/SBN 34) as 'time in its first appearance to the mind is always conjoin'd with a succession of changeable objects' (T 1.2.3.9/SBN 36). The features of adjacency and seriality are the form in which the impression is represented by the imagination, what Hume calls the 'manner of their appearance'.

While the notion of 'manner' in this context might at first seem obscure, it characterises nothing more mysterious than the way a certain impression is experienced. After all, the complex idea of an apple, to cite Hume's example, is the representation of the compound of certain qualities – colour, taste, smell – and not any additional impression above or beyond them. Recall that Hume also uses the notion of 'manner of conceiving' in his discussion of belief (T 1.3.8.7/SBN 101), which involves a 'transition of the fancy' via resemblance, contiguity or cause and effect that imparts force and vivacity to the corresponding idea: a picture of an absent friend, closeness to home, and religious relics as the effects of some saint all enliven their corresponding ideas and produce belief. The increased force and vivacity comprises the 'manner' in which the idea strikes the imagination. In the case of space and time, of course, we are dealing not with extant ideas (a friend, home or saint), but trying to discover the origin of those ideas themselves; as with belief – and the complex idea of apple – Hume is emphasising the way impressions appear and it is this appearance that strikes the imagination and is copied by it to create the idea. If we accept that ideas of space and time are compound impressions, it follows that Hume must be relying on some ordering principle that holds the compound together (either before, one assumes, or in the course of the copying) such that the ideas in question can arise. Some have pointed out that this is a blatant contradiction of Hume's most cherished epistemological principles, others that it requires only an amendment to resolve.

The final word on Hume's inconsistency notwithstanding, it remains the case that he takes the genuine ideas of space and time to be explicable in terms of the manner of appearance of sense experience; the same is not true of a vacuum (empty space) and time without change, both fictions that are to be distinguished from their genuine counterparts. Since space is nothing but the manner of appearance of coloured points, Hume reasons, 'we can form no idea of a vacuum, or space, where there is nothing visible or tangible' (T 1.2.5.1/SBN 53), and if the idea of time is derived from the succession of changeable objects, where impressions of such are absent, there can be no idea of time (T 1.2.5.28–9/SBN 64–5). 'Or in other words', as Hume puts it succinctly, ''tis impossible to conceive either a vacuum and extension without matter, or a time, when there was no succession or change in any real existence' (T 1.2.4.3/SBN 40). Hume is well aware, of course, that these ideas have been subjects of considerable philosophical controversy, which would imply that disputants have at least some notion of them (see T 1.2.5.3 and 1.2.5.28/SBN 54–5 and 64–5). The idea of a vacuum has additional observations in its favour. We can conceive an empty vessel where all matter has been annihilated and where the walls and roof still come into contact in the absence of matter and, in accord with the maxim that what is conceivable is possible, we are apparently forced to embrace a 'something else' to explain this, namely the idea of a vacuum (T 1.2.5.3/SBN 55). Moreover, the idea of a vacuum seems to be a necessary and unavoidable conclusion of the thought that bodies move into and occupy place; how could they do so were there no space void of matter into which they can move? (T 1.2.5.4/SBN 55).[17]

Hume's response to these objections is to argue that, strictly speaking, we do not have genuine ideas of a vacuum or time without change at all; rather, what we take to be ideas of putatively real phenomena are fictions: unlike their genuine counterparts (space and time), they arise from the propensity of the imagination to seek an easy transition among its ideas, which it accomplishes by creating a fiction of misapplication, taking two genuine ideas and confusing them to form a third that encompasses both. To reveal the error behind the idea of a vacuum, Hume shows that we actually have two ideas of distance. The first is the genuine idea of space already explained, namely the idea of extension from the experience of coloured points from which the idea of space is inseparable. The second idea of distance is also genuine but does *not* involve space; it arises from measuring the interval between objects – points of light in the dark, for example – where the interval is absent tangible impressions: darkness is not a positive idea, Hume maintains, but the 'negation of light, or more properly speaking, of colour'd and visible objects' (T 1.2.5.5/SBN 55); it is 'without parts, without composition, invariable and indivisible' (T 1.2.5.11/SBN 57) and so cannot be a basis for our idea of space.

While these two ideas of distance are quite distinct – one involving genuine space and extension, the other not – they are 'the same or resembling' (T 1.2.5.21/SBN 61) and present the imagination with a 'close relation betwixt that distance, which conveys the idea of extension, and that other, which is not fill'd with any colour'd or solid object' (T 1.2.5.18/SBN 59). The close relation consists, first, in the fact that objects at a distance from each other without tangible objects (the luminous points in the dark) strike the senses in the same way as if there were such objects in between (genuine space or extension); second, that invisible distances 'are capable of receiving the same extent' (T 1.2.5.16/SBN 59), that is, of becoming extended, and, third, that qualities of objects such as heat and light diminish proportionally whether or not the distance involves real existence. In its desire to find some easy transition, the imagination apparently overlooks the differences between the two ideas and focuses on the similarities, associating them through resemblance, a process Hume describes in terms of 'animal spirits', which 'falling into the contiguous traces, present other related ideas in lieu of that, which the mind desir'd at first to survey'. Whatever the correct physiological aetiology, Hume's point remains that an error of misapplication results: we are not 'sensible of the change', he remarks, 'but continuing still the same train of thought, [we] make use of the related idea, which is present to us, and employ it in our reasonings, as if it were the same with what we demanded' (T 1.2.5.20/SBN 61). We thus 'substitute the idea of distance, which is not consider'd either as visible or tangible, in the room of extension, which is nothing but a composition of visible and tangible points dispos'd in a certain order' (T 1.2.5.21/SBN 62). The supposed idea of a vacuum is thus born of misapplying the term 'extension' to form a fiction that is the composite of and includes both – empty space – where we only 'imagine that we have an idea of extension without the idea of any object either of the sight or feeling' (T 1.2.5.19/SBN 60).

Hume takes the second fiction – that of time without change or of a steadfast object with duration – to run parallel to his explanation for empty space; it is an idea that arises because 'we apply the idea of time, even to what is unchangeable, and suppose, as is common, that duration is the measure of rest as well of as motion' (T 1.2.3.11/SBN 37).[18] Some commentators have criticised the argument for its circularity (that it assumes we can recognise the temporality of an unchanging object, the very phenomenon Hume purports to explain) and Ainslie, although defending Hume against this charge, points out that when the 'idea of a vacuum is properly distinguished from the idea of the unchanging, it becomes clear that Hume cannot assume that his prior account of the former can easily be transformed into an account of the latter'.[19] Be that as it may, there is general agreement that Hume refers the fiction in question to the imagination unwittingly confusing ideas and carrying on as if nothing had happened. There is a 'psychological mechanism of confounding' related ideas, as Don Baxter puts it, and then, being unaware that the 'wrong idea has been substituted, we continue thinking as if no substitution had been made and thinking that the characteristics presented by the substitute idea apply to what we began thinking about'; 'perceived changes in other objects and the successiveness of our perceptions in observing an object is made the basis', as

Allison describes it, 'for the attribution of a fictitious duration to the object observed'; or while the 'unchanging object, thought of in isolation', in Ainslie's characterisation, 'does not yield an idea of temporality, the fact that we are aware of it as surrounded by changing objects allows us to treat it as if it were changing and thus in time'.[20] This substitution, attribution or treating amounts to a fiction of misapplication, where two genuine ideas, which can be traced to real existence and matter of fact (time and a steadfast object) are confounded to produce their fictional counterpart, time without change or an unchanging object in time.

The first idea we have considered already: it is that of time, which Hume has explained as the manner of appearance of a succession of changeable objects: 'there is a continual succession of perceptions in our mind' so the 'idea of time' is 'ever present with us' (T 1.2.5.29/SBN 65). The second idea is that of an unchanging object, which does *not* involve time. On the face of it, it might seem that Hume is helping himself to an idea the origin of which is at best obscure: what could it mean to have an impression of an unchanging object? This difficulty disappears if one recalls that, for Hume, the idea of time depends on the succession of our perceptions. For this reason, when asleep or focused on a particular thought, the perception of a changeable succession ceases and time effectively disappears. Similarly, time speeds up or slows – it 'appears' longer or shorter – according to the increased or decreased rapidity of impressions. The experience of time is thus constrained by the capacity of the imagination to copy impressions. To use Hume's example,

> If you wheel about a burning coal with rapidity, it will present to the sense an image of a circle of fire; nor will there seem to be any interval of time betwixt its revolutions; merely because 'tis impossible for our perceptions to succeed each other with the same rapidity, that motion many be communicated to external objects.

This does not mean that there is no 'real succession in the objects' (T 1.2.3.7/SBN 35), but it is perfectly compatible, in Hume's thinking, to conceive – as Baxter puts it – of 'intervals of time when we have a perception but not successive perceptions, even when there is a succession elsewhere'. The single perception – a 'steadfast perception' – is precisely the impression that yields the idea of a steadfast object. [21]

With the origin of these two ideas made clear, we can see how Hume explains the origin of the fiction in question, where the idea of time and the idea of a steadfast object are confused. Hume writes:

> When we consider a steadfast object at five-a-clock, and regard the same at six, we are apt to apply to it that idea [of time that is 'ever present' to us] in the same manner as if every moment were distinguish'd by a different position, or an alteration of the object.

The first and second appearances of the object are 'compar'd with the succession of our perceptions' and 'seem equally remov'd as if the object had really chang'd'. As with the genuine ideas of distance, the two ideas of time (from the succession of perceptions) and an unchanging object (from a single perception) resemble one another insofar as they arise from similar causes: the perceptions of the unchanging object appear to be temporally separate as if change had in fact taken place; we know from experience that the object could have undergone such change; and the qualities of the unchanging object are increased or diminished in the same way as if there were succession perceived by the senses. The imagination then confuses one idea with the other by focusing on their resemblance at the expense of their differences, and combines the idea of time involving succession with that of an unchanging object. Here we have 'two appearances, which make us fancy we have that idea' (T 1.2.5.29/SBN 65), Hume insists, which is a composite of and includes both: *time without change*. Or ''tis by a fiction of the imagination', as he writes, 'by which the unchangeable object is suppos'd to participate of the changes of the co-existence objects, and in particular of that of our perceptions' (T 1.4.2.29/SBN 200–1). As in the case of a vacuum, this is a confusion of ideas that produces a fiction, which cannot be traced to any real existence or matter of fact.

Liberty and Necessity

Hume does not use the term 'fiction' (or any equivalent) in either section 8 of the first *Enquiry* or in T 2.3.1–2, the main texts where he addresses the issues of liberty and necessity (or, to use more contemporary terminology, free will and determinism), but he clearly identifies the debate as a confusion involving the imagination, and for that reason it is not implausible to understand what he says in terms of a fiction of misapplication, the imagination drawing connections where none otherwise exist. Indeed, Hume situates his discussion squarely in the context of philosophical debates and the 'meaning of the terms' employed by disputants to them. As in the case of the fictions of space and time, one might expect proponents on either side to have a clear idea of or reached consensus about the language they use. That the controversy has neared no conclusion, however, suggests the very opposite: rather than arriving at the 'true and real subject of the controversy', Hume observes, philosophers have been led into a 'labyrinth of obscure sophistry' (EHU 8.2/SBN 81), and disputants continually 'affix[ed] different ideas to the terms employed' (EHU 8.1/SBN 80). For this reason, he concludes that philosophical disagreements have 'hitherto turned merely on words' (EHU 8.3/SBN 81). As this assessment readily suggests, Hume's interest lies not in discovering the nature of free will and determinism – that would be to engage in the spurious controversy the nature of which needs to be exposed – but in showing that there is a mistake in the meanings attached to the terms themselves. Tracing the ideas to their origin in real existence and matter of fact will clarify the 'reasonable sense' of these terms (EHU 8.3/SBN 81) and explain how their fictitious counterparts arise. Presumably, Hume thinks vulgar reasoners know what they mean when they speak of 'liberty' and 'necessity'; philosophers are the ones responsible for the errors and the spurious, unresolved controversies that have ensued.

As in his discussion of space and time, Hume's strategy is to isolate, first, the genuine ideas of liberty and necessity, and to show, second, how correspondingly fictitious versions of them arise from the tendency of the imagination to confuse and conflate terms: the genuine idea of necessity as *constant conjunction* is replaced with *absolute determinism*, and the genuine idea of liberty meaning *freedom from constraint* is supplanted by liberty understood as *freedom from causes*. Hume accomplishes the first task by invoking conclusions he has reached already concerning causal necessity. When we speak of necessity, we refer to nothing more or less than our experience of constant conjunction, how objects in the world or our ideas of those objects in the mind are connected together. This is true not only in the case of 'natural evidence' about the 'operation of bodies', but with respect to 'moral evidence' as well. We expect and assume a regular and uniform order in human behaviour and employ it routinely and unreflectively in connecting actions with motives. Where people act out of character – when they do not behave according to our expectations based on our past experience of them – it is due to and explicable by some other intervening cause: a sudden frenzy determines a trusted friend unexpectedly to stab me in the back (EHU 8.20/SBN 91) or a peevish response from one of usually 'obliging disposition' can be traced to a toothache or the fact that 'he has not dined' (EHU 8.15/SBN 88). Intervening courses of this sort are no more mysterious than unexpected events in the natural world, such as a sudden earthquake that destroys one's house. Indeed, as Hume points out, the connections drawn in the case of the moral world are no less strong than those made in the material: a prisoner 'discovers the impossibility of his escape, as well when he considers the obstinacy of the gaoler, as the walls and bars, with which he is surrounded' (EHU 8.19/SBN 90); similarly, a 'man who leaves his purse full of gold on the pavement at Charing Cross, may as well expect that it will fly away like a feather, as that he will find it untouched an hour after' (EHU 8.20/SBN 91).

Having grasped that the genuine idea of necessity is one with cause, the genuine idea of liberty follows as a matter of course. When we speak of voluntary action, we are referring to the will, which, on the basis of the copy principle, Hume defines as 'nothing but *the internal impression we feel and are conscious of, when we knowingly give rise to any new motion of our body, or new perception of our mind*' (T 2.3.1.2/SBN 399). Or, as he puts it in the first *Enquiry*, 'By *liberty*, then, we can only mean *a power of acting or not acting, according to the determinations of the will*; that is, if we choose to remain at rest, we may; if we choose to move, we also may' (EHU 8.23/SBN 95). A voluntary action is not divorced from necessity but involves the same regularity and uniformity of action indicated by the latter term; this is 'hypothetical liberty' (EHU 8.23/SBN 95) or 'liberty of *spontaneity*' (T 2.3.2.1/SBN 407) that involves freedom from constraint. Rather than being opposed to causality, the genuine idea of liberty is identical with it, arising from our experience of a regular and uniform order and the expectation that a given motive will lead to a certain action or that a certain action will spring from a given motive. There is no difference in the perception of the mind when I freely choose to act as when I expect one billiard ball to be moved by another. The mimetic imagination copies and represents this feeling to produce the idea of liberty.

Explaining the origin of our genuine ideas of liberty and necessity, then, at once shows the proper meaning of these terms. Moreover, Hume emphasises, this is in fact how we use the terms in common discourse when we speak of being free or at liberty to act in one way rather than another. It is displayed in judgements we make about the natural world (external objects and the changes that attend the ageing of the human body) as well as the moral (that human beings organise themselves in societies and political associations, and make routine judgements about one another's character) (T 2.3.1.6–9/SBN 401–2).[22] 'Thus it appears', as Hume puts it, 'not only that the conjunction between motives and voluntary actions is uniform, as that between the cause and effect in any part of nature; but also that this regular conjunction has been universally acknowledged among mankind, and has never been the subject of dispute, either in philosophy or common life' (EHU 8.16/SBN 88; see 8.21/SBN 92). Given this, what exactly has been the subject of dispute, and why, if the true meaning of 'liberty' and 'necessity' is so easily obtained, do philosophical debates turn on the same words used in quite different ways?

Hume's response to this question, and the second part of his strategy, is to show that the genuine idea of liberty has a fictitious counterpart that does not count as an idea in his technical sense. Hume refers to this as a 'fantastical system of liberty' (T 2.3.1.15/SBN 404) or simply the 'doctrine of liberty' (T 2.3.2.1/SBN 407). First, he argues, the genuine idea of necessity is subverted when philosophers cannot rest content with the discovery of cause and effect in constant conjunction, but take it as an inherent spring or principle in the world itself. 'But though this conclusion concerning human ignorance be the result of the strictest scrutiny of this subject', he observes, 'men still entertain a strong propensity to believe, that they penetrate farther into the powers of nature, and perceive something like a necessary connexion between the cause and the effect' (EHU 8.21/SBN 92). Philosophers spiritualise nature and take necessity as an independent power inherent in matter. On this view:

> Every object is determin'd by an *absolute fate* to a certain degree and direction of its motion, and can no more depart from that precise line, in which it moves, that it can convert itself into an angel, or spirit, or any superior substance. (T 2.3.1.3/SBN 400, emphasis added)

Once the spurious idea of necessity has arisen, the fact that liberty also involves the necessity of causes is obscured, and liberty in the sense of spontaneity – freedom from constraint – is transformed into the 'liberty of *indifference*' (T 2.3.2.1/SBN 407), that is, freedom from causes of the sort Descartes famously refers to when the mind is not 'compelled by reason':

> But the indifference I feel when there is no reason pushing me in one direction rather than another is the lowest grade of freedom; it is evidence not of any perfection of freedom, but rather of a defect in knowledge or a kind of negation. For if I always saw clearly what was true and good, I should never have to deliberate about the right judgement or choice; in that case, although I should be wholly free, it would be impossible for me ever to be in a state of indifference. (AT 7:58; CSM 2:40)

Liberty in this sense, Hume emphasises, 'by removing necessity, removes also causes, and is the very same thing with chance' (T 2.3.1.18/SBN 407). It is absurd, because it robs liberty of the very uniformity and regularity that constitute it. We thus confound the liberty of spontaneity (freedom from constraint) with liberty of indifference (freedom from causes) and produce the idea of chance that involves both, an idea – uncaused freedom – that is as unintelligible as empty space or changeless time.

Hume explains the conflation of the two ideas of liberty by pointing to the tendency of the imagination to create a fiction where '*resembling* objects are readily taken for each other' (T 2.3.2.2/SBN 408, emphasis added), as is found in the feelings that accompany voluntary action. Hume emphasises that freedom is not a quality in persons, but arises 'in any thinking or intelligent being, who may consider the action, and consists of the determination of this thought to infer its existence from some preceding objects'. Strictly speaking, then, there is no experience of the will or of freedom on the part of agents when they act, but we 'imagine that we feel that the will itself is subject to nothing'; imagination still produces 'something like it', a '*false sensation or experience*' that the will is absolutely free, namely, free from causes (T 2.3.2.2/SBN 408). This is precisely the mistake Descartes makes when he says of the will that 'the idea of any greater faculty is beyond my grasp' (AT 7:57; CSM 2:40). Though liberty is not in the agent at all, Hume concludes, and is at best 'an image or faint motion', we still 'perswade ourselves' that it 'cou'd have been completed into the thing itself', that is, that there is an impression of liberty, which *could* be fully experienced on some next occasion. All 'these efforts are in vain', however, and though we 'may imagine we feel a liberty within ourselves' (T 2.3.2.2/SBN 408), it is but a trick of the fancy that leads us to take what resembles an impression of absolute freedom as the thing itself; we thus accept the doctrine of liberty, a fiction of misapplication, even in the face of overwhelming experience to the contrary.[23]

Before leaving Hume's treatment of liberty and necessity, it is worth noting how it informs two phenomena that he treats later in Book Three of the *Treatise*; these properly fall under Hume's reflections on the nature of political society, but both depend on his conclusion that the idea of free will is a fiction of misapplication. The first concerns the obligation of promises, a fact that might easily be explained through public utility as a solution to the problems posed by self-interest and the unstable nature of property. As we will see in the next chapter, in the section on imagination and political society, Hume employs this argument to explain our motive to produce various 'artificial' contrivances to avoid the dangers of social disorder. If promising were natural, he reasons, 'there must be some act of mind attending these words, *I promise*; and on this act of the mind must the obligation depend'. On examination, however, no such act can be discovered, and Hume concludes that we actually 'feign a new act of the mind, which we call the *willing* an obligation; and on this we suppose the morality to depend' (T 3.2.5.12/SBN 523). In actuality, there is no such act, it being a fiction of misapplication, although we come to see it as a mysterious phenomenon comparable to the mystery of '*transubstantiation*, or *holy orders*, where a certain form of words, along with a certain intention, change entirely the nature of an external object, and even of a human creature' (T 3.2.5.14/SBN 524). The principal difference – and a profound one at that – is that promising arises with a view to public interest, and for this reason takes many forms relative to the particularities of time and place. The 'monstrous doctrines of mere priestly inventions', by contrast, have no such tie but, once established, 'follow more directly the current of reason and good sense'. Hume suggests that theologians came to recognise that words, being 'mere sound', thus required some intention 'to make them have efficacy', and subsequently connected the power of the sacrament to the intention of the priest, with the result that a secret withdrawal of intention would destroy that power. No such parallel ever occurred in the case of promising, however, since it arises on the basis of public good, which would be quickly undermined were the obligation involved reduced mysteriously to thought alone (T 3.2.5.14/SBN 524–5).

The second phenomenon in which Hume's treatment of the will is implicated concerns the attention we pay to wealth and our desire to acquire it. As we will see in Chapter 3, Hume takes property in general to be a 'particular species of causation' (T 2.1.10.1/SBN 310), where the mind moves easily between the idea of a proprietor and the property he owns. As one might expect, real objects connected to our own person excite pleasure or pain and inspire the passions of pride or humility, but the same applies, less obviously, to our felt power of acquiring property, which has the same effect even when it goes unrealised. The prospect of a probable or even possible acquisition produces pleasure, even more so when we realise it to be in our own power to take or leave the object, and that nothing hinders our enjoyment if we choose to acquire it. In this case, our 'imagination easily anticipates the satisfaction', Hume observes, 'and conveys the same joy, as if they [men] were perswaded of its real and actual existence' (T 2.1.10.8/SBN 314). The object is rendered contiguous by the power of thought, and even a miser can enjoy his wealth, albeit unspent, because he '*imagines* it to approach nearer' whenever he has the freedom to employ it (T 2.1.10.9/SBN 314). The basis for this phenomenon, Hume suggests, is the 'false sensation of liberty, which makes us imagine we can perform any thing, that is not very dangerous or destructive'. When there are no impediments to a person's action we 'judge from experience, that the pleasure will exist, and that he will probably obtain it. But when ourselves are in that situation, we judge from an *illusion of the fancy*, that the pleasure is still closer and more immediate'. In this way, the 'the will seems to move easily every way, and casts a shadow or image of itself, even to that side, on which it did not settle'. The result is the same 'lively satisfaction, as if it were perfectly certain and unavoidable' (T 2.1.10.9/SBN 315). The same fiction explains our humility when others have power over us, and pride when we consider ourselves free to act. When we compare ourselves to others with fewer riches and less power than ourselves, the sense of our own potency increases, but only because the 'imagination finds it in the very subject: The passage of the thought to its conception is smooth and easy and this augments its influence (T 2.1.10.12/SBN 316). Complex and profound these results might be, but they are all founded on the fiction of free will.

General Rules of the Imagination

I noted above – taking issue with Ainslie – that Hume's discussion of general or abstract ideas does not provide hard evidence for classing them as fictions: Hume does not identify any contradiction to escape from which the imagination creates a new idea, nor does he describe a case of misapplication where the faculty confuses ideas and inadvertently takes one for another. The fact that some ideas are 'general in their representation' might point to a case of 'idea substitution', but they remain explicable through custom, features of natural language and the mechanism of reviving ideas; general ideas are not, in short, fictions. One place where such a fiction does seem to occur, however, is in the creation of a certain species not of general ideas but of 'general rules', which Hume traces to the imagination. Hume does not use the term 'fiction' when discussing them, but he does identify a confusion into which the faculty falls, and this follows a pattern similar to the one we have identified in the other fictions of misapplication.

Hume distinguishes general rules of the imagination from 'general rules of the understanding', which facilitate a form of probabilistic reasoning, inferences made on the basis of experience that ought to guide our judgements about cause and effect, moral judgements and beauty. These rules express and abridge our experience of constantly conjoined objects and enable us to connect motives and actions, or decipher proper objects of aesthetic appreciation by reflecting upon what has pleased and displeased over time. Born of reason and experience, they enable us to transfer past experience to the future so that our judgements are based on matter and fact. They are thus reliable – though not infallible – guides to conduct and they effectively divide correct judgements from their incorrect counterparts. Hume observes:

> By [such rules] we learn to distinguish accidental circumstances from the efficacious causes; and when we find that an effect can be produc'd without the concurrence of any particular circumstance, we conclude that that circumstance makes not a part of the efficacious cause, however frequently conjoin'd with it. (T 1.3.13.11/SBN 149)

While general rules of the understanding thus have a basis in experience and guide the wise man in his judgement, general rules of the imagination represent an 'unphilosophical species of probability' (T 1.3.13.7/SBN 146), are even *contrary* to observation and experience' (T 1.3.13.7/SBN 147, emphasis added) and effectively subvert it. They arise from the very same principle as those of the understanding – experience – but continue to guide action even though the original circumstances that gave rise to the idea no longer exist; they are 'extended beyond the principle, whence they first arise' (EPM 4.7/SBN 207). The same habit that determines the mind to move among ideas and generate general rules of the understanding is also responsible for the transition from one idea to another that creates general rules of the imagination. Hume observes:

> Our judgements concerning cause and effect are deriv'd from habit and experience, and when we have been accustom'd to see one object united to another, our imagination passes from the first to the second, by a natural transition, which precedes reflection, and which cannot be prevented by it. (T 1.3.13.8/SBN 147)

The imagination thus completes a union in the absence of or despite a present impression and 'naturally carries us to a lively conception of the usual effect', Hume writes, 'tho' the object be different in the most material and most efficacious circumstances from that cause' (T 1.3.13.12/SBN 148).

As with the other fictions of misapplication, Hume explains this transition by emphasising the tendency of the imagination to confuse objects that resemble one another but are not the same. He writes:

> Now 'tis the nature of custom, not only to operate with its full force, when objects are presented, that are *exactly the same* with those to which we have been accustom'd; but also to operate in an inferior degree, when we discover such as are *similar*; and tho' the habit loses somewhat of its force by every difference, yet 'tis seldom entirely destroy'd, where any considerable circumstances remain the same. (T 1.3.13.8/SBN 147, emphases added)

The result is a confused notion on the part of the imagination and, while its results should be rejected, the general ideas in question overpower the judgement and become rules that, for good or ill, guide our actions.

This might seem a trivial matter, but it is an extraordinary phenomenon and far-reaching in its effects. It accounts for the behaviour of the man who moves easily from one kind of fruit to another when his favourite is not in season, the drunk who moves effortlessly to white wine when red is not available (T 1.3.13.8/SBN 147), and explains why great heights cause fearful ideas of 'fall and descent, harm and death', even when present impressions teach us that our situation (Hume speaks of a man suspended securely in a cage from a high tower) is quite safe (T 1.3.13.10/SBN 148). More perniciously, general rules of the imagination explain the origin of prejudice and ground some of our deeply held moral beliefs. These judgements are mistakes and thus open to review and correction, on occasions by evoking general rules of the understanding. 'Custom soon reconciles us to heights and precipices', Hume points out, for example, 'and wears off . . . [the] false and delusive terrors' to which they give rise (EPM 5.14), as judgement leads to revisions of the inequalities of our 'internal emotions and impressions . . . and preserves us from error, in the variations of images, presented to our external senses'. For 'we know, that, on our approach to it, its image would expand on the eye, and that the distance consists not in the object itself, but in our position with regard to it' (EPM 5.41).

While understanding can and should, in all cases, prevail over the imagination, this is not always the case. The opposition between understanding and imagination takes the form of what Kant later describes as an antinomy since, as Hume presents it, there are no unassailable grounds for adopting arguments in favour of one idea rather than the other.[24] In Kantian language, these ideas would qualify as 'illusion', syllogisms that 'contain no empirical premises' in which 'we conclude from something which we know to something else of which we have no concept, and to which . . . we yet ascribe objective reality' (KrV A339/B397). General rules of the imagination do not arise from the antinomy but, once created by the imagination and encouraged by the force and vivacity of ideas, they set in motion a dialectical movement that lacks any final solution. Where impressions are copied through the power of memory, judgement and reason prevail; when the imagination takes over, the process is subverted, only to be corrected in turn by sound reasoning, the results of that again undermined by the power of the imagination. 'Sometimes the one, sometimes the other prevails', Hume observes, 'according to the disposition and character of the person' (T 1.3.13.12/SBN 150). General rules of the imagination, then, are fictions of misapplication, but they do not qualify unequivocally as artificial, since they reflect a universal tendency of human beings not only to make mistakes but also to commit errors that cannot be rectified. In the final analysis, Hume thinks that they are partially correctable, but the conflict between imagination and reason is insoluble because the competing influences of the rules to which they give rise can never be resolved. This conflict and the antimony it occasions is a pattern that emerges whenever the imagination holds sway, especially, as we shall see in later chapters, in the areas of religion and philosophy, where the fictions are powerful and exert a considerable influence over the minds of believers and practitioners, respectively.

Fictions of invention

Fictions of invention, we recall, are cases where the imagination invents an idea to resolve a contradiction, and this is the way Hume proceeds in trying to account for the ideas of continued and distinct existence, primary and secondary qualities, objective causal power, substance as a substratum and personal identity. In some cases Hume's discussion makes it difficult to say unambiguously that he has invention in mind and in others it is difficult to decipher whether the fiction in question is of the vulgar or philosophical kind. His discussion of personal identity suffers under the latter constraint and his path to continued existence is labyrinthine, to say the least, the fiction being explained as a matter of invention by way of others that are cases of misapplication (identity and its application to interrupted perceptions). It is with this fiction that we begin.

Continued and distinct existence

At the end of Part 2 of Book 1 of the *Treatise*, Hume makes it clear that the ideas of 'existence' and 'external existence' can be explained in terms of his copy principle. Since all impressions and ideas are conceived as existing, the only difficulty is to decide whether the idea of existence is 'deriv'd from a distinct impression, conjoin'd with every perception or object of our thought, or must be the very same with the idea of the perception or object' (T 1.2.6.2/SBN 66). Hume rejects the former possibility – there being no 'distinct impression' of existence that accompanies 'every impression and idea' (T 1.2.6.3/SBN 66) – and accepts the second: the idea of existence is the 'same with the idea of what we conceive to be existent' and 'Whatever we conceive, we conceive to be existent' (T 1.2.6.4/SBN 67). Conversely, if we attempt to supplement the perception of any object with the idea of existence, we find that we add nothing at all to it. The same reasoning, Hume then urges, accounts for our idea of external existence. We cannot conceive of anything other than the way it appears to us, that is, as existing independently and it is an 'absurdity' to take external existence 'for something specifically different from our perceptions' (T 1.4.2.2/SBN 188). Both existence and external existence are thus genuine ideas because they can be traced to impressions and the representational power of the mind to copy and represent.

Thus, when Hume discusses existence in T 1.4.2, his main interest is neither 'external existence' (the 'absurdity' of which he takes himself to have shown already in T 1.2.6) nor whether objects actually exist (something we simply 'take for granted in all our reasonings'), but what *causes induce us to believe in the existence of body* (T 1.4.2.1/SBN 187) or, as he breaks the question down, the mutually supporting beliefs in 'continued existence' – that objects endure, though perceived intermittently – and 'distinct existence' – that they are external in position and independent in existence and operation. The two ideas are closely related, as Hume points out, because if objects exist continuously then it follows that they do so independently as well (T 1.4.2.2/SBN 188). Hume then considers the three possibilities that might explain continued and distinct existence: the senses, reason and imagination. The senses cannot give us an idea of continued existence since they only function intermittently (we disrupt such existence when we turn away, blink or sleep), and do not give rise to distinct existence because we have single perceptions rather than evidence of 'double existence' – of both representation and represented object – and we cannot separate the object from the perception of the object in the first place. Reason, in turn, cannot be the origin of the ideas because those who lack recourse to such arguments – the vulgar – still have the ideas in question and, besides, because we take our perceptions to be the same as objects, there are no independent grounds to infer the existence of the latter from the former. Thus, Hume concludes, the ideas of continued and distinct existence 'must be entirely owing to the IMAGINATION' (T 1.4.2.14/SBN 193).

Having isolated this faculty as the likely explanation, Hume isolates the 'peculiar qualities in our impressions, which makes us attribute to them a distinct and continu'd existence' (T 1.4.2.17/SBN 194). First, all objects exhibit regularity in their order of appearance, or constancy, even after sense perception has been interrupted (my pen and paper are in the same place when I return to my desk as when I left it) and, where this is lacking (through absence or prolonged interruption), we find, second, regularity in their dependence on each other, or coherence, according to the relation of cause and effect (a fire in the grate that is extinguished when I return conforms to my causal reasoning about fires that have run out of fuel). The question, then, is why the constancy and coherence of impressions should give rise to the specific ideas of continued and distinct existence. Hume responds by arguing that we move from one to the other as a result of the supposing tendency of the imagination: the idea of coherence leads the imagination to invent continued existence to remove a contradiction, and that of constancy leads to the same from confusing resembling ideas. It is worth noting that Hume's discussion suggests that constancy and coherence are two distinct and potentially alternative routes for the imagination to reach the idea of continued existence; coherence, he maintains, is 'too weak to support alone so vast an edifice' and must be 'joined' with constancy to provide a 'satisfactory account' (T 1.4.2.23/SBN 199). Hume is silent on the reasons why coherence alone is inadequate, as he is on how the two might join to produce the idea in question.[25]

COHERENCE

Hume begins by discussing the idea of coherence, pointing out that there are many occasions where the dependence of one object upon another seems to fail us. A creaking door that I hear without seeing its movement contradicts my past experience of the sound being the perceived effect of a door opening, as somebody bringing a letter up to my apartment, unless the person did so contrary to my experience of gravity, must have used stairs that exist, although I do not perceive them. There is a contradiction between my experience of the world – creaking doors have to be opened and human beings do not fly – and the fact that the phenomenon in question (the cause of the motion and the stairs) is unperceived. 'Here I am naturally led to regard the world, as something real and durable', Hume observes, 'and as preserving its existence, even when it is no longer present to my perception' (T 1.4.2.20/SBN 197).

It might appear that Hume is appealing here to the associative principle of cause and effect – that we ascribe identity through custom and past experience – which leads us to conclude that 'if we had kept our eye or hand constantly upon it [the object], it wou'd have conveyed an invariable and uninterrupted perception' (T 1.3.2.2/SBN 74). The principle does not operate in this case, however, because the habit of supposing something to exist in the absence of an impression fails to satisfy what is required to explain the connection, namely, the constant conjunction of objects. We are here bestowing on objects a *greater regularity* than what is observ'd in our mere perceptions' (T 1.4.2.21/SBN 197, emphasis added). Hume suggests, instead, that the idea of continued existence is a creation of the imagination, a fiction of invention, where the faculty works according to its principle of easy transition to complete a whole, and, to recall Hume's metaphor, 'like a galley put in motion by the oars, carries on its course without any new impulse'. Once the mind is 'in the train of observing a uniformity among objects, it naturally continues, till it renders the uniformity as compleat as possible', providing a 'much greater regularity among objects' than would the senses alone. The imagination thus overcomes the contradiction between our experience of the world and the unperceived events through the 'simple supposition' of an object's continued existence (T 1.4.2.22/SBN 198), even though we have no experience of the phenomenon to which the idea putatively refers.[26]

CONSTANCY

Hume's account of how we move from the constancy of perceptions to the idea of continued existence appeals to the same principles of imagination as does coherence, namely, as he says in his 'sketch of abridgement' of the discussion to follow, resembling perceptions that are confused and a 'kind of contradiction' from which the imagination frees us by way of a 'disguise' or 'supposing' that 'interrupted perceptions are connected by a real existence, of which we are insensible' (T 1.4.2.24/SBN 199). This brief synopsis glosses a good deal of complexity that Hume subsequently reveals by identifying 'four things' that are requisite (T 1.4.2.25/SBN 200) to reach the idea of continued existence, what might be seen as stages or steps in a sort of natural history of vulgar thought,[27] with the presence of the imagination felt throughout. Continued existence is a fiction of invention that the imagination creates to solve a contradiction, but, in order to reach it, the faculty is called upon to produce a fiction of misapplication in the form of identity, to apply that idea to our experience of interrupted perceptions, and to raise the force and vivacity of the idea so that continued existence becomes an object of belief.

FROM UNITY AND NUMBER TO IDENTITY

We have already had occasion to consider Hume's explanation of identity in considering his view of the self, a fiction of misapplication that he explains in terms of his earlier treatment of identity in general. The latter appears as the first part of the 'system' and explains how we move from unity or number to identity as a 'medium' that 'must lie in something that is neither of them' but is 'betwixt' the two, a peculiar notion, as Hume himself admits, there being no conceivable 'medium' between those ideas than there is between 'existence and non-existence' (T 1.4.2.28/SBN 200). Baxter goes so far as to call it a 'mongrel idea'.[28] Hume's attempt to 'remove this difficulty' is really a step around it, a reformulation of the problem that shows the medium to be a fiction of misapplication that the imagination produces – 'identity' – according to the same mechanism that gave rise to an unchanging temporal object: identity is a fiction 'by which the unchangeable object is suppos'd to participate of the changes of the co-existent objects, and in particular of that of our perceptions' (T 1.4.2.29/SBN 201).

The idea of identity poses a problem for Hume because there is no direct impression to which it can be traced. The available options are unpromising: the idea cannot be derived from the perception of a single object, which only provides for unity (the idea that 'an object is the same with itself' means 'nothing' [T 1.4.2.26/SBN 200]), or from perception of a multiplicity, since even when the objects are virtually indistinguishable, this yields only the idea of entities that are 'entirely distinct and independent'. In the case of time, to recall, the idea of fictional duration arises when an unchangeable object is taken to participate in changes of other objects, which, in certain respects, it resembles; the genuine idea of time is confused with a steadfast object to yield an object in time that does not change. Hume urges that a comparable 'fiction

of the imagination' explains how a single object perceived without
interruption or variation leads to the idea of identity. In the latter
case, we confuse the idea of the object in time (genuine because
time is nothing but succession) with the perception of an uninterrupted object (steadfast object), to yield the idea of something in
time without variation or interruption (steadfast object in time),
and this, Hume says – the '*invariableness* and *uninteruptedness* of
any object, thro' a suppos'd variation of time' – is precisely what
we mean by identity. 'Here then is an idea, which is a medium
betwixt unity and number; or more properly speaking, is either of
them, according to the view, in which we take it: And this we call
the idea of identity' (T 1.4.2.29/SBN 200).

FROM INTERRUPTED PERCEPTIONS TO IDENTITY

The second part of Hume's discussion is to explain why the resemblance of interrupted impressions leads us to attribute identity to
them, or at least 'one of the essential qualities' of it, 'invariableness'. This also amounts to a fiction of misapplication, and Hume
refers again to the principle he has articulated already in his discussion of space and time: the tendency of imagination to move easily
and blindly among resembling ideas, mistaking one for another,
'without a strict attention, of which, generally speaking, 'tis
wholly incapable' (T 1.4.2.33/SBN 203). Hume first identifies the
'disposition' of the mind when viewing an object that is constant
through a succession of moments – what Hume also calls 'perfect
identity' (T 1.4.2.24/SBN 199) – where, he discovers, rather than
bothering to form a new image or idea at each moment, the 'faculties of the mind repose themselves in a manner, and take no more
exercise, than what is necessary to continue that idea, of which
we were formerly possest, and which subsists without variation or
interruption' (T 1.4.2.33/SBN 203). It is not then 'very difficult',
Hume observes, to discover other objects that place the mind in a
similar disposition and dispose it to seek the same uninterrupted
passage, namely a succession of related objects, where, though we
perceive objects that are different, the imagination 'slides along the
succession with equal facility, as if it consider'd only one object;
and therefore confounds the succession with the identity' (T 1.4.2
34/SBN 204). The 'mistake', moreover, is a 'very natural' one for
us make, so that without effort or notice, we simply take 'different interrupted perceptions for one constant and uninterrupted
perception' (T 1.4.2.35/SBN 204), a fiction pervasive among 'all

the unthinking and unphilosophical part of mankind, (that is, all of us, at one time or another)' (T 1.4.2.36/SBN 205).

FROM IDENTITY TO CONTINUED EXISTENCE AND BELIEF

The third part of Hume's discussion, then, involves showing how this idea of perfect identity gives rise to that of continued existence; the fourth, and shortest, part then examines why we believe the absence of impressions and the ideas related to them. Hume describes an antimony where perfect identity is undermined by our experience of interrupted appearances of the same object, which gives rise to the idea of 'distinct beings, which appear after certain intervals', or what, in discussing personal identity, Hume calls 'imperfect identity' (T 1.4.6.9/SBN 256). This 'contradiction' causes a 'perplexity', which 'produces a propension to unite these broken appearances by the fiction of continu'd existence' (T 1.4.2.36/SBN 205). Hume emphasises how the 'opposition' between identity and interruption gives rise to 'uneasiness', from which the hedonistic imagination will naturally seek relief. When I perceive objects such as the sun or the ocean at different moments in time, I take them to be 'individually the same', but at once cannot ignore the fact that experience shows me the 'first impression as annihilated, and the second newly created' (T 1.4.2.24/SBN 199). The idea of sameness, in other words, immediately contradicts our experience that perceptions of objects – the ocean and the sun – are interrupted and *not* therefore of the same object. Yet the 'smooth passage of the imagination along the ideas of the resembling perceptions makes us ascribe to them a perfect identity', Hume urges. 'The uninterrupted manner of their appearance makes us consider them as so many resembling, but still distinct beings, which appear after certain intervals' (T 1.4.2.36/SBN 205). These two ideas, then – that objects are the same (resembling) and distinct (interrupted) – form a 'kind of contradiction' (T 1.4.2.24; 199), 'opposite opinions' in the face of which the imagination feels perplexed and 'uneasy' and from which it 'will naturally seek relief' (T 1.4.2.37/SBN 206).

The contradiction, moreover, amounts to an antinomy in the sense urged above, there being no unassailable grounds for adopting one idea in favour of the other:

> Since the uneasiness arises from the opposition of two contrary principles, it [the imagination] must look for relief by sacrificing the one to

the other. But as the smooth passage of our thought along resembling perceptions makes us ascribe to them an identity, we can never without reluctance yield to that opinion. We must, therefore, turn to the other side, and suppose that our perceptions are no longer interrupted, but preserve a continu'd as well as an invariable existence, and are by that means entirely the same. But here the interruptions in the appearance of these perceptions are so long and frequent, that 'tis impossible to overlook them. (T 1.4.2.37/SBN 206)

The 'sensible uneasiness' arises from being unable to yield either to perfect identity or uninterrupted existence; the transition of ideas in the former is too strong to resist, the experience of the latter too palpable to overlook. The only option, Hume proposes, is that we free ourselves from the contradiction by adopting, as quoted above, a 'disguise' or 'by *supposing* perceptions are connected by a real existence, of which we are insensible' (T 1.4.2.24/SBN 199, emphasis added). 'The perplexity arising from this contradiction', he concludes, 'produces a propension to unite these broken appearances by the fiction of a continu'd existence' (T 1.4.2.36/SBN 205), 'feigning a continu'd being, which may fill those intervals [of interrupted existence], and preserve a perfect and entire identity to our perceptions' (T 1.4.2.40/SBN 208). The idea, however, is a fiction:

> The imagination is seduc'd into such an opinion only by means of the resemblance of certain perceptions; since we find they are only our resembling perceptions, which we have a propension to suppose the same. The propension to bestow an identity on our resembling perceptions, produces the fiction of continu'd existence; since that fiction, as well as the identity, is really false, as is acknowleg'd by all philosophers, and has no other effect than to remedy the interruption of our perceptions, which is the only circumstance that is contrary to their identity. (T 1.4.2.43/SBN 209)

The contradiction cannot be resolved, but it is practically overcome through inventing an idea that allows us to conceive an object as being both present and absent to the mind – both perceived and unperceived – without any change in its existence. Needless to say, this is an idea that has no correspondence to any impressions or matter of fact.

The fourth and final part of Hume's account of continued existence aims to explain how 'we are led after this manner, by the natural propensity of the imagination' (T 1.4.2.43/SBN 209), to believe the idea in the absence of impressions and the ideas related to them. In the case of continued existence, there is another 'principle' at work, which Hume finds in the faculty of memory. He writes:

> Our memory presents us with a vast number of instances of perceptions perfectly resembling each other, that return at different distances of time, and after considerable interruptions. The resemblance gives us a propension to consider these interrupted perceptions as the same; and also a propension to connect them by a continu'd existence, in order to justify this identity, and avoid the contradiction, in which the interrupted appearance of these perceptions seems necessarily to involve us. (T 1.4.2.42/SBN 209)

The idea rises to the level of belief, then, due to this propensity to 'feign the continu'd existence of all sensible objects; and as this propensity arises from some lively impressions of memory, it bestows a vivacity on that fiction; or in other words, makes us believe the continu'd existence of body' (T 1.4.2.42/SBN 209). Moreover, this is not a belief over which we have any control; we assent to it even though no arguments can be marshalled in its favour. 'Nature has not left this to his choice', Hume concludes, referring to a pretended sceptic, 'and has doubtless esteem'd it an affair of too great importance to be trusted to our uncertain reasonings and speculations' (T 1.4.2.1/SBN 187).

Substance as a substratum

Hume's treatment of substance owes much to Locke, who argues famously in the *Essay* that, while we have ideas of particular substances, using the term generically involves 'supposing' that qualities inhere in an unknown something or substratum of which we have no idea. Locke writes:

> every one upon Enquiry into his own thoughts, will find that he has 'no other *Idea* of any *Substance* ... but what he has barely of those sensible *Qualities*, which he supposes to inhere, with a supposition of such a *Substratum*, as gives as it were support to those *Qualities*, or simple *Ideas*, which he has observed to exist united together. (*Essay* 2.23.6, 298; see also 2.13.18–19, 174–5)

'We have no such *clear idea* at all', Locke concludes, 'and there-fore signify nothing by the word *Substance*, but only an uncertain supposition of we know not what' (*Essay* 1.4.18, 95). Locke does not deny that this is a mistake confined to philosophers, but the tenor of his discussion suggests that the suppositional nature of the idea will become apparent to 'any one' who cares to 'examine himself' concerning it (*Essay* 2.23.2, 295).

Hume adopts both the form and content of this view, including the ambiguity of whether it involves a vulgar error or falls within the purview of philosophers. When Hume first broaches the issue (T 1.1.6), he suggests the latter, asking 'those philosophers' who trade in the idea and its relata whether they can be traced either to impressions of sensation or reflection, since neither appear to be good candidates. With respect to the latter, Hume points out that while the senses supply our perceptions of colour, sound, taste and the like, substance itself cannot be identified with any particular percept. 'None will assert', he remarks, 'that substance is either a colour, or a sound, or a taste'. At the same time, substance cannot be counted among the former – impressions of reflection – since these resolve into passions or emotions, and, like impressions of sense, cannot themselves represent a substance. Strictly speaking, then, 'We have therefore no idea of a substance', Hume observes, 'distinct from that of a collection of particular qualities, nor have we any other meaning when we either talk or reason concerning it' (T 1.1.6.1/SBN 16). Philosophers might not be aware of it, but when they speak of substance they can mean 'nothing but a collection of simple ideas, that are united by the imagination, and have a particular name assign'd to them, by which we are able to recal, either to ourselves or others, that collection' (T 1.1.6.2/SBN 16). Philosophers thus trade on the practice of common life where, when we speak of 'gold' (to use Hume's example), we just mean something of a particular colour, weight and malleability. Assuming that they do have this clear idea in mind, when philosophers speak of 'substance' they simply capture in general and technical terms the way that non-philosophers speak and think. Here, then, we might think, is a genuine idea of substance, meaning a collec-tion of particular qualities, the origin of which can be traced to experience.

Hume complicates this picture, however, by suggesting that even this vulgar idea of substance involves a 'fiction' (he uses the term explicitly), where qualities that form the substance are 'referr'd to an unknown *something*, in which they are suppos'd to inhere' (T 1.1.6.2/SBN 16). Hume does not mention the imagination by name, but one can see how the principle of easy transition explains it: unsatisfied with a mere collection of simple ideas, the faculty is driven to seek a whole, which it finds in the idea, to use Locke's term, of a substratum, a fiction of invention that cannot be traced to any real existence or matter of fact. Hume clearly associates this fiction with vulgar reasoning and even presents it as part of the process whereby we are able to expand our concepts by adding other qualities to those already contained in the idea when new facts about it are discovered. The discovery that gold dissolves in *aqua regia* adds a new quality to the substance – dissolubility – which is added to those of its colour, weight, malleability and fusibilty. Even this addition of a quality, however, involves the propensity to move from what is present to an otherwise absent attendant: 'we suppose it [dissolubility] to belong to the substance as much as if its idea had from the beginning made a part of the compound one'. This certainly comes close to qualifying as an idea that inspires a first-order natural belief, not a malady that can be corrected but something indispensable for making the world a coherent place. Hume also suggests that the fiction is not inevitable, although he insists that even 'granting this fiction shou'd not take place', the qualities in question 'are at least suppos'd to be closely and inseparably connected by the relations of contiguity and causation' (T 1.1.6.2/SBN 16). This opens the possibility that Hume regards the fiction of a substratum as a malady of which we can be cured, but the imagination remains indispensable for providing some 'principle of union' that is held to bind qualities together and provide 'entrance' for the addition of new ones.

That the substratum view of substance is originally a vulgar fiction finds support in Hume's discussion of substance in T 1.4.3, where he shows what the fiction of a substratum consists in (identity and simplicity) and how the imagination reaches it (as a resolution of contradictions supplied by experience).[29] The section is advertised as an examination of the 'fictions of antient philosophy' (T 1.4.3.1/SBN 219), substances, substantial forms, accidents and occult qualities, and informs his 'abandoning utterly' the dispute over the materiality or immateriality of the soul, where disputants do not really understand the meaning of the question because they have no clear idea of what they mean by the terms – *substance* and *inhesion* – they use (T 1.4.5.6/SBN 234). Before Hume diagnoses these artificial fictions of philosophers, however, he explains in some detail how the compound formed of taking qualities to inhere in an unknown something (a substratum) involves and trades on the vulgar fiction and natural belief people have in the simplicity and identity of objects: why we regard a compound of qualities – the object – as 'ONE thing, and as continuing the SAME under very considerable alterations' (T 1.4.3.2/SBN 219). We arrive at the fiction of a substratum through the imagination, which immediately contrasts with our experience of things as composites and subject to variation. These are 'evident contradictions' into which we 'almost universally fall' and that 'we endeavour to conceal' (T 1.4.3.2/SBN 219). The fictions of ancient philosophers are 'unreasonable and capricious', but Hume recognises that they have a 'very intimate connexion with the principles of human nature' (T 1.4.3.1/SBN 219).

The first contradiction Hume considers is between the identity and diversity of objects. The imagination moves easily along a chain of related qualities to produce the idea of one continued object. 'The smooth and uninterrupted progress of the thought, being alike in both cases, readily deceives the mind, and makes us ascribe an identity to the changeable succession of connected qualities' (T 1.4.3.3/SBN 220). Hume adds that there is a tendency to confuse succession with an unchanging object because the 'acts of mind' in each case are 'similar' (T 1.4.3.4/SBN 220). When we compare objects not through successive points in time but at different times, however, variation becomes obvious and the previously perceived identity of the object is destroyed by diversity. In order to 'reconcile' the contradiction, Hume says, the 'imagination is apt to feign something unknown and invisible, which it supposes to continue the same under all these variations, and this unintelligible something it calls a *substance*, or *original and first matter*' (T 1.4.3.4/SBN 220).

The second contradiction is between simplicity and complexity. Hume here appeals to the fact that there is no discernible difference to the imagination between a simple indivisible object and one that is a composite of different parts connected by some 'strong relation'. The resemblance of one to the other means that we tend to take objects as simple even though they have discernible parts; these are the 'primary and more natural notions' of objects. Hume writes:

> The imagination conceives the simple object at once, with facility, by a single effort of thought, without change or variation. The connexion of parts in the compound object has almost the same effect, and so unites the object within itself, that the fancy feels not the transition in passing from one part to another. (T 1.4.3.5/SBN 221)

At the same time, experience also shows that the qualities of objects are 'different, and distinguishable, and separable from each other', a view that undermines the idea of simplicity, which 'obliges the imagination to feign an unknown something, or *original* substance and matter, as a principle of union or cohesion among those qualities' (T 1.4.3.5/SBN 221).

Again, as in the earlier section (T 1.1.6), Hume does not make it clear whether these fictions give rise to first- or second-order natural beliefs, but if they are a malady it is difficult to see what correction of them would look like: they are 'principles of human nature' after all, and intimately bound with how we order the world and make our experience of it seamless and coherent. What is clear, however, from the discussion that ensues is that Hume takes the vulgar fiction of a substratum to be the basis for a variety of philosophical fictions that *are* the offspring of a diseased mind: doctrines that are 'like specters in the dark, and deriv'd from principles, which, however common, are neither universal nor unavoidable in human nature' (T 1.4.4.2/SBN 226). These fictions not only depart from the genuine idea of substance as a collection of simple ideas united by the imagination, but follow the imagination beyond the natural fiction of vulgar reason to the point where it creates a system that is 'entirely incomprehensible', even though it is 'deriv'd from principles as natural as any of those above-explain'd', namely the vulgar fiction of a substratum (T 1.4.3.8/SBN 222). Hume describes a natural progression of philosophical thought from post-Aristotelian views that reduce diversity (fire, water, earth and air) to the same substance 'perfectly homogenous in all bodies' (T 1.4.3.6/SBN 221), through substantial form assigned to different species of objects, and the discovery of accidents to accommodate properties of bodies that require a 'subject of inhesion to sustain and support them' (T 1.4.3.6/SBN 222). Here these philosophers 'both suppose a substance supporting, which they do not understand, and an accident supported, of which they have as imperfect an idea'. Carrying 'their fictions still farther' into the realm of occult qualities (T 1.4.3.8/SBN 222) is then little more than admission of failure, a return, albeit by a different path, to the 'situation of the vulgar' (T 1.4.3.9/SBN 223).

Objective Causal Power

The same process that explains the fictitious idea of substance also accounts for the fictional idea of causal connection, and, again, we appear to have an artificial fiction of philosophy that trades in an error that human beings naturally make. The idea of objective causal power is the counterpart to the genuine idea of causal necessity that arises from the power of memory to recall past experience of constantly conjoined events and the manner of their appearance as resembling, which strikes the imagination in such a way as to give rise to belief. The puzzle Hume faces in accounting for the genuine idea is that, while we have the idea of causal power, we do not have any impression to which it can be directly traced. At the same time, if we *are* to 'assert that we really have such an idea', he acknowledges, we 'must find some impression' to which it corresponds (T 1.3.14.1/SBN 155). Hume solves this puzzle – though in a way so counter-intuitive that he thinks it will fall largely on deaf ears – by appealing to memory, the powers of imagination and the effect of custom or a certain habit of mind, to conclude that it is 'an internal impression of the mind, or a determination to carry our thoughts from one object to another' (T 1.3.14.20/SBN 165).

Hume reaches this conclusion by observing, first, that causality is something in which we have a justified belief, a case where we readily 'mark the difference between something preserv'd by the mind in a steady and uniform manner for some considerable time, as opposed to the comparatively faint and languid ideas of imagination'. It is not a fiction, he urges, and should be distinguished explicitly from ideas such as continued existence, from which it is 'at bottom considerably different' (T 1.4.2.21/SBN 197). Causal necessity must be an idea that is both genuine (corresponds to some matter of fact) and adequate (the relations, contradictions and agreements of the ideas are all applicable to the objects). Hume observes:

> If I see a billiard-ball moving towards another, on a smooth table, I can easily conceive it to stop upon contact. This conception implies no

> contradiction; but still it *feels very differently* from that conception,
> by which I represent to myself the impulse, and the communication of
> motion from one ball to another. (EHU 5.11/SBN 48, emphasis added)

Here we find that 'difference between a *fiction* and *belief*, [which]
lies in some sentiment or feeling, which is annexed to the latter,
not to the former, and depends not on the will, nor can be commanded at pleasure' (EHU 5.11/SBN 48). In the case of cause and
effect, the imagination is required to combine these ideas together
but it is the *customary* transition that eases its path: 'when we have
been accustom'd to see one object united to another, our imagination passes from the first to the second, by a natural transition,
which precedes reflection, and which cannot be prevented by it'
(T 1.3.13.8/SBN 147).

Second, while memory 'raise[s] up the images of past perceptions' (T 1.4.7.18/SBN 260), that same faculty does not have the
power to relate those ideas together, a feat that only the imagination, as the seat of the natural principles of association, is able to
accomplish. The ideas of memory strike the passive imagination
because of the secret union or natural attraction they exhibit, and
the imagination actively combines them in regular and uniform
ways. It will do so when the relations between events resemble one
another in terms of succession and contiguity. The imagination is
then influenced more or less strongly by the degree to which events
are more or less constantly conjoined in experience, and thus
recalled by memory, and gives rise to that feeling, which constitutes
belief; the degree of conviction is always probabilistic, however,
proportional to our experience of constant conjunction. Where
one event is regularly conjoined with another – one billiard ball
has always imparted motion to another – the feeling or belief that
it will do so again is 'entire'; where the conjunction is less regular
– rhubarb or opium are *not* always followed by their purging or
soporific effects (EHU 6.4/SBN 57–8) – the feeling or belief will be
partial or imperfect. In all cases, the 'essence of necessity', Hume
contends, is 'that propensity, which custom produces, to pass from
an object to the idea of its usual attendant' (T 1.3.14.22/SBN 165)
or, as he expresses his view in the first *Enquiry*, 'This connexion,
. . . which we *feel* in the mind, this customary transition of the
imagination from one object to its usual attendant, *is the sentiment or impression*, from which we form the idea of power or
necessary connection' (EHU 7.28/SBN 75, emphasis added).

How, then, we might ask, is the idea 'formed'? Hume insists that nothing is 'either discover'd or produc'd in any objects by their constant conjunction' – the ideas 'represent not any thing' (T 1.3.14.19/SBN 164) – but the '*observation* of this resemblance produces a new impression *in the mind*, which is its real model' (T 1.3.14.20/SBN 165). 'What alteration has happened to give rise to this new idea of *connexion*?' Hume asks of the man having seen several instances of one billiard ball hitting another. 'Nothing', he replies, 'but that he now feels these events to be connected in his imagination, and can readily foretell the existence of one from the appearance of the other' (EHU 7.28/SBN 75–6). The repetition of resembling instances strikes the passive imagination and gives rise to a sentiment, which is then copied and represented through its mimetic power in the form of a new appearance, namely the 'original idea' of causal necessity (T 1.3.14.16/SBN 163). As noted above, Hume distinguishes belief in necessary connection from a fiction of the imagination; we are convinced that a billiard ball will impart motion to another because the idea can be traced to an internal impression, that is, a matter of fact with real existence. It is thus born of the mimetic power of the imagination, but is an idea both adequate and genuine and capable of inspiring true belief.

While the idea of causal necessity can be traced to experience, the same cannot be said of its fictional counterpart, which takes it to be a real or objective power in the world itself. Here we go further and, as Hume puts it, 'ascribe a power or necessary connexion to ... objects' (T 1.3.14.28/SBN 168–9) and 'do not understand our own meaning in talking so', he urges, 'but ignorantly confound ideas, which are entirely distinct from one another' (T 1.1.3.27/SBN 168). What is the cause of this mistake, and why do we imagine a conjunction where none exists? Hume's answer to this question develops along similar lines to his treatment of substance. We 'transfer the determination of the thought to external objects', Hume observes, 'and suppose any real intelligible connexion betwixt them; that being a quality, which can only belong to the mind that considers them' (T 1.3.14.27/SBN 168). He writes:

'Tis a common observation that the mind has a great propensity to spread itself on external objects, and to conjoin with them any internal impressions, which they occasion, and which always make their appearance at the same time that these objects discover themselves to the senses. Thus as certain sounds and smells are always found to attend certain visible objects, we naturally imagine a conjunction, even in place, betwixt the objects and qualities, tho' the qualities be of such a nature as to admit of no such conjunction, and really exist no where. ... the same propensity is the reason, why we suppose necessity and power to lie in the objects we consider, not in our mind, that considers them ... (T 1.3.14.25/SBN 167)

As in the case of substance, the imagination creates a new relation, which takes the quality of causal relation that arises properly from the experience of constant conjunction and transfers it to objects themselves. Reflection traces the quality to constant conjunction and impressions of reflection (that constitute the genuine idea of causal necessity), yet imagination completes the union that renders the transition easy and natural. We fail to perceive the opposition, and so, instead of renouncing either side of the antinomy, suppose causal power to have a place where none exists. Again, this is tantamount to saying that a 'thing is in a certain place, and yet is not there' (T 1.4.5.13/SBN 238), an unintelligible idea, which strikes the imagination nonetheless with sufficient force and vivacity to constitute belief, albeit false.

Reification

In the course of unmasking the confusions involved in debates over the materiality or immateriality of the soul, Hume considers an argument employed by the latter camp, to the effect that since extension and qualities are incompatible, they can never – as the materialists propose – 'incorporate into one subject' (T 1.4.5.7/SBN 234). Hume does not respond to this claim argument directly, but observes instead that the issue it raises concerns not whether the soul is really a substance but why qualities are given a spatial location in the objects of which they are predicated. The real question, then, concerns the soul's 'local conjunction with matter' (T 1.4.5.8/SBN 235). Pursuing this question, Hume identifies a vulgar fiction of invention (he calls it an 'illusion'), which he traces to the imagination and its principle of easy transition. On the basis of this fiction and the natural belief that attends it, the philosophical doctrine of materialism arises because proponents are tempted by the principles of imagination to 'conjoin all thought with extension' (T 1.4.5.15/SBN 239). We can think of this as a species of reification, the fallacy of misplaced concreteness, where, due to the imagination, we take certain qualities, such as taste and smell, and produce a 'new relation' that confers spatial location or 'local conjunction' (T 1.4.5.8/SBN 235) on them that they do not otherwise possess.[30]

Hume's argument involves defending the maxim *that an object may exist, and yet be no where* (T 1.4.5.10/SBN 235). Drawing on his earlier discussion, Hume emphasises that space or extension requires what is 'colour'd and tangible' and, where qualities that lack these features occur with others that have them, that we are apt to associate them and confer on the former a real existence they do not possess. Hume offers the following example:

> Thus supposing we consider a fig at one end of the table, and an olive at the other, 'tis evident, that in forming the complex ideas of these substances, one of the most obvious is that of their different relishes; and 'tis as evident, that we incorporate and conjoin these qualities with such as are colour'd and tangible. The bitter taste of the one, and sweet of the other are *suppos'd to lie* in the very visible body, and to be separated from each other by the whole length of the table. (T 1.4.5.11/SBN 236, emphasis added)

The creation of this new relation can be explained through the 'inclination of our fancy by which we are determin'd to incorporate the taste with the extended object' (T 1.4.5.13/SBN 238). The imagination has a tendency to 'compleat the union' among ideas, rendering the 'transition more easy and natural', in the course of which 'we feel a satisfaction in joining the relation of contiguity to that of resemblance, or the resemblance of situation to that of qualities' (T 1.4.5.12/SBN 237). Reflection immediately shows us the 'impossibility of such a union', and the result is a dialectic between two contradictory but equally unassailable alternatives. Hume observes:

> Being divided betwixt these opposite principles, we renounce neither one nor the other, but involve the subject in such confusion and obscurity, that we no longer perceive the opposition. We suppose, that taste exists within the circumference of the body, but in such a manner, that it fills the whole without extension, and exists entire in every part without separation. . . . Which is much the same, as if we shou'd say, that thing is in a certain place, and yet is not there.

Indeed, this means that 'our most familiar way of thinking' coincides with the scholastic principle that the 'whole is in the whole, and the whole in every part' (*totum in toto et totum in qualibet parte*) (T 1.4.5.13/SBN 238).

This is obvious in the case of objects of thought and perceptions of smell and hearing, which are actually incompatible with the idea of spatial location, contiguity or distance. It is also true, though less evident, with objects of sight and feeling, where we take the bitter taste of the olive and the sweetness of the fig to be within the perceived objects. The same might be said of sentiments and passions, which are taken to be within the person who exhibits them, though they are really ways of assessing or accounting for behaviour that, when collected together, we call character.[31] Hume insists that this maxim and the judgements that fall under it are not the result of an artificial connection drawn between ideas, but part of 'our most familiar way of thinking' (T 1.4.5.13/SBN 238), a 'notable and so natural an illusion' (T 1.4.5.11/SBN 236), which amounts to accepting that something can be in a certain place and yet not be there. As offensive to reason as it might be, the principle pervades common life and, while it can be explained as a fiction of invention to resolve a contradiction, it cannot be eradicated.

Primary and Secondary Qualities

Hume discusses the distinction between primary and secondary qualities under the rubric of 'modern philosophy', and he appears to take the doctrine as a defining feature of the tradition. Hume's diagnosis of the fiction involved is closely connected to his criticism of the substratum view of substance, an idea the imagination invents to explain how a bundle of qualities can at once partake in and designate a single being. Once we have this vulgar idea, it is a short step for the philosopher to attach certain qualities (primary ones) to it. Hume acknowledges that the distinction itself is on firm ground insofar as observation teaches that impressions do vary while the appearance of the object remains the same: changes in distance and perspective alter the colours of an object, and the same food is sweet to one person while to bitter to another as it is both sweet and bitter at different times to the same person in altered states of health. The explanation for this phenomenon, moreover, is as just as the observation is accurate. We do not assume that every colour perceived due to change of perspective is caused by a resembling quality in the object, and, on the assumption that like effects follow from like causes, we reasonably conclude that the different appearances are all 'deriv'd from a like origin' (T 1.4.4.4/SBN 227).[32] Once this point has been granted, however, the imagination moves quickly to the conclusion that, since no sensible (now 'secondary') qualities have 'continu'd independent existence', the only real qualities of which we have any notion must be ones inhering in the object, the 'primary' ones of 'extension and solidity, with their different mixtures and modifications' (T 1.4.4.5/SBN 227). As we have seen, Hume thinks it a 'notable and natural illusion' that we accept the idea of something being in a certain place and yet not being there (being 'no where'), for which reason we place the taste in an object: it 'exists within the circumference of the body, ... and fills the whole without extension, and exists entire in every part without separation' (T 1.4.5.13/SBN 230). Following this tendency, the imagination moves smoothly to place primary qualities, of which we have no idea, into matter (substance as a substratum) of which we also have no idea. This is a spurious philosophical doctrine and, as Hume goes on to show, in an argument already made famous by Berkeley, the doctrine terminates in complete scepticism by annihilating the object entirely: if secondary qualities are merely perceptions of the mind, then nothing stops the same being true of primary qualities as well.[33]

Personal Identity or Self

The final fiction of invention in which the imagination looms large – and the final fiction of metaphysics we will consider in this chapter – is that concerning personal identity, or the self, that Hume discusses in T 1.4.6. This section of the *Treatise* has proved notoriously difficult to interpret in any decisive way, a state of affairs exacerbated by the doubts Hume expresses later in the Appendix about his solution and an apparent rejection of at least some of his earlier conclusions. These doubts are quite specific, however, and concern only his professed inability to 'explain the principles, that unite our successive perceptions in our thought or consciousness' (T Appx.20/SBN 636), it being beyond his power to reconcile what he characterises as 'two principles' that he 'cannot render consistent' (T Appx.21/SBN

636). As commentators routinely observe, Hume actually leaves untouched (and even reaffirms) much of his earlier discussion, including the two central elements that are relevant in the present context: that the self is a 'fiction' (a term he uses explicitly), the origin of which is to be explained by the imagination and the principle of easy transition that governs it.[34] Hume does not raise either of these as problematic parts of the 'labyrinth' in which he claims to have involved himself (T Appx.10/SBN 633), and we should expect no less: to question these would effectively cast doubt on the many other areas of his thought where he appeals to the imagination, including its proclivity for inventing fictions.

Hume's argument is motivated famously by the observation that, while we seem to possess an idea of the self as something that exists and has continued existence, there is no 'impression constant and invariable' (T 1.4.6.2/SBN 251) to which it can be traced. Reflection reveals only a 'bundle or collection of different perceptions', the mind being a 'kind of theatre' with mental players variously appearing, gliding away and mingling with each other, and lacking both simplicity and identity (T 1.4.6.4/SBN 252–3). Hume focuses on the latter (although he takes his argument to apply equally to simplicity [T 1.4.6.22/SBN 263]) and then asks whence the 'propension' to ascribe identity to successive perceptions, such that we reach the idea in question in the absence of the required impression. In answering this question, Hume effectively recapitulates the argument he has already supplied in T 1.4.2 ('Of scepticism with regard to the senses'), where, as we have seen, he explains identity as a fiction of misapplication that occurs when different interrupted perceptions are taken as one constant and uninterrupted perception, to yield the *'invariableness* and *uninteruptedness* of any object, thro' a suppos'd variation of time.' Here (to repeat his conclusion quoted above) is an idea that is a 'medium betwixt unity and number; or, more properly speaking, is either of them, according to the view, in which we take it: And this we call the idea of identity' (T 1.4.2.29/SBN 200). As Hume explains, referencing his earlier argument:

> The identity, which we ascribe to the mind of man, is only a fictitious one, and of a like kind with that which we ascribe to vegetable and animal bodies. It cannot, therefore, have a different origin, but must

proceed from a like operation of the imagination upon like objects. (T 1.4.6.15/SBN 259)

If personal identity is explicable as a specific case of general identity, we might conclude that the former, like the latter, is really a fiction of misapplication, and that is indeed the way Hume proceeds, which really involves two steps. The first involves explaining how the fiction of self arises. On the one hand, he observes, we have the idea of identity or sameness (an invariable and uninterrupted object through a supposed variation of time) and, on the other, that of diversity (different objects in succession), but through an 'action of the imagination' one is 'confounded' with the other: both are the 'same to feeling', and this resemblance leads to 'confusion and mistake, and makes us substitute the notion of identity, instead of that of related objects'. This 'mistake' follows from a 'biass of the imagination' to which we are compelled to 'yield' (T 1.4.6.6/SBN 254). Hume then elaborates the various phenomena that induce the imagination to make its smooth passage among the ideas it finds: small changes are hardly noticed; change is judged in proportion to the relevant whole rather than absolutely; and changes that are gradual and insensible do not enter into judgements of identity.

Having discovered the source of the fiction, the second step is to demonstrate that identity is 'merely a quality, which we attribute to them [different perceptions], because of the union of their ideas in the imagination, when we reflect upon them' (T 1.4.6.17/SBN 260). Hume considers two of the principles of association to explain this union. The first (as we might expect from the confounding of ideas involved in the fiction) is resemblance, which leads the imagination to move 'more easily from one link to another' in a chain of images raised by memory to 'make the whole seem like the continuance of one object'. Memory is crucial, Hume emphasises, because it both 'discovers' identity and 'contributes to its production' by 'producing' the relation of resemblance among the perceptions it raises (T 1.4.6.18/SBN 261).[35] The second and, to Hume's mind, more fundamental principle is that of cause and effect:

As to *causation*, we may observe, that the true idea of the human mind, is to consider it as a system of different perceptions or different existences, which are link'd together by the relation of cause and effect, and mutually produce, destroy, influence, and modify each other.

This observation inspires Hume to draw an analogy between the mind and a commonwealth in which members, laws and constitutions might change without taking away its identity (T 1.4.6.19/SBN 261). In this case, memory does not so much '*produce*' as '*discover* personal identity, by showing us the relation of cause and effect among our different perceptions' (T 1.4.6.20/SBN 262), upon which the imagination then works to 'feign' an identical self to which the distinct but causally related perceptions are taken to belong.

What, then, given Hume's diagnosis, makes personal identity a fiction of invention rather than one of misapplication? To answer this question, we need to consider whether the self is an idea that arises in the course of vulgar reasoning and thus inspires natural belief, or whether it falls under the purview of philosophy and should be regarded as only a matter of persuasion. When Hume introduces the issue in T 1.4.6, he certainly advertises it as a case of the latter, and he criticises 'some philosophers' (T 1.4.6.1/SBN 251) who claim knowledge about its existence, identity and simplicity above what can be demonstrated and, more importantly, experienced. Given this opening salvo, it is tempting to regard the entire ensuing discussion as an attack on philosophical doctrines: after all, as Allison notes, Hume's bundle view of mind is 'not one that would occur to the vulgar', and one might think, with Ainslie, that his 'findings are primarily *philosophical*, rather than relevant to our everyday concerns' since they require 'taking up the reflective posture in which we observe our mental states', one quite different from the 'posture of everyday life', where we are aware only of their content and not the states themselves.[36]

One feature that sets the idea of personal identity apart from other fictions, however, is that the idea is not of some external object but is a matter of internal impressions of what one calls oneself; the object and its identity, as unified through time, only appears upon reflection.[37] Only on reflection are we faced with a contradiction that requires a solution: 'However at one instant we may consider the related succession as variable or interrupted, we are sure the next to ascribe to it a perfect identity, and regard it as invariable and uninterrupted' (T 1.4.6.7/SBN 254). The 'propensity to this mistake' is so strong because of the resemblance of the ideas that 'we fall into it before we are aware' and are unable to correct it for long through reflection, despite knowing its existence to be an 'absurdity'. Our 'last resort is to yield to it [the bias of imagination], and boldly assert that these different related objects are in effect the same, however interrupted and variable'. Yielding in this way involves justifying the absurdity to ourselves by feigning 'some new and unintelligible principle' that acts as a 'disguise' for our inability either to resist the mistake or otherwise explain it. The idea thus invented is what we call 'self' or 'personal identity'. As in the other fictions we have considered, this fulfils the imagination's desire for satisfaction and its tendency to move easily from one idea to another:

> and as the very essence of these relations in their producing an easy transition of ideas; it follows, that our notions of personal identity, proceed entirely from the smooth and uninterrupted progress of the thought along a train of connected ideas . . . (T 1.4.6.16/SBN 260)

The idea of self is not simply a confusion of terms – not 'merely a dispute concerning words' (T 1.4.6.7/SBN 255) – but a conceptual or 'grammatical' difficulty (T 1.4.6.21/SBN 262). As Hume puts it,[38] it is an entirely 'new principle' the imagination invents in order to account for the propensity of assigning identity to cases of succession. The imagination creates these ideas not from its power to represent and copy or combine through the principles of association, but from its power to produce original ideas that cannot be traced to matter of fact or real existence.

Which principle one settles on depends, moreover, on whether one speaks with the vulgar or as a philosopher: as a fiction of the former it inspires natural, first-order belief, and as a fiction of the latter a belief-like state that only persuades practitioners. As in some of the other fictions we have considered in this chapter – continued existence, substance as a substratum and the tendency to give spatial location to intangible objects – personal identity is a fiction that is fundamentally vulgar in origin but at once forms the basis for the creation of artificial fictions when philosophers follow the principles of imagination further. The precise referents of 'our' and 'we' in Hume's discussion of self may be murky, but he writes clearly of the profound effect of the 'principles of imagination' on a 'great genius' (he is speaking of Anthony Ashley Cooper, Third Earl of Shaftesbury) *and* 'mere vulgar' alike (T 1.4.6.6n50/SBN 254n1). Philosophically inclined or not, a mind still seeks 'something unknown and mysterious, connecting parts, beside their relation' (T 1.4.6.6/SBN

254), as when the vulgar resort to the artifice of a '*common end or purpose*' to account for a ship being the same even though most of its parts have been replaced (T 1.4.6.11/SBN 257), or to ascribe 'identity . . . to plants and vegetables' (T 1.4.6.11/SBN 255). This purpose is strengthened when '*sympathy* of parts' is added to it: an oak that grows from a small plant into a large tree or an infant that becomes a man and is 'sometimes fat, sometimes lean' are taken to do so without a change of identity (T 1.4.6.12/SBN 257). Philosophers, on the other hand, make the same move, but, thick with theories and blind to their own prejudices, they follow the imagination further and 'run into the notion of a *soul*, and *self*, and *substance*' to explain the same (T 1.4.6.6/SBN 254), more rarefied, abstract and sophisticated formulations of the same tendency found among non-philosophers.[39] Thus in the hands of Shaftesbury, the vulgar notion of purpose and sympathy blossoms into a 'uniting principle' that finally explains the universe as a whole (T 1.4.6.6n50/SBN 254n1).[40]

In this chapter we have seen that Hume explains the origin of metaphysical fictions by showing them to arise either through misapplication or invention. The productive imagination confuses and confounds genuine ideas to produce a fictitious idea that combines or incorporates both (a vacuum and time without change, liberty and necessity, identity and those connected with general rules of the imagination), or it creates a new idea to solve a contradiction that has no reference to matter of fact at all (continued and distinct existence, substance as a substratum, objective causal power, reification, primary and secondary qualities, and personal identity). As noted at the outset, these ideas might also be divided according to whether they qualify as fictions of vulgar reasoning that inspire natural first-order beliefs or artificial philosophical fictions, which inspire only belief-like states that can and should be corrected. In the former case, the imagination joins ideas on the basis of natural attraction, which gives rise to first-order natural beliefs that are unavoidable and necessary. In the latter case, the imagination draws connections where none otherwise exist, giving rise to second-order natural beliefs, maladies that can and should be corrected. Some of the fictions (and belief in them) that we have considered in this chapter, then, make life possible and without them 'human nature must immediately perish and go to ruin'. It is fitting that we leave Hume's treatment of metaphysics by emphasising the indispensible role that some fictions play in ordering experience. These ideas might even be thought of as part of what Hume refers to on one occasion as:

> a kind of pre-established harmony between the course of nature and the succession of our ideas; and though the powers and forces by which the former is governed be wholly unknown to us; yet our thoughts and conceptions have still, we find, gone on the same train with the other works of nature. (EHU 5.21/SBN 54–5)

Belief in a world recreated with every blink of the eye or a self broken up in time and place are terrifying propositions; the weakness (or strength) of the imagination spares us such terrors, and while philosophy of the sort pursued by Hume allows temporary and fleeting glimpses into the anatomical horrors of the universe, it is a view that cannot be long maintained. For this, more than in any other area of our lives, we should be immensely grateful.

Notes

1. For an up-to-date discussion and overview, see Peter van Inwagen and Meghan Sullivan, 'Metaphysics', *The Stanford Encyclopedia of Philosophy* (spring 2015 edn), Edward N. Zalta (ed.), http://plato. stanford.edu/archives/spr2015/entries/metaphysics/ (last accessed 30 July 2017).
2. See Streminger, 'Hume's Theory of Imagination', pp. 92–3, who emphasises that metaphysics also involves a *critique* of metaphysics, since Hume is at once attempting to 'constrain' its traditional tendency to follow prejudice, fall prey to anthropomorphism and generalise from experience to '"extra-mental" objects', all products of the imagination when that faculty is followed 'blindly'. A critique of metaphysics thus goes hand in hand with a critique of the imagination, since clarifying the nature and function of the latter should involve clarifying proper parameters of the former.
3. McRae, 'The Import of Hume's Theory of Time', p. 124, emphasis added. See also Wilbanks, *Hume's Theory of Imagination*, pp. 81–2, Sokolowski, 'Fiction and Illusion in David Hume's Philosophy', p. 193, and Passmore, *Hume's Intentions*, who recognises the inventive function in his remark about 'metaphysics' being a set of 'doctrines' that 'illustrate the tendency of our minds to construct 'fictions', in order to reconcile apparent conflicts in our experience' (p. 70).

Cf. Jonathan Cottrell, 'A Puzzle about Fictions in the *Treatise*', *Journal of the History of Philosophy*, 54: 1 (2016), pp. 47–73, who distinguishes between 'application fictions' and 'concealment fictions'. The former, he says (following McRae) 'consist in, or are produced by, applying an idea or term improperly and inexactly', 'while the latter arise because we then "feign" a further fiction to "conceal" the one already created' (p. 61). Cottrell frames the distinction from considering the case of 'unity and simplicity' (an application fiction) and 'unitary substance' (a concealment fiction), and although he suggests that it might be applied to others as well, it appears too narrow to accommodate all the fictions of a metaphysical sort and inadequate for isolating the origin of the fictions in question, which is better accomplished in the manner suggested.

4. *Hume's True Scepticism*, pp. 64 and 75. Ainslie does not mention McRae, but this mechanism appears to be equivalent to the latter's 'fiction of misapplication', although I take the fiction to be a new, hybrid idea rather than one of simple substitution.

5. Ainslie suggests that the case of general ideas satisfies Hume's description of a fiction at T 1.2.3.11/SBN 37: 'Ideas always represent the objects or impressions, from which they are deriv'd, and can never without a fiction represent or be apply'd to any other.' It is not clear, however, that Hume intends this as a complete definition of a fiction or even a definition at all: it suggests only that a fiction is required for an idea to refer to something other than the impression it represents, but not that the substitution is itself what constitutes a fiction.

6. Cf. Ainslie, *Hume's True Scepticism*, pp. 76–89, who treats these under the auspices of 'idea substitution'.

7. Cf. McRae, 'The Import of Hume's Theory of Time', who distinguishes duration in the 'philosophical and vulgar' sense from 'Humean time and succession'. The former, McRae argues, is 'for Hume, a "fiction", something falsely attributed to objects' (p. 120).

8. See Lorne Falkenstein, 'Hume on Manner of Disposition and the Ideas of Space and Time', *Archiv für Geschichte der Philosophie*, 79: 2 (1997), pp. 179–201.

9. These ideas do not, then, have the same origin as the idea of causal necessity, where the imagination copies an internal impression, the feeling of expectation that a given event will be followed by its customary effect or that an effect is the product of its customary cause.

10. Falkenstein, 'Hume on Manner of Disposition and the Ideas of Space and Time', p. 187, emphasis added.

11. Ibid. pp. 188–9.

12. Ibid. pp. 188.
13. Michael Costa, 'Hume, Strict Identity, and Time's Vacuum', *Hume Studies*, 16: 1 (1990), writes that 'it is clear that Hume intends this account of abstract ideas to apply to the ideas of space and time' (p. 3), and Marina Frasca-Spada, 'Some Features of Hume's Conception of Space', *Studies in History and Philosophy of Science*, 21: 3 (1990), concludes that 'the origin of the idea of space . . . is the same as for abstract ideas' (p. 403).
14. See Berkeley, *Treatise*, Introduction, §11–20.
15. See Costa, 'Hume, Strict Identity, and Time's Vacuum', pp. 2–4.
16. Falkenstein, 'Hume on Manner of Disposition', p. 190.
17. See Ainslie, *Hume's True Scepticism*, who suggests that 'Hume is willing to countenance talk of a vacuum *when it is properly understood* in terms of what we think of when the mind substitutes ideas for another' (p. 83). Ainslie cites a passage from the Appendix (that Hume intended to be inserted as a note at T 1.2.5.26) to support the observation, although the definition of 'vacuum' Hume there provides is rather thin and effectively avoids the issue of whether 'space' can be 'empty' or not: 'A vacuum is asserted: That is, bodies are said to be plac'd after such a matter, as to receive bodies betwixt them, without impulsion or penetration. The real nature of this position of bodies is unknown. We are only acquainted with its effects on the sense, and its power of receiving body' (T 1.2.5.26n12.2/SBN 639). Ainslie does not identify a parallel in the case of an unchanging object.
18. While the idea of a vacuum is a clear case of a doctrine that arises from philosophical speculation, the idea of fictional duration appears less equivocally so: Hume writes that it is the 'common opinion of philosophers as well as the of the vulgar' (T 1.2.3.11/SBN 37) and, when referring to it in his later discussion of continued existence, he says that the 'fiction of the imagination' in question 'almost universally takes place' (T 1.4.2.29/SBN 201). Hume surely had philosophical doctrines primarily in mind, and, like its counterpart in the case of space, it seems like a technical concept that requires philosophical reflection to attain. For that reason, I treat it as an artificial, philosophical fiction, though one cannot rule out the possibility that Hume conceived it to relate in some way to natural fictions of vulgar reasoning.
19. The charge of circularity is made by Stroud, *Hume*, pp. 103–4, and, citing him, Allison, *Custom and Reason*, p. 240. Ainslie's objections, *Hume's True Scepticism*, pp. 87–8, rest on the observation that in the 'case of the vacuum and its temporal analogue, we try to have an

idea of the *manner of appearance* relevant to space or time without objects so appearing. In the case of the unchanging object and its spatial analogue, we try to have the idea of an *object* in space or time *without the appropriate manner of appearing*.' His response to Stroud and Allison is found on pp. 85–7. Cf. Costa, 'Hume Strict Identity, and Time's Vacuum', pp. 7–8, who emphasises the parallel between Hume's account of a vacuum and time without change. Donald L. M. Baxter, *Hume's Difficulty: Time and Identity in the Treatise* (New York, Routledge, 2008), notes that we have 'deeply held commonsense convictions' about the difference between time and space (that he takes Hume's account to capture), and that 'there is no spatial analogue to a steadfast object' (p. 41), although neither of these points affect the structure of Hume's explanation.

20. Baxter, *Hume's Difficulty*, p. 44; Allison, *Custom and Reason*, p. 240; and Ainslie, *Hume's True Scepticism*, p. 84.

21. See the discussion in Baxter, *Hume's Difficulty*, Ch. 4, to which I am indebted. The quotations are from pp. 32 and 33. Baxter responds convincingly (pp. 33–6) to interpreters (T. H. Green, Price, Jonathan Bennett and Waxman), who deny that Hume identifies perceptions of this sort to which steadfast objects might be traced. Cf. Ainslie, who appears to equivocate between taking the fiction in question as the 'steadfast object in time' and the 'steadfast object' itself. See *Hume's True Scepticism*, pp. 83–4 and 89, respectively. When Hume uses the term 'stedfast', he does so to mean unchanging, which is not a fiction.

22. Hume does not explicitly make the same claim in his discussion of the genuine ideas of space and time, but a similar observation would seem to apply. When I speak of my desk being a foot from the wall or of a song being three minutes long, I do not separate the ideas of space and time from the impressions that constitute space and duration, respectively.

23. Hume repeats this argument, almost verbatim, in EHU 8.22.n18.

24. On the comparison between Hume and Kant on this point, see Manfred Kuehn, 'Hume's Antinomies', *Hume Studies*, 9: 1 (1983), pp. 25–45; Dorothy Coleman, 'Hume's Dialectic', *Hume Studies*, 10: 2 (1984), pp. 139–55; Donald W. Livingston, *Philosophical Melancholy and Delirium: Hume's Pathology of Philosophy* (Chicago: Chicago University Press, 1998), Ch. 2; and Timothy M. Costelloe, *Aesthetics and Morals in the Philosophy of David Hume* (London: Routledge Press, 2007), Ch. 4.

25. For discussion of this issue and a suggested explanation of Hume's reservations about the coherence, see Ainslie, *Hume's True*

Scepticism, pp. 73–4, and Loeb, *Stability and Justification in Hume's 'Treatise'*, pp. 207–14. Ainslie also proposes a way in which coherence and constancy might be 'integrated' (pp. 91–7).

26. Cf. Ainslie, *Hume's True Scepticism*, pp. 72–3, who rather downplays Hume's emphasis on the fact that imagination solves a contradiction, and focuses instead on 'our causal expectations for things of that kind' to explain the fiction in question. This is hard to square with Hume's claim that causal reasoning *cannot* account for the move from coherence to continued existence, which is precisely the reason why a 'disguise' or 'supposition' is required.

27. See Baxter, *Hume's Difficulty*, who sees in Hume's discussion an 'order of acquisition of ideas', which means that identity comes later and only after 'we realise that we are thinking of the steadfast object as both one and many' (p. 44). A similar emphasis is found in Ainslie, *Hume's True Scepticism*, pp. 94–7. Ainslie acknowledges that 'Hume himself never mentions – or even hints at – a developmental story', though it 'seems not only plausible, but altogether mandated for someone who thinks that mental habits are at the root of the explanandum's beliefs, and that such habits are acquired in experience' (pp. 95–6). Hume certainly treats his 'four things' less like stages than ingredients, analytically distilled, that hang together in a logical rather than temporal way.

28. Baxter, *Hume's Difficulty*, p. 33.

29. Cf. Ainslie, *Hume's True Scepticsim*, who describes the section as 'on its own terms, unexciting, in that it mostly revisits points he had made much earlier [in T.1.16]' (p. 152). Ainslie emphasises that 'Hume's greatest concern in AP ['Of the antient philosophy'] is how philosophers tend to respond to the imaginatively generated content' (p. 153), which tends to downplay the fact that Hume takes the first five paragraphs to explain how the substratum view arises first as a *vulgar* fiction.

30. Hume refers the reader to his earlier discussion of continued existence in T 1.4.2. ('towards the end'), which, as I present it below, is also a vulgar fiction of invention.

31. I have made a case for understanding Hume's conception of character along these lines in Timothy M. Costelloe, 'Beauty, Morals, and Hume's Conception of Character', *History of Philosophy Quarterly*, 21: 4 (2004), pp. 397–415.

32. It is for this reason, one may surmise, that Hume *endorses* (or at least employs the language of) the distinction between primary and secondary qualities insofar as there are indeed qualities that are internal

but taken to be in the object. Moral sentiments and the quality of beauty are 'secondary' in this sense.

33. See Berkeley, *Principles*, Part 1, sects. 9–15. Berkeley, of course, moves from this argument to the doctrine of immaterialism, while Hume simply rejects the doctrine as a fiction.

34. For a useful survey of the various interpretations of Hume's discussion, including attempts to decipher the nature of his second thoughts in the Appendix, see Udo Thiel, *The Early Modern Subject: Self-consciousness and personal identity from Descartes to Hume* (Oxford: Oxford University Press, 2011), Chs. 12 and 13.

35. For an emphasis on the place Hume gives to memory in his account of personal identity, see, among others, Donald L. M. Baxter, 'Hume's Labyrinth concerning the Idea of Personal Identity', *Hume Studies*, 24: 2 (1998), pp. 203–34; Wayne Waxman, 'Hume's Quandary Concerning Personal Identity', *Hume Studies*, 18: 2 (1992), pp. 233–54; Oliver Johnson, '"Lively" Memory and "Past" Memory', *Hume Studies*, 13: 2 (1987), pp. 343–59; and Traiger, 'Hume on Memory and Imagination'.

36. Allison, *Custom and Reason*, p. 244, and Ainslie, *Hume's True Scepticism*, p. 205.

37. This point is emphasised by Ainslie: we 'believe it [the mind or self] is unified because we associate our ideas of our perceptions when we reflect on them'. See *Hume's True Scepticism*, pp. 188 and 205–8. Ainslie takes this aspect to be a central difference between Hume's and Locke's treatment of personal identity.

38. Hume makes this claim directly after explaining the origin of the self, which makes it clear that 'identity' here refers to *personal* identity.

39. See Ainslie, *Hume's True Scepticism*, p. 193, who points out that nowhere in his discussion of the idea of self does Hume invoke any notion of substance and that those who take him to be attacking this notion are 'misled by Hume's later claim that the philosophers he criticises rely on "the notion of a *soul*, and *self*, and *substance*"'. Thus a substance view, where we imagine a 'local conjunction' between our impressions of self and suppose them to 'inhere' in something of which we have no clear idea, is just 'one option'; the 'Lockian "self"' is another option', and that of Shaftesbury (one assumes) still another.

40. Shaftesbury writes, for example: 'For my own share ... I have a MIND in my possession, which serves, such as it is, to keep my body and its Affections, my Passions, Appetites, Imaginations, Fancys, and the rest, in tolerable *Harmony* and *Order*. But *the order of the*

UNIVERSE, I am persuaded still, is much better of the *two*. ... I consider, That as there is *one* general Mass, *one* Body of the Whole; so to this Body is *an Order*, to this *Order* a MIND: That to this *general* MIND each *particular-one* must have a relation; as being of like Substance, ... alike active upon Body, original to Motion and Order; alike simple, uncompounded, individual; of like Energy, Effect, and Operation; and more like still, if it co-operates with it to the general Good, and strives to will according to the best of *Wills'*. Anthony Ashley Cooper, Third Earl of Shaftesbury, *The Moralists; a Philosophical Rhapsody*, in *Characteristicks of Men, Manners, Opinions, Times*, 3 vols (Indianapolis: Liberty Fund, [1711] 2001), 2: pp. 200–1.

3

Morals and Politics

In this chapter, we turn to Hume's treatment of morals and politics, areas in which the imagination looms large, although one would hard hardly know it from the secondary literature, much of which tends either to gloss over the issue or ignore it entirely.[1] Hume regards morals and politics as two sides of the same coin – and for that reason it makes sense to consider them in the same chapter – though, as an exegetical matter, it is possible to disentangle the two and trace the way he draws on the imagination in each case. On the side of morals, the faculty is implicated in the process of moral judgement through which virtue and vice and their attendant sentiments are constituted, a process that depends in turn on the capacity to sympathise with others and the ability to put oneself in the disinterested attitude that Hume calls the 'general point of view', both desiderata furnished by the imagination. The capacity to sympathise depends on the mimetic power of the faculty to copy the sentiment of the other as an idea in the observer; its productive power to draw connections between the object (the sentiment in the other) and the observer; and the capacity to feel the pleasure that sympathetic connection with others produces. The 'general point of view' relies on the imagination to produce an ideal standard from which to reflect upon and correct the consequences of partiality and prejudice.

On the side of politics, the imagination makes an appearance in two ways. First, in its preference for the contiguous over the remote, the faculty encourages short-term gain over long-term interests; the result is an ongoing threat to social order, a problem for which the imagination also provides the solution in the form of the general point of view and reflection, from which arise the institutions and various contrivances that ensure furtherance of the public good. Imagination also enters, second, to explain the rules that determine property. These, too, arise with a view to public utility, but are only possible through the tendency of the imagination to make as easy a transition as possible among its ideas, and its power to invent a vulgar fiction that inspires a first-order natural belief. Property, Hume urges, is a species of cause and effect that binds persons to objects in an invisible relation of constant possession that cannot be traced to experience or matter of fact. Once established, property follows its own natural history, each subsequent rule generated by the tendency of the imagination to create a new relation that resembles those that already exist. The imagination might seem a weak basis on which to build so substantial an edifice as government or property, but that makes the fact of its role no less true nor, indeed, does it make those institutions any less stable.

Moral Judgement

Hume's ethical writings are concerned fundamentally with the nature of moral value, its source and subsequent expression in the form of virtues and their respective vices, which he sorts according to utility and agreeableness and their origin as sentiments in ourselves (the possessor) or in others. This yields four categories of qualities: those *useful to the others* (the 'social virtues') promote the public good (laws between nations encourage trade, for example, chastity further the nurturing of young, and allegiance to government ensures peace and social order); those *useful to ourselves* promote the good of the individual who possesses them (discretion furthers success, as industry leads to good fortune); those *immediately agreeable to ourselves* raise pleasure in the possessor (including greatness of mind, dignity of character and a proper degree of pride and self-value); and those *immediately agreeable to others* (the 'companionable virtues') raise pleasure in the observer who witnesses them (such as wit and ingenuity, for instance, the spirit of dialogue and conversation, eloquence and cleanliness). Some virtues, Hume emphasises, 'derive their merit from complicated sources' and thus fall into more than one category. Honesty, fidelity and truth, for example, are praised for promoting the interests of society (useful to others), but once established are seen as 'advantageous to the person himself' (useful to the possessor) (EPM 6.13/SBN 238). Similarly, chastity

promotes good reputation (useful to the possessor) and strengthens the stability of relationships for nurturing the young (useful
to others), while courage is a quality useful to the 'public and
person possessed of it' and, due to its 'peculiar luster', the source
of 'sublimity and daring confidence' (agreeable to the possessor)
that also catches the eye of every spectator (agreeable to others)
(EPM 7.11–15/SBN 254–5).

Hume argues, further, that whereas all virtues and vices depend
ultimately on pleasure and pain, they are not 'entirely natural' in
origin. A specific set – the social virtues connected with the institutions of government and political society – arise from utility alone,
and are appropriately termed 'artificial' because they form as 'mere
contrivances for the interest of society' (T 3.3.1.9/SBN 577), to
solve, that is, problems posed by scarce resources, limited benevolence and human impotence, contingencies that otherwise prevent
or interfere with the progress of a commodious and well-ordered
life. Hume conducts a thought experiment to prove his point: a
country with either profuse abundance or extended benevolence
would avoid the obstacles – competition over limited resources
and the acquisitive effects of self-interest – that hinder the fair
and peaceful distribution of goods and services, thus obviating the
need for artifice to regulate the whole. At the same time, Hume is
careful to emphasise (thought experiments notwithstanding) that
wherever human beings form society, the institutions of government and the associated virtues always do emerge. Once established, moreover, these artificial virtues require the same affective
power as their entirely natural counterparts if they are to raise
specifically moral sentiments. While the origin of these artificial
virtues is singular, the process through which they are constituted
as virtues is the same: all virtues (and vices), whether natural or
artificial, arise from an amiableness or beauty that affects a person
prior to 'all precept and education' (EPM 5.4/SBN 214), and they
are explicable in terms of moral judgement in which, as we will see
in what follows, the imagination takes centre stage. The distinction between natural and artificial virtues, on the one side, and
between utility and agreeableness, on the other, overlaps but does
not coincide.

As the title of the second *Enquiry* makes clear, Hume develops these distinctions in pursuit of a philosophical principle to
understand and explain virtue and vice, and in this endeavour the
imagination is involved only indirectly, insofar as it enters into the

practice of philosophy itself. We shall see in the final chapter that Hume has a good deal to say about this matter, but in his approach to morals, at least, the imagination plays quite a different role, that of providing the condition that facilitates and makes possible the practice of moral judgement through which pleasure and pain are transformed into moral sentiments, and 'qualities' of persons, actions and events become virtues and vices. Hume supposes that people possess certain stable features that compose the underlying disposition for the formation of what we call character. 'If any action be either virtuous or vicious', he proposes, ''tis only as a sign of some quality or character. It must depend upon durable principles of the mind, which extend over the whole conduct, and enter into the personal character' (T 3.3.1.4/SBN 575). Hume need not commit to any particular position concerning the nature or origin of these dispositional qualities (although claims have been made on his behalf),[2] since all he requires is that they are visible in the activities in which people engage, and when viewed cause 'pleasure or uneasiness of a particular kind' in the possessor or viewer of the quality. 'To have the sense of virtue', as Hume writes, 'is nothing but to *feel* a satisfaction of a particular kind from the contemplation of a character. The very *feeling* constitutes our praise or admiration' (T 3.1.2.3/SBN 471). On this view, qualities thus displayed produce sentiments of pleasure (or pain), which inspire in turn approbation (or disapprobation) through which the action (and by extension the person) is constituted as virtuous (or vicious). The virtue (or vice) can then be categorised under one or more headings of Hume's fourfold principle, with the logic of the process varying slightly depending on whether the source of the praise lies in utility or agreeableness and/or in ourselves or others: with qualities useful to others, the feeling arises in an observer who sees the public good furthered; with qualities useful to ourselves, the pleasure arises in the observer who recognises that the good of an individual is furthered; and where the cause is immediate agreeableness the pleasure arises first either in the possessor or in the observer.

Sympathy

The crucial component in each of these four cases is that certain qualities of action and character are not simply agreeable but that the pleasure they produce is attended with *moral* approbation, and this is only possible, Hume urges, due to the singular human capacity for sympathy, a subject that (along with its conceptual kin, the 'general point of view'), has generated a good deal of discussion in the literature even if the role of the imagination has been largely passed over in favour of emphasising it as a 'mechanism' of 'communication'.[3] The qualities that constitute the social virtues excite approbation due to 'a *sympathy* with public interest' (T 3.2.2.24/SBN 499); those that further the good of the individual presuppose that others partake in the 'ideas of happiness, joy, triumph, and prosperity' of the person whose good is furthered (EPM 6.3); those immediately agreeable to ourselves require that observers 'enter into the same humour [as the possessor], and catch the sentiment, by a contagion or natural sympathy' (EPM 7.2/SBN 251); and a quality that forms a companionable virtue works its magic by 'communicating, on its first appearance, a lively joy and satisfaction to every one who has any comprehension of it' (EPM 8.3/SBN 262).

Hume's main discussion of sympathy occurs in T 2.1.11, which, as James Farr among others has observed, is considerably more elaborate than in the second *Enquiry*, by which time Hume seems to have doubted that it can be treated – as he does in the earlier work – as an 'instantiation of association'. Sympathy remains important in the later work but, rather than attempt a psychological aetiology, Hume describes it simply as a 'principle of human nature' and subject to the proviso that 'there are, in every science, some principles, beyond which we cannot hope to find any principle more general'; for this reason it is 'needless to push our researches so far as to ask, *why* we have humanity or fellow-feeling with others' (EPM 5.17n19/SBN 219–20n1, emphasis added).[4] In the *Treatise* account he introduces it as a preamble to explaining the love of fame, a secondary cause of pride and humility explicable only through the relations we have with others. Praise and blame, reputation and infamy, are not original causes, Hume urges, because they are reducible to the more fundamental capacity we have to sympathise with others. This 'remarkable' quality of human nature means that sentiments arising first in other people produce, through some natural and unavoidable mechanism, a similar sentiment in us; it is nothing but the propensity 'to receive by communication' the 'inclinations and sentiments' of others, 'however different from, or even contrary to our own' (T 2.1.11.2/SBN 316). It enables an observer to conceive or create a sentiment or passion even though he or she may never have experienced it originally.

Sympathy, along with its effects, might be remarkable but it is not inexplicable, these being one instance of the general process whereby an idea of a passion or emotion is enlivened and 'converted into an impression'.[5] Indeed, Hume regards the 'principle of sympathy or communication' as 'nothing but the conversion of an idea into an impression by the force of imagination' (T 2.3.6.8/SBN 427). In order to understand what 'conversion' means in the context of sympathising with others, it is useful to consider first the analogous case of its operation in our own person. Recalling or imagining an occasion that produced or could produce anger, for example, gives rise to an *impression* of anger, which, though fainter than the original, gains sufficient force and vivacity to reach the status of a new impression and constitute a new feeling of anger. Like all impressions, it can then be copied to form a new idea, itself capable of conversion into another impression. We then *become* angry, not by witnessing an event or seeing an object but through effectively 'converting' an idea into an impression by imbuing it with increased forced and vivacity so that it approaches the original.[6]

'Sympathy', as Hume uses the term, is the same process whereby an idea of a passion is enlivened itself to become a passion, except that it takes place with other people; we do not, after all, sympathise with ourselves.[7] 'When I see the *effects* of passion in the voice and gesture of any person', Hume writes, 'my mind immediately passes from these effects to their causes, and forms such a lively idea of the passions, as is presently converted into the passion itself' (T 3.3.1.7/SBN 576). In this way 'an idea of a sentiment or passion, may . . . be so enliven'd as to *become* the very sentiment or passion', and 'we enter so deep into the opinions and affections of others, whenever we discover them' (T 2.1.11.7/SBN 319, emphasis added); they thus 'operate upon us . . . in the very same manner, as if they had been originally deriv'd from our own temper and disposition' (T 3.3.2.3/SBN 592). The important difference, then, between converting an idea into an impression in my own person and entering into the sentiments of others is that the idea, which forms the object of the conversion, has its origin not in our own recollection of anger or in some imagined cause of it, but in an impression originally in somebody else, that is, *their* feeling of anger. Expressing this insight, Hume writes:

> 'Tis indeed evident, that when we sympathise with the passions and sentiments of others, these movements appear at first in *our* mind as mere ideas, and are conceiv'd to belong to another person, as we conceive any other matter of fact. 'Tis also evident, that the ideas of the affections of others are converted into the very impressions they represent, and that the passions arise in conformity to the images we form of them. (T 2.1.11.8/SBN 319)

These passions and emotions are not, moreover, mysterious mental items trapped in minds accessible only through some peculiar intuitive magic. On the contrary, Hume supposes that people 'infer' them routinely from their 'effects' as 'external signs' in 'countenance and conversation' (T 2.1.11.3/SBN 317) or in the 'voice and gesture of any person' (T 3.3.1.7/SBN 576). Through sympathy, the conversion takes place when the sentiment felt by the other and inferred from their behaviour is copied and represented in the observer as an idea, which is subsequently enlivened to form a new impression, that is, a sentiment similar to the one experienced by the other. It can be traced originally to the passion in somebody else, but the idea copied from it by the spectator 'acquires such a degree of force and vivacity, as to become the very passion itself, and produce an equal emotion, as any original affection' (T 2.1.11.3/SBN 317). Hume sometimes describes the entire process as 'conversion', although, strictly speaking (and as he generally makes clear), the object converted is not the passion of the other – which is *copied* – but the *idea of that passion*, which becomes an impression of the same kind as the sentiment that appeared first in somebody else. As the maxim concerning the relative force and vivacity of impressions and ideas would lead one to expect, the new sentiment is fainter than the original from which it is derived, although the difference is often imperceptible and the power of the feeling generated by sympathy considerable. Indeed, Hume suggests that through sympathy the enlivening of the idea is more intense precisely because 'Our affections depend more upon *ourselves*, for which reason they arise more naturally from the imagination, and from every lively idea we form of them' (T 2.1.11.7/SBN 319, emphasis added). For sympathy to function in this way presupposes capacities that only the imagination can provide: the mimetic power of that faculty to copy the sentiment of the other as an idea in the observer; its productive power to draw connections between the object (the sentiment in the other) and the observer; and the capacity to feel the pleasure that sympathetic connection with others produces. We can consider each in turn.

Sympathy and the Mimetic Power of Imagination

First, as should be clear already from the language Hume uses, the capacity to sympathise depends fundamentally on the mimetic power of the imagination to copy and represent the impression originally in the other (the sentiment or passion expressed in behaviour) as an idea in the observer. Hume's various characterisations of the process suggest that sympathy occurs passively, adventitiously and spontaneously whenever we perceive, remember, or imagine the event in question: the sentiments of others are 'thrown ... upon me', so that 'I find myself' in the same humour with others; or I feel myself 'under the dominion of the beneficent affections' and 'transported' by them.[8] The sentiments of others 'strike upon the soul', are 'communicated' and 'infused'; they 'transfuse themselves' and 'diffuse over our minds' or, to use Hume's musical metaphor, a passion has a certain pitch that gives it motion like the sounds of an instrument that the listener cannot fail to hear. 'As in strings equally wound up', he remarks, 'the motion of one communicates itself to the rest; so all the affections readily pass from one person to another, and beget correspondent movements in every human creature' (T 3.3.1.7/SBN 576). In perhaps the most striking image, Hume describes the effect of sympathy as a 'contagion' that spreads like a disease or mood, affecting its victims as if by magic. 'We enter, I shall suppose, into a warm, well-contrived apartment', Hume writes, in an image that cannot fail to arouse sympathy in the reader. He continues:

> We necessarily feel the pleasure from its very survey, because it presents us with pleasing ideas of ease, satisfaction, and enjoyment. The hospitable, good-humoured, humane landlord appears. ... His whole family, by the freedom, ease, confidence, and calm enjoyment, diffused over their countenances, sufficiently express their happiness. I have a pleasing sympathy in the prospect of so much joy, and can never consider the course of it, without the most agreeable emotions. He tells me, that an oppressive and powerful neighbour had attempted to dispossess him of his inheritance, and had long disturbed all his innocent and social pleasures. I feel an immediate indignation arise in me against such violence and injury. (EPM 5.19–21/SBN 220–1)

The same movement is exemplified in other contexts where the imagination is touched by the drama or intensity of a passion. A crowd will always gather around the card game at which the most dramatic play is unfolding, even though it does not involve the best players; for the 'view, or, at least, imagination of high passions, arising from great loss or gain, affects the spectator by sympathy, gives him some touches of the same passions, and serves him for a momentary entertainment' (E 217). Similarly, somebody entering the theatre is 'immediately struck with the view of so great a multitude, participating in one common amusement; and experiences, from their very aspect, a superior sensibility or disposition of being affected with every sentiment, which he shares with his fellow-creatures' (EPM 5.24/SBN 221). That parents protect their children is explained by the same feature of human nature, as is the action of a generous man rushing to the aid of friends from a 'direct tendency or instinct', without calculation or even due regard for the possible consequences (EPM Appx.3.2/SBN 303).

Sympathy and the Productive Power of Imagination

While sympathy involves the imagination being moved by the sentiment of the other, the productive power of that faculty is also engaged actively in drawing connections between the object (the sentiment in the other) and ourselves, according to the principles of association, successfully effecting an easy transition between the two. Hume writes:

> In a word, no ideas can affect each other, either by comparison, or by the passions they separately produce, unless they be united together by some relation, which may cause an easy transition of the ideas, and consequently of the emotions or impressions attending the ideas; and may preserve the one impression in the passage of the imagination to the object of the other. (T 2.2.8.20/SBN 380)

In sympathy, this unity is achieved primarily (though not exclusively) through resemblance rather than contiguity or cause and effect because there is a marked similarity between our own passions and those we recognise in others, even if – as is sometimes the case – we have not experienced the passion with the same intensity or, indeed, have no direct knowledge of it. Of course, the 'stronger the relation is betwixt ourselves and any object', Hume points out, 'the more easily does the imagination make the transition, and convey to the related idea the vivacity of conception, with which we always form the idea of our own passion' (T 2.1.11.5/SBN 318).[9] We still have some notion of a friend's distress at the death of a loved one, however, even when we have never lost anybody comparably dear. Indeed, there is such a 'general resemblance' among human beings with respect to the structure of mind and body, and human nature is sufficiently uniform that there is hardly a passion or principle in others 'of which, in some degree or other, we may not find a parallel in ourselves' (T 2.1.11.5/SBN 318).

We should note, also, that while resemblance is the primary principle of association operating in the mechanism of sympathy, it receives added force from the other two and, indeed, 'must be assisted by [them]' if we are to 'feel the sympathy in its full perfection' (T 2.1.11.8/SBN 320) or have the passions 'communicate themselves entirely' (T 2.1.11.6/SBN 318). Without contiguity of time and place, a person is effectively reduced to solitude, and sympathy fails 'because the movements of his heart are not forwarded by correspondent movements in his fellow-creatures' (EPM 5.18/SBN 220). Cause and effect, on the other hand, perfects the process by forming a 'tie' between self and others in relations of blood or acquaintance, according to the principle that 'in the original frame of our mind, our strongest attention is confin'd to ourselves; our next is extended to our relations and acquaintance; and 'tis only the weakest which reaches to strangers and indifferent persons' (T 3.2.2.8/SBN 488). The imagination is affected more by ties that are close – between parents and children, for example, or those we have come to know intimately over a long course of time – when the idea is most lively and vivacious; the degree of connection loosens, by contrast, as the vivacity decreases and the further we move from those with whom we share a form of life, from neighbours through colleagues and fellow countrymen to strangers, where, being struck with less force, the imagination can establish but weak connections. Through causality, then, sympathy forms a web of invisible threads that bind us with more or less strength to other human beings or, like a pebble dropped in a pond, we stand at the centre of progressively faint circles moving outwards, every one a more distant effect that weakens at each remove.

Sympathetic Pleasure

In addition to its mimetic and productive powers, the imagination is also required to register the pleasure and pain involved in the sympathetic movement of the sentiments.[10] There are two ways in which these sensations are aroused. On the one hand, there is pleasure and pain involved in the communication of the passion through sympathy. When the idea of the original in somebody else is converted into a like impression in us, it naturally carries with it the same sensation of pleasure or pain depending on the passion in question: the 'very aspects of happiness, joy, prosperity, gives pleasure; that of pain, suffering, sorrow, communicates uneasiness' (EPM 5.18/SBN 220). Thus, Hume remarks:

> In general, it is certain, that, wherever we go, whatever we reflect on or converse about, every thing still presents us with the view of human happiness or misery, and excites in our breast a sympathetic movement of pleasure or uneasiness. In our serious occupations, in our careless amusements, this principle still exerts its active energy. (EPM 5.23/SBN 221)

We do tend to receive more pleasure when sympathising with a man in the throws of passions that produce agreeable sentiments, however, and less when the effects are disagreeable. In the former case, 'Our imagination, entering into his feelings and disposition, is affected in a more agreeable manner', Hume observes, 'than if a melancholy, dejected, sullen, anxious temper were presented to us' (EPM 7.2/SBN 251).

On the other hand, distinct from the pleasure and pain that accompany a passion communicated through conversion, Hume considers the act of sympathy itself to be the source of a distinct pleasure that arises regardless of whether that passion communicates pain or pleasure; this sympathetic pleasure originates not in the passion aroused – pleasure at another's prosperity, say, or pain in their suffering – but in the process of conversion through which an idea becomes a passion. Hume explains this phenomenon by emphasising again the universality of human nature, there being no greater pleasure possible, he thinks, than when we gain insight into the lives of others. The imagination responds to the equivalent of an entertainment involving new and foreign objects that produces a 'lively sensation' and 'excites the spirits'. Hume writes:

On the appearance of such an object, it [the mind] awakes, as it were, from a dream: The blood flows with a new tide: The heart it elevated: And the whole man acquires a vigour, which he cannot command in his solitary and calm moments. (T 2.2.4.4/SBN)

The effect of this novelty is greatest, moreover, and the entertainment most satisfying when confronting another person:

> the liveliest of all objects, *viz.* a rational and thinking being like ourselves, who communicates to us all the actions of his mind; . . . Every lively idea is agreeable, but especially that of a passion, because such an idea becomes a kind of passion, and gives a more sensible agitation to the mind, than any other image or conception. (T 2.2.4.4/SBN 353)

It should be emphasised again, however, that, like the imagination on which it depends, sympathy has its limits. Hume expresses confidence that 'there is no human, and indeed no sensible, creature, whose happiness or misery does not, in some measure, affect us, when brought near to us, and represented in lively colours' (T 3.2.1.12/SBN 481), but it does not follow that we are always moved, and when we have little or no acquaintance with the person or event in question, the colours grow so dim as to barely register at all. The imagination is like a keyboard upon which effects are registered most distinctly when they fall within the range of human hearing, or like a canvas on which objects stand within the scope of our perceptual field. At either end of its range – as the pitch grows higher and lower, as the object moves closer or farther away – the sounds and the images grow indistinct, and beyond a certain point nothing is audible or visible at all. Hume seems to regard one's countrymen as the outer limits to which sympathy meaningfully reaches, though that one's compatriot in another country (or a human on the moon) is a friend 'proceeds only from the relation to ourselves; which in these cases gathers force by being confin'd to a few persons' (T 3.2.1.12/SBN 482).[11] When it comes to those qualities of character remote in time and place – the cruelty of Nero or Alexander's dignity of mind – approval or condemnation is possible because the case resembles others that are contiguous and familiar. The fact remains that when objects are 'very remote, our sympathy is proportionably weaker, and our praise or blame fainter and more doubtful' (T 3.3.3.2/SBN 603). This is no moral failing for which people should be condemned but an outer limit beyond which sympathy cannot penetrate, a lack originating in the very faculty that makes sympathy possible.

The 'General Point of View'

While sympathy is central to Hume's approach to morals, and decisive for the process of moral judgement, it presupposes a further and more fundamental condition that the imagination also supplies, what Hume calls variously the 'general point of view', the perspective of the 'unprejudiced' or 'judicious spectator', and the viewpoint of a 'man in general'. The presence of this concept in Hume's thought has led to something of a puzzle for interpreters, since assigning it weight skews the whole tenor of his moral philosophy away from 'sentimentalism', where moral judgement is based on or identical to feelings of pleasure and pain, and towards that of an 'ideal spectator' – 'fully informed, entirely objective and not self-interested', as Elizabeth Radcliffe characterises it – that makes virtue and vice the product of projected rather than real sentiments.[12] Different readers have tended to regard the choice between these options as disjunctive – Hume must be *either* a sentimentalist *or* an ideal observer theorist – though there seems no barrier to combining them, especially if one takes the spectator to be a position from which to reflect on and correct judgements that arise immediately and adventitiously. Moral judgements are, indeed, as the sentimentalist Hume argues, a matter of pleasure and pain, but these are not the final word and must succumb to some more reliable standard, even if scrutiny yields only better judgements – a new 'appearance' and revised 'language' – rather than altered sentiments, feelings often remaining 'stubborn or unalterable' (see EPM 5.41n24/SBN 228n1; and T 3.3.1.16/SBN 582). 'The imagination is sure to be affected', Hume acknowledges, 'though the passions excited may not always be so strong and steady as to have a great influence on the conduct and behaviour' (EPM 5.31/SBN 223). That reflection produces conclusions and courses of action contrary to feelings and desires is actually an accurate description of the phenomenology of our moral lives: sometimes one prevails and sometimes the other.

Hume's appeal to the idea of a spectator, moreover, is part and parcel of the eighteenth-century discovery of 'disinterestedness', a philosophical concept that finds its first explicit formulation in the neo-Platonic aesthetics of Shaftesbury, and that in ethical theory receives its most sophisticated expression in the guise of the 'impartial spectator' developed by Hume's friend and contemporary, Adam Smith.[13] It also finds striking and underappreciated application in Lord Kames' concept of 'ideal presence', a sort of 'waking dream' that imbues a fiction with the same 'truth and reality' as if it were a 'real existence'.[14] To speak of an 'ideal' in this sense is not to impute any perfection to the presence in question, but to emphasise its status as the product of mind. Very much in the same spirit, Hume also regards the general point of view as a mental state or attitude that effects an imaginary 'change' of 'situation' (T 3.3.3.2/SBN 603) in and through which one distances oneself psychically – as Edward Bullough later described the same phenomenon in the context of aesthetic experience – from the various interests and prejudices that otherwise interfere with calm reflection and sound judgement.[15] It is from this 'view' – a term Hume uses to exploit the analogy with sight – that spectators free themselves to be moved by actions and characters, which, as described above, begin the process whereby pleasure is transformed into approbation and qualities into virtues. As everybody with normal eyesight brackets the variations following on different perspectives in order to see the same object, so individuals can transcend the particularities of their own person to view the same qualities and react to them in the proper way, as anybody would when freed of partiality and prejudice. Only through this imaginative projection can we explain how the 'good qualities of an enemy are hurtful to us; but may still command our esteem and respect. 'Tis only when a character is consider'd in general', Hume writes, 'without reference to our particular interest, that it causes such a feeling or sentiment, as denominates it morally good or evil' (T 3.1.2.4/SBN 472).

Indeed, as an impartial attitude in this sense, the general point of view is best understood as a remedy or solution for two weaknesses in human nature and the problem they pose. The first arises from self-interest, our 'very limited ... generosity', which determines that we 'remain constantly in that situation and point of view, which is peculiar to us' (T 3.3.3.2/SBN 603). The second weakness follows from the limits of sympathy, whose effects tend to weaken the farther we move beyond the narrow circle of family and friends. Self-interest and limited sympathy raise barriers to the general intercourse of society and conversation, and undermine the universality that moral judgement requires and presupposes.

The imagination, in the form of the general point of view, solves this problem by producing an ideal standard from which to reflect upon and correct the consequences of partiality and prejudice. The process is the internal analogue to the adjustments routinely made when objects of outer sense appear to diminish with distance. Our reaction is not to think that they actually grow smaller, but 'correcting the appearance by reflection, [we] arrive at a more constant and establish'd judgement concerning them' (T 3.3.3.2/SBN 603). In doing so, Hume urges, we effectively replace the 'original standard' given by sense with a 'general unalterable' alternative derived from reason.

The same is true in the sphere of morals. Judgement 'corrects the inequalities of our internal emotions and perceptions in like manner, as it preserves us from error, in the several variations of images, presented to our external senses.' Hume continues:

> The same object, at a double distance, really throws on the eye a picture of but half the bulk; yet we imagine that it appears of the same size in both situations; because we know, that, on our approach to it, its image would expand on the eye, and that the difference consists not in the object itself, but in our position with regard to it. And, indeed, without such a correction of appearances, both in internal and external sentiment, men could never think or talk steadily on any subject; while their fluctuating situations produce a continual variation on objects, and throw them into such different and contrary lights and positions. (EPM 5.41/SBN 227–8)

In the case of both external and internal perception, the analogy suggests, initial judgements are corrected by considering what an object or action would look like were we to change our position and perspective. Moral perception provides an 'original standard', but the demands of social intercourse and the dictates of moral conduct require that individuals depart from their own perspective and 'form some general and inalterable standard, by which we may approve or disapprove of characters and manners' (T 3.3.3.2/SBN 603). The standard often presents views and courses of action that contradict our passions and desires, but this shows only the power of reason to correct the corrupting influences of the imagination on internal sentiments as it does the erroneous perceptions of outer sense. One discovers here, then, a curious cooperation between faculties more often than not in conflict and contradiction: imagination provides the general point of view that allows reason to reflect on judgements and courses of action, and reason enters to sift accidental circumstances from the efficacious causes and replace the unphilosophical species of probability born of imagination with the more reliable one supplied by the understanding.

The faculties cooperate in the same way to further the inculcation of morals and the progress of our own characters, found in that

> constant habit of surveying ourselves, as it were, in reflection, [which] keeps alive all the sentiments of right and wrong, and begets, in noble creatures, a certain reverence for themselves as well as others; which is the surest guardian of every virtue. (EPM 9.10/SBN 276)

There is a twist, as Hume goes on to explain, because the motive to this habit lies in the propensity of the imagination to be affected by self-love or the love of fame, the opinions that others have of us throwing into relief the opinion we form of ourselves. It is thus from 'our continual and earnest pursuit of a character, a name, a reputation in the world, [that] we bring our own deportment and conduct frequently in review, and consider how they appear in the eyes of those, who approach and regard us' (EPM 9.10/SBN 276). To explain this phenomenon, Hume turns to sympathy and the process of conversion it facilitates. Affects are known by their effects in the form of those outward signs in countenance and conversation, and the ensuing idea is converted to an impression that acquires such vivacity to become the passion itself and produce the same affection as any original passion. The sentiments of others resemble ones we find in ourselves and the 'stronger the relation is betwixt ourselves and any object, the more easily does the imagination make the transition, and convey to the related idea the vivacity of conception, with which we always form the idea of our own person' (T 2.1.11.5/SBN 318). From the force of imagination, then, the other's impression of us is converted into the same impression of ourselves, and this forms a motive for reflecting on our own conduct.

It is important to emphasise, however, that while the imagination works towards a corrective of its own corrupting influence, the general point of view does not alter in any material way the facts of human nature that produce the difficulty in the first place. In many instances, we continue to follow 'the *natural* and *usual* force of the passions, when we determine concerning vice and virtue; ... A man naturally loves his children better than his nephews', Hume points out, 'his nephews better than his cousins, his cousins better than strangers, where every thing else is equal. Our sense of duty always follows the common and natural course of our passions' (T 3.2.1.18/SBN 483–4). For this reason we often cling tenaciously to our prejudices despite evidence to the contrary – that an '*Irishman* cannot have wit, and a *Frenchman* cannot have solidity' (T 1.3.13.7/SBN 146) – where, as we saw in Chapter 2, general rules of the imagination persist and guide judgement beyond the original circumstances that first gave rise to them. Such errors can never be eradicated entirely, Hume suggests, but continue to arise and inspire belief from the powerful influence they have on the mind.

Imagination and Political Society

As we have already noted, Hume considers government and political society 'mere contrivances' designed to overcome threats to peace and stability that spring from limited benevolence and scarce resources. Actions that support these arrangements further the good of the whole and through the process of moral judgement are constituted as virtues. In addition to its function in explaining the virtues associated with political society, however, Hume also draws on the imagination to explain the origin of government and the complicated arrangements governing property.[16]

First, Hume emphasises the role of imagination in the foundation of government; the faculty is implicated both in the problems to which political society is a solution and in the solution itself. The problems spring from the fact that human beings are 'mightily governed by the imagination' and moved more by an object's appearance than any 'real intrinsic value' it contains (T 3.2.7.2/SBN 534); the contiguous vanquishes what is remote and 'present motives and inclinations' obscure courses of action that would actually promote more valuable and worthy ends. Hume writes:

> [When] objects approach nearer to us, or acquire the advantages of favourable lights and positions, which catch the heart or imagination; our general resolutions are frequently confounded, a small enjoy-

ment preferred, and lasting shame and sorrow entailed upon us. And however poets may employ their wit and eloquence, in celebrating present pleasure, and rejecting all distant views to fame, health, or fortune; it is obvious, that this practice is the source of all dissoluteness and disorder, repentance and misery. (EPM 6.15/SBN 239)

Were this tendency felt only in the course of a few individual lives, its wider impact would be nugatory; the shame and sorrow of a minority would be of little consequence to society at large. Hume considers the tendency general, however, with trivial, present advantage being routinely preferred 'to the maintenance of order in society, which so much depends on the observance of justice' (T 3.2.7.1/SBN 534). The tendency of the imagination to be moved more by the contiguous than the remote inclines people to courses of action that undermine peace and order, and this 'infirmity' is a perennial threat with potentially devastating consequences; on a cursory view, moreover, it appears 'incapable of remedy' (T 3.2.7.4/SBN 535).

There is a remedy, however, and like the problem it lies in the imagination. The 'infirmity of human nature becomes a remedy to itself', Hume proposes, 'and that provision we make against our negligence about remote objects, proceeds merely from our natural inclination to the negligence' (T 3.2.7.5/SBN 536). Hume's reasoning on this point is of a piece with his discussion of the attitude that defines the general point of view and the process of reflection and correction it facilitates. Again, drawing an analogy with the sense of sight illuminates his point. Objects seen close up have a detail and resolution that strikes the imagination with sufficient force and vivacity to incline the viewer towards them, but when the same are considered 'at a distance, all their minute distinctions vanish, and we always give the preference to whatever is in itself preferable, without considering its situation and circumstances' (T 3.2.7.5/SBN 536). When viewing the same object for a second time, it appears in a new light, details that made the object striking on a first view fading in comparison to what is now recognised as its real and intrinsic value. The same is true, Hume urges, with actions and their consequences in which – as in a future action one resolves to perform – the general point of view and the 'general and more discernible qualities of good and evil' reveal 'circumstances ... at first over-look'd', and these are what now come to have an 'influence on my conduct and affections' (T 3.2.7.5/SBN 536).

In this way, a new resolution comes to replace the old, nature remedying itself by providing a restraint where study, reflection, meditation, repeated resolution and advice of friends alone have limited effect.

The same reasoning discovers, second, the origin of political society and allegiance, a 'cure' for the 'natural weakness' that drives individuals with a 'violent propension to prefer contiguous to remote'. This dangerous propensity requires correction, but since it is impossible to change anything 'material in our nature', the only recourse is to 'change our circumstances and situation, and render the observance of the laws of justice our nearest interest, and their violation our most remote' (T 3.2.7.6/SBN 537). This being impractical for everybody, the responsibility falls to a few who have little or no interest in acts of injustice, namely the civil magistrates, kings, ministers and other rulers deemed worthy or at least suitable for the fair administration of justice and impartial resolution of disputes concerning its statutes. In effect, government and the individuals who compose it embody the general point of view by ensuring that actions deriving from self-interest and prejudice are corrected by other actions that promote the common good. Large-scale cooperative action invariably occasions particular and therefore competing and contradictory points of view, which would render the planning and execution of any project impossible and impose expense and trouble upon a few. 'Political society remedies both these inconveniences', Hume observes, for officials who decide in favour of or against such plans and forward its completion 'find no interest in it, either immediate or remote'. Their single motivation is the public good and only on such a basis can the long-term complex projects that define a full life be undertaken and completed: 'bridges are built; harbours open'd; ramparts raised; canals form'd; and armies disciplined' in spite of the 'human infirmities' that mark the individuals who execute and compose these and like plans (T 3.2.7.8/SBN 539).

Property and Its Natural History

The role of imagination in Hume's discussion of property is both striking and original, and amounts to a case where the faculty invents an idea – a fiction – to reconcile contradictory and irreconcilable propositions that otherwise cause pain and bewilderment. Judgements about an apparently 'real relation' actually 'rest upon an illusion', as Miller describes the view that Hume develops.[17] Hume's discussion develops in response to two issues. The first concerns the origin of property, the explanation for which proceeds along the same lines proposed for the origin of government. Hume characterises property as 'nothing but those goods, whose constant possession is establish'd by the laws of society; that is, by the laws of justice' (T 3.2.2.11/SBN 491) and he traces property to the 'same artifice' as government and justice, it too being a contrivance to solve otherwise intractable problems caused by human nature. In this case Hume does not call the imagination by name, but its presence is clearly felt. The real and intrinsic value of objects is obscured by the force and vivacity excited by the 'love of gain', an affection so powerful that vanity, pity and revenge pale by comparison. 'This avidity alone', Hume writes, 'of acquiring goods and possessions for ourselves and our nearest friends, is insatiable, perpetual, universal, and directly destructive of society' (T 3.2.2.12/SBN 491–2). Like the preference for what is contiguous over remote, this passion is a material part of our nature and cannot be expunged, although it can be redirected. As the origin of government proceeds from accepting the need to curb self-interest and the desire for short-term gain, so reflection teaches that 'possession must be stable', the acquisition and enjoyment of goods being more likely under conditions of social order than under its solitary, forlorn and violent alternative. Human nature is its own cure, for with the aid of reason the destructive passion constrains itself by submitting to a general rule of the understanding that it recognises as the best way to achieve its goal: restraint triumphs over wanton liberty, and the desire for gain succumbs to the rules of justice. The idea of stable or constant possession, then, is the first and most primitive idea of property, arising as it does spontaneously from reflection on the passion for acquisition.

This victory of reason over imagination, however, does not yet explain a second issue: namely how and why the stable possession is 'determined', that is, particularised in such a way as to assign ownership and enjoyment of certain goods to some while excluding others from the same. Hume rejects straight away the idea that such principles might be discovered in the advantage of objects to the persons who possess them, since it could never prevent multiple individuals from claiming the same relationship and the ensuing controversy would threaten the very stability required for property to arise and persist in the first place. The rule must be tight enough to remove the possibility of discord but sufficiently universal to transcend person and place: justice is blind, after all, to the miser, generous and spendthrift alike. Hume's ensuing discussion takes the form, instead, of tracing a natural history of property, a narrative the moral scientist reconstructs by inference from experience, delineating the progress of property from the most simple through more complex societies, each subsequent rule being a stronger guarantor of stability than its predecessor: occupation (first possession), prescription (long possession), accession (acquiring new property by extending what one owns already), and succession (passing property on to others). Given Hume's view of property as an artificial contrivance to remedy the infirmities of human nature, one might expect these rules to be explicable from social utility, and in the main body of the *Treatise* where Hume treats the question (T 3.2.3), with the exception of accession where the imagination alone is responsible, this is indeed where the emphasis lies: objects under present possession remain changeable and uncertain; rights from occupation grow obscure through time; prescription obviates disputes over objects potentially alienable from one's property; and succession is passed to those 'dearest to [the owners], in order to render them more industrious and frugal' (T 3.2.3.11/SBN 510–11). In each case, progress is a product of reflection, the forming and framing of rules driven by the demands of utility to ensure the stability of external goods.

In the lengthy footnotes, however, Hume traces the causes not to reason and utility but to the imagination, 'leaving it to the reader's choice, whether he will prefer those deriv'd from public utility, or those deriv'd from the imagination'. Hume expresses some ambivalence throughout the discussion as to the final winner, but clearly ultimately favours the latter, for while there are 'no doubt, motives of public interest for most of the rules, which determine property', he ventures, 'still I suspect, that these rules are principally fix'd by the imagination, or the more frivolous properties of our thought and conception' (T 3.2.3n71.1/SBN 504n1). Utility might be a motive for the rule, but its formation is explicable only by the imagination. This nod to the imagination clearly springs from Hume's appreciation of the concept of property, that it denotes at bottom an idea that expresses an intangible relation between an individual and an object, where owner and thing owned are connected as causes to their effects: 'all relations are nothing but a propensity to pass from one idea to another' (T 2.10.9.13/SBN 309). Hume writes:

> We are said to be in possession of any thing, not only when we immediately touch it, but also when we are so situated with respect to it, as to have it in our power to use it; and may move, alter, or destroy it, according to our present pleasure or advantage. This relation, then, is a species of cause and effect; and as property is nothing but a stable possession, deriv'd from the rules of justice, or the conventions or men, 'tis to be consider'd as the *same species of relation*. (T 3.2.3.7/SBN 506, emphasis added)

The 'species of causal power' in question is not what we have seen to be the genuine idea arising from the power of memory to recall past experience of constantly conjoined events, but its fictional counterpart, an invention the imagination conjures when a quality of the mind is transferred to and taken to inhere in external objects. Without this propensity of the imagination to 'spread itself on external objects', the relation of possession and objects we call property could never arise. The idea transcends possible experience and cannot be traced to matter of fact, but it inspires a belief nonetheless, expressed in the rules that determine property and its natural history. The fiction is a natural one of vulgar reasoning that arises as a 'natural instinct' or 'propensity of human nature' that inspires a first-order natural belief and, however good our intentions or however well we understand their causes, they remain intractable. That the origin and stability of property should be a function of the imagination and arise from a fiction might seem paradoxical but, as Hume makes clear, the ensuing rules are no less universal or weaker for deriving from that source.

Evidence in favour of Hume's proposed explanation can be marshalled from the fact that property and possession are a continual source of disputes that are not, moreover, easily resolved. This is precisely because they arise from the imagination:

> 'tis in many cases impossible to determine when possession begins or ends; nor is there any certain standard, by which we can decide such controversies. A wild boar, that falls into our snares, is deem'd to be in our possession, if it be impossible for him to escape. But what do

we mean by impossible? How do we separate this impossibility from an improbability? And how distinguish that exactly from a probability? Mark the precise limits of the one and the other, and show the standard, by which we may decide all the disputes that may arise, and, as we find by experience, frequently do arise upon this subject? (T 3.2.3.7/SBN 506)

The imagination is affected by a complex of qualities that 'run so insensibly and gradually into each other' (T 3.2.3n73.1/SBN 504n1) as to leave the matter contingent or at least uncertain: a hare stolen from its hunter is theft due to the mobility of the hunter, for example, but the immobility of an apple makes it the property of whoever takes it first, even when plucked from the tree felicitously before another's outstretched hand; similarly, where an object is hidden or obscure, sight is sufficient to establish possession, although proprietary intention is sometimes required as well. To drive home the 'frivolous' character of the imagination in such decisions, Hume relates a story from Plutarch of two Grecian colonies both claiming ownership of an uninhabited territory, the messenger from one having arrived in the city first, but not before a slower counterpart had landed a spear moments before at the gates. The 'dispute is impossible to decide', Hume concludes, 'and that because the whole question hangs upon the fancy, which in this case is not possess'd of any precise or determinate standard, upon which it can give sentence' (T 3.2.3.7n73.4/SBN 508n1). While imagination cannot determine a standard, however, its principles still furnish the rules that determine property, which are as hard and resilient as the physical objects they transform, as if by magic, from mere things into the property. In each case the imagination feigns a relation from its propensity to seek the path of least resistance and, as we saw with those fictions discussed under the rubric of metaphysics in the previous chapter, invents the idea of a relation where none previously existed; the rules of property are fictions, ideas not traceable to experience and matter of fact.

Thus, present possession, Hume proposes, expresses the natural affection for and attachment to what one owns already, there being a 'natural propensity to join relations', especially 'resembling ones' where the imagination 'finds a kind of fitness and uniformity' in the union (T 3.2.3.10n75.2/SBN 509n2). This love of order leads us to arrange resembling objects contiguously (books in a library), place them in corresponding positions (chairs in a parlour), or combine parts into wholes (institutions composing a society). So great in this propensity that, on some occasions, the imagination will 'feign' an 'absurd' relation, much as – to recall the discussion of reification in the previous chapter – it gives spatial location to the bitter taste of the olive and sweetness of the fig. 'As property forms a relation betwixt a person and an object, 'tis natural to found it on some preceding relation', Hume then proposes, 'and as property is nothing but a constant possession, secur'd by the laws of society, 'tis natural to add it to the present possession, which is a relation that resembles it' (T 3.2.3n71.2/SBN 504–5n). Once established, occupation proceeds from present possession in the same way, formed when the imagination adds to the existing relation an invented one that resembles it. Prescription follows from the same course, property 'produc'd by time, . . . [being] not any thing real in the objects, but . . . the offspring of the sentiments, on which alone time is found to have any influence' (T 3.2.3.9/SBN 509), as does succession, which 'depends, in a great measure, on the imagination' (T 3.2.4.11n76/SBN 513n1) as it moves easily from the established relation of children to parents and connects the former to the property of the latter. Hume also emphasises how the imagination determines the extent of occupied property. Somebody landing on a small island is deemed to have acquired the whole because the object is 'bounded and circumscrib'd in the fancy, and at the same time is proportion'd to the new possessor', but the same person arriving on a large island owns only that part he occupies. The same principle explains that where colonists are numerous they are 'esteemed the proprietors of the whole from the instant of their debarkment' (T 3.2.3.8/SBN 507).

Hume's most elaborate consideration of the imagination and property concerns the acquisition of objects by accession, the cause of which, as noted above, Hume treats as wholly independent of and 'unmix'd' with any considerations of public utility: it is a 'source of property [that] can never be explain'd but from the imagination' (T 3.2.3.10n75.1/SBN 509n2). The rule determines that objects are acquired because connected with objects we already own – fruits from our garden or the offspring of our cattle – and this is explicable only through a 'kind of taste or fancy, arising from analogy, and a comparison of similar instances' (T 3.2.3.4n71.1/SBN 504n1):

> Where objects are connected together in the imagination, they are apt to be put on the same footing, and are commonly suppos'd to be endow'd with the same qualities. We readily pass from one to the other, and make no difference in our judgements concerning them; especially if the latter be inferior to the former. (T 3.2.3.10/SBN 509)

As this observation makes clear, one would expect the principle of easy transition to determine that the imagination move from small to great, according to which the 'right of accession must encrease in strength, in proportion as the transition of ideas is perform'd with greater facility'; it would then follow that 'when we have acquir'd the property of any small object, we shall readily consider any great objects related to it as an accession, and as belonging to the proprietor of the small one'. Accession works in quite the opposite direction, however, as when a large island like Great Britain is given natural dominion over its contiguous islands, whereas authority over the latter carries no claim to the larger country. This seems to contradict the maxim *'that the ascribing of property to accession is nothing but an effect of the relations of ideas, and of the smooth transition of the imagination'* (T 3.2.3.10n75.4/SBN 510n). As Hume points out, this very same maxim operates, albeit modified by the 'agility and unsteadiness of the imagination' and its capacity to place its objects in 'different views' (T 3.2.3.10n75.5/SBN 510n). The imagination naturally joins together objects that are the property of the same person, where the strength of the relation is proportional to the size of the object owned. Where a small and a great object are thus related and the owner strongly related to the larger, he is automatically related strongly to both; where strongly related to the smaller, by contrast, he will not be so strongly related to both, the reason being that the lesser part is 'not apt to strike us in any great degree' (T 3.2.3.10n75.5/SBN 511n). The mind thus moves from greater object to lesser – from Britain to its islands – but not vice versa where the idea contains less force and vivacity and the imagination is unmoved. Contrary to first appearances, then, the principle of easy transition still operates and the smooth passage among its ideas accounts for the rule of accession; where the transition is interrupted and no conjunction can be made, the property relation is terminated.

Hume collects a number of conspicuous examples to illustrate his point. The Rhine and Danube strike the imagination as 'too large . . . to follow as an accession to the property of the neighbouring fields' for which reason ownership falls to the larger entity of the nation, an object of 'suitable bulk to correspond with them, and bear them such a relation in the fancy' (T 3.2.3.10n75.7/SBN 511n). Similarly, the imagination grasps the idea of alluvial deposits on lands adjacent to rivers as a way of connecting one piece of property to another, and though the physical connection is made 'insensibly and imperceptibly', the 'circumstances . . . mightily assist the imagination in the conjunction'. Concomitantly, a portion of land that breaks from one bank and settles on another fails to become the property of the latter 'till the trees or plants have spread their roots into both. Before that, the imagination does not sufficiently join them' (T 3.2.3.10n75.8/SBN 511n). The same principle is at work in deciding ownership of properties that are conjoined and cannot be separated. Where the objects can be divided but not separated – as in bushels of wheat mingled as one – the imagination supposes the whole to be common property and divides it proportionally according to the number of parts contributed by each owner.

As Hume points out, these considerations account for a distinction in Roman law between 'confusion' and 'commixtion': in the former, parts are mixed so as to become indistinguishable (as in different liquids), whereas in the latter bodies are blended but remain obviously and visibly separate (in the bushels of wheat). In cases of confusion, the imagination is unable to distinguish parts and will establish the object as property of an entire community and divide it proportionally; in cases of commixtion, by contrast, where it 'is able to trace and preserve a distinct idea of the property of each', the right of each proprietor is maintained, though, as Hume notes, the practical difficulties of such a conclusion may force the same division as that produced by confusion (T 3.2.3.10n75.10/SBN 512n). When neither division nor separation is possible – as when somebody builds a house on another's land – the imagination is struck more strongly by what is greater and the whole is then regarded as the property of the person who owns the largest portion. This raises the further question of which quality makes something the 'most considerable part, and most attractive to the imagination' (T 3.2.3.10n75.12/SBN 512n) and, as one would expect from the faculty's frivolous nature, these are often various and contradictory – constancy and durability, economic value, size, separate and independence existence – and, since human nature cannot fix a standard, the law steps in to decide by fiat so that decisions become effectively conventional.

Even where decisions of this sort have argument and reason in their favour, the principles of imagination are sure to be at work. Hume cites the dispute between Proclus and Sabinus, jurists of first-century Rome, over who owns a cup or ship made by one from the metal or wood of another. Sabinus, Hume reports, awarded the object to the owner of the raw material, arguing that the substance or matter is the incorruptible foundation and therefore superior to any form imposed on it, whereas Proclus gave it to the craftsman on the basis of the form, that being the main criterion in terms of which any given body is classified as one species of object rather than another. Hume discovers no grounds for preferring one side over the other in the dispute, but cites a solution offered later (in the sixth century) by Tribonia: 'that the cup belongs to the proprietor of the metal, because it can be brought back to its first form: But that the ship belongs to the author of its form for a contrary reason'. Hume is quick to add that 'however ingenious this reason may be, it plainly depends upon the fancy', which 'finds a closer connexion and relation betwixt a cup and the proprietor of its metal, than betwixt a ship and the proprietor of its wood, where the substance is more fix'd and unalterable' (T 3.2.3.10n75.15/SBN 513n). In this case, a dispute appears to be resolved by reason and argument, but they belie the silent workings of the imagination beneath.

Hume's final observation about property and imagination concerns transference: not a rule, strictly conceived, but clearly central to the stability of ownership. Like the rules determining property, the underlying convention springs from 'plain utility and interest'; reflection finds a medium between rigid rules and uncertainty by fixing on the idea that possession should be stable except where the owner agrees to bestow his property on another. This solution alone, however, does not overcome a considerable difficulty in the way in which the property is transferred. Being a creation of the imagination, the quality that relates persons to property is 'perfectly insensible, and even inconceivable', and we can form no 'distinct notion, either of its stability or translation' unless that property is connected in some tangible way to our sentiments. It is then 'from more trivial reasons' – that is, from the imagination – that civil law requires '*delivery*, or a sensible transference of the object' (T 3.2.4.2/SBN 515). Hume then proposes that:

In order to aid the imagination in conceiving the transference of property, we take the sensible object, and actually transfer its possession to the person, on whom we wou'd bestow the property. The suppos'd resemblance of the actions, and the presence of the sensible delivery, deceive the mind, and make it fancy, that it conceives the mysterious transition of the property. (T 3.2.5.2/SBN 515)

The result is an invented 'symbolical delivery, to satisfy the fancy, where the real is impracticable': the keys to the granary symbolise delivery of the corn, and samples of stone and earth represent the transference of a manor. Hume calls this a 'superstitious practice in civil laws' comparable to the way Roman Catholics represent and render present by a 'taper, or habit, or grimace' the 'inconceivable mysteries' of their religion. So 'lawyers and moralists', Hume remarks, 'have run into like invention for the same reason, and have endeavour'd by those means to satisfy themselves concerning the transference of property by consent' (T 3.2.4.2/SBN 515–16).

As we shall see with religious ideas (see Chapter 6), the fact that, in Hume's view, imagination lies at the root of property – which is an artificial contrivance to remedy the infirmities of human nature – by no means impugns the power of the fiction involved, nor does it undermine the strength of the belief-like state it inspires, natural and born of an irresistible propensity. As we have seen in this chapter, the same is true of moral practice and political institutions in general, phenomena that arise and endure from the secret workings of the very faculty that also has the power to bring their continued existence into question.

Notes

1. Admittedly, specific issues discussed by commentators in one context or another often do not call for the imagination to be placed front and centre, which goes some way to explaining the neglect. It is still surprising, however, that a subject that plays a foundational role in Hume's moral and political thought should have received so little attention in an extensive literature. See below, nn. 3 and 16. It is absent from the discussion of Hume in J. B. Schneewind, *The Invention of Autonomy: A History of Modern Moral Theory* (Cambridge: Cambridge University Press, 1998), and the relevant chapter in Stephen Darwall, *The British Moralists and the Internal 'Ought': 1640–1740* (Cambridge: Cambridge University Press,

1995). Even Jonathan Harrison's *Hume's Moral Epistemology* (Oxford: Clarendon Press, 1976), its title notwithstanding, does not have an index entry for the subject.

2. Some commentators have tended to regard these qualities as having some independent existence as metaphysical entities or physiological conditions that exist prior to and independent of the process of moral judgement. For a discussion of these views and an alternative to them, see Costelloe, 'Beauty, Morals, and Hume's Conception of Character'.

3. Substantial treatments of sympathy and the general point of view that either mention imagination only in passing or ignore it all together include Julia Driver, 'Pleasure as the Standard of Virtue in Hume's Moral Philosophy', *Pacific Philosophical Quarterly*, 85: 2 (2004), pp. 173–94; Jacqueline Taylor, 'Hume on the Standard of Virtue', *Journal of Ethics*, 6: 1 (2002), pp. 43–62, and the relevant sections (primarily Ch. 2) in her more recent *Reflecting Subjects: Passion, Sympathy, & Society in Hume's Philosophy* (Oxford: Oxford University Press, 2015); Christine M. Korsgaard, *The Sources of Normativity* (Cambridge: Cambridge University Press, 1996), and 'The General Point of View: Love and Moral Approval in Hume's Ethics', *Hume Studies*, 25: 1 and 2 (1999), pp. 3–41; John Bricke, *Mind and Morality: An Examination of Hume's Moral Psychology* (Oxford: Clarendon Press, 1996); J. L. Mackie, *Hume's Moral Theory* (London: Routledge & Kegan Paul, 1980); Harrison's *Hume's Moral Epistemology*; Carole Stewart, 'The Moral Point of View', *Philosophy*, 51: 196 (1976), pp. 177–87; and Páll S. Árdal, *Passion and Value in Hume's Treatise* (Edinburgh: Edinburgh University Press, 1966), Ch. 3. Árdal (pp. 133–7) appears to have little trouble recognising the role of the faculty in Adam Smith's *Theory of Moral Sentiments*, but overlooks it in the case of Hume, a tendency also evident in Phillip Mercer, *Sympathy and Ethics: A Study of the Relationship between Sympathy and Morality with Special Reference to Hume's Treatise* (Oxford: Clarendon Press, 1972), and, in the more distant past, Glenn R. Morrow, 'The Significance of the Doctrine of Sympathy in Hume and Adam Smith', *Philosophical Review*, 32: 1 (1923), pp. 60–78. The imagination is given brief consideration by Gerald J. Postema, '"Cemented with Diseased Qualities": Sympathy and Comparison in Hume's Moral Psychology', *Hume Studies*, 31: 2 (2005), pp. 249–98 (see pp. 259 and 293–4 n. 36); hovers behind much of the discussion in Donald C. Ainslie, 'Sympathy and the Unity of Hume's Idea of the Self',

in *Persons and Passions: Essays in Honor of Annette Baier*, ed. Joyce Jenkins, Jennifer Whiting and Christopher Williams (Notre Dame: University of Notre Dame Press, 2005), pp. 143–72; and is mentioned *en passant* by A. E. Pitson, 'Sympathy and Other Selves', *Hume Studies*, 22: 2 (1996), p. 262. Cf. Ryu Susato, *Hume's Sceptical Enlightenment*, pp. 39–46; James Baillie, *Hume on Morality* (London: Routledge, 2000), pp. 190–5; Rachel Cohon, 'The Common Point of View in Hume's Ethics', *Philosophy and Phenomenological Research*, 57: 4 (1997), pp. 827–50, incorporated into Ch. 5 of *Hume's Morality: Feeling and Fabrication* (Oxford: Oxford University Press, 2008), esp. pp. 139–42; the discussion in Jennifer A. Herdt, *Religion and Faction in Hume's Moral Philosophy* (Cambridge: Cambridge University Press, 1997), pp. 74–5; R. W. Altmann, 'Hume on Sympathy', *Southern Journal of Philosophy*, 18: 2 (1980), pp. 123–36; and Laird, *Hume's Philosophy of Human Nature*, pp. 197 and 220.

4. See Farr, 'Hume, Hermeneutics, and History', pp. 292–6, and Taylor, *Reflecting Subjects*, who emphasises how Hume treats sympathy as something that 'operates with an immediacy akin to instinct' (p. 44). Farr speculates that one reason for the change between the *Treatise* and second *Enquiry* is that Hume came to recognise the limits of associationism, namely that it involves passivity, when sympathy is something Hume thinks we can 'control and regulate', and imagination – on which sympathy depends – is an 'active, creative, and regulative propensity or faculty' (p. 296). As we have seen, however, since the imagination is the basis for association and imagination is a creative faculty, imagination and association can hardly be opposites in the way Farr suggests. Besides, as Farr points out, the 'important point, nonetheless, is that Hume retains sympathy, and the conclusions that can be drawn from it' (p. 295).

5. Cf. Mercer, *Sympathy and Ethics*, who juxtaposes Hume's mechanism of conversion with Smith's appeal to imagination, as if the former excluded that faculty entirely: 'Whereas Hume held that sympathy consists in the idea of an emotion being converted into the emotion itself through the enlivening association with the impression of self, according to Smith sympathy involves imagining oneself in the other person's situation and thus, in one's imagination, going through the emotional experiences he would be going through' (p. 85).

6. Hume's notion of conversion has been a source of debate on the part of readers, especially its use to solve the 'problem of tragedy' and explain how and why an object or event that would ordinarily cause

pain and distress brings an 'unaccountable pleasure' to the spectator when represented in a literary work (E 216). As we shall see in the next chapter, when Hume speaks of 'conversion' in the context of tragedy, he assumes the discussion of the *Treatise*, but adds to it the pleasure aroused by aesthetic representation.

7. Sympathy does not, however, as Taylor rightly emphasises, 'involve imagining oneself in the place of the other'. See Taylor, *Reflecting Subjects*, p. 42.

8. On this point I am indebted to the discussion in Samuel Fleischacker, 'Sympathy in Hume and Smith: A Contrast, Critique, and Reconstruction', in *Intersubjectivity and Objectivity in Adam Smith and Edmund Husserl*, ed. Christel Fricke and Dagfinn Føllesdal (Frankfurt: Ontos), pp. 273–312. See also Miller, *Philosophy and Ideology in Hume's Political Thought*, pp. 53–4.

9. See Rachael M. Kydd, *Reason and Conduct in Hume's Treatise* (Oxford: Oxford University Press, 1946), pp. 132–5, who emphasises the effect on the imagination of contiguity and distance in time and space; the result is that the imagination 'distorts' our ideas and passions (p. 135).

10. See in this context, Driver, 'Pleasure as the Standard of Virtue in Hume's Moral Philosophy'. Driver does not mention the role of imagination, but argues (incorrectly to my mind) that a trait is 'reasonable or justified' insofar as it is 'beneficial and agreeable. And that is all the general point of view is' (p. 180).

11. In this context, see Mark Collier, 'Hume's Theory of Moral Imagination', *History of Philosophy Quarterly*, 27: 3 (2010), pp. 255–73, who distinguishes 'associative' sympathy (our capacity to feel vicariously the pain of others) from 'cognitive' sympathy (our ability to reflect what we would feel in somebody else's place). The latter, Collier urges, is what enables us to enter the afflictions of distant strangers.

12. See Elizabeth S. Radcliffe, 'Hume on Motivating Sentiments, the General Point of View, and the Inculcation of "Morality"', *Hume Studies*, 20: 1 (1994), pp. 37–58; the quote is from p. 37. A similar emphasis is found in Geoffrey Sayre-McCord, 'On Why Hume's "General Point of View" Isn't Ideal – and Shouldn't Be', *Social Philosophy and Policy*, 11: 1 (1994), pp. 202–28. The older interpretation of Hume as a proponent of the Ideal Observer model is to be found in an earlier generation of commentators, and appears now to be universally rejected. Harrison's reading, *Hume's Moral Psychology*, pp. 113–14, is typical of the now discredited view.

13. See Shaftesbury, *Characteristicks* 2: pp. 221–2, and Adam Smith, *The Theory of Moral Sentiments*, ed. D. D. Raphael and A. L. Macfie, in *The Glasgow Edition of the Works and Correspondence of Adam Smith*, 7 vols (Oxford: Oxford University Press, [1759] 1976), esp. 1: pp. 9–26.

14. Henry Home, Lord Kames, *Elements of Criticism. The Sixth Edition. With the Author's Last Corrections and Additions*, 2 vols (Indianapolis: Liberty Fund, [1785; 1st ed. 1762] 2005), 1: pp. 66–77. See Timothy M. Costelloe, *The British Aesthetic Tradition. From Shaftesbury to Wittgenstein* (Cambridge: Cambridge University Press, 2012), Ch. 3, and for an application of Kames' theory in the field of aesthetics, Eva Dadlez, 'Ideal Presence: How Kames Solved the Problem of Fiction and Emotion', *Journal of Scottish Philosophy*, 9: 1 (2011), pp. 115–33.

15. See Edward Bullough, 'Psychical Distance', *British Journal of Psychology*, 5 (1912), pp. 87–117, and for a critique of the doctrine in general, George Dickie, *Art and The Aesthetic: An Institutional Analysis* (Ithaca: Cornell University Press, 1974).

16. The role of imagination in Hume's political thought has received more attention than it has in treatments of his moral philosophy, although it is still undervalued or (one assumes) simply not considered pertinent to the discussions at hand, which in many cases tend to focus on Hume's science of politics per se rather than the philosophical underpinnings of it. By far the most extensive, comprehensive and sympathetic treatment is found in Miller, *Philosophy and Ideology in Hume's Political Thought*, esp. Chs. 3 and 4. It is touched on by Forbes, *Hume's Philosophical Politics*, pp. 9–15, and figures in the relevant discussion in Baillie, *Hume on Morality*, Ch. 6. It is considered briefly by Mackie, *Hume's Moral Theory*, pp. 95–6, who summarily dismisses it, and is raised in various contexts by Jonathan Harrison in *Hume's Theory of Justice* (Oxford: Clarendon Press, 1981); this stands in contrast to his earlier *Hume's Moral Epistemology*, where it is hardly mentioned, although even in the later work Harrison shows little patience with Hume's view (see esp. pp. 96–103). Stewart, *The Moral and Political Philosophy of David Hume*, emphasises the importance of the faculty in Hume's theory of belief formation but largely ignores it later in the book when discussing the political philosophy, and omits mention of it entirely in his later *Opinion and Reform in Hume's Political Philosophy* (Princeton: Princeton University Press, 1992). The same is true of Whelan, *Order and Artifice in Hume's Political Philosophy*, who

devotes a section to the 'principles of the imagination' (pp. 96–117), but barely mentions it later when considering the substance of Hume's political thought. It receives only passing mention in Neil McArthur, *David Hume's Political Theory: Law, Commerce, and the Constitution of Government* (Toronto: University of Toronto Press, 2007), is largely absent from both Russell Hardin, *David Hume: Moral and Political Theorist* (Oxford: Oxford University Press, 2007) and Andrew Sabl, *Hume's Politics: Coordination and Crisis in the 'History of England'* (Princeton: Princeton University Press, 2012), although the latter does mention the importance of political principles (Magna Charta and settled rules of royal succession) being 'vivid to the imagination' (p. 143) and cites on more than one occasion 'partiality and short-sightedness' as psychological factors that make conventions necessary (see p. 31 *passim*). As noted above, the imagination finds no place at all in Árdal, *Passion and Value in Hume's Treatise*, even in Ch. 8, which concerns the artificial virtue of justice.

17. Miller, *Philosophy and Ideology in Hume's Political Thought*, pp. 71–2. See also Forbes' *Hume's Philosophical Politics*, pp. 9–12.

4

Aesthetics

In this chapter we consider the place of the imagination in Hume's approach to aesthetics, and how it explains artistic creativity, audience receptivity and the origin of the particular kind of value associated with such terms as 'beauty' and 'the sublime'. Most of Hume's remarks in this area are made about literature, with references to painting, music and architecture only fleeting and, in the estimate of some, inconsequential.[1] Hume uses the term 'literature' broadly to include poetry, comedy, tragedy and eloquence; sometimes even history falls under the heading as well, although, as we shall see in the next chapter, historical writing bears a different relationship to the imagination that effectively distinguishes it from literary works more narrowly conceived. Since the majority of Hume's examples are drawn from various poetic forms – lyrical, dramatic, pastoral and epic – my consideration of his aesthetics will focus on these, and, following Hume, I shall use the terms 'literature' and 'poetry' interchangeably. In principle, however, there is no reason why his views on imagination and literature cannot be applied *mutatis mutandis* to other art forms as well.

We begin with an overview of the main features of Hume's philosophical aesthetics before showing how the productive power of the imagination underlies and informs his approach. The poet exploits the productive imagination to create artificial fictions, or a 'poetical system of things' (T 1.3.10.6/SBN 121) as Hume describes it, which, through the manipulation of language and application of techniques, creates a fanciful world of ideas that the audience is enticed to enter and take as real. The imagination is the source of both poetic creativity, in the shape of literary genius, and aesthetic receptivity that allows an audience to experience the pleasure that writers bring about; when refined, this is what, in the tradition of the eighteenth century, Hume calls 'delicacy of taste'.

Literary fictions are artificial and an audience does not believe in the existence of the objects to which they ostensibly refer but is persuaded by them for the pleasure the work brings.

To be successful in achieving their effects, however, poets must procure an easy transition among the ideas in the imagination, which is only possible by creating a poetical system that gives the appearance of reality. They do this according to three principles: by transforming ordinary experience into something extraordinary; creating ideas that are agreeable to an audience; and bringing about their effects deliberately. At the same time, poets can only achieve their results by appealing to principles of human nature, for when poetry becomes too artificial it ceases to have the desired effect on the audience. Striking this balance between nature and artifice is something that any work of literature is obliged to do, and for this reason the principles of the poetic arts can be understood as specifying rules of art or literary criticism, which, extracted from poetic practice, determine whether a work will be successful or not. Hume thus shows what constitutes good literature and he specifies normative rules that, if followed in a certain manner, should result in the production of good or even great literary works.

Hume's Aesthetics

Before we can appreciate the role of the imagination in literary creativity and aesthetic receptivity, it will be useful to outline briefly the main features of Hume's aesthetics, since they are assumed as background to his various discussions. Hume's view of beauty and the arts is part of a tradition that has its immediate philosophical impetus in Locke's influential treatment of language in Book 3 of the *Essay*, which, as Stephen Land emphasises, gave to eighteenth-century aesthetics a dominant semantic theory in which 'Words are thought to work like pictures; they "represent" things either by convention or by virtue of actual resemblance'.[2] This tradition can be traced to other figures from which Hume draws inspiration – especially the Abbé Jean-Baptiste Dubos, Addison and Francis Hutcheson – and its influence, as Land argues, can be seen well into the nineteenth century.[3] There is much debate concerning particular aspects of Hume's aesthetics but consensus over the general outlines of his approach, which displays four main features.[4]

First, the beauty and deformity of art and nature can be traced to sentiments or feelings that arise in an individual as a result of the relationship between that individual and the object in question. In 'Of the Standard of Taste' Hume writes:

> Though it be certain that beauty and deformity, more than sweet and bitter, are not qualities in objects, but belong entirely to the sentiment, internal or external; it must be allowed, that there are certain qualities in objects, which are fitted by nature to produce those particular feelings. (E 235)

Or as he puts it in the second *Enquiry*:

> in all decisions of taste or external beauty, all the relations are beforehand obvious to the eye; and we thence proceed to feel a sentiment of complacency or disgust, according to the nature of the object, and the disposition of our organs. (EPM Appx.1.13/SBN 291)

At least in part, Hume follows Locke and takes beauty to be a secondary quality in an audience rather than an objective feature of the world itself.[5]

Second, as the above quotes suggest, Hume assumes that human beings are constituted in such a way that there is a natural 'fit' – a 'match' or 'natural aptness' as some commentators have called it[6] – between the aesthetic object and the subject who, by virtue of a natural receptivity, is capable of being affected in a certain manner. 'Beauty is such an order and construction of parts', as Hume writes in the *Treatise*, 'as either by the *primary constitution* of our nature, by *custom*, or by *caprice*, is fitted to give a pleasure and satisfaction to the soul' (T 2.1.8.2/SBN 299; see also EPM 5.38/SBN 224–5 and E 63–5). For this reason Hume is sometimes seen as holding a 'causal' theory of taste, the view that there is some decipherable causal connection linking objects with the sentiments they elicit.[7]

Third, Hume argues that beauty and deformity arise due to the sentiments of pleasure and pain elicited by the object and, in some cases, the utility or fitness it exhibits in achieving its end. Judgements of beauty and deformity – normative claims about good and bad – are then expressions of these sentiments. So '*beauty* of all kinds gives us a peculiar delight and satisfaction; as *deformity* produces pain' (T 2.1.8.1/SBN 298), Hume remarks, and the view of well-cultivated fields appeals to us more than 'briars and brambles' (EPM 2.9/SBN 179). Generally, Hume takes pain/pleasure and utility as a single principle. A 'machine, a piece of furniture, a vestment, a house well contrived for use and conveniency, is so far beautiful', he observes, for instance, 'and is contemplated with pleasure and approbation' (EPM 2.10/SBN 179). Thus 'From innumerable instances of this kind . . . we may conclude that beauty is nothing but a form, which produces pleasure, as deformity is a structure of parts, which conveys pain' (T 2.1.8.2/SBN 299).[8]

Fourth, and finally, Hume emphasises that the mere presence of beautiful objects and the capacity of human beings to be affected by them do not translate automatically into appropriate sentiments and correct judgements. There is a natural basis for being affected by objects and experiencing them as beautiful, but the extent of the satisfaction depends upon the degree to which spectators have cultivated their taste and can be affected by the work in question. Ongoing critical reflection on one's judgements is required to educate the sentiments and achieve a 'delicacy of taste'. For only a mind that is 'susceptible to those finer sensations' is in a position to 'give praise to what deserves it' (EPM App. 1.16/SBN; see T 3.1.2.4/SBN 472). Hume writes:

> When you present a poem or a picture to a man possessed of this talent, the delicacy of his feeling makes him be sensibly touched with every part of it; nor are the masterly strokes perceived with more exquisite relish and satisfaction, than the negligencies or absurdities with disgust and uneasiness. (E 4)

Perfection in such delicacy is 'impossible to be attained', and those who come close to it are rare, but achieving even a modicum of good taste promises great satisfaction, and Hume thinks it is something for which we could and should strive over the course of a lifetime.[9]

Poetry and the Imagination

With these four main features of Hume's aesthetics in mind, we can now turn to his treatment of poetry, which depends on the productive power of the imagination. Poets take ideas produced by the former and through the power of the latter proceed to mix, compound, separate and divide them to form new and original ideas of objects that do not correspond to anything in the world.

The poet thus represents experience and subverts it in a particular way. These creations are unlike complex ideas such as 'apple', the discrete constituents of which can be traced to impressions of sense, but comparable to those of the New Jerusalem and a gold mountain, which can still be traced ultimately to original impressions but do not arise directly from real existence. As such, the poet creates a class of artificial fictions, or 'poetical fictions' as Hume sometimes calls them. The poet represents experience so that in the 'fables we meet with in poems and romances . . . Nature there is totally confounded, and nothing mention'd but winged horses, fiery dragons, and monstrous giants' (T 1.1.3.4/SBN 10). Poetry treats the world not as an object to be understood, but as a subject of aesthetic representation limited in the first instance by the poetic genius of the author in question. This can be seen as a weakness insofar as poetic ideas lack the force and vivacity of original impressions, but also as a strength, since, unless liberated from repeating matters of fact, the poetic arts would be impossible.

These fictions, however, gain their specifically poetic character when authors confer a certain status on them by virtue of placing them in a 'poetical system of things'. They are not natural fictions of a vulgar sort, but arise from artifice, where the poet self-consciously connects ideas and draws relations in ways that, in many cases, they would not otherwise or obviously exhibit. This does not give the objects to which the ideas refer real existence, but, Hume says, serves as 'sufficient foundation for any fiction' (T 1.3.10.6/SBN 121). There are three discernible characteristics the poetic arts display and are required for ideas to attain their poetic status: the magical power to transform ordinary experience into something extraordinary; the capacity to create ideas that are agreeable to an audience; and the ability to bring about this effect deliberately. The second of these constitutes delicacy of taste in the audience, while the other two form what we can refer to as 'poetic genius'.

The Transformation of Ordinary Experience

Given his place in the eighteenth-century tradition, it is not surprising to find in Hume's aesthetics an emphasis on the force of language and, in particular, a version of the view that well-chosen words can produce ideas in a reader that are more vivid than those that arise from a direct perception, although they do not inspire belief in real existence. 'The reader finds a Scene drawn in stronger

Colours', as Addison puts it in one of his essays in *The Spectator*, 'and painted more to the Life in his Imagination, by the help of Words, than by an actual survey of the Scene which they describe' (No. 416, 560). Hume expresses the same thought, that poets are like magicians or conjurors who use their pens to represent the world with such 'strong and remarkable' strokes that they 'convey a lively image to the mind' (E 191–2) and thereby transform ordinary experience into something extraordinary and marvellous.[10] In Hume's view,

> All poetry, being a species of painting, brings us nearer to the objects than any other species of narration, throws a stronger light upon them, and delineates more distinctly those minute circumstances, which ... serve mightily to enliven the imagery, and gratify the fancy. (EHU 3.11)[11]

Like Addison, Hume emphasises that the transformative power of poetic language embellishes the world; poetry sheds light on the topography of experience, highlighting certain details while casting others into shadow so that through its lens what is in reality ugly, repellent or mundane appears beautiful, appealing or in some way fascinating.

Thus there is a difference between the straightforward representation of the world involved in the creation of any idea and – to use Land's phrase – a 'true poetic imitation', a distinction which, as Land emphasises, can be traced to John Dryden's *Essay of Dramatic Poesy* (1668), where we find a neo-Platonic alternative to the prevailing Lockean picture theory of language. As Land observes:

> The orthodox position expounded by Crites [in the *Essay of Dramatic Poesy*] sees the true symbol as essentially a copy of the actual, but Dryden holds that the true symbol cannot in principle be a copy but must be a deliberate distortion of the natural in the direction of something greater.[12]

Whether Hume had this work in mind or not, he certainly expresses the same idea that poetry distorts, albeit for aesthetic purposes, the subject matter it treats; poetry draws not on imitation per se, but on the productive power of the imagination to subvert experience. He writes:

Sentiments, which are merely natural, affect not the mind with any pleasure, and seem not worthy of our attention. The pleasantries of a waterman, the observations of a peasant, the ribaldry of a porter or hackney coachman, all of these are natural, and disagreeable. What an insipid comedy should we make of the chit-chat of the tea-table, copied faithfully and at full length? Nothing can please persons of taste, but nature drawn with her graces and ornaments, *la belle nature*. (E 191–2)

Thus, in the '*poetical* fiction of the *golden age*', for example, everything frightening and threatening about the world is expunged, and the representation contains only what is 'charming and most peaceable'. Hume continues:

The seasons, in that first period of nature, were so temperate, if we credit these agreeable fictions, that there was no necessity for men to provide for heat and cold: The rivers flowed with wine and milk: The oaks yielded honey; and nature spontaneously produced her greatest delicacies. Nor were these the chief advantages of that happy age. Tempests were not alone removed from nature; but those more furious tempests were unknown to human breasts, which now cause such uproar, and engender such confusion. Avarice, ambition, cruelty, selfishness, were never heard of: Cordial affection, compassion, sympathy were the only movements with which the mind was yet acquainted. Even the punctilious distinction of *mine* and *thine* was banished from among that happy race of mortals, and carried with it the very notion of property and obligation, justice and injustice. (EPM 3.14)

To represent the world in its 'merely natural' aspect would be to replicate, like memory, the empirical content of experience in all its mundane detail; the poet, on the other hand, creates an alternative reality, as in the golden age, where the world is adorned, rendered beautiful and effectively perfected by the power of language.

The Creation of Agreeable Ideas

Second, as Hume's description of the golden age makes clear, in transforming and embellishing experience the poet at once creates ideas that are agreeable to an audience and satisfy the imagination's desire for the pleasure it derives from relating ideas and completing a whole. Hume notes at one point that the imagination's love of totality and the satisfaction it finds there is the reason poets employ synecdoche and 'frequently draw their images and metaphors' to make part stand for the whole, as in a gate to represent a city (T 3.2.3n73.5/SBN 508n). When poets achieve their effects, they do so by transforming merely natural objects and scenes into things of beauty, deliberately arousing a corresponding pleasure in the audience. As Garrett points out, 'literary and other arts derive their primary appeal *from* the imagination and have their primary appeal *to* that faculty'.[13] While poetic genius reflects the active side of the imagination, its passive role is manifest as an audience's capacity to be moved by images the poet has created and the ideas raised in their minds as a result. Poets rely on the receptive capacity of the audience and the same mechanism of sympathy that we have seen to be central to moral life. For, Hume writes:

> it is a rule in criticism, that every combination of syllables or letters, which gives pain to the organs of speech in the recital, appears also, from a species of sympathy, harsh and disagreeable to the ear. Nay, when we run over a book with our eye, we are sensible of such unharmonious composition; because we still imagine, that a person recites it to us, and suffers from the pronunciation of these jarring sounds. So delicate is our sympathy! (EPM 5.37/SBN 224)

As in the case of actions that give rise to sentiments that constitute virtue and vice, human beings cannot be indifferent to beauty and deformity, but are moved by the view of certain scenes that give rise to pleasure or pain. The same applies to works of literature, where

> Every movement of the theatre, by a skilful poet, is communicated, as it were by magic, to the spectators; who weep, tremble, resent, rejoice, and are enflamed with all the variety of passions, which actuate the several personages of the drama. (EPM 5.26/SBN 221–2)

'But no passion, when well represented', Hume adds later, 'can be entirely indifferent to us; because there is none, of which every man has not, within him, at least the seeds and first principles' (EPM 5.30/SBN 222). For this reason, an audience feels anxiety and concern when the happiness or good fortune of a favourite literary character is thwarted, and 'where their sufferings proceed from the treachery, cruelty, or tyranny of an enemy, our breasts are affected with the liveliest resentment against the author of these calamities' (EPM 5.27/SBN 222).

A fundamental difference, however, between reality and its poetic counterpart is that poetic ideas are always a source of pleasure rather than pain, the agreeableness arising from the effect of sympathy and a quality immediately agreeable to ourselves. The compositions of 'poets and other authors ... [are] chiefly calculated to please the imagination' (E 228), Hume writes, and:

> When poets form descriptions of the ELYSIAN fields, where the blessed inhabitants stand in no need of each other's assistance, they yet represent them as maintaining a constant intercourse of love and friendship, and sooth our fancy with the pleasing image of these soft and gentle passions. (EPM 7.20/SBN 257)

Poetry achieves this effect more easily when it paints 'lively pictures of the sublime passions, magnanimity, courage, disdain of fortune; or those of the tender affections, love and friendship; which warm the heart, and diffuse over it similar sentiments and emotions'. Yet 'even the most disagreeable, such as grief and anger', he continues, 'are observed, when excited by poetry, to convey a satisfaction, from a mechanism of nature, not easy to be explained' (EPM 7.26/SBN 259). Pain, after all, is a real sentiment born of impressions or arising when sentiments are rekindled through memory; however weak a real sorrow may be, 'yet in none of its gradations will it ever give pleasure' (E 221). In a poetical reality, by contrast, the passion is transformed; poetry does not simply reproduce the original sentiment but refashions it in such a way that it becomes a source of pleasure rather than pain.

Poets are unlikely to have any theoretical grasp of this process, but they know that human passions *can* be engaged and, if possessed of the requisite genius, they will know how to do it: by depicting characters, conduct and events in the bright colours necessary to warm the imagination, enflame the passions, and arouse agreeable sentiments. 'All the passions, excited by eloquence, are agreeable in the highest degree' (E 219), Hume observes, even if the subject matter it treats would ordinarily be a source of pain. 'From Homer down to Dr Young, the whole inspired tribe have ever been sensible, that no other representation of things would suit the feeling and observation of each individual' (DNR 95–6). Hence the 'unaccountable pleasure', as

Hume characterises it in 'Of Tragedy', 'which the spectators of a well-written tragedy receive from sorrow, terror, anxiety and other passions, that are in themselves disagreeable and uneasy' (E 216). Here, he writes,

> The whole art of the poet is employed, in rousing and supporting the compassions and resentment of his audience. They are pleased in proportion as they are afflicted, and never are so happy as when they employ tears, sobs, and cries to give vent to their sorrow, and relieve their heart, swoln with the tenderest sympathy and compassion. (E 216–17)

For 'the same object of distress, which pleases in a tragedy, were it really set before us, would give the most unfeigned uneasiness' (E 218). Some have dubbed this Hume's 'Principle of Conversion' or 'Conversion Hypothesis',[14] because, as Hume puts it, 'from that very eloquence, with which the melancholy scene is represented. ... [T]he whole impulse of those [melancholy] passions is converted into pleasure, and swells the delight which the eloquence raises in us' (E 219–20).

There has been much debate over the form and content of Hume's principle and its application to the case of tragedy, and various proposals – and much criticism – of exactly what it amounts to and whether it solves the problem in question; many have charged that Hume fails to account for the relevant facts of aesthetic experience and at least one commentator has suggested that in the final analysis he is not really discussing tragedy at all.[15] Hume's attempt to explain the phenomenon clearly assumes his discussion of 'conversion' in the *Treatise*, although, as noted in Chapter 2, he does there appear to be using the term in a different sense. As we have seen, Hume initially discusses conversion in the context of sympathy to designate that process whereby a passion or emotion is enlivened to the point where it approaches the force and vivacity – is 'converted into' – an impression. This 'mechanism of nature, not easy to be explained' can take place in our own person or, via sympathy, among different individuals. In the discussion of tragedy, this is clearly relevant since it explains *what* the phenomenon of conversion amounts to: we feel the passion portrayed in the drama because the sentiment in the characters becomes an idea in us and is then enlivened to the point where it appears as a new impression in the audience. It does not, however, explain what is at issue in the case of tragedy, namely, that we feel pleasure in a passion that would otherwise cause pain or, to express it differently, we take pleasure in another's pain, and that is the whole 'problem' Hume is trying to solve.

One way to clarify what Hume is proposing as a solution here, and to show the place of the imagination in it, is to recognise that he is confronting, if not clearly distinguishing, two distinct issues: the psychological mechanism of conversion – which we have already met in the *Treatise* account of sympathy – that explains how one emotion apparently replaces another, and the literary depiction of the emotion through which 'the melancholy scene is *represented*' (E 219, emphasis added) and, in Hume's view, forms the necessary cause for the effect of conversion to come about.[16] The conversion thus takes place when the melancholic passions are redirected by the sentiments of beauty that arise from poetic representation by softening the degree of belief involved and thus 'enlivening the mind, and fixing the attention' (T 1.3.9.15/SBN 115). 'The latter [sentiments of beauty], being the predominant emotion', Hume adds, 'seize the whole mind, and convert the former into themselves, at least tincture them so strongly as totally to alter their nature' (E 220). We do not take pleasure in another's pain, then, but in the beauty of the representation. There are limits to this process, scenes so 'bloody and atrocious', as Hume writes, that the horror roused 'will not soften into pleasure' (E 224); such is the case, for example, with the scene of self-mutilation in playwright Nicholas Rowe's *Ambitious Stepmother* (1699).[17] With the exception of such graphic violence, however, Hume holds that poetic representations of otherwise painful emotion contain less force and vivacity than the original and transform reality into fiction, giving rise to sentiments of beauty and the pleasure that attends them.[18]

Poetic Deliberation

Clearly – and this is the third characteristic that makes an idea a poetic fiction – authors do not produce such agreeable sentiments by accident, but employ their skills and techniques to bring them about deliberately as a particular response in the audience. Poets must have some knowledge of the principles of human nature and especially the fact that the imagination should not be strained, but engaged in such a way that it can move freely and easily among its ideas according to the principles of association. This deliberate use of poetic skill is a double-edged sword, however, since one cannot embellish the world in a fictional way without exaggeration and artifice. This ambiguity reflects the Janus-faced character of the imagination, its positive and negative sides, which make human creativity possible only by subverting experience. Depending on one's emphasis, then, one might laud the genius of poetry for achieving its effects or condemn its power of manipulation through which reality is turned into fiction. When Hume acknowledges the positive side of the imagination he has only praise for poets, but when he recognises the negative side he denounces them as a source of artifice and deceit.

On the one hand, to be effective in transforming the world, poets must possess a certain genius, taste or spirit as well as a firm grasp of the principles governing human nature; without these qualities poets would create ideas that are dull and unable to convince, move or otherwise affect an intended audience. In Hume's view, the essence of genius is identical to the presence of a particularly strong active imagination, the perfection of the 'fancy to run from one end of the universe to the other in collecting ideas, which belong to the subject'. Hume refers to this as a 'kind of magical faculty of the soul, which, tho' it be always most perfect in the greatest geniuses, and is properly what we call genius, is however inexplicable by the utmost efforts of human understanding' (T 1.1.7.15/SBN 24). The poet has the singular capacity to create 'beauties of the imagination' (E 220) that can entertain an audience:

> The genius required to paint objects in a lively manner, the art employed in collecting all the pathetic circumstances, the judgment displayed in disposing them: the exercise, I say, of these noble talents, together with the force of expression, and beauty of oratorical numbers, diffuse the highest satisfaction on the audience, and excite the most delightful movements. (E 219–20)

Who can doubt, Hume asks, that this ability of poets to move the passions is a 'considerable merit; and being enhanced by its extreme rarity, may exalt the person possessed of it, above every character of the age in which he lives?' (EPM 7.27/SBN 259). Partly for this reason, Hume's list of 'Great Poets' is as short (E 550–1) as his list of bad ones is long (H 5.149–55).

Hume's own passion for literature is well known, discovered
and tended early in his youth and still alive and well as he lay on
his deathbed: Adam Smith recounts that Hume passed his final
days 'very well with assistance of amusing books' (E xlvi). These
included Lucian's *Dialogues of the Dead* and (what so shocked
Samuel Johnson) George Campbell's *The Philosophy of Rhetoric*.[19]
As Ernest Campbell Mossner documents, Hume was also a great
promoter and patron of Scottish writers.[20] Given his love and
knowledge of literature, one would expect Hume to appreciate
and praise poets for their skill in transforming the world and their
gift for giving pleasure to a reader, including one close to death.
'Such a superiority do the pursuits of literature possess above every
other occupation', he remarks at one point, 'that even he, who
attains but a mediocrity in them, merits the pre-eminence above
those that excel the most in the common and vulgar professions'
(H 5.155). Hume surely had himself in mind with such remarks,
not only given his own aspirations to become a man of letters and
self-styled 'Ambassador from the Dominions of Learning to those
of Conversation' (E 535), but also because he took such care in
perfecting the literary presentation of his philosophy (the *Essays*
alone went though nine separate editions in Hume's lifetime).

While Hume himself cuts a fine literary figure and praises
the rarity, merit and creative power of poetic genius, he at once
expresses genuine suspicion of poets and their art, and strikes a
note of deadly seriousness in tracing the fine line between genuine
creativity and cynical manipulation. For the very same virtue
of eloquence that adorns a character – his included, one must
assume – can become vicious when used to conceal sinister ends.
'Eloquence . . . when it rises to an eminent degree, and is employed
upon subjects of any considerable dignity and nice discernment'
is immediately agreeable and meritorious (EPM 8.7/SBN 263),
Hume declares, but a 'little art or eloquence' can also be employed
cynically, 'as best suits the purpose of [one's] discourse' (EPM, A
Dialogue 19/SBN 330).

It is worth noting that this decrying of eloquence is entirely
conventional, with Hume striking the same familiar tone set by
Locke in his *Essay* where he disparages *'figurative speeches'* as the
imperfection and abuse of language (*Essay* 3.10.34, 508), itself
part of an agonistic tradition going back to Plato's dismissal of
rhetoric as anathema to truth and virtue and Aristotle's willingness
to categorise it as a branch of dialectic, albeit an art of popular

persuasion rather than a science of systematic inquiry.[21] It is also reflected more generally in the unease felt by Hume's contemporaries who realised, as Leopold Damrosch puts it, that when works of art 'do their work effectively they intoxicate readers into analogous bondage'. Such bondage may be part of the aesthetic experience – embracing 'captivity to a higher and a nobler mind', as Johnson says of reading Milton – but, Damrosch adds, 'the mere existence of metaphor, let alone of elaborate fictions, is a threat to the integrity of language and thought'.[22] As Adam Potkay has argued, in this light one can read Hume as reflecting a widespread tension in the eighteenth century between the model of ancient eloquence to move the 'just passions of civic assembly', on the one hand, and the restraints of polite style, on the other. This found its philosophical counterpart, Potkay observes, in the view that 'experimental ideal, procedural rigor and a transparent language of argumentation should supplant the deceptions of eloquence in all essays addressed to the understanding'.[23] In this spirit, Hume suspects poetry of involving some inherent and unavoidable corruption, and while his mistrust might be conventional, it expresses at once his view that the imagination plays the dual role of facilitating and subverting experience: it brings pleasure through creative activity while using artifice and manipulation to do so. The poetic imagination is beholden to experience if an audience is to be engaged, but it requires departing from experience if it is to craft more than mere copies of memory and successfully achieve its effects.

This is a difficult tension to manage, especially where the difference between ideas of memory and those of imagination is found only in the degree of force and vivacity each exhibits, and that passion and reason are locked in a 'struggle' or 'war' where the movement of the former can too easily be mistaken for the 'conclusions only of our intellectual faculties' (T 2.3.8.13/SBN 437). Ideas of beauty and deformity are calm impressions of reflection, but they become violent when the 'raptures of poetry and music frequently rise to the greatest height; while those other impressions . . . may decay into so soft an emotion, as to become, in a manner, imperceptible' (T 2.1.1.3/SBN 276). Skilful writers possess a 'native enthusiasm' (E 139) and can sweep an audience away in a wave of passion. The 'strong spirits' they conjure in viewers are characteristic of and comparable to a corrupt religious state, for under the sway of a poetic enthusiasm the 'warm imagination' is swelled 'with great, but confused conception', individuals enjoy 'raptures, transports, and surprising flights of fancy', and at its summit may experience a kind of frenzy in which 'every whimsy is consecrated' (E 74). Literature and the sympathy on which it depends can exhibit just these symptoms. Hume remarks:

> A man, who enters the theatre, is immediately struck with the view of so great a multitude, participating of one common amusement; and experiences, from their very aspect, a superior sensibility or disposition of being affected with every sentiment, which he shares with his fellow creatures. He observes the actors to be animated by the appearance of a full audience, and raised to a degree of enthusiasm, which they cannot command in any solitary or calm moment. (EPM 5.24–5/SBN 221)

When overheated, the imagination becomes disordered and incapable of distinguishing truth from falsehood because 'every loose fiction or idea' is received on the same footing as ideas of memory. The result is a state of persuasion that can even reach to delirium. 'This is common to both poetry and madness', Hume writes, 'that the vivacity they bestow on the ideas is not deriv'd from the particular situations or connexions of the objects of these ideas, but from the present temper and disposition of the person' (T 1.3.10.10/SBN 630). The poet gives a 'bent to the imagination [and] draws along the passion, in the same manner as if its proper object were real and existent' (T 2.2.5.12/SBN 362). The imagination has the power to bring objects closer to us so that we are tempted to enjoy the present advantage of aesthetic pleasure over and above what we know to be the dictates of judgement and the sanity of experience. The poet is implicated in such schemes, for 'however poets may employ their wit and eloquence, in celebrating present pleasure, and rejecting all distant views to fame, health, or fortune; it is obvious, that this practice is the source of all dissoluteness and disorder, repentance and misery' (EPM 6.15/SBN 239). Yet there is something seductive and irresistible about the images they conjure and, as Hume remarks:

> 'Tis difficult for us to withold our assent from what is painted out to us in all the colours of eloquence; and the vivacity produc'd by the fancy is in many cases greater than that which arises from custom and experience. We are hurry'd away by the lively imagination of our author or companion; and even he himself is often a victim to his own fire and genius. (T 1.3.10.8/SBN 123)

Unlike cases of actual madness, however, poetic enthusiasm is a temporary state, and while poetry works by creating a fanciful world, neither poets nor readers actually believe in the reality they create; poetic reality consists of artificial fictions of the imagination – 'counterfeit on belief and judgement' – and while the faculty might be able to set objects before us in their 'true colours', it cannot, Hume insists, 'of itself, reach belief':

> [I]n the warmth of a poetical enthusiasm, a poet has a counterfeit belief, and even a kind of vision of his objects . . . [where the] blaze of poetical figures and images . . . have their effect upon the poet himself, as well as upon his readers. (SBN 123)[24]

In contrast to memory, whose ideas correspond to matters of fact and give rise to justified belief, the productive power of imagination exploited by the poet produces only fictions and even these are not the natural beliefs of the sort associated with primary propensities of the imagination that make life possible. Despite the increased force and vivacity they contain, even in the midst of a poetic enthusiasm poetic ideas still *feel* different from those arising from those of vulgar reasoning; events, characters and conduct in a literary work belong only to the world of the poetic imagination and the artifice of drawing relations where none naturally exist. Hume is convinced that poetic fictions are never as strong as even the lowest probability of belief derived directly from experience. As a result, we can distinguish the 'feeling' of 'serious conviction' from ideas aroused by the 'fervours of poetry and eloquence', which are the 'mere *phantom of belief or perswasion*' (T 1.3.10.10/SBN 630, emphasis added). Hume writes:

> We observe, that the vigour of conception, which fictions receive from poetry and eloquence, is a circumstance merely accidental, of which every idea is equally susceptible; and that such fictions are connected with nothing that is real. This observation makes us only *lend ourselves*, so to speak, to the fiction: But causes the idea to feel very different from the external establish'd perswasions founded on memory and custom. They are somewhat of the same kind: But the one is much inferior to the other, both in its causes and effects. (T 1.3.10.11/SBN 631–2, emphasis added)[25]

The same is true of passions aroused in real life and those merely persuasive ones 'excited by poetical fictions'; there is a perceptible difference between the two, and despite poetic magic a real passion is never confused with one inspired by literature, a point reflected in the pleasure afforded by passions that would otherwise be a source of pain. 'A passion, which is disagreeable in real life, may afford the highest entertainment in a tragedy, or epic poem. In the latter case it lies not with that weight upon us: It feels less firm and solid' (T 1.3.10.10/SBN 631). As Hume puts it succinctly in the Abstract, 'Poetry, with all its art, can never cause a passion, like one in real life. It fails in the original conception of its objects, which never *feel* in the same manner as those which command our belief and opinion' (T Abstract, 22/SBN 654). The imagination can imbue its creations with such force and vivacity that they strike the imagination to persuade an audience, but not to the point where they believe in the real existence of objects to which the ideas refer.

The fact that poet and audience can always distinguish poetic fiction from matter of fact, however, does not mean that poetry cannot be abused as well as used wisely. On the one hand, poetry improves the temper and encourages elegance of sentiment; it excites soft emotions, draws the mind away from hurry and business, teaches us to cherish reflection, and encourages tranquillity and agreeable melancholy (see E 7, 534 and 549). The charms of poetry can also aid the philosopher – the 'painter' as we shall see in Chapter 7 – in engaging the imagination to make us 'feel the difference between vice and virtue' (EHU 1.1/SBN 6) and encourage the reader to bestow praise and blame on what deserves it (see E 228). A strong imagination, on the other hand, also undermines the critical faculty, and makes it more difficult to resist an idea when it is painted out 'in all the colours of eloquence' (T 1.3.10.8/SBN 123). Poets address themselves to the passions, which, when encouraged, become intemperate and a potential vehicle for vice (see E 567). Poetry should aim at a mean between dull repetition and the distracting adornment of nature but, given the pleasure the imagination takes in novelty and surprise, over-refinement and excessive ornament are ever-present temptations. The dangers here are no worse than affectation, conceit and degeneracy of taste (see E 196), not to be wished for, perhaps, but less pernicious than the potential effects of false religion and philosophy, which (as we shall see in Chapter 7), Hume regards as having damaging consequences in the rounds of social, political and moral life.

When Hume emphasises the distorting power of the poetic arts, then, and their proclivity to produce temporary states of persuasion, he sees them as inherently deceitful. Poetry is always one remove from reality, which it disguises in the bright colours of its representations (see E 240). There is never, to use Keats' phrase, any 'truth' of imagination; in transcending experience, poets trade actuality for fiction, and only under the influence of some poetic enthusiasm can they believe they have arrived at knowledge and achieved the 'right relationship with the world'.[26] The business of poetry is to give pleasure by appealing to the passions, and, consequently, the only possible coin of the poet's trade is fiction, the deliberate employment of language to manipulate an audience. In this spirit Hume writes that the 'beauties [of poetry] are founded on falsehood and fiction, on hyperboles, metaphor, and an abuse and perversion of terms from their natural meaning' (E 231), which puts them in the company of priests and allegorists, who corrupted real events and heroes and thus 'successively improved the wonder and astonishment of the ignorant multitude' (NHR 5.6). 'Painters too and sculptors came in for their fair share of profit in the sacred mysteries;' he adds, 'and furnishing men with sensible representations of their divinities, whom they cloathed in human figures, gave great encrease to the public devotion, and determined its object' (NHR 5.7).

It is in this vein that Hume goes so far as to call poets 'liars by profession, [who] always endeavour to give an air of truth to their fictions' (T 1.3.10.5/SBN 121). Since the 'whole art of the poet is employed, in rouzing and supporting the compassion and indignation, the anxiety and resentment of his audience' (E 217), they have much in common with 'harmless' or 'common' liars whose 'universal intention is to please and entertain' and whose behaviour is condemned on account of the general love of truth that is universally approved (EMP 8.6/SBN 263).[27] He writes:

> We find that common liars always magnify, in their narrations, all kinds of danger, pain, distress, sickness, deaths, murders, and cruelties; as well as joy, beauty, mirth, and magnificence. It is an absurd secret, which they have for pleasing their company, fixing their attention, and attaching them to such marvellous relations, by the passions and emotions, which they excite. (E 217–18)

Much 'vulgar lying' of this sort, Hume argues, is a way for those whose lives are devoid of real adventures to satisfy their vanity by inventing events or, where the events are real, forging a connection to them that otherwise does not exist (T 2.1.8.6/SBN 301). Poets achieve their effects in similar ways, and as the mendacity of harmless liars finds its place in 'humorous stories' that are 'agreeable and entertaining' (EMP 8.6), so poets mix reality with fable (E 422) and, like Homer, throw themselves 'headlong into chimæra', unable to treat their subjects 'without a multitude of false subtilties and refinements' (E 115). Poets of this sort might seem dangerous, but their fictions are always artificial, and however profound the poetic enthusiasm appears, it is always fleeting and the professed belief a phantom one.

The Rules of Art

In aesthetics, as in other areas of human life, Hume praises the great advance of empirical or 'practical' science in discovering regularities or general principles amid the diversity of human experience. These principles are appropriately thought of as abridgements, since they express formally the regularities that give order to the practices in question. Thus, in judgements of beauty and deformity, it is possible to isolate 'what has been universally found to please in all countries and in all ages', as Hume writes in 'Of the Standard of Taste', and thus to allow 'rules of composition' to be 'fixed'; reflection reveals common features of works that have as a matter of fact elicited pleasure rather than pain.[28] Once discovered, this standard of taste can be used to reconcile the various sentiments that different individuals necessarily express. Hume does not deny that in practice there are differences in the actual judgements that individuals make, but since beauty and deformity are based on principles of human nature, they are explicable in terms of obstructions – ignorance, prejudice, lack of sense, want of delicacy and dearth of practice – that intervene between the potential to experience beauty and the appropriate sentiment of pleasure that constitutes it. 'But when these obstructions are removed', Hume writes, 'the beauties, which are naturally fitted to excite agreeable sentiments, immediately display their energy; and while the world endures, they maintain their authority over the minds of men'. For this reason Homer was admired in Athens and Rome and, while his greatness may be temporarily dulled by fad and fashion, over the course of historical time 'All the changes of climate, government, religion, and language, have not been able to obscure his glory' (E 233). When these regularities in taste over long periods of time are made explicit, there is good reason, in Hume's view, to speak of general or universal principles, or what he often refers to as 'rules of criticism' or 'rules of art'.

As some commentators have emphasised, as in his deprecation of linguistic distortion, the content Hume gives to these rules is largely conventional, and although, as Mossner points out, they are empirical rather than a priori, there is some truth to the observation that along with his eighteenth-century contemporaries, Hume wanders little from the 'well-worn highroad of seventeenth-century reason and Neo-Classical taste'.[29] As in his orthodox view of language and metaphor, however, this easy assessment threatens to obscure the real philosophical foundations of Hume's approach to criticism and his elucidation of principles governing works of great literature. These principles arise from reflecting on experience, and can be taken either as philosophical or critical. As philosophical principles, they have descriptive or explanatory value for the moral scientist, since they show how poets achieve their effects by creating ideas that conform to human nature and elicit agreeable sentiments in an audience. As critical principles, on the other hand, they have prescriptive or normative value for the creative artist by offering guidelines for writing great poetry. Like following a recipe, successful application of the rules is never straightforward or automatic, and the active imagination of the poet is required to use the recipe to good effect. Indeed, writers of genius never follow such rules explicitly, and though a 'perfect' imagination or that 'magical faculty of the soul' is always obvious in great works of art, the cause of the satisfaction it conveys often remains elusive (EPM 8.14).[30]

As the imagination itself displays 'universal principles' that make it 'uniform with itself in all times and places' (T 1.1.4.1/SBN 10), so do the creative arts that arise from it. Poetry 'can never submit to exact truth', but must at the same time 'be confined by rules of art, discovered to the author either by genius or observation' (E 231). These, in turn, are 'founded on qualities of human nature; and the quality of human nature, which requires a consistency in every performance, . . . which renders the mind incapable of passing in a moment from one passion and disposition to a quite different one' (T 2.2.8.18/SBN 379). Even in works of genius, in the lines of Homer and the notes of Beethoven, the work must conform to rules of criticism without which the art would fail to elicit further the movement of the imagination among its ideas. Moreover, as we have seen already, the genius of the poet consists in eliciting this response in an audience, which depends in turn on natural principles governing the passive imagination; the success of any literary work, therefore, depends on the degree to which a writer satisfies the criteria governing whether or not the intended response is brought about. These criteria are identical to the natural principles of the passive imagination that determine whether a poetic representation of the world is correct, that is, whether it has produced the appropriate ideas in the mind of the audience and facilitated the easy transition of ideas that produces pleasure: the imagination should be enlivened without becoming enervated. Accordingly, we can specify three general rules of criticism that Hume considers tantamount to techniques, which, if followed, facilitate this movement but if violated hinder it; poets whose works do not display these rules have effectively failed in the art of poetry.

Poetic Ideas as Plausible Fictions

First, in order to create a world that engages an audience, poetic depictions must be plausible fictions. The poet has the express task of persuading or convincing an audience about the poetic reality of events and thus enflaming the audience with the same passions that 'actuate' the figures in the work (EPM 5.26/SBN 222). For this reason, a 'painter, who intended to represent a passion or emotion of any kind, wou'd endeavour to get a sight of the person actuated by a like emotion, in order to enliven his ideas, and give them a force and vivacity superior to what is found in those, which are mere fictions of the imagination' (T 1.3.5.5/SBN 85). To produce indifference or check the 'progress of the passions' is a recipe for poetic failure (EPM 5.28/SBN 222). The imagination is satisfied as long as it can make an easy transition among its ideas, and while this does not reproduce experience and inspire true belief, the force and vivacity must be sufficient to bring about a temporary state of persuasion; the ideas must approximate truth while remaining distinct from real existence and matter of fact. ''Tis certain', Hume observes, 'we cannot take pleasure in any discourse, where our judgement gives no assent to those images which are presented to our fancy'. Poets might be 'liars by profession', but where they fail in giving an 'air of truth to their fictions ... their performances, however ingenious, will never be able to afford much pleasure'. 'In short', he concludes, 'we may observe, that even when ideas have no influence on the will and passions, truth and reality are still requisite, in order to make them entertaining to the imagination' (T 1.3.10.5/SBN 121).

The 'truth' and 'reality' of poetry, however, cannot be of the sort associated with impressions and copies made by memory, since poetic fictions can never satisfy the condition that the idea produces the 'same effect with those impressions, which are immediately present to the senses and perception' (T 1.3.10.3/SBN 119). 'All the colours of poetry, however splendid', Hume writes, 'can never paint natural objects in such a manner as to make the description be taken for a real landscape. The most lively thought is still inferior to the dullest sensation' (EHU 2.1/SBN 17). While there is no question of producing belief, the poet must still succeed in facilitating the easy transition of the imagination among its ideas. The force and vivacity of poetic ideas should transform the world *and* have a foothold in common life. Excess or deficiency of either will produce passions that are overheated and enthusiastic, on one side, or cool and disinterested, on the other. In both cases, the audience becomes disconnected from the action and the work must fail. If poets aim to elicit an emotional response in the audience *and* give pleasure, they must be guided by experience and certain facts of human nature.

At the same time, if poetical fictions are free of experience completely – if they are too artificial or over-contrived – the passions would not be engaged and the poetry would be ineffectual. It is thus 'the business of poetry', Hume writes, 'to bring every affection near to us by lively imagery and representation, and make it *look like truth and reality*: A certain proof, that, wherever that reality is found, our minds are disposed to be strongly affected by it' (EPM 5.30/SBN 222–3, emphasis added). Poetry, in other words, creates its effects by allowing reality to enter, but never with the force and vivacity that accompanies belief arising from memory or belief-like states of natural fictions. The poet elicits 'fictitious sentiments' produced in a poetic reality rather than real sentiments experienced in common life, and for this reason we take pleasure in the poem, even if the sentiments – such as loss, sorrow, anguish and despair experienced in tragedy – are otherwise a source of pain to the literary character or would be to the spectator experiencing the same emotions outside the literary depiction (T 2.2.7.3/SBN 369).

In order to achieve this fine balance, poets require techniques to make ideas 'enter into the mind with facility, and prevail upon the fancy', that 'procure a more easy reception into the imagination for those extraordinary events, which they represent' (T 1.3.10.6/SBN 122). Thus:

> It is here esteemed contrary to the rules of art to represent any thing cool and indifferent. A distant friend, or a confident, who has no immediate interest in the catastrophe, ought, if possible, to be avoided by the poet; as communicating a like indifference to the audience, and checking the progress of the passions. (EPM 5.28/SBN 222)

At the same time, if the idea is to be plausible, it must refer to experience; for where the 'justness of the representation is lost', Hume contends, '. . . the mind is displeased to find a picture, which finds no resemblance to any original' (E 192). A poetic description of the Elysian fields, for example, is made more convincing when the poet has a beautiful meadow or garden in view (T 1.3.9.5/SBN 109), and good 'tragedians always borrow their fable, or at least the names of their principal actors, from some known passage in history'. Comic poets, on the other hand, are not required to go to such lengths because their characters are more familiar and 'enter easily into the conception, . . . even tho' at first sight they be known to be fictitious and the pure offspring of the fancy' (T 1.3.10.6/SBN 122).

The same rule applies to the depiction of characters in literary works. 'The persons introduced in tragedy and epic poetry', Hume writes, 'must be represented as reasoning, and thinking, and concluding, and acting, suitably to their character and circumstances; and without judgement, as well as taste and invention, a poet can never hope to succeed in so delicate an undertaking' (E 240). The words and actions of literary personae must be proportionate to the situations in which they find themselves, but without repeating scenes in every detail, which would be tedious and mundane. For 'with what pretence', Hume asks, 'could we employ our criticism upon any poet or polite author, if we could not pronounce the conduct and sentiments of his actors, either natural or unnatural, to such characters, and in such circumstances?' (EHU 8.18/SBN 90).

Poetic Works and Design

Second, a work of literature must exhibit order and coherence by having a plan and a design, created by the poet in conformity with the principles of association. Hume largely accepts the Aristotelian unities of time, place and action in this regard, but replaces the 'necessity of reason' with the 'novel explanation' of the principles of association to explain how these unities worked.[31] For Hume, what is true of experience generally is true of poetry in particular: even in our wildest and most wandering poetic reveries, our thoughts cannot 'be allowed to run at adventures, if we would produce a work, which will give any lasting entertainment to mankind' (EHU 3.10). For 'every kind of composition, even the most poetical, is nothing but a chain of propositions and reasonings; not always, indeed, the justest and most exact, but still plausible and specious, however disguised by the colouring of the imagination' (E 240). Without the active imagination of the author employed to discover and express the connections in this chain, the passive imagination of the audience is left without direction and it is impossible to take pleasure in the work. Hume writes:

> In all compositions of genius ... it is requisite, that the writer have some plan or object; and though he may be hurried from his plan by the vehemence of thought, as in an ode, or drop it carelessly, as in an epistle or essay, there must be some aim or intention, in his first setting out, if not in the composition of the whole work. A production without a design would resemble more the ravings of a madman, than the sober efforts of genius and learning. (EHU 3.5)

The poet enjoys some freedom in bringing this unity about, and may choose from different principles as long as regular connections are forged and an overall design emerges. The events in Ovid's *Metamorphoses*, for example, resemble one another in being fabulous transformations brought about by the power of the gods (EHU 3.7), as Homer unifies the life of Achilles through the hero's anger (EHU 3.10 and 16).

There are, however, limits to the poet's freedom of expression in creating unified literary works imposed by the general end that poetry has in view – to give pleasure – and the natural principles of the imagination that have to be propitiated if the easy transition between ideas that produces the agreeable sentiments is to be achieved. This proportioning of means to ends must be kept 'constantly in our view', Hume says, 'when we peruse any performance; and we must be able to judge how far the means employed are adapted to their respective purposes' (E 240). This is the case most notably in epic narratives familiar from Antiquity, exemplified by the *Odyssey* and the *Æneid*, which are unified by tracing causal connections among events (EHU 3.12). The poet unifies the whole by connecting events in a causal chain, but the literary form and the nature of human faculties effectively limit the writer. Hume makes this point by comparing poetry to the demands of historical and biographical narrative:

> The unity of action . . . to be found in biography or history, differs from that of epic poetry, not in kind, but in degree. In epic poetry, the connexion among the events is more close and sensible: The narration is not carried on through such a length of time: And the actors hasten to some remarkable period, which satisfies the curiosity of the reader. This conduct of the epic poet depends on that particular situation of the *Imagination* and of the *Passions*, which is supposed in that production. The imagination, both of writer and reader, is more enlivened, and the passions more enflamed than in history, biography, or any species of narration, which confine themselves to strict truth and reality. (EHU 3.10)

Given that epic achieves its end *poetically*, by representing the world to bring pleasure to an audience, it must unify events by achieving a fine balance between reality and fiction, enlivening the imagination enough to engage the audience but without the prolonged intensity that enervates them. Epic poets are therefore not entitled to recount events according to 'strict truth and reality'; this would be a memorial reiteration, and tracing connections to a distant origin – as Hume begins his *History* with an account of the ancient Britons, for example – would result in a work that, in literature at least, would extend to a tedious and exhausting length. The poet must still be careful to include sufficient reference to 'minute circumstances' in order to engage and amuse readers, but not so many details as to bore and exhaust them. Time itself must be represented poetically, sequences condensed and events glossed if the imagination is not be hindered in its movements. As Hume points out, the reader of the *Iliad* does not want to be informed every time Achilles ties his shoelaces, but there must be sufficient detail for the reader to engage with the unfolding action. Voltaire's play *La Henriade* suffers from insufficient detail, since 'events are run over with such rapidity, that we scarcely have leisure to become acquainted with the scene or action' (EHU 3.11). As Hume notes, ancient epics achieve this effect by employing the technique of 'oblique narrative' (storytelling through a character in retrospect) to ensure that 'events follow with rapidity, and in a very close connection: And the concern is preserved alive, and, by means of the near relations of the objects, continually encreases, from the beginning to the end of the narration' (EHU 3.12).

Further, poets should avoid making any abrupt and complete transition from one event, theme or character to another, which would interfere with the progress of the imagination. For

> were the poet to make a total digression from his subject, and introduce a new actor, nowise connected with the personages, the imagination, feeling a breach in the transition, would enter coldly into the new scene; would kindle by slow degrees; and in returning to the main subject of the poem, would pass, as it were, upon foreign ground, and have its concern to excite anew, in order to take part with the principal actors. (EHU 3.12)

For the same reason, a tragedian should never represent the hero as too ingenious and witty, which would interrupt the 'regular flowing of the passions and sentiments' and leave the audience untouched by the unfolding events (T 1.4.1.11/SBN 185–6), nor should serious and profound sentiments or different styles be combined in a single work. In such cases, Hume insists, the audience is obliged to compare things that are different in kind: a tragedy abounding in comic beauties and a comedy in tragic elements are contradictions in terms; the imagination is obliged continually to break from one and start afresh with the other. Where consistency is breached in such a manner, the imagination is interrupted and the effect of the writing lost.[32]

Poetic Works and Simplicity

Third, literature must exhibit simplicity – in thought, expression and composition – a virtue Hume prized in his work and his character.[33] Since the noblest works of art are 'beholden for their chief beauty to the force and happy influence of nature' (E 139), this aim can only be realised if the poet imitates nature itself. There is no reason for the poet to do more than put touches on a canvas already completed. When poets acknowledge themselves as understudies to the master and guide of nature, a world of poetic possibilities opens up as they at once discover techniques that can hardly fail to arouse sentiments of pleasure necessary to satisfy the imagination. Hume writes:

> It is a great mortification to the vanity of man, that his utmost art and industry can never equal the meanest of nature's productions, either for beauty or value. Art is only the under-workman, and is employed to give a few strokes of embellishment to those pieces, which come from the hand of the master. Some of the drapery may be of his drawing; but he is not allowed to touch the principal figure. Art may make a suit of clothes: But nature must produce a man. (E 138)

Objects are beautiful, in part, because they are structured in a way that fits our capacity to be affected; we take pleasure from harmonious compositions (EPM 5.37/SBN 224) and figures that are balanced (EPM 6.28/SBN 245), like the parts of an animal moving together in a perfect whole or a pillar slender at its top and wider at its base. 'From innumerable instances of this kind', Hume writes, '. . . we may conclude that beauty is nothing but a form, which produces pleasure, as deformity is a structure of parts, which conveys pain' (T 2.1.8.2/SBN 299). The same is true of poetic objects, where there is a natural fit between the beauty and unity of poetic representations and the capacity of the imagination to be affected by them. Hume observes:

> In all nobler productions of genius, there is a mutual relation and correspondence of parts; nor can either the beauties or blemishes be perceived by him, whose thought is not capacious enough to comprehend all those parts, and compare them with each other, in order to perceive the consistence and uniformity of the whole. (E 240)

At the same time as poets must not obscure the beauty of nature through excessive ornamentation and artifice, they must still represent rather than reiterate her features. Nature already possesses poise and balance, and her forms are fitted to produce pleasure in those with sufficient taste to detect them, but poetry nevertheless should offer readers *la belle nature* rather than the mere repetition of detail. Literature should aim to balance the imitation of nature's inherent simplicity and refinement with a representation of her with embellishment enough to engage the imagination (see E 191–6).

Such a balance is difficult to attain – it is the work of genius – but poetry is more likely to be realised successfully if poetic representations follow nature as closely as possible. Art conceived and executed in this manner will bring lasting enjoyment and endure through the ages: 'A pleasant comedy, which paints the manners of the age, and exposes a faithful picture of nature, is a durable work, and is transmitted to the latest posterity' (H 6.153).

In short, the general rule for poets is to avoid any hint of Locke's figurative speeches, flourishes that distort natural language and inhibit the easy movement of the imagination. The imagination is pleased by the novelty of innovative productions, but those 'which are merely surprising', Hume writes, 'without being natural, can never give any lasting entertainment to the mind. To draw chimeras is not, properly speaking, to copy or imitate' (E 192). 'Fine writing', on the other hand, '. . . consists of sentiments, which are natural, without being obvious' (E 191), so that 'Uncommon expressions, strong flashes of wit, pointed similes, and epigrammatic turns . . . are a disfigurement, rather than an embellishment of discourse'. Such flourishes in literary works are equivalent to the multiplicity of ornaments on a Gothic building: as the eye is 'distracted . . . and loses the whole by its minute attention to the parts; . . . [so] the mind, perusing a work overstocked with wit, is fatigued and disgusted with the constant endeavour to shine and surprise' (E 192–3). For this reason, Hume considers the pastoral form of poetry to be the most entertaining since it mimics nature as closely as poetry is able and presents scenes that are best fitted to arouse agreeable sentiments in an audience. The 'chief source of its pleasure', Hume writes, 'arises from those images of a gentle and tender tranquillity, which it represents in its personages, and of which it communicates a like sentiment to the reader'. So naturally suited are these scenes to the imagination of an audience that there is hardly need to convert painful scenes into a source of pleasure. Consequently, where ideas of pain and suffering *are* included in pastorals, they produce the opposite of the intended effect. Thus, in Hume's estimation:

> [The Italian poet] Sannazarius, who transferred the scene to the sea-shore, though he presented the most magnificent object in nature, is confessed to have erred in his choice. The idea of toil, labour, and danger, suffered by the fishermen, is painful; by an unavoidable sympathy, which attends every conception of human happiness or misery. (EPM 5.29/SBN 222)

Hume's idea of simplicity and refinement is manifest most clearly in the literature of Antiquity, the age of Augustus and the Greeks at the height of Athenian culture, distinguished by their 'correctness and delicacy' (H 6.543) and 'an amiable simplicity, which ... is so fitted to express the genuine movements of nature and passions' (H 5.149). Homer, Hume writes, 'copies true, natural manners, which, however rough or uncultivated, will always form an agreeable and interesting picture' (H 4.386). From 'the simple purity of Athens', however, Hume discerns an increasing desire for novelty, a gradual move away from the simple depiction of nature to increasing artifice and adornment, which leads authors 'wide of simplicity and nature' and encourages a 'degeneracy of taste' (E 196). 'The glaring figures of discourse, the pointed antithesis, the unnatural conceit, the jingle of words; such false ornaments were not employed by early writers' (H 5.149). This 'general degeneracy of style and language' becomes pronounced in 'that tinsel eloquence, which is observable in many of the Roman writers, from which Cicero himself is not wholly exempted, and which so much prevails in Ovid, Seneca, Lucan, Martial, and the Plinys' (H 5.150), comes of age in the rebirth of letters in Europe in the sixteenth and seventeenth centuries, and reaches fruition in the Restoration dramas in the reign of Charles II. 'The productions, represented at that time on the state, were such monsters of extravagance and folly', Hume declares, 'so utterly destitute of all reason or even common sense; that they would be the disgrace of English literature, had not the nation made atonement for its former admiration of them, by the total oblivion to which they are now condemned' (H 6.542). Even before that, under Elizabeth Tudor and the Stuarts, learning was 'attired in the same unnatural garb, which it wore at the time of its decay among the Greeks and Romans', as is evident in Shakespeare, whose works involve irregularities, absurdities and deformities (H 5.151); Johnson, who did little more than translate 'into bad English the beautiful passages of the Greeks' (H5.151); and John Donne, whose satires, in Hume's view, though they contain 'some flashes of wit and ingenuity ... are totally suffocated and buried by the harshest and most uncouth expressions, that is anywhere to be met with' (H 5.152).

In fact, Hume gives praise only when writers come close to the Augustan/Greek model, and then it is for elements or particular works rather than for a corpus as a whole. For example, he writes that Edmund Spenser contains great beauties, a sweet and harmonious versification, easy elocution, a fine imagination. Yet does the perusal of his work become so tedious, that one never finishes it from the mere pleasure which it affords: It soon becomes a kind of task-reading; and it requires some effort and resolution to carry us on to the end of his long performance. (H 4.386)

In comparison with Homer, the 'pencil of the English poet [in *The Faerie Queen*] was employed in drawing the affectations, and conceits, and fopperies of chivalry, which appear ridiculous as soon as they lose the recommendation of the mode' (H 4.386). Hume also finds much to praise in the 'great poet' John Milton (DNR 10.13) and bemoans his neglect. Yet 'Even in the Paradise Lost, his capital performance', he remarks, 'there are very long passages, amounting to near a third of the work, almost wholly destitute of harmony and elegance, nay, of all vigour of imagination' (H 6.150–1). Similarly, Hume sees great genius in some of Dryden's compositions – *A Song for St Cecilia's Day* and *Absalom and Achitophel* – but considers his plays to be 'utterly disfigured by vice or folly or both. . . . Even his fables are ill-chosen tales, conveyed in an incorrect, though spirited versification'. Some pieces, Hume concludes, constitute the 'refuse of our language' (H 6.543).

Hume's criticisms might be harsh and are certainly contestable, but they are neither arbitrary nor inconsistent with his view of literature and the rules governing good composition. The rules of art are abridgements of practice and express an ideal at which poets should aim. It is in the nature of genius to create rare works that come close to this perfection, judged as such by their success in engaging the imagination to produce pleasure. This is only possible if the poet attends to the principles governing that faculty, since these are the criteria, the satisfaction of which determines the success of a poetic work. As Hume's comments on various writers make clear, there is still much value in writing that falls short of genius, and literature remains a source of great pleasure even if it does not follow all the rules of criticism or follows particular ones imperfectly. Hume is quick to point out, though, that as in apparently miraculous violations of the laws of nature, where the event is accountable by way of intervening and equally regular causes (EHU 10.12/SBN 114–15), when a work violates the rules *and* gives pleasure, other elements that do conform to good taste will be found. The Italian Renaissance poet Ariosto, for example, repels insofar as he breaks some rules – 'by monstrous and improbable fictions, by his bizarre mixture of the serious and comic styles, by the want of coherence in his stories, or by the continual interruptions of his narration' – but charms in conforming to others – 'by the force and clearness of his expression, by the readiness and variety of his inventions, and by his natural pictures of the passions' (E 232). Similarly, that the English dramatist Matthew Prior successfully combined the comic and the tragic in a single volume does not undermine the rule against such juxtapositions, and is explicable in terms of the reader who 'considers these performances as entirely different, and by this break in the ideas, breaks the progress of the affections, and hinders the one from influencing or contradicting the other' (T 2.2.8.18/SBN 380).

At work here is that productive power of the imagination to create poetic fictions by transposing and changing its ideas and following its tendency to move easily among them, with a view to creating a whole and feeling the pleasure that brings. Where this smooth and easy passage is lost, the art of poetry is wanting. Whether poetic ideas are viewed positively as the offspring of genius or negatively as the bastard of deceit, poetry rearranges ideas and departs from experience, and in so doing pleasantly deceives its willing audience by setting up a new and a poetic reality, distinct from but in important respects beholden to matter of fact. In Hume's view, the imagination is both the active source of poetic genius and the means by which an audience is passively affected by poetic artifice. Poets are thus constrained by certain principles of human nature if they are to achieve the emotional response they desire. These principles are manifest as poetic techniques or, otherwise conceived, rules of criticism that abridge poetic practice and offer guidelines for the creation of entertaining and even great literary works. At the same time, because poetical fictions are self-conscious creations, they never rise to the status of belief.

Despite his strong words about the inherent mendacity of the poetic arts, Hume recognised and enjoyed them as part of a refined, tasteful and civilised existence, and since the objects in a poetic reality are easily distinguished from those with real existence, even minds lifted high on the wings of poetry do not pose dangers of the sort associated with the gloomy fictions of religion or the ideological ones of philosophy. For this reason, we might expect Hume to have banished philosophers rather than poets from the polis, preferring the company of those who entertain and inspire their audience rather than others who are more likely to depress or threaten it.

Notes

1. See Peter Kivy, 'Hume's Neighbour's Wife: An Essay on the Evolution of Hume's Aesthetics', *The British Journal of Aesthetics*, 23: 3 (1983), p. 201, and Peter Jones, 'Hume's Literary and Aesthetic Theory', in *The Cambridge Companion to Hume*, ed. David Fate Norton (Cambridge: Cambridge University Press, 1993), p. 256. More generous evaluations of Hume's interest in the arts are to be found in Laird, *Hume's Philosophy of Human Nature*, pp. 276–7, and James Noxon, 'Hume's Opinion of Critics', *Journal of Aesthetics and Art Criticism*, 20: 2 (1961), pp. 157 and 161.

2. Stephen K. Land, *From Signs to Propositions: The Concept of Form in Eighteenth-Century Semantic Theory* (London: Longman, 1974), p. 22.

3. See Land, *From Signs to Propositions*, Ch. 2. For the place of Hume in eighteenth-century aesthetics more generally, see Guyer, *A History of Modern Aesthetics,* vol. 1, Ch. 2; Costelloe, *The British Aesthetic Tradition*, Ch. 2; Dabney Townsend, *Hume's Aesthetic Theory: Taste and Sentiment* (New York: Routledge, 2001), Chs. 1 and 2; Peter Jones, *Hume's Sentiments: Their Ciceronian and French Context* (Edinburgh: Edinburgh University Press, 1982); Peter Kivy, *The Seventh Sense: Francis Hutcheson and Eighteenth-Century British Aesthetics*, 2nd edn, rev. (Oxford: Clarendon Press, [1976] 2003), esp. Ch. 1; and Teddy Brunius, *David Hume on Criticism*. Figura 2. Studies Edited by the Institute of Art History, University of Uppsala (Stockholm: Almquist & Wiksell, 1952), Ch. 6.

4. For an overview of literature (up to 2004 at least) relevant to the discussion in this chapter, see Timothy M. Costelloe, 'Hume's Aesthetics: The Literature and Directions for Future Research', *Hume Studies*, 30: 1 (2004), pp. 87–126. For extended treatments of Hume's aesthetics, see Townsend, *Hume's Aesthetic Theory*, and Costelloe, *Aesthetics and Morals in the Philosophy of David Hume*.

5. See also T 2.1.8.6/SBN 301; EMP Appx. 1.14/SBN 291–2, and E 165, 235. Hume's view also reveals important points of departure

from Locke. See Kivy, 'Hume's Neighbour's Wife'; William H. Halberstadt, 'A Problem in Hume's Aesthetics', *Journal of Aesthetics and Art Criticism*, 30: 2 (1971), pp. 209–11; Carolyn W. Korsmeyer, 'Hume and the Foundations of Taste', *Journal of Aesthetics and Art Criticism*, 35: 2 (1976), pp. 201–15; and George Dickie, *The Century of Taste: The Philosophical Odyssey of Taste in the Eighteenth Century* (Oxford: Oxford University Press, 1996), pp. 123–4. Cf. Simon Blackburn, 'Hume on the Mezzanine Level', *Hume Studies*, 19: 2 (1993), pp. 273–88, and Theodore A. Gracyk, 'Rethinking Hume's Standard of Taste', *Journal of Aesthetics and Art Criticism*, 52: 2 (1994), pp. 169–82.

6. See Peter Railton, 'Aesthetic Value, Moral Value, and the Ambitions of Naturalism', in Jerrold Levinson (ed.), *Aesthetics and Ethics: Essays at the Intersection* (Cambridge: Cambridge University Press, 1998), pp. 67 and 93; and Nick Zangwill, 'Hume, Taste, and Teleology', *Philosophical Papers*, 23: 1 (1994), p. 9.

7. See Peter Jones, 'Hume's Aesthetics Reassessed', *Philosophical Quarterly*, 26 (1976), pp. 48–62; Jeffrey Wieand, 'Hume's Two Standards of Taste', *Philosophical Quarterly*, 34: 135 (1984), pp. 129–42; and Roger A. Shiner, 'Hume and the Causal Theory of Taste', *Journal of Aesthetics and Art Criticism*, 54: 3 (1996), pp. 237–49.

8. Similar remarks are to be found *inter alia* at T 2.3.9.4/SBN 439, EPM 5.1, 6.22 and 6.28.

9. For commentary that emphasises this aspect of Hume aesthetics, see Katherine Everett Gilbert and Helmut Kuhn, *A History of Esthetics*, 2nd edn, rev. (Westport, CT: Greenwood Publishers, [1939] 1972), p. 246; Redding S. Sugg, Jr, 'Hume's Search for the Key with the Leather Thong', *Journal of Aesthetics and Art Criticism*, 16: 1 (1957), pp. 96–102; Harold Osborne, 'Some Theories of Aesthetic Judgment', *Journal of Aesthetics and Art Criticism*, 38: 2 (1979), pp. 135–44; Paul Guyer, 'The Standard of Taste and the "Most Ardent Desire of Society"', in *Pursuits of Reason: Essays in Honor of Stanley Cavell*, ed. Ted Cohen, Paul Guyer and Hilary Putman (Lubbock: Texas Tech University Press, 1993), p. 41; James Shelley, 'Hume and the Nature of Taste', *Journal of Aesthetics and Art Criticism*, 56: 1 (1998), pp. 29–38, and Rochelle Gurstein, 'Taste and the "Conversible World" in the Eighteenth Century', *Journal of the History of Ideas*, 61: 2 (2000), pp. 203–21.

10. On this point, see Ralph Cohen, 'The Rationale of Hume's Literary Inquiries', in *David Hume: Many-sided Genius*, ed. Kenneth R.

Merrill and Robert W. Shahan (Norman: University of Oklahoma Press, 1976), pp. 97–115, esp. 104–6.

11. The final sentences of EHU 3.3 and 3.4–18 in their entirety do not appear in the 1777 edition of the first *Enquiry* used by SBN, but do appear in all editions from 1748 to 1772, and are included by Beauchamp (pp. 102–7).

12. Land, *From Signs to Propositions*, pp. 31 and 35. See John Dryden, *On Dramatic Poesy and Other Critical Essays*, ed. George Watson (London: Dent & Dutton, 1962).

13. Don Garrett, 'The Literary Arts in Hume's Science of the Fancy', *Kriterion*, 44: 108 (2003), p. 168.

14. See, for example, Margaret Paton, 'Hume on Tragedy', *British Journal of Aesthetics*, 13: 2 (1973), p. 121, and Mark Packer, 'Dissolving the Paradox of Tragedy', *Journal of Aesthetics and Art Criticism*, 47: 3 (1989), p. 212.

15. See Alex Neill, 'Yanal and Others on Hume and Tragedy', *Journal of Aesthetics and Art Criticism,* 50: 2 (1992), p. 152, and 'Hume's Singular Phænomenon', *British Journal of Aesthetics*, 39: 2 (1999), pp. 112–25. For an overview of the debate and some contributors to it, see Costelloe, 'Hume's Aesthetics', pp. 107–9.

16. See Neill, 'Hume's Singular Phænomenon', p. 113.

17. Hume also points out that disposition and national character sometimes determine where such limits are drawn. The English are so modest and of good sense that 'their comic poets, to move them, must have recourse to obscenity; their tragic poets to blood and slaughter: And hence their orators, being deprived of any such resource, have abandoned altogether the hopes of moving them, and have confined themselves to plain argument and reasoning' (E 622).

18. Hume sees the same principles at work in religion where, through conversion, the 'most dismal and gloomy passions' are a source of pleasure (T 1.3.9.15/SBN 115). I discuss this in more detail in Chapter 6.

19. See Adam Smith's letter to William Strahan (dated 9 November 1776), L2: 450–2, and Adam Potkay, *The Passion for Happiness: Samuel Johnson and David Hume* (Ithaca: Cornell University Press, 2000), pp. 194–6.

20. Ernest Campbell Mossner, 'Hume's "Of Criticism"', in *Studies in Criticism and Aesthetics, 1660–1800. Essays in Honor of Samuel Holt Monk*, ed. Howard Anderson and John S. Shea (Minneapolis: University of Minnesota Press, 1967), pp. 244–5.

21. See Richetti, *Philosophical Writing*, pp. 5–6.

22. Leopold Damrosch, *Fictions of Reality in the Age of Hume and Johnson* (Madison: University of Wisconsin Press, 1989), p. 58. See also Land, *From Signs to Propositions*, pp. 50–74; Gilbert and Kuhn, *A History of Esthetics*, Ch. 8; and M. A. Box, *The Suasive Art of David Hume* (Princeton: Princeton University Press, 1990), Ch. 2.

23. See Adam Potkay, *The Fate of Eloquence in the Age of Hume* (Ithaca: Cornell University Press, 1994), esp. Chs. 1 and 2. The quotes are taken from pp. 2 and 4. Potkay regards Hume's 'Of Eloquence' as an ambivalent expression of disappointment at and celebration of the fact that Athenian warmth had been defeated by the coolness of English manners: in the essay, Potkay proposes, 'Hume attests to the loss of eloquence that he regrets in the very act of writing about it with analytic distance' (p. 49).

24. Norton deletes this passage entirely without reproducing the original; SBN keeps the original and lists the addendum in the Appendix (see SBN 630–2).

25. This passage appeared in Hume's Appendix with instructions to be inserted at the end of T 1.3.10. In the penultimate sentence, Hume's original has 'eternal' (SBN 632), which Norton changes to 'external' in his edition. For present purposes, nothing material hinges on whether one chooses the original or the amended reading.

26. See Keats' letter 31, in *The Poetical and Other Writings of John Keats* Vol 6: p. 98, and for a discussion of the concept, Andrew J. Welburn, *The Truth of Imagination* (New York: St Martin's Press, 1989), pp. 3–4.

27. On at least one occasion, Hume is willing to credit poets with 'a certain taste or common instinct' that led them to recognise the artificial character of justice, a fact that had escaped the philosophical mind, at least. See T 3.2.2.15–16/SBN 493–4.

28. See, in this context, Garrett, 'The Literary Arts in Hume's Science of the Fancy', pp. 173–4, and Costelloe, *Aesthetics and Morals in the Philosophy of David Hume*, Ch. 1.

29. Gilbert and Kuhn, *A History of Esthetics*, p. 233. See also Mary Mothersill, 'Hume and the Paradox of Taste', in George Dickie, Richard Scalfani and Ronald Roblin (eds), *Aesthetics: A Critical Anthology*, 2nd edn (New York: St Martin's Press, 1989), pp. 269–86, and Mossner, 'Hume's "Of Criticism"', pp. 199 and 243.

30. The concept of rules as abridgements is borrowed from Michael Oakeshotte, 'Rationalism in Politics', in Michael Oakeshotte, *Rationalism in Politics and Other Essays*, new and expanded edn (Indianapolis: Liberty Fund, [1962] 1991), pp. 5–42.

31. See Gilbert and Kuhn, *A History of Esthetics*, p. 235.
32. See EPM 8.12/SBN 266 and T 2.2.8.18/SBN 379–80. Hume follows Horace and Addison in decrying the tragic-comic style. See, for example, Horace, *The Art of Poetry* 2.1–9.23, in *Satires, Epistles, The Art of Poetry*, trans. H. Rushton Fairclough, Loeb Classical Library (Cambridge, MA: Harvard University Press, 1926), and Addison, *Spectator* No. 409, p. 530.
33. Hume wrote to Hugh Blair of an experience in Paris: 'what gave me chief pleasure was to find that most of the elogiums bestowed on me turned on my personal character; my naivety and simplicity of manners, the candour and mildness of my disposition &c.' (L I, 437), quoted in Damrosch, *Fictions of Reality in the Age of Johnson and Hume*, p. 19.

5

History

In this chapter we focus our attention on the role of the imagination in Hume's approach to history. Hume is rare among philosophers for being also a practising historian, and in his own lifetime and for a century thereafter he was better known for his seven-volume *History of England* than for the *Treatise*, *Enquiries* and *Essays*, for which he is now principally famous. As David Fate Norton and Richard Popkin document, the *History* had a long and illustrious career: it remained in print until the last decade of the nineteenth century, going through six editions while Hume was alive and (on their estimate, writing in 1965) 'about 175' posthumously. It remained the standard work on the subject until eclipsed by Thomas Babington Macaulay's *History of England* (1848), a work considerably narrower in historical scope.[1] As an active philosopher and practising historian, it is not surprising that Hume was sensitive both to matters of historiography – the methodological issues pertaining to the practice of isolating sources, selecting evidence and crafting a narrative – and to issues that fall (anachronistically) under 'philosophy of history', concerning historical understanding, historical knowledge and literary representation. The line between Hume's historiographical and philosophical concerns is rarely, if ever, clearly demarcated, but the complex issues they raise come together in what he refers to as 'philosophical history'.[2]

In order to appreciate what Hume means by this term, and to elucidate more generally how he understands the relationship between imagination, history and historical practice, I propose to frame the discussion in terms of aesthetics, extending some of the insights from the previous chapter. This approach might at first appear arbitrary or unwarranted, but we may put such worries to rest by noting how Hume himself provides impetus for pursuing this line of inquiry. In numerous remarks, he explicitly juxtaposes the craft of the historian against the art of the poet in order to highlight the strong connection of the former to the faculty of memory rather than imagination, emphasising how it is beholden to fact rather than fiction: unlike the poet who creates a poetic reality by subverting experience, the historian aims to depict it by reiterating the sequence of past events as accurately as possible, and when historians depart from matter of fact their narrative becomes false. At the same time, Hume emphasises how historians also rely on the imagination, for two reasons. First, the subject matter of history is available only indirectly, through the existence of written record, itself based largely on the testimony of others, which has to be made available through reconstructing the past; a historical depiction is thus a recreation, a tensed representation of experience, direct access to which is by definition impossible. Second, historians are obliged to represent historical events in a way that enlivens the imagination of the audience and procures a smooth and easy transition among the ideas they create in order to inspire true belief in the narrative they construct.

For these reasons, historians find themselves in a position that is both different from and compatible with that of the poet. On the one hand, they must embrace the principles of memory to copy the world with accuracy and truth, and reject the tendency of the imagination to lead them into fictions that depart from matter of fact and real existence. On the other hand, they depend upon the imagination both to bring past events into a vivid present and portray them in such a way that carries conviction for the reader. In so doing, they transform ordinary experience, create agreeable ideas, and do so deliberately, requirements that can be framed as rules of historical art comparable to the rules of criticism, which, as we saw in the previous chapter, govern what counts as good literature. In the final analysis, Hume acknowledges, historical facts are qualitatively indistinguishable from poetic fictions, but they can be differentiated from them in the same way as ideas of memory differ from fictions of the imagination, namely by the amount of force and vivacity they contain, and, due to their source in impressions of sense and memory, the degree of belief and conviction they ultimately inspire.

Testimony and Historical Testimony

Before considering Hume's approach to history, it is important to understand clearly what he means by a concept central to it, namely that of 'testimony' and, more specifically, 'historical testimony', upon which the practice of the historian depends. That Hume has a 'theory' of testimony, as some have proposed, seems doubtful, but he does clearly indicate what he means by the term. Considered from the point of view of his theory of ideas, testimony consists (to paraphrase Tony Pitson's characterisation) of words (written or spoken) that are connected causally as effects with ideas, which in turn represent facts in the world, and of which the testimony is intended as a report. The ideas also *resemble* the facts – a point Hume exploits to explain the human tendency to credulity – which is a singular feature of testimony:

> Other effects only point to their causes in an oblique manner; but the testimony of men does it directly, and is to be consider'd as an image as well as an effect. No wonder, therefore, we are so rash in drawing our inferences from it, and are less guided by experience in our judgments concerning it, than in those upon any other subject. (T 1.3.9.12/SBN 113)

Historians rely on testimony and for that reason must take pains not to be so rash in drawing their conclusions as their evidence might tempt them to be.[3]

Hume's view of testimony has been seen to involve two questions. The first speaks to the 'epistemology of testimony', to employ a phrase from Alvin Goldman, which '. . . concerns the conditions or circumstances in which a hearer is *justified or warranted* in accepting a speaker's testimony that p'.[4] Responses to this question among contemporary epistemologists resolve largely into one of two camps, either the 'non-reductionist' whose proponents (to quote Jennifer Lackey's characterisation) hold that 'testimony is *just as basic* a source of justification (warrant, entitlement, knowledge, etc.) as sense perception, memory, inference, and the like', or the 'reductionist', whose members hold that 'hearers must have sufficiently good positive reasons for accepting a given report, reasons that are themselves ineliminably based on the testimony of others', which means that the 'justification of testimony is *reduced* to the justification we have for sense perception, memory, and inductive inference'.[5] Largely as a result of the influential treatment by C. A. J. Coady, Hume has been placed among the reductionists and his view thus interpreted criticised as incoherent.[6]

In the present context, this debate is relevant insofar as Hume's defenders have often emphasised that not only is he not a reductionist and thus immune from the criticisms levelled by Coady, but that he is also interested in quite a different question – the second one mentioned above – concerning how we *acquire beliefs through testimony*.[7] This elision of the justification and acquisition of beliefs, and the misreading of Hume that follows upon it, is well illustrated in debate over the interpretation of an important passage from the *Treatise* where Hume describes the 'chains' of cause and effect that give rise to belief in historical narratives. He writes:

> [W]e may choose any point in history, and consider for what reason we either believe or reject it. Thus we believe that CAESAR was kill'd in the senate-house on the *ides* of *March*; and that because this fact is establish'd on the unanimous testimony of historians, who agree to assign this precise time and place to that event. Here are certain characters and letters present either to our memory or senses; which characters we likewise remember to have been us'd as the signs of certain ideas; and these ideas were either in the minds of such as were immediately present at that action, and receiv'd the ideas directly from its existence; or they were deriv'd from the testimony of others, and that again from another testimony, by a visible gradation, till we arrive at those who were eye-witnesses and spectators of the event. 'Tis obvious all this chain of argument or connexion of causes and effects, is at first founded on those characters or letters, which are seen or remember'd, and that without the authority either of the memory or senses our whole reasoning wou'd be chimerical and without foundation. Every link of the chain wou'd in that case hang upon another; but there wou'd not be any thing fix'd to one end of it, capable of sustaining the whole; and consequently there wou'd be no belief nor evidence. And this actually is the case with all *hypothetical* arguments, or reasoning upon a supposition; there being in them, neither any present impression, nor belief of a real existence. (T 1.3.4.2/SBN 83)

Debate over this passage is due in large part to G. E. M Anscombe's claim that in it Hume is arguing that our belief 'that Caesar was killed in the senate-house on the ides of March' requires inferring the existence of a chain of testimony: 'Hume is arguing not merely that we must have a starting-point', she writes, 'but that we must *reach* a starting point in the justification of these inferences'. Even effecting the 'revision' required to render Hume's writing 'coherent', Anscombe contends, only serves to reveal the 'position as incredible'.[8] We are more certain that the event took place than we are certain about the chain of cause and effect that constitutes the testimony, and since the belief depends on justification of the latter, we are forced to doubt the original belief such that, as Donald Livingston puts it in the course of responding to Anscombe, the 'existence of Caesar' becomes 'an hypothesis that can be freely doubted'.[9]

Anscombe is surely correct that the view she takes Hume to be defending is 'incredible', but her objection only has force if Hume is attempting to justify historical beliefs when he is actually describing how we acquire them through testimony. Hume is thus offering an 'analysis of the structure of historical beliefs', to quote Livingston again, or, as Pitson has put it more recently, an explanation of *how* such beliefs arise 'by relating them to impressions of sense or memory construed as the effects of ideas in the minds of historians whose testimony contributes links to a chain of such testimony'.[10] Hume is emphasising that at bottom there is some present impression or real existence that anchors a chain of historical narrative in the bed of lived experience and which guides the historian in writing a true narrative; the testimony established in the record is one link in the chain, and the judgements of historians more again. In principle, there is an original scene (the chain is 'fix'd to one end of it') 'beyond which there is no room for doubt or enquiry' (T 1.3.4.1/SBN 83) and the historian aims to reach it. The idea of Rome, for example, is painted out from 'conversation and books of travellers and historians', links in the causal chain that make the idea acquire the requisite force and vivacity that make it feel different from ideas of the mimetic imagination. As such, Rome is an object of true belief because it refers ultimately to memory, even though the imagination is required to represent historical time and past events. At the same time, the original cannot be displayed by cutting the past at its joints; the past is not an open book to be read but a scene of interpretation to be reconstructed, and this is precisely what historians do and how they are read (and expect to be read) by others. The documents, written and oral, are thus transformed into historical knowledge because, as Livingston puts it, 'they express "the unanimous testimony of historians"'

[(T 1.3.4.2/SBN 83)] about the facts of Caesar's death, that is, they are understood to express propositions within the body of what we believe to be historical knowledge'.[11] There is a chain, to follow Hume's metaphor, which leads from the present into remote regions of the past, but the links are images of events and the natural connections between them shadows to be illuminated by historical reason regarding testimony in a certain manner, namely by *weighing* or *evaluating evidence*. In broaching this subject, Hume speaks directly to the nature of historical inquiry.

One way to appreciate Hume's approach is by way of a distinction drawn by Michael Welbourne between a 'default' and (though not his term exactly) 'critical' response to testimony. The default response presupposes that testimony is accepted, and only when faced with reports of extraordinary or miraculous events will that be overridden with a more critical view: we then 'begin to treat [testimony] differently', Welbourne observes, applying a 'calculus of probabilities', such as whether the speaker is trustworthy or the likelihood that we are being deceived.[12] This puts Hume in the unlikely company of his contemporary and critic Thomas Reid and his *'principle of credulity'*, an 'original principle implanted in us by the Supreme Being' in the form of a 'disposition to confide in the veracity of others, and to believe what they tell us'.[13]

The default response is evident in a passage from the first *Enquiry*, one that has become the *locus classicus* and starting point for the debates over Hume's view. It is worth quoting in full:

> there is no species of reasoning more common, more useful, and even necessary to human life, than that which is derived from the testimony of men, and the reports of eye-witnesses and spectators. This species of reasoning, perhaps, one may deny to be found on the relation of cause and effect. I shall not dispute about a word. It will be sufficient to observe, that our assurance in any argument of this kind is derived from no other principle than our observation of the veracity of human testimony, and of the usual conformity of facts to the reports of witnesses. It being a general maxim, that no objects have any discoverable connexion together, and that all the inferences, which we can draw from one to another, are founded merely on our experience of their constant and regular conjunction; it is evident, that we ought not to make an exception to this maxim in favour of human testimony, whose connexion with any event seems, in itself, as little necessary as any other. (EHU 10.5/SBN 111)

In this passage Hume understands belief in the testimony of others to be based on the principle of cause and effect, which in this instance involves our experience of the constant conjunction between testimony ('reports of witnesses') and things testified ('facts'). We do this, moreover, because there is a default tendency to accept testimony, given that we expect people, on the basis of our experience of the regular principles of human nature, to tell the truth.[14] Hume observes in this spirit:

> When we receive any matter of fact upon human testimony, our faith arises from the very same origin as our inferences from causes to effects, and from effects to causes; nor is there anything but our *experience* of the governing principles of human nature, which can give us any assurance of the veracity of men. (T 1.3.9.12/SBN 113)

As he expresses it even more clearly, again in the first *Enquiry*:

> Were not the memory tenacious to certain degree; had not men commonly an inclination to truth and a principle of probity; were they not sensible to shame, when detected in a falsehood: Were not these, I say, discovered by *experience* to be qualities in human nature, we should never repose the least confidence in human testimony. A man delirious, or noted for falsehood and villainy, has no manner of authority with us. (EHU 10.5/SBN 112)

In the absence of reasons to believe otherwise, this principle of veracity – of truth, or probity – that we discover in the conduct of our fellow human beings inclines us to believe the testimony of others automatically.[15]

So strong is this principle of veracity, in fact, that Hume sees it turning easily into a weakness, that of credulity, or a '*too easy* faith in the testimony of others' from a 'remarkable tendency to believe whatever is reported, even concerning apparitions, enchantments, and prodigies, however contrary to daily experience and observation' (T 1.3.9.12/SBN 113, emphasis added), especially when these are of a religious sort. 'A wise man ... proportions his belief to the evidence' (EHU 10.4/SBN 110), as Hume remarks famously, and in such cases we can and should reflect upon and if need be correct our initial judgements in the light of the available evidence. Such occasions arise when the default response to testimony breaks down and the basis for assent is undermined, that is, when 'contrariety of evidence' calls into question the assumption of the veracity of the witnesses. The causes of this are myriad, as Hume points out in the course of discussing miracles, arising variously

> from the opposition of contrary testimony; from the character or number of the witnesses; from the manner of their delivering their testimony; or from the union of all these circumstances. We entertain a suspicion concerning any matter of fact, when the witnesses contradict each other; when they are but few, or of doubtful character; when they have an interest in what they affirm; when they deliver their testimony with hesitation, or on the contrary, with too violent asseverations. There are many other particulars of the same kind, which may diminish or destroy the force of any argument, derived from human testimony. (EHU 10.7/SBN 112–13)

This critical response to testimony is not the norm in everyday life, though it can and does arise, but it sets the standard when it comes to writing history. Indeed, as Welbourne observes, much of the discussion of testimony in the first *Enquiry* concerns the critical rather than the default response, and in many passages quoted by his critics Hume is actually speaking as a 'philosophical historian interested in the principles by which the testimony should be evaluated from a historian's point of view. It is a mistake to think he is commenting on what he conceives to the basis of receiving testimony'.[16] Historians are in the business of weighing evidence and comparing contradictory reports in order to decide on one version of events over another. In doing so, they draw on experience and observation to make informed judgements, inferences about the relative likelihood of competing reports. Weighing testimony in this way is still a species of causal reasoning since the 'ultimate standard . . . is always derived from experience and observation' (EHU 10.6/SBN 112), but it is employed to discover 'hidden causes' where the customary causal reasoning that defines the default response has been called into question.[17] This is precisely the situation Hume is describing when he speaks of history as being 'philosophical' and 'true' as opposed to 'monkish' and 'false', terms that will make a lot more sense now that Hume's general view of 'testimony' and 'historical testimony' has been made clear.

Philosophical History

The importance of these concepts is on display right at the beginning of the *History of England*, which Hume commences with an
expression of 'regret that the history of remote ages should always
be much involved in obscurity, uncertainty, and contradiction'
(H 1.3), and a promise in his own efforts to supplant the 'fables,
which are commonly employed to supply the place of true history'
with a consideration of the language, manners and customs that
puts history on a firm empirical foundation (H 1.4). The historian is beholden to evidence based on written records, for which
reason, in Hume's view, the invention of modern printing marks
an important milestone in historiography as it overcomes one of
the great barriers to accurate historical writing. As Hume writes in
the *Natural History*:

> An historical fact, while it passes by oral tradition from eyewitnesses
> and contemporaries, is disguised in every successive narration, and may
> at least retain but very small, if any, resemblance to the original truth,
> on which it was founded. The frail memories of men, their love of exag-
> geration, their supine carelessness; these principles, if not corrected by
> books and writing, soon pervert the account of historical events; where
> argument or reasoning has little or no place, nor can ever recall the
> truth which has once escaped those narrations. (NHR 1.8)[18]

In preserving the record and saving it from the vagaries of human
nature, the printing press is the beginning of the 'useful, as well
as the more agreeable part of modern annals', Hume observes,
events 'preserved by printing' being equivalent to truths frozen
in time from which the historian selects, confident that the events
occurred as reported and that the narration they compose is certain
(H 3.82). This allows history to realise its task of

> distinguish[ing] between the *miraculous* and the *marvellous*; to reject
> the first in all narrations merely profane and human; to doubt the
> second; and when obliged by unquestionable testimony, to receive as
> little of it as is consistent with the known facts and circumstances.
> (H 2.398)

Hume captures this idea that history should be beholden to facts
and respond critically to testimony in his conviction that it should

be 'true' or 'philosophical'. As Livingston has pointed out, many earlier interpreters of Hume emphasised what they saw as a discontinuity between his philosophy and historical writing, claiming that Hume deserted the former for the latter, lacked any historical sense, or even judged his approach to the past as 'anti-historical'.[19] More recent commentators, by contrast, inspired in part by Duncan Forbes' influential re-evaluation of Hume's *History*, have argued for a fundamental continuity in Hume's concern with philosophy and history, understanding them as mutually supportive components of his overall approach to the 'science of man'.[20] Mossner, for example, says that, for Hume, philosophy and history 'are closely akin because the development of the human mind, which it is the historian's task to trace, provides the materials from which the philosopher derives the very principles of thinking and conduct',[21] and Livingston bases his comprehensive interpretation of Hume's thought by treating the 'philosophical and historical work as mirrors to each other'. 'Hume considered his historical writings as an application and extension of this philosophical work', Livingston proposes. 'From the beginning and throughout his career as a writer, he was engaged in historical work as well as in the philosophical problems to which such work gives rise'.[22] In a similar vein, Gregory Moses argues that for Hume, the 'roles of historian and philosopher compliment each other and in some places even overlap', and that any differences between the two come down to a difference in emphasis rather than one of kind. Both concern '*historical events* and *principles*', Moses concludes; both are pursued as a result of natural curiosity, and 'what counts as an explanation in one or the other is also the same'.[23] Victor Wexler, on the other hand, finds Hume to be uncovering a 'new scene of historical thought' by extending the sceptical approach of his philosophy into the arena of history,[24] and Farr and S. K. Wertz, finally, have emphasised the importance of sympathy as being as central to Hume's historiography as it is to other parts of his philosophy.[25] James Harris has recently brought this line of thinking to its logical conclusion by placing the *History* on a par methodologically with Hume's other writings, emphasising that under Hume's penmanship 'History made itself philosophical by shifting focus away from the actions of individual historical agents and towards general principles able to explain long-term and large-scale social, political, economic, and cultural change'.[26]

To urge that history should be philosophical in this sense –

sceptical, unbiased and in search of universal principles – will no doubt strike the modern reader as unsurprising, although in the eighteenth century it was a significant departure from accepted practice. As Popkin emphasises, at the time Hume's attitude was revolutionary since it marked a decisive break with a tradition of 'theological' history that until recently had regarded the Bible as a historical document. In dismissing 'providential and prophetic history totally', Popkin writes, Hume '. . . set a pattern for purely secular history and the secular examination of man. . . . [He] constructed a different kind of historical world for man to live in . . . a world in which the prophetic and miraculous were so unlikely that all that one could profitably study was the actual normal course of events'.[27] This was recognised by no less a figure than Edward Gibbon, who went out of his way to describe Hume as 'our philosophical historian',[28] and, as Laurence Bongie shows in his study of the *History*'s reception in late-eighteenth-century France, the close connection between Hume's philosophical views and his historical work was immediately apparent to a readership whose taste demanded that history should follow the model of '*l'histoire raisonnée* as opposed to *l'histoire simple*', the writing of which only 'profound thinkers' like Hume with a sufficiently 'reflective turn of mind' were qualified to undertake.[29]

Hume's rejection of prophetic or theological history is evident in his derision towards 'monkish' historians, whose writings he sees as reflecting the general ignorance and superstition of the times in which they wrote and the narrow horizons of their form of life. The works of medieval chroniclers and annalists reflect individuals who

> lived remote from public affairs, considered the civil transactions as entirely subordinate to the ecclesiastic, and besides partaking of the ignorance and barbarity, which were then universal, were strongly infected with credulity, with the love of wonder, and with a propensity to imposture; vices almost inseparable from their profession, and manner of life. (H 1.25)

On occasion, Hume sees these chroniclers as succeeding only in giving voice to their own beliefs, reporting miracles as fact and celebrating various 'monkish virtues' (H 1.38, 133); at other moments, he accuses them of bombast, inaccuracy, exaggeration and 'spurious erudition' (H 2.88, 328 and 477) or outright 'invention and artifice' designed to blacken the name of those who challenged ecclesiastical privilege (H 1.85, 132 and 241). The Reformation spread with such speed, in Hume's view, precisely because the Church of Rome was both unacquainted with 'true literature' and a stranger to open debate (H 3.142), which made it easier for individuals to perceive the 'defect in truth and authenticity' in the Catholic appeal to the purportedly 'divine origin' of ecclesiastical power (H 3.140). Protestant historians were no less guilty of expressing their own commitments, which were clearly displayed, Hume reports, in those of their persuasion who 'spread out the incidents' of the reign of Henry III in such a way as 'to expose the rapacity, ambition, and artifices of the court of Rome' (H 2.4), and in others who 'endeavoured to throw many stains' on James V of Scotland because he had opposed the Protestants during his reign (H 3.294).

Religious dogmatism is only one way in which history can be diverted from its true path, however, it being but the most common instance of hypothetical argument or 'reasoning upon a supposition' that supplants the disinterested search for truth (T 1.3.4.2/SBN 83). Corruption of a similar sort also occurs when historians choose to relate the '*secret* history' of events to excite curiosity (E 564); where 'national prepossessions and animosities have place', as Hume reports of English historians writing of Athelstan, the tenth-century Saxon king in the line of Alfred the Great (H 1.84); or when accounts are 'delivered by writers of the hostile nations, who take pleasure in exalting the advantages of their own countrymen, and depressing those of the enemy' (H 6.277). Similarly, 'controversies of faction' affect the honest weighing of evidence – exemplified in historians' attempts to assess the nature and consequences of the Norman invasion of 1066 (H 1.227) – as do the tendencies of 'passionate historians' to draw inferences based on sentiments rather than sound reasoning (H 4.40). In general, Hume considers the early history of nations and those who chronicled them to be so thoroughly soaked in the stain of superstition and ignorance that the philosophical historian should condemn them to obscurity rather than risk inserting hypotheses where sound matter of fact should have place. He writes:

It is evident what fruitless labour it must be, to search in those barbarous and illiterate ages, for the annals of a people, when their first leaders, known in any true history, were believed by them to be the fourth in descent from a fabulous deity, or from a man, exalted by ignorance into that character. The dark industry of antiquaries, led by imaginary analogies of names, or by uncertain traditions, would in vain attempt to pierce into that deep obscurity, which covers the remote history of those nations. (H 1.17)

Of course, Hume does not rule out the possibility of honest errors, occurring despite the good faith of historians, and even where elements of superstition tarnish an otherwise true narrative they do not impugn the integrity of the whole. Tacitus, Hume notes, is not beyond including accounts of miracles in his history – that Vespasian cured a blind man through his spittle and a lame man by the touch of his foot (EHU 10.25/SBN 122) – as Quintus Curtius reports without question the 'supernatural courage' of Alexander the Great 'by which he was hurried on singly to attack multitudes' and 'his supernatural force and activity, by which he was able to resist them' (EHU 8.8/SBN 84). While Hume never entertains such reports as part of a true narrative, on occasion he is himself willing to admit extraordinary events into the historical record. He reports without comment, for example, Herodutus' account that the Scythians 'after scalping their enemies, dressed the skin like leather, and used it as a towel; and whoever had the most of those towels was most esteemed among them' (EPM 7.14/ SBN 255).

Some mistakes, moreover, are unwitting and arise from simple ignorance and inexperience (H 5.469), or are oversights due to benign prejudice. Such is the case with Livy's portrayal of Hannibal (EPM Appx. 4.17/SBN 320) and Timæus' partiality in describing Agathocles, reproached by that author for his tyranny but unsung for his 'talents and capacity for business' (EPM Appx. 4.20/SBN 321). Historians can also be forgiven mistakes that are 'natural and almost unavoidable, while the events are recent' (H 2.173), and for going astray either because of the sheer complexity of the narrative or where obscure evidence is a barrier to interpretive accuracy. Hume considers naval battles to suffer unavoidably from the former disadvantage, where the historian confronts confusions 'derived from the precarious operations of winds and tides, as well as from the smoke and darkness, in which every thing there is involved. No wonder, therefore, that accounts of those battles are apt to contain uncertainties and contradictions' (H 6.277). Of the latter kind, he emphasises the difficulty of deciphering the conflict between the Houses of York and Lancaster:

> There is no part of English history since the Conquest, so obscure, so uncertain, so little authentic or consistent, as that of the wars between the two Roses: Historians differ about many material circumstances; some events of the utmost consequence, in which they almost agree, are incredible and contradicted by records; ... All we can distinguish with certainty ... is a scene of horror and bloodshed, savage manners, arbitrary executions, and treacherous, dishonourable conduct in all parties. (H 2.469)

It is the great benefit of historical investigation, however, that errors of this sort can be corrected through review and reflection, either by contemporary narrators themselves or, as is usually the case, by subsequent generations of historians who peruse extant histories with the wisdom of hindsight and an improved or more accurate knowledge of human motives and conduct (EHU 8.9/SBN 84–5). This is not to say that the historian cannot err, and Hume's own *History* has been widely criticised for straying from the path of impartiality. Laird Okie, for example, argues that Hume owed a good deal to 'pro-Royalist' writers for his account of the Revolution and Civil War, and that at crucial points he 'parroted Clarendon's commentary in an unscholarly manner that does not measure up to the critical, skeptical method attributed to him by his recent champions',[30] while Donald Siebert observes that 'Hume's way of writing history is to shape the historical fact for a desired instructive or emotional impact', which, on occasion, leads him to 'abandon his normal care in establishing historical truth to tell a morally invigorating story'.[31] In a similar vein, writing of the *Natural History of Religion*, Christopher Wheatley accuses Hume of 'making a radical departure from accuracy ... in the interest of forceful presentation' in order to persuade readers of the 'unattractive' nature of Christianity.[32] Whether the historian should be making moral judgements at all is a long-standing debate, and some have argued that, rather than moral instruction being a form of prejudice, it is part and parcel of Hume's method where, as Wertz describes it, 'presenting the information' both 'informs the understanding of the readers' and makes it possible that 'moral sentiment arises as an impression within them'.[33]

At the same time, Hume himself provides instances in his own work of a critical response to reports and subsequent confirmation or correction of the record. The veracity of the aforementioned report of Quintus Curtius on Alexander's supernatural courage is 'much to be suspected' and is easily exploded as a 'forgery in history' when we realise that the actions ascribed to him 'are directly contrary to the course of nature, and that no human motives, in such circumstances, could ever induce him to such a conduct' (EHU 8.8/SBN 84). Similarly, the 'whole tenor of English history', he observes, confirms the once disputed fact that 'it would be difficult to find in all history a revolution more destructive, or attended with a more complete subjection of the ancient inhabitants' than the Norman Conquest of Britain (H 1.226–7), and in the standard narrative concerning Cardinal Wolsey's illegitimate assumption of papal authority in ecclesiastical courts, Hume observes 'many circumstances' that are 'very suspicious, both because of the obvious partiality of the historian, and because the parliament, when afterwards they examined Wolsey's conduct, could find no proof of any material offence he had ever committed' (H 3.125n). The actions of King John, by contrast, serve to reveal his vicious character and thus confirm the 'disagreeable picture' of him – exaggerated though it might appear – painted by ancient historians (H 1.453). Moreover, even where there is no direct evidence available, a general knowledge of historical circumstances will support the likelihood of something having been the case. Hume reasons in this manner when considering whether well-born thanes resisted the rise of merchants or ceorles through the ranks of medieval society, and suggests that:

> Though we are not informed of any of these circumstances by ancient historians, they are so much founded on the nature of things, that we may admit them as a necessary and infallible consequence of the situation of the kingdom during those ages. (H 1.170)

Errors can also be corrected by giving the benefit of the doubt to contemporary reports; writers with a stake in events are more likely to be better informed and more accurately report events than others whose interest is more academic. For instance, Hume writes:

> The circumstances, which attended [Robert the] Bruce's first declaration [to free Scotland from English rule], are variously related; but we

> shall rather follow the account given by the Scottish historians; not that their authority is in general anywise comparable to that of the English; but because they may be supposed sometimes better informed concerning the fact, which so nearly interested their own nation. (H 2.137)

Indeed, the true historian has not only opportunity to correct errors in these ways, but is under an obligation to do so. While contemporary writers can be forgiven for imputing all errors of a reign 'to the person who had the misfortune to be entrusted with the reins of empire' – as Hume writes of the unfortunate Edward III – historians should draw on the benefit of hindsight and the perspective of distance to aid their judgement; it is thus 'a shameful delusion in modern historians', Hume charges, 'to imagine, that all the ancient princes, who were unfortunate in their government, were also tyrannical in their conduct' (H 2.173–4).

For this reason, history is particularly suited to be a source of instruction because it provides a general point of view, the same principle already met with in Hume's moral philosophy but here made transcendent, a vantage point from which to extract general truths about human nature and learn lessons about the present. Its 'chief use', Hume observes in the first *Enquiry*,

> is only to discover the constant and universal principles of human nature, by showing men in all varieties of circumstances and situations, and furnishing us with materials, from which we may form our observations, and become acquainted with the regular springs of human action and behaviour. These records of wars, intrigues, factions, and revolutions, are so many collections of experiments, by which the politician or moral philosopher fixes the principle of his science. (EHU 8.7/SBN 83–4)

Given that history 'affords materials for disquisitions of ... [manners, finances, arms, commerce, arts and sciences]', as Hume expresses the same thought in the *History*, '... it seems the duty of an historian to point out the proper inferences and conclusions' (H 6.140). Since 'each incident has a reference to our present manners and situation', he writes, 'instructive lessons occur every moment during the course of the narration' (H 3.82). For this reason, as Hume remarks of the English people looking back on their history:

An acquaintance with the ancient periods of their government is chiefly *useful* by instructing them to cherish their present constitution, from a comparison or contrast with the condition of those distant times. And it is also *curious*, by shewing them the remote, and commonly faint and disfigured originals of the most finished and most noble institutions, and by instructing them in the great mixture of accident, which commonly concurs with a small ingredient of wisdom and foresight, in erecting the complicated fabric of the most perfect government. (H 2.525)

Specific courses of events may even be a source of wisdom for the art of politics. From the history of English revolution, Hume is convinced, 'we may naturally deduce the same useful lesson, which Charles himself, in his later years, inferred: that it is dangerous for princes, even from the appearance of necessity, to assume more authority, than the laws have allowed them', as well as 'another instruction, no less natural, and no less useful, concerning the madness of the people, the furies of fanaticism, and the danger of mercenary armies' (H 5.545–6).

In contrast to these honest, sometimes unavoidable, and at least partly correctable errors, as well as the wisdom and instruction that can be gleaned from a disinterested contemplation of the past, genuine corruptions of the historical record are the result of systematic and principled distortion, something true historians avoid by scrutinising evidence and reiterating events as they occurred. Ideally, history is a true copy, a veridical depiction, in contrast to the speculation of narratives that – from error, fancy or dogmatism – depart from matter of fact. For this reason, Hume writes in 'Of the Populousness of Ancient Nations', 'The first page of THUCYDIDES is . . . the commencement of real history. All preceding narrations are so intermixed with fable, that philosophers ought to abandon them, in great measure, to the embellishment of poets and orators' (E 422). The historian who understands the nature of his enterprise, as Hume puts it,

traces the series of actions according to their natural order, remounts to their secret springs and principles, and delineates their most remote consequences. He chooses for his subject a certain portion of the great chain of events, which compose the history of mankind: Each link in this chain he endeavours to touch in his narration . . . And always, he is sensible, that the more unbroken the chain is, which he presents to his reader, the more perfect is his production. (EHU 3.9)

Thus, if the poet personifies the power of imagination to subvert experience, the historian reflects the force of memory to present and preserve it, as far as possible, in its original form, due position and temporal sequence. Past events are equivalent to impressions, and the products of the historian to adequate ideas; the latter are thus fainter images of the former, but they still correspond to them and ideally preserve them in their original order. Unlike those who exploit the imagination to falsify reality for aesthetic effect, historians memorialize the past; and where they depart from the original it is due to some defect or imperfection in the process of writing, namely when some corruption or another turns true, philosophical history into its false, unphilosophical counterpart. Historians avoid this fate in as far as they 'confine themselves to strict truth and reality' (EHU 3.10), to matter of fact (E 564) and to explanation based on causes rather than reasons speculatively attributed to individual actors. Hume writes of Charles' peace with the Scots in 1639, for example, 'What were the *reasons*, which engaged the king to admit such strange articles of peace, it is vain to enquire: For there scarcely could be any. The *causes* of that event may admit of a more easy explication' (H 5.267). The historical writer regards the past with a disinterested eye and bears witness to it as it happened, though not necessarily as it was reported, by stripping away falsehood and allowing 'all human race [to] appear in their true colours, without any of those disguises, which, during their life-time, so much perplexed the judgements of the beholders' (E 567). Historians, in short, distinguish fact from fiction, as ideas of memory can be separated from those of imagination; they discern the real shape of events under the clutter with which contemporary reports and time have effectively masked them.

History and Imagination

On the face of it, then, the empirical character of philosophical history, a pursuit to be distinguished sharply from the corrupt forms of its speculative counterparts, leaves little room for truck with the imagination, the faculty that trades precisely in the sort of fictions and loose reveries that distort the true narrative of past events. Indeed, the origin of false history lies in the effects of prejudice, credulity, fear and superstition that take hold because the imagination is open to suggestion and easy persuasion. Moreover, in memorialising the past, historians must reject the productive power of the imagination exploited by poets to separate, mix and compound the evidence of sense and experience into new and fantastic creations; this has no place in a discipline constrained by the strict injunction to separate fact from fiction. Poets, we might recall, borrow from history to give some reality to their inventions, and while they 'commonly have some foundation for their wildest exaggerations', where they are the sole historians 'they disfigure the most certain history by their fictions, and use strange liberties with truth' (H 1.22). For historians to flirt with the creative power of the fancy is thus to court an ally who will inevitably prove their undoing.

Yet, while Hume emphasises the ideally philosophical character of historical writing and its relationship to memory and matter of fact, he also acknowledges that the historian relies upon resources that only the imagination can provide. Far from freeing historians from the influence of that faculty, the nature of historical investigation ties them to it; history, in fact, depends upon the power of the productive imagination and without it the historian's task would be impossible. This stems from the fact that, unlike memory, which corresponds directly to impressions, history has only indirect access to the originals it copies, and this gives rise in turn to two features of history that impose peculiar constraints on how it is pursued and written.

First, the historian's originals are events long gone, temporally and spatially remote and available only in and through a historical narrative. Historians bring the past to life by performing the function Hume attributes to the memory when it recalls past impressions: reinvigorating them with something approaching their original force and vivacity. The historian extends the power of memory by transferring the past into the future, turning it into a source of knowledge and instruction on the basis of which judgements about the present and predictions about the future can be made. 'History, the great mistress of wisdom', Hume writes, 'furnishes examples of all kinds; and every prudential, as well as moral precept, may be authorised by those events, which her enlarged mirror is able to present to us' (H 5.545–6). As Hume says in 'Of the Dignity or Meanness of Human Nature':

[man is] a creature . . . [who] looks backward to consider the . . . history of the human race; casts his eye forward to see the influence of

his actions upon posterity, and the judgments which will be formed of
his character a thousand years hence. (E. 82)

The historian thus 'extends our experience to all past ages, and to
the most distant nations; making them contribute as much to our
improvement in wisdom, as if they had actually lain under our
observation' (E 566–7). This task is made possible by the historian's
capacity to annihilate the distance of time and space and bring
events into a vivid present, which the reader can experience. This,
in turn, can only be achieved by drawing on the power of the
imagination, which allows the writer to project him or herself into
the past, reviving events that compose it and giving reality to what
would otherwise be inaccessible. A 'man acquainted with history',
as Hume writes, 'may, in some respect, be said to have lived from
the beginning of the world, and to have been making continual
additions to his stock of knowledge in every century' (E 567). This
is a function of the imagination, however, and not of memory alone.

Second, even though historians rely on memory, they at once
interpret and represent the past. When the memory recollects past
impressions it refers directly back to the immediacy of lived experience, but the originals of the historian are beyond living memory;
they are reports in the form of written record or the judgements
of other historians. Thus they are already images, or images of
images, copied by others and available as their testimony of events,
which, in many or most cases, they never directly experienced. The
historian effectively proceeds

> by passing thro' many millions of causes and effects, and thro' a chain
> of arguments of almost an immeasurable length. Before the knowledge
> of the fact [some point in antient history] cou'd come to the first histo-
> rian, it must be convey'd thro' many mouths; and after it is committed
> to writing, each new copy is a new object, of which the connexion
> with the foregoing is known only by experience and observation.
> (T 1.3.13.4/SBN 145)

This feature gives history a peculiar method that reflects its dual
nature: of being both an extended form of memory – the power of
recollection extended into a distant past – and an act of interpretation in which the event is reconstructed, and this is something that
requires the representational power of imagination.

These two features of historical evidence – the remoteness of past events and the interpreted nature of the testimony it involves – stamp history with a character that contrasts with Hume's other characterisation of it as a straightforwardly empirical discipline distinguished by an emphasis on veridicality and connection to memory. History is, indeed, constrained by recollecting matter of fact, but it is at once a species of 'invention' (E 567), and this complicates considerably the injunction that the historian be 'impartial' or free of 'prejudice'. True historians might abjure the creative fictions of literature, but, like poets, they craft scenes in a way that places them in a historical system of things and confers a certain status on the ideas involved. This does not give them real existence, but – to extend Hume's observation about poetry – still serves as a sufficient foundation for any historical fact. The historian is also obliged to produce a narrative that enlivens the imagination of the reader by facilitating an easy transition among ideas in the imagination. As Addison observed in his essays on the imagination, the historian expresses events in such a way that the audience enters into the narrative, and 'this shews more the Art than the Veracity of the Historian', a characteristic exemplified by Livy:

> He describes every thing in so lively a manner, that his whole History is an admirable Picture, and touches on such proper Circumstances in every Story, that his reader becomes a kind of Spectator, and feels in himself all the variety of Passions, which are correspondent to the several Parts of the Relation.[34]

Recognising that in this respect historian and poet share a similar goal, Hume understands that the historian's craft is also guided by the same three qualities that characterise literary creativity: the magical power to transform ordinary experience into something extraordinary; the capacity to create ideas that are agreeable to an audience; and the rare gift of historical genius to bring about this effect.

The Transformation of Ordinary Experience

As poets work upon ordinary experience to create something marvellous, so historians employ the productive imagination to transform the past, by highlighting certain aspects of it and casting others into shadow. As in poetry, the creation of agreeable ideas involves embellishing the world or, as Hume puts it in the case of history, 'adorning' the facts in the process of selecting what is relevant for the narrative (H 3.82). In a historical narrative, what was in reality ugly, repellent or mundane appears beautiful, appealing or in some way fascinating. There is a difference between straightforward memorial representations of events and their historical representation in a true narrative, which casts doubt on the claim, as Wertz has it, that Hume is simply describing events as 'presenting information'. Wertz is correct to emphasise sympathy as the means by which the historian draws the reader into the narrative by 'converting' ideas roused by it into internal impressions that is '"lived" again in those readers',[35] but this does not occur by happenstance or follow as an unintended consequence of writing, any more than it follows from prejudice or lack of objectivity; it is, rather, an effect brought about deliberately by transforming reported 'facts' in the past into the historical 'facts' of a narrative.

Historians achieve this transformation in two related ways. First, they approach the past as the sedimentation of action and events, from which the heavier elements are dredged and placed before the reader as relevant facts. History memorialises the past, but copying it 'faithfully and at full length' – to recall Hume's remark on poetry – would make a history as insipid as a comedy that simply repeated the chit-chat of the tea-table; it would make for what Friedrich Nietzsche aptly calls 'antiquarian' history, a mere collection of artefacts laid out on a narrative table.[36] 'History', Hume writes, in a preamble to considering the reign of Henry III,

> ... being a collection of facts which are multiplying without end, is obliged to adopt such arts of abridgement, to retain the more material events, and to drop all the minute circumstances, which are only interesting during the time, or to the persons engaged in the transactions. ... What mortal could have the patience to write or read a long detail of frivolous events as those with which it [the reign of Henry III] is filled, or attend to a tedious narrative which would follow, through a serious of fifty-six years, the caprice and weaknesses of so mean a prince as Henry? (H 2.3–4)

From a mass of mundane details, the drama of history is revealed as true by way of events that are deemed important to the matter at hand. The historical lens brings events closer, but in a way that focuses on a select number while pushing the rest into the background. To some degree, the narrative depends on the writer and the kind of history being written and, as a result, there might be more than one true history or correct representation of the past; while different true histories are available, their content and philosophical status still depend on satisfying the criteria governing what count as relevant facts. Such selection might even be guided, as Siebert has argued, by Hume's desire that his writing have 'instructive or emotional impact' so that he would then be 'shaping [it] for his own artistic and political purposes', making it 'didactic history'.[37] As John Vladimir Price writes, commenting on the description of Cromwell's character (H 7.107–10), 'Hume arranges his facts to speak for themselves, knowing that adroitly arranged facts could be far more impressive than slander or abuse'.[38]

Second, while in accord with the principles of memory, historians retain the original form and due position of events in temporal sequence. Like poets who condense sequences and gloss events, they are obliged to transform *time* by representing it in a more or less foreshortened way. A history is not a transcription of events, but a temporal representation of them to suit the purposes of historical narration. To some degree, this reflects the amount, quality and availability of evidence that tends to become more adequate as the historian moves forward through increasingly contiguous events and more extensive written testimony: in the *History*, Hume's account of Anglo-Saxon England – from the Roman Empire circa 55 AD to the death of Harold and the Norman Conquest in 1066 – is compressed into some 160 pages of narrative, and he does not begin dating events systematically until the reign of Egbert in 827–38 (H 1.55ff). More significantly, narrative time reflects the importance attached by the author to the events under discussion. As Hume examines events of increasing importance, detail and drama – those leading up to the dissolution of the Long Parliament and Restoration of Charles II, for example (H 6.111–54) – the narrative grows protracted and the temporal sequence slows, sometimes abruptly, from years to months, days and even, as in the events preceding the murder of Thomas à Becket, to a matter of hours (H 1.328–34).

The Creation of Agreeable Ideas

The dramatic representation the historian achieves by transforming and embellishing the past also produces ideas that are agreeable to an audience. Hume explicitly characterises the aim of history in terms of instruction, but he also emphasises that bringing the past into the present is a source of 'entertainment to the fancy' (H 1.4), affording 'occupation or agitation of the mind' that is 'commonly agreeable and amusing' (T 3.3.4.14/SBN 613; see also H 1.4). History entertains because it opens up the world in a unique way, so that

> Those, who consider the periods and revolutions of human kind, as represented in history, are entertained with a spectacle full of pleasure and variety, and see, with surprise, the manners, customs, and opinions of the same species susceptible of such prodigious changes in different periods of time. (E 97)

'In reality', Hume writes,

> what more agreeable entertainment to the mind, than to be transported into the remotest ages of the world, and to observe human society, in its infancy, making the first faint essays towards the arts and sciences: . . . In short, to see all the human race, from the beginning of time, pass, as it were, in review before us; . . . What amusement, either of the senses or imagination, can be compared with it? Shall those trifling pastimes, which engross so much or our time, be preferred as more satisfactory, and more fit to engage our attention? How perverse must that taste be, which is capable of so wrong a choice of pleasures? (E 565–6)

Like poets, historians also rely upon the receptivity of an audience and that same mechanism of sympathy so central to the social and moral life of human beings. 'The perusal of a history seems a calm entertainment;' Hume writes, 'but would be no entertainment at all, did not our hearts beat with correspondent movements to those which are described by the historian' (EPM 5.32/SBN 223). In this respect, the historian might be compared to the tragedian whose literary depiction of a scene provides occasion through sympathy for the conversion of pain experienced by those at the scene into pleasure for the reader. Hume makes this point when commenting on Cicero, whose speeches brought pleasure through his power of eloquence even while the audience was convinced of the reality of the events narrated:

> When he had raised tears in his judges and all his audience, they were then the most highly delighted, and expressed the greatest satisfaction

with the pleader. The pathetic description of the butchery, made by
VERRES of the SICILIAN captains, is a masterpiece of this kind: But
I believe that none will affirm, that the being present at a melancholy
scene of that nature would afford any entertainment. Neither is the
sorrow here softened by fiction: For the audience were convinced of
the reality of every circumstance. (E 219)

Even where readers believe in the facts of the matter, there is a
difference between the events as they happened, and the passions
they would ordinarily elicit, and the historical depiction of them
in a narrative. In the latter, the force and vivacity of the original is
transformed, and the effect of pleasure arises from 'that very eloquence, with which the melancholy scene is represented' (E 219).

The historical drama, however, must not be painted in colours
that are *too* vivid. Analogous to theatrical scenes that disturb an
audience because of their contiguity in space – the self-mutilation
in playwright Nicholas Rowe's *Ambitious Stepmother*, to recall
Hume's example – some events from history are not amenable to
narrative transformation because they lie too contiguous in time.
As Damrosch points out, there are occasions when 'an actual event,
for those who have lived through it, may remain too emotionally
fraught to be capable of artistic transformation'.[39] Such is the
case with the massacre of the English in Ireland during O'Neal's
rebellion (1641) where 'To enter into particulars would shock
the least delicate humanity. Such enormities, though attested by
undoubted evidence, appear almost incredible' (H 5.342). Hume
acknowledges the same attitude in Clarendon's account of the
execution of Charles I, 'too horrid a scene to be contemplated with
any satisfaction, or even without the utmost pain and aversion'.
Hume remarks:

He [Clarendon] himself, as well as the readers of that age, were too
deeply concerned in the events, and felt a pain from subjects, which
an historian and a reader of another age would regard as the most
pathetic and most interesting, and, by consequence, the most agreeable. (E 223–4)

Historical Deliberation

As in poetry, historians do not produce such agreeable sentiments
by accident but, as already noted, by deliberately bringing about a

response in the reader by employing certain skills and techniques. In poetry, as we have seen, this deliberate use of poetic skill is a double-edged sword because a fictional embellishment of the world cannot be achieved without the aid of exaggeration and artifice, which can be traced in turn to the fact that imagination supplies both the creative power of the poet and the receptivity of the audience, respectively. Historical narratives do not suffer from this problem so acutely, since, instead of transforming reality into fiction, they represent matter of fact as accurately as possible. For this reason, Hume does not denounce history as an essentially corrupt discipline but one that becomes false contingently, when it distorts the empirical record through hypothetical reasoning. As such, it is still a case where the reader is manipulated by the imagination securing an easy transmission of its ideas and making a smooth and easy transition among them.

In achieving this effect, historians tread a fine line between representing events to bring about agreeable ideas and achieving 'true and establish'd judgement' (T 1.3.9.14/SBN 115). They are obliged at once to memorialise events while engaging the sympathy of the reader and to inspire conviction without becoming antiquarian or departing from matter of fact that changes fact into fiction. In Hume's view, this balance is possible because history refers to matter of fact and aims at bringing about conviction rather than false belief or persuasion. Recollecting events of a history evoke a different feeling from that which accompanies the effects of literature, not because of any 'intrinsic' difference between the ideas of each but because one involves testimony and is based in a tradition of knowledge about the past, while the other involves neither.[40] 'Every particular fact is there the object of belief. Its idea is modify'd differently from the loose reveries of a castle-builder' (T App. 4). As Hume observes in a revealing passage:

> If one person sits down to read a book as a romance, and another as a true history, they plainly receive the same ideas, and in the same order; nor does the incredulity of one, and the belief of the other hinder them from putting the very same sense upon their author. His ideas produce the same ideas in both; tho' his testimony has not the same influence on them. The latter has a more lively conception of all the incidents. He enters deeper into the concerns of the persons: Represents to himself their actions, and characters, and friendships, and enmities: He even goes so far as to form a notion of their features, and air, and person.

While the former, who gives no credit to the testimony of the author, has a more faint and languid conception of all these particulars; and except on account of the style and ingenuity of the composition, can receive little entertainment from it. (T 1.3.7.8/SBN 97–8)

Hume makes the same point when he recalls sending a copy of Plutarch's *Lives* to a female admirer, 'assuring her . . . that there was not a word of truth in them from beginning to end. She perused them very attentively', he continues, "till she came to the lives of ALEXANDER and CÆSAR, whose names she had heard by accident; and then returned me the book, with many reproaches for deceiving her' (E 564).

In these instances, a poetic romance is distinguished from a historical narrative by the degree of belief each inspires, which depends on the degree of force and vivacity they contain and on the way they strike the imagination, their 'manner of appearance'. Dugald Stewart, for one, later identified Hume's ability to capture this manner as a mark of the *History*'s success. 'There are few books more interesting than Hume's *History of England*', Stewart writes, 'but, if we conceived the events to be fictitious, it would make a very indifferent romance'.[41] 'A poetical description may have a more sensible effect on the fancy than an historical narration', as Hume realises.

> It may collect more of those circumstances, that form a compleat image or picture. It may seem to set the object before us in more lively colours. But still the ideas it presents are different to the *feeling* from those, which arise from the memory and the judgement. There is something weak and imperfect amidst all that seeming vehemence of thought and sentiment, which attends the fictions of poetry. (T 1.3.10.10/SBN 631)

Since poetic and historical ideas are similar in kind and differ only according to the degree of force and vivacity they contain, there will be a tendency for the former to come close to the latter and for historical ideas to fade into poetic ones. Poetry enlivens the imagination and passions, whereas history does not (see EPM 5.41), and there is still a sensible difference between the fictions of the former and the facts of the latter. For this reason, history can be false, but never enthusiastic in the manner of a poetic reverie. One does not, after all, rise on the wings of history as one does on those of poetry.

Historical conviction, as Hume makes clear, is ultimately secured by the impression of real existence that lies at the end of the chain of the narrative that anchors the account in the bed of lived experience, at which point doubt and inquiry come to an end. At first sight, the fact that historical evidence takes the form of testimony is a natural barrier to historical truth, since, according to the copy principle, belief *diminishes* as the distance from the original impression increases, and reasoning over a long period of time and through many transitions requires having 'a very strong and firm imagination to preserve the evidence to the end, where it passes thro' so many stages' (T 1.3.13.3/SBN 144). Perhaps the ancient history is 'lost in time' then, since belief consisting only in vivacity would 'decay by the length of the transition, and must at last be utterly extinguished' (T 1.3.13.4/SBN 145). While each link in the historical chain is of this kind, connections between cause and effect *resemble* each other in the same way that a copy of a book resembles the original:

> One edition passes into another, and that into a third, and so on, till we come to that volume we peruse at present. There is no variation in the steps. After we know one, we know all of them; and after we have made one, we can have no scruple as to the rest. This circumstance alone preserves the evidence of history, and will perpetuate the memory of the present age to the latest posterity. . . . [A]s most of these [historical] proofs are perfectly resembling, the mind runs easily along them, jumps from one part to another with facility, and forms but a confus'd and general notion of each link. By this means a long chain of argument, has as little effect in diminishing the original vivacity, as a much shorter wou'd have, if compos'd of parts, which were different from each other, and of which each requir'd a distinction consideration. (T 1.3.13.6/SBN 146)

History involves belief that carries conviction, even though events are already images enshrined only in the testimony of others; it can do this because it effectively takes a critical view of testimony and crafts the results into a historical narrative. Unlike poetical fiction, historical inference is 'proportioned to the constancy of the conjunction. On this is founded our belief in witnesses, our credit in history, and indeed all kinds of moral evidence, and almost the whole conduct of life' (T Abstract 33/SBN 661).

The Rules of Historical Art

Despite Hume's emphasis on the philosophical character of historical writing, then, like poets, historians are obliged to transform experience and produce agreeable ideas by manipulating an audience through the active and passive power of the imagination. As Hume points out, historical ideas differ not in kind from their poetical counterparts but in the way the force and vivacity they contain elicit a particular response in the audience. The nature of its evidence and the causal reasoning involved supply historical narratives with their truth, constituted by the feeling accompanying the sentiments they arouse. As such, there exists what we might term the rules of historical art comparable to those that govern poetry, the satisfaction of which determines the success of a historical narrative. These criteria govern the effective production of appropriate ideas in the mind of the audience and the easy movement of the imagination that brings about pleasure and conviction. As in the case of poetry, the imagination is the active source of historical genius and the means by which an audience is passively affected by historical representation. These general rules of historical criticism are likewise abridgements of historical practice, techniques that govern the success or failure of historical writing.

Historical Ideas and Conviction

First, where the poet brings about plausible fictions, historians must produce ideas that carry conviction by painting an historical picture with colours bright enough to warm the passions of an audience, fill the imagination and satisfy its desire to form a whole, allowing readers to enter into the characters and events related in the narrative. For this reason, Hume maintains, some themes are more suitable than others for treatment by the historian, since the imagination is naturally affected by events that influence it most, in the case of history those that are dramatic and of greater consequence. He remarks:

> The histories of kingdoms are more interesting than . . . those of small cities and principalities: And the history of wars and revolutions more than those of peace and order. We sympathise with the persons that suffer, in all the various sentiments which belong to their fortunes. The

mind is occupy'd by the multitude of the objects, and by the strong passions, that display themselves. (T 3.3.4.14/SBN 613)

For the same reason,

> THUCYDIDES and GUICCIARDIN support with difficulty our attention; while the former describes the trivial reencounters of the small cities of GREECE, and the latter the harmless wars of PISA. The few persons interested, and the small interest fill not the imagination, and engage not the affections. The deep distress of the numerous ATHENIAN army before SYRACUSE; the danger, which so nearly threatens VENICE; these excite compassion; these move terror and anxiety. (EPM 5.33/SBN 223)

Even when narrating events that have this natural appeal to the audience, history must include sufficient detail to engage the reader without producing a merely antiquarian narrative or – as Hume remarks while commenting on James V's unwise relationship with his favourite, Robert Carr, Viscount Rochester – dwelling on demeaning trivialities: 'History charges herself willingly with a relation of the great crimes, and still more with that of the great virtues of mankind; but she appears to fall from her dignity, when necessitated to dwell on such frivolous events and ignoble personages' (H 5.53). In some cases, however, the details themselves constitute what is interesting about the subject under discussion. Thus, while considering the reign of Elizabeth, Hume writes:

> We have related these incidents at greater length, than the necessity of our subject may seem to require: But even trivial circumstances, which show the manners of the age, are often more instructive, as well as entertaining, than the great transactions of wars and negociations, which are nearly similar in all periods and in all countries of the world. (H 4.44)

Where details are sparse, by contrast, the imagination remains unaffected; the colours of the narrative are dull, the passions cold and the audience distant from the events narrated. As Hume writes:

> The indifferent, uninteresting style of SUETONIUS, equally with the masterly pencil of TACITUS, may convince us of the cruel depravity

of NERO or TIBERIUS: But what a difference of sentiment! While the former coldly relates the facts; and the latter sets before our eyes the venerable figures of a SORANUS and a THRASEA, intrepid in their fate, and only moved by the melting sorrows of their friends and kindred. What sympathy then touches every human heart! What indignation against the tyrant, whose causeless fear or unprovoked malice gave rise to such detestable barbarity! (EPM 5.34/SBN 223–4)

Historical Works and Design

Second, a historical narrative should not run to adventures but must exhibit order and coherence by having a plan and a design created by the historian in conformity with the principles of association. As 'a certain unity is requisite in all productions', Hume writes, 'it cannot be wanting in history more than in any other' (EHU 3.14). As in poetry, the historian has some latitude in choosing the connections that give unity to the diversity of events. Contiguity in space and time might suffice, in which case 'All events, which happen in that portion of space and period of time, are comprehended in his design, though in other respects different and unconnected' (EHU 3.8). The same can be achieved by focusing on particular themes that distinguish a period, as in the civil transactions that Hume sees as the 'great ornament of history' under the Stuarts (H 5.469), or the 'catalogue of reversals ... fluctuation and movement' that unifies the history of ancient Britain (H 2.311).

Given that history memorialises the past and secures conviction by tracing a chain of events to an original scene of action, however, the historian more usually produces unity through cause and effect, accomplished by the imagination that actively draws relations between events that already display a natural attraction (see EHU 3.9). Hume follows this method in his own historical writing, which, as he remarks before embarking on an account of Anglo-Saxon Britain, aims to 'give a succinct account of the successions of kings, and of the more remarkable revolutions in each particular kingdom' (H 1.25). Only out of respect for the rule of reporting relevant detail does he depart from this model, as in the case of Henry III, for instance, where he warns the reader that 'till the end of the reign, when the events become more memorable, we shall not always observe an exact chronological order' (H 2.4–5).

In this respect, historical technique is of a piece with epic poetry, where the writer is also obliged to construct a narrative through a chain of cause and effect. Since the difference between the two forms of narrative lies

> only in the degrees of connection, which bind together those several events, of which their subject is composed, it will be difficult, if not impossible, by words, to determine exactly the bounds, which separate them from each other. That is a matter of taste more than of reasoning; and perhaps, this unity may often be discovered in a subject, where, at first view, and from an abstract consideration, we should least expect to find it. (EHU 3.15)

Epic poetry differs from history, however, according to the nature of the writing and the effect it aims to bring about. The composer of epic inflames and enlivens the passions to a degree not required of the historian (EHU 3.10); the links he forges in the chain of events are 'closer and more sensible', Hume emphasises, 'on account of the lively imagination and strong passions, which must be touched by the poet in his narration' (EHU 3.14). The historian carries the narrative over a greater period of time and, being more interested in truth, is less concerned than the composer of epic poetry with affecting the imagination.

Historical Works and Veracity

Third, and finally, history must achieve veracity by attempting to imitate nature. History, to recall and extend Hume's remark on poetry (E 138), works with images that cannot be equal to the actuality of events; the historian too is an 'under-workman' who gives a 'few strokes of embellishment' to the past on which he works. The poet satisfies this requirement by simultaneously copying the simplicity and refinement of nature and representing her in all her beauty, *la belle nature*. Historians follow the same rule in two ways.

First, their depictions are successful when the characters approximate human beings, as they are experienced in common life. If the figures the historian sketches are too artificial, they leave the imagination cold and unmoved. 'What would become of history', Hume asks, 'had we not a dependence on the veracity of the historian, according to experience, which we have had of mankind?' (EHU 8.18/SBN 90). This is especially pleasing to the reader when the virtues are drawn in bright and lively colours. As Hume remarks:

> Place in opposition the picture, which TACITUS draws of VITELLIUS, fallen from empire, prolonging his ignominy from a wretched love of life, delivered over to the merciless rabble; tossed, buffeted, and kicked about; constrained, by their holding a poinard under his chin, to raise his head, and expose himself to every contumely. . . . Yet even here, says the historian, he discovered some symptoms of a mind not wholly degenerate. To a tribune, who insulted him, he replied 'I am still your emperor'. (EPM 7.9/SBN 253)

Second, historians also imitate nature in attempting, as far as possible, to copy the 'natural order' of events and preserve the original form. As we saw above, Hume himself represents time in a way that serves a dramatic purpose relevant to the subject matter at hand, but the historian, he maintains, should follow the temporal sequence as accurately as possible because the imagination is pleased more when allowed to pass easily from one idea to another along an orderly and intelligible causal chain. For this reason, Hume observes:

> An historian may, perhaps, for the more convenient carrying on of his narration, relate an event before another, to which it was in fact posterior; but then he takes notice of this disorder, if he be exact; and by that means replaces the idea in its due position. (T 1.1.3.3/SBN 9)

In general, he writes:

> We always follow the succession of time in placing our ideas, and from the consideration of an object pass more easily to that, which follows immediately after it, than to that which went before it. We may learn this, among other instances, from that order, which is always observ'd in historical narrations. Nothing but an absolute necessity can oblige an historian to break the order of time, and in his *narration* give the precedence to an event, which was in *reality* posterior to another. (T 2.3.7.7/SBN 430)

To interfere unnecessarily with the natural order in this way at once interrupts the flow of events depicted and produces unease, which hinders the movement of the imagination in the direction in which it is moving and breaks the relation of ideas that bring it pleasure.

Hume's references to historical writers are relatively few compared to his more elaborate discussions of literary figures. Where he does offer critical observations, he clearly reveals his preference for ancient authors whom he takes to exemplify the rules of historical art most perfectly and considers the best and most trustworthy models for modern writers to follow. Tacitus, in particular, stands out for his 'candour and vivacity' and Hume ranks him as 'the greatest and most penetrating genius, perhaps, of all antiquity' (EHU 10.25/SBN 123). Hume's esteem for ancient historians is also reflected in his many references to them for illustrations of virtue and vice – an honour he does not confer on poets, one might observe – and for the details of religious practice they provide;[42] where modern historians receive praise it is largely by comparison with their ancient forbears. For instance, Hume writes:

> Camden's history of queen Elizabeth may be esteemed good composition, both for style and matter. It is written with simplicity of expression, very rare in that age, and with a regard to truth. It would not perhaps be too much to affirm, that it is among the best historical productions which have yet been composed by any Englishman. It is well known that the English have not much excelled in that kind of literature. (H 5.154)

He observes on another occasion:

> If the reader of Raleigh's history can have the patience to wade through the Jewish and Rabbinical learning which compose the half of the volume, he will find, when he comes to the Greek and Roman story, that his pains are not unrewarded. Raleigh is the best model of that ancient style, which some writers would affect to revive at present. (H 5.154)

Again, like literary works, historical writing is still of value even when it does not satisfy all the rules of historical art. Such is the case with Clarendon who, writing of the English Revolution, manages to mix a 'prolix and redundant' style with an integrity that made it difficult for him to falsify the facts even though clearly partial to the Royalist cause (H 6.154).

We have seen in this chapter how Hume regards history as

philosophical, insofar as it memorialises the past and is beholden to the evidence of matter of fact, but also acknowledges its connection to the imagination, which alone enables the historian to reclaim the past in a historical narrative that at once transforms and adorns events so that they entertain, educate and convince a reader. The imagination is both the active source of historical genius and the means by which an audience is passively affected by historical representation. These principles are manifest as historical techniques or, otherwise conceived, rules of historical criticism that abridge historical practice and offer guidelines for the creation of true and entertaining historical work. In these respects history has features in common with poets, although whereas the poet trades in creative fictions, the ideas produced by the historian feel different, rise to the status of true belief and carry conviction. If history coincides with poetry in its dependence on the imagination to achieve its effects, it departs from it significantly in anchoring its investigations in matter of fact, even though they are lost temporally to a past that requires reconstruction and adornment. This feature of the historical craft, moreover – that it at once memorialise *and* embellish – gives to history the unique function of painting the past in such a way that it can be a source not only of instruction and wisdom but of moral virtue as well. For 'the historians', Hume observes, comparing them favourably with poets and philosophers whose track record in this regard he considers poor, 'have been, almost without exception, the true friends of virtue, and have always represented it in its proper colours, however they may have erred in their judgements of particular persons' (E 567).

At the same time, given the historian's reliance on the imagination, one might legitimately ask whether it is a naive oversight on Hume's part to cite 'impartiality' as the *sine qua non* of the historian's task, and more than a little disingenuous to declare allegiance to *l'histoire raisonnée* as if reason could overcome the power of prejudice and passion for party, especially when Hume omits, includes or emphasises certain facts to suit his own purposes. Impartiality itself involves adherence to a certain kind of practice, and surely that can be called into question in the same way as any other article of philosophical faith. Indeed, as Bongie points out, this was Hume's own fate: by the time of the French Revolution, he reports, it is not 'Hume's famous impartiality' that was doubted, but 'what is impugned is *impartiality itself*'.[43] This issue is especially pressing in the case of Hume, who is hardly sanguine about the power of reason over passion, and, as we shall see, finds fault with philosophers for basking too much in the warmth of enthusiasm and succumbing too easily to the appeal of a 'favourite principle' to which they reduce 'every phænomenon, though by the most violent and absurd reasoning' (E 159). Some philosophers of the 'painterly' kind, moreover, employ their art deliberately to engage readers, rouse their sentiments and inspire virtue in them.

In Hume's view, this sort of tension seems unavoidable, although the fact that there is at bottom some matter of fact to which historical work is ultimately accountable means that it does not rise to the status of an antinomy of the sort to be met with in metaphysics, religion or even philosophy itself (as we shall see in the two final chapters). By the very nature of their craft, historians cannot help painting the world in an artful way, and they must recognise that the colours they choose are variable and acknowledge that even the most impartial of histories is subject to the various passions that animate different sects of men. Perhaps in the writing of history, as Moses suggests, 'passions are not so much repressed as *redeployed*'.[44] At the same time, that readers of the *History* were, and perhaps still are, incapable of taking the general point of view does not undermine the attempt to write history, which, if pursued with a philosophical spirit, will at least have accuracy as its goal and come closer to achieving it than those that start out from prejudice, dogma or abstract principle alone.[45] Unlike poetry, religion and philosophy, it is real existence that is the final arbiter of historical pronouncements, and true history can form models of virtue and wisdom from which those willing to listen might learn how to resist the more wayward forces of the imagination on which the historian also depends.

Notes

1. See 'Introduction' in *David Hume: Philosophical Historian*, ed. David Fate Norton and Richard H. Popkin (New York: Bobbs-Merrill, 1965), pp. 109–10 and 413–17. Macaulay's *The History of England from the Accession of James the Second* covers the years 1685 to 1702, ending with the death of William III. Hume's *History*, as its subtitle advertises, runs from the invasion of Julius Caesar in 55AD to the Glorious Revolution of 1688.
2. Some commentators have seen Hume as anticipating the theory of

'imaginative reconstruction' associated with R. G. Collingwood and Herbert Butterfield. See Herbert Butterfield, *History and Human Relations* (London: Collins, 1951) and R.G. Collingwood, *The Idea of History*, rev. edn (Oxford: Oxford University Press, [1946] 1993). For a discussion of Hume's views in the context of those of Butterfield, Collingwood and later philosophy of history, see S. K Wertz, 'Moral Judgements in History: Hume's Position', *Hume Studies*, 22: 2 (1996), pp. 339–67, and his earlier 'Collingwood's Understanding of Hume'. Collingwood, ironically, accused Hume of having abandoned philosophy for history and for holding an anti-historical view of human nature. For a discussion and defence of Hume in this regard, see Livingston, *Hume's Philosophy of Common life*, pp. 219–24.

3. See Tony Pitson, 'George Campbell's Critique of Hume on Testimony', *Journal of Scottish Philosophy*, 4: 1 (2006), pp. 1–15. Pitson is inclined to think that when 'Hume is concerned with testimony as a source of belief he generally has in mind historical narratives which purport to provide knowledge of past events' (p. 5). This seems to place an unnecessarily narrow restriction on how Hume understands 'testimony'.

4. Alvin I. Goldman, *Pathways to Knowledge: Public and Private* (Oxford: Oxford University Press, 2002), p. 201, emphasis added.

5. Jennifer Lackey, 'Introduction', in Jennifer Lackey and Ernest Sosa (eds), *The Epistemology of Testimony* (Oxford: Oxford University Press, 2006), pp. 4 and 7. Lackey's discussion also serves as a useful introduction to the various positions – non-reductionist, reductionist, and 'hybrid' – that contemporary writers have taken. See also Goldman, *Pathways to Knowledge*, pp. 201–2.

6. C. A. J. Coady 'Testimony and Observation', *American Philosophical Quarterly*, 108: 2 (1973), pp. 149–55, incorporated as Ch. 4 into his *Testimony: A Philosophical Study* (Oxford: Clarendon Press, 1992). See also Frederick F. Schmitt, 'Justification, Sociality, and Autonomy', *Synthese*, 73: 1 (1987), pp. 43–85, and Mark Owen Webb, 'Why I Know About as Much as You: A Reply to Hardwig', *Journal of Philosophy*, 90: 5 (1993), pp. 260–70.

7. Defenders of Hume against Coady et al. include Sarah Wright, 'Hume on Testimony: A Virtue-Theoretic Defense', *History of Philosophy Quarterly*, 28: 3 (2011), pp. 247–65; Fred Wilson, 'Hume and the Role of Testimony in Knowledge', *Episteme*, 7: 1 (2010), pp. 58–78, esp. 69–70 and 73–4; Michael Root, 'Hume on the Virtues of Testimony', *American Philosophical Quarterly*, 38: 1

(2001), pp. 19–35; and Paul Faulkner, 'David Hume's Reductionist Epistemology of Testimony', *Pacific Philosophical Quarterly*, 79: 4 (1998), pp. 302–13. Cf. Saul Traiger, 'Humean Testimony', *Pacific Philosophical Quarterly*, 74: 2 (1993), pp. 135–49, and 'Experience and Testimony in Hume's Philosophy', *Episteme*, 7: 1 (2010), pp. 42–57, who argues that Hume is actually an '*anti*-reductionist.'

8. See G. E. M. Anscombe, 'Hume and Julius Caesar', *Analysis*, 34: 1 (1973); reprinted in *The Collected Philosophical Papers of G. E. M. Anscombe*, 3 vols (Minneapolis: University of Minnesota Press, 1981), vol. 1, pp. 86–92. The quotations are from pp. 87 and 86, respectively.

9. See Donald W. Livingston, 'Anscombe, Hume and Julius Caesar', *Analysis*, 35: 1 (1974–5), pp. 13–19. The quotation is from p. 13.

10. Livingston, 'Anscombe, Hume and Julius Caesar', p.14, and Pitson, 'George Campbell's Critic of Hume on Testimony', p. 4. Livingston's initial point against Anscombe has been much repeated. In addition to Pitson, see Traiger, 'Experience and Testimony', pp. 46–7, and 'Humean Testimony', pp. 138–9; Faulkner, 'David Hume's Reductionist Epistemology of Testimony', pp. 308 and 312, n. 24; and Welbourne, 'The Community of Knowledge', pp. 312–13.

11. Livingston, 'Anscombe, Hume and Julius Caesar', pp. 15–16.

12. See Michael Welbourne, *Knowledge* (Montreal: McGill-Queen's University Press, 2001), pp. 85–91, and 'Is Hume Really a Reductivist?', *Studies in History and Philosophy of Science*, 33: 2 (2002), pp. 407–23, esp. 415–18. A similar emphasis is found in Wilson, 'Hume and the Role of Testimony in Knowledge', and in Livingston, *Hume's Philosophy of Common Life*, p. 232. Welbourne observes that 'critics of Hume such as Coady ... have tended to mistake a discussion of the questions of when and how testimony should be weighed or evaluated, when the default response should be withheld, for a theory of how testimony should be received in the first place' (*Knowledge*, p. 90).

13. See Thomas Reid, *An Inquiry into the Human Mind on the Principles of Common Sense*, ed. Derek R. Brookes (Edinburgh: Edinburgh University Press, [1764] 1997), p. 194. Pitson observes that George Campbell framed a similar principle concerning testimony requiring some 'original grounds of belief' somewhat earlier. See George Campbell, *A Dissertation on Miracles: Containing an Examination of the Principles Advanced by David Hume, Esq; in An Essay on Miracles*, 2nd edn (Edinburgh: Kincaid & Bell, [1762] 1766), p. 13,

and Pitson, 'George Campbell's Critique of Hume on Testimony'. On the similarity between Hume and Reid, see Wellbourne, *Knowledge*, pp. 90–1, and on Reid's view more generally, James Van Cleve, 'Reid on the Credit of Human Testimony', in Lackey and Sosa, *The Epistemology of Testimony*, pp. 50–74; Goldman, *Pathways to Knowledge*, pp. 173–9; Coady, *Testimony*, pp. 120–9; and Root, 'Hume on the Virtues of Testimony', pp. 26–7.

14. See Faulkner, 'David Hume's Reductionist Epistemology of Testimony', pp. 305–7, who rightly emphasises this aspect of Hume's view. See also Root, 'Hume on the Virtues of Testimony', who argues (on the basis of the discussion of the virtues in the *Treatise*) that Hume takes testimony to depend on the virtues of 'veracity' and 'credibility'; he points out that this has the advantage of endowing testimony with a 'forward looking' aspect rather than the exclusively 'backward looking' perspective to which it is confined when based solely on the past experience of constant conjunction.

15. In this respect at least, insofar as he locates a natural principle to explain why we believe others, Hume appears to be in, or very near to, the same 'non-reductionist' camp established and occupied by Reid and Campbell. This point is made by Welbourne in *Knowledge*, pp. 90–1, and 'Is Hume Really a Reductivist?', pp. 418–22.

16. Welbourne, *Knowledge*, pp. 88. Obviously, the failure to draw the distinction between the default and critical responses to testimony (and the kinds of inference attending each) goes a good way to explaining how Coady and others are at least partially mistaken in glossing Hume's entire position as 'reductionist.'

17. This point is brought out nicely by Wilson, 'Hume and the Role of Testimony in Knowledge', pp. 70–1. See, in this context, Hume's juxtaposition of a false belief in the immortality of the soul with a 'true and establish'd judgement; such as is deriv'd from the testimony of travellers and historians' (T 1.3.9.14/SBN 114–15).

18. It is worth noting that, writing at the beginning of the nineteenth century, Stewart viewed Hume's *Natural History* as an example of what he termed 'conjectural history', a method that, in the absence of direct empirical evidence, allows for inferring the likelihood of probable conduct on the basis of the principles of human nature and knowledge of circumstances. Whether or not this is an accurate characterisation of the *Natural History*, it is not Hume's method in the *History of England*. For a discussion of the sense in which Hume's method coincides and diverts from Stewart's methodological maxim, see Simon Evnine, 'Hume, Conjectural History, and the Uniformity

of Human Nature', *Journal of the History of Philosophy*, 31: 4 (1993), pp. 589–606, and, more recently, Juan Samuel Santos Castro, 'Hume and Conjectural History', *Journal of Scottish Philosophy*, 15: 2 (2017), pp. 157–74.

19. For an outline of these earlier views, see Livingston, *Hume's Philosophy of Common Life*, pp. 210–12; Laird Okie, 'Ideology and Partiality in David Hume's *History of England*', *Hume Studies*, 11: 1 (1985), pp. 1–32, esp. 1–4; and, more recently, Claudia M. Schmidt, 'David Hume as a Philosopher of History', in Mark G. Spencer (ed.), *David Hume: Historical Thinker, Historical Writer* (University Park, Pennsylvania: The Pennsylvania State University Press, 2013), pp. 161–79.

20. See Duncan Forbes, 'Introduction' to David Hume, *History of Great Britain: The Reigns of James I and Charles I*, ed. Duncan Forbes (Harmondsworth: Penguin, 1970), and *Hume's Philosophical Politics*, Chs. 8 and 9.

21. Mossner, *The Life of David Hume*, p. 301.

22. Livingston, *Hume's Philosophy of Common Life*, pp. ix and 214.

23. Gregory Moses, 'David Hume as Philosophical Historian', *Australian Journal of Politics and History*, 35: 1 (1989), pp. 81 and 83–5. See also David Fate Norton, 'History and Philosophy in Hume's Thought', in *David Hume: Philosophical Historian*, pp. xxxii-l; Stephen Paul Forster, 'Different Religions and the Difference they Make: Hume on the Political Effects of Religious Ideology', *Modern Schoolman*, 66: 4 (1989), pp. 253–4; and Donald T. Siebert, *The Moral Animus of David Hume* (Newark: University of Delaware Press, 1990), pp. 119–20.

24. Victor G. Wexler, 'David Hume's Discovery of a New Scene of Historical Thought', *Eighteenth-Century Studies*, 10: 2 (1976–7), pp. 185–202.

25. Farr, 'Hume, Hermeneutics, and History'; and Wertz, 'Moral Judgments in History', esp. pp. 343–6. See also Douglas Long, 'Hume's Historiographical Imagination', in Mark G. Spencer (ed.), *David Hume: Historical Thinker, Historical Writer* (University Park, Pennsylvania: The Pennsylvania State University Press, 2013), pp. 201–24. A similar emphasis is found earlier in Livingston, *Hume's Philosophy of Common Life*, pp. 214–24. Cf. Donald T. Siebert, 'The Sentimental Sublime in Hume's *History of England*', *Review of English Studies, New Series*, 40: 159 (1989), pp. 352–72, who calls the *History* a 'good example of sentimental literature', which celebrates the 'hero of feeling' (pp. 353 and 354).

26. Harris, *Hume: An Intellectual Biography*, p. 20. 'The philosophical spirit', Harris writes later in his discussion of Hume's volume on the Stuarts, 'expressed itself most clearly of all in those passages in which Hume sought to reduce political debates to their most essential and abstract principles, by balancing the best case that could be made on one side against the best that could be made on the other, and then presenting a considered judgement to the strengths and weaknesses of each argument' (p. 339).

27. Richard H. Popkin, 'David Hume: Philosophical versus Prophetic Historian', in Kenneth R. Merill and Robert W. Shahan (eds), *David Hume: Many-sided Genius* (Norman: University of Oklahoma Press, 1976), pp. 83, 89–90 and 92.

28. Edward Gibbon, *The History of the Decline and Fall of the Roman Empire*, quoted in Siebert, *The Moral Animus of David Hume*, p. 119.

29. Laurence L. Bongie, *David Hume: Prophet of the Counter-Revolution*, 2nd edn (Indianapolis: Liberty Fund, 2000), p. 5. Making a somewhat different point, Harris, *Hume: An Intellectual Biography*, reports that in Hume's time, among writers both at home and abroad, it was 'commonplace' opinion – 'almost a cliché' – that party politics had made an objective account of English history impossible (p. 308).

30. Okie, 'Ideology and Partiality in Hume's *History of England*', pp. 16–17. Okie is referring to Edward Hyde, First Earl of Clarendon (1609–74), politician, statesman and author of *The History of the Rebellion and Civil Wars in England* (1702–4). Okie explains what he sees as Hume's lack of partiality in the following terms: 'When Hume began work on his History . . . he had other concerns in mind besides political philosophy. Hume . . . had an axe to grind: The History was, in part, a "vehicle" for attacking the Whigs because Hume resented the Whig monopoly of place, position and literary taste' (p. 24). See also Robert J. Roth, S. J., 'David Hume on Religion in England', *Thought*, 66 (1991), pp. 51–64, who argues that 'it was an anti-Presbyterian and anti-Puritan bias which coloured his [Hume's] whole view of the history of that [early Stuart] period' (p. 52; see also pp. 53 and 62), and for a different view, Victor G. Wexler, *David Hume and the 'History of England'* (Philadelphia: The American Philosophical Society, 1979), pp. 8 and 22–3.

31. Siebert, *The Moral Animus of David Hume*, pp. 55 and 58. Cf. pp. 121–2, where Siebert makes a similar point while discussing Hume's treatment of 'three religious heroes': Thomas à Becket, Joan

of Arc and Sir Thomas More. See also his remark that 'Hume's *History* projects a moral vision by its ability to reshape the past, to impose meanings on the past, creating patterns that imply a corresponding beauty in human nature – all too seldom instantiated in human life, it is true, but nonetheless capable of being discovered, indeed created in the fiat of narrative, by the historian's moral imagination' (p. 21).

32. Christopher J. Wheatley, 'Polemical Aspects of Hume's Natural History of Religion', *Eighteenth-Century Studies*, 19: 4 (1986), pp. 502–14. The quotations are taken from p. 513.

33. Wertz, 'Moral Judgments in History', p. 343. See also Livingston, *Hume's Philosophy of Common Life*, pp. 243–6; Farr, 'Hume, Hermeneutics, and History', pp. 301–2; and for a discussion of the issue beyond Hume, Adrian Oldfield, 'Moral Judgments in History', *History and Theory*, 20: 3 (1981), pp. 260–77. Cf. Harris, *Hume: An Intellectual Biography*, who places Hume's impartiality in the context of the battle between Whig and Tory interpretations of history, of which he provides a useful overview (pp. 308–19). Hume, Harris writes, 'realised that . . . a separation of the politics of the present from the politics of the past opened the way to a new kind of historical impartiality' (p. 321), although he also acknowledges that Hume's readers were 'encouraged, coerced even, into a sympathetic emotional engagement with the victims of history, both small and great', and the result in some cases was 'to blur the distinction between history on the one hand and fiction on the other' (pp. 348–9).

34. Addison, *Spectator* No. 420, p. 574. He also observes that 'As the Writers in Poetry and Fiction borrow their several Materials from outward Objects, and join them together at their own Pleasure, there are others who are obliged to follow Nature more closely, and to take entire Scenes out of her. Such are Historians, natural Philosophers, Travellers, Geographers, and, in a Word, all who describe visible Objects of a real Existence.'

35. See Wertz, 'Moral Judgments in History', pp. 340 and 343–4. Elsewhere (pp. 348, 351, *passim*) Wertz does credit historians with some 'skill' in animating their personages, but he appears to assume that the effects of the narrative somehow emerge without deliberate intent on the part of the historian. Cf. Oldfield, 'Moral Judgments in History', on which Wertz draws approvingly. Oldfield is less inclined to rule out authorial intent, but he, too, suggests that moral judgement and moral education emerge from the historian 'telling us about the moral dilemmas which faced the men of the past, and

about the ways in which these dilemmas were resolved, and by allowing contemporaries to speak for themselves. ... The richly diverse resources of the historian can thus be harnessed to the task of moral education, without his having to crack his own whip' (p. 275).

36. See Friedrich Nietzsche, *The Uses and Abuses of History for Life*, in *Untimely Meditations*, trans. R. J. Hollingdale (Cambridge: Cambridge University Press, 1997).

37. Siebert, 'The Sentimental Sublime in Hume's *History of England*', pp. 366, 368–9 and 372. Siebert notes of Hume's treatment of Mary Queen of Scots: 'Closer examination reveals that Hume has de-emphasised or suppressed certain details, given others greater prominence, and added interpretive commentary. These touches urge the narrative towards that thematic conclusion and emotional effect Hume desires' (p. 357).

38. John Vladimir Price, *The Ironic Hume* (Austin: University of Texas Press, 1965), p. 83.

39. Damrosch, *Fictions of Reality in the Age of Hume and Johnson*, p. 64.

40. On this point see Livingston, 'Anscombe, Hume and Julius Caesar', p. 16.

41. *The Collected Works of Dugald Stewart*, ed. Sir William Hamilton, 11 vols (Edinburgh: Thomas Constable & Co.) 5: p. 273.

42. See, for example, EPM 6.16, 7.9, 13–15/SBN 240, 253, 254–5; and NHR 4.6–9, 12.20–1.

43. Bongie, *David Hume*, p. 136, emphasis added.

44. See Moses, 'David Hume as Philosophical Historian', pp. 87–9.

45. On this point, see Mossner, 'Was Hume a Tory Historian?', pp. 115–17.

6

Religion

In this chapter we turn our attention to Hume's approach to religion, an area where, as in studies of his moral and political philosophy, the imagination has received little attention from commentators despite the prominent role it plays in many of his discussions. The literature has tended to focus on specific substantive areas, such as the nature of religious belief, Philo's 'reversal' at the end of the *Dialogues*, and the essay on miracles in the first *Enquiry*, along with attempts to decipher the nature of any religious beliefs he might himself have held: Hume has been characterised variously as an 'atheist', an 'aesthetic theist', a 'philosophical theist', an 'agnostic', an 'attenuated deist', a 'moral atheist', a 'religious sceptic' and a 'sceptical fideist'.[1]

As with the scholarly focus on specific areas of Hume's approach to morals and politics, addressing the subject of religion in many instances does not require consideration of the imagination directly, although the extent to which it has been passed over – even in book-length studies of the subject – is still surprising.[2] In some ways, moreover, religion is the most difficult area in which to identify precisely the place Hume assigns the imagination, not only because of the well-known interpretive quandaries endemic to deciphering his enigmatic writings on the subject but also to the very topic of religion itself, which, as Hume acknowledges explicitly, poses special problems for the philosopher. In 'theological reasonings' we are 'strangers in a strange land', as Philo says early in the *Dialogues*, travellers who not only seek objects 'too large for our grasp', but who do so without the compass of 'common sense and experience' that guides methods and strengthens conclusions when considering trade, morals, politics or criticism (DNR 1.10). Hume almost certainly lost whatever personal commitment he ever had to Christianity while still in his teens, but his many writings on religious matters suggest that he felt 'constrained, ever and again, almost in spite of himself', as Kemp Smith puts it, 'to speculate anew on it. It was so many-sided and so ambiguous in its manifestations, so puzzling in its lack of conformity to the other, more ordinary, aspects of human existence!'[3]

Considering Hume's view of this singular aspect of human experience and the imagination's place in it, I want to focus on the fictions that compose 'polytheism' and 'popular theism', the two species of 'false' superstitious religion with which Hume is principally concerned. The former consists of artificial fictions of the sort we have considered already in Hume's writing on metaphysics and aesthetics: they involve drawing connections where none otherwise exist and they produce a species of persuasion about the existence of objects to which the ideas putatively refer. The latter, popular theism, involves vulgar fictions and natural beliefs, although, since they are not necessary, required and universal, they are secondary (involving a propensity) rather than first order. Part of Hume's point in the case of religion and the reason, perhaps, that he singled it out as distinct from other areas of life is that religious ideas have a particular appeal to the imagination so that, despite being ideas that merely persuade (polytheism) or inspire belief-like states (popular theism), they have a tendency to endure even when they are revealed as groundless and unjustified. The reasons for this are to be found in the imagination's principle of easy transition, coupled with its tendency to facilitate and encourage enthusiasm, along with the pleasure it takes in being terrified by religious images and in the gloomy passions that accompany them. At the same time Hume also discovers a species of religion that is 'true', the kind of theism he terms 'philosophical', which, like its counterpart in history, is based on reason and proportioned to evidence derived from experience and thus free of fictions that dominate religion in its false forms. Since it involves a species of belief, however, even this refined theism depends on the imagination, which, unwilling to be silenced, re-emerges to do battle with the faculty that deposed it. The result is a dialectic between true and false religion – philosophical theism and superstition – that takes the form of an antinomy, a conflict that can be explicated and diagnosed but never resolved.

Religion and Religious Fictions

In the *Natural History*, Hume says that 'religion' involves 'belief of invisible, intelligent power' (NHR Intro.1; see also 4.1), a definition general enough to encompass a potentially wide range of different systems that, as Falkenstein observes, form a spectrum on which each finds a place 'depending on how refined a conception of invisible intelligent power they put forward'.[4] The move from the specific and concrete to the general and abstract is the fulfilment of a 'natural progress of thought', a thesis that Hume proposes and defends in the *Natural History*. Whether a specific set of beliefs on the spectrum Falkenstein describes counts as 'true' or 'false', however, depends not on its status as a religion per se but on the origin of the beliefs in question. True religion, as we shall see later in this chapter, is based on reasoning from evidence (which Hume identifies with a version of the design argument) and the way belief in a designing God strikes the imagination. Religions that are false, by contrast, arise from the 'changeable, weak and irregular' principles of imagination, involve fictions, and are characterised by persuasion or belief-like states that can and should be corrected. Hume distinguishes these false forms under the broad division of 'polytheism', intended to encompass 'primitive' – that is, pre-monotheistic belief systems characteristic of early human societies – and 'theism' of the 'vulgar', 'traditional' or 'popular' kind, which involves a monotheistic system centred on a benevolent, omnipotent, omniscient Supreme Being, creator of the world with the particular providential power to oversee and intervene in the affairs of individuals, about whose welfare this Being is intimately concerned.[5] It might also include the occurrence of miracles that contravene the laws of nature and involve belief in the immortality of the soul that brings promise of an afterlife or 'future state', although these are neither necessary nor sufficient for a system to be theistic.[6]

Despite the profound difference in the tenets of these respective religious forms, both share the feature of being superstitious; they arise, that is, from fear in response to the vagaries and misfortunes of human life – health and sickness, plenty and want, life and death – and a profound ignorance of their real causes. Early and 'uninstructed' peoples respond to 'unknown causes' (NHR 3.1) by inventing 'invisible powers' – versions of themselves with passions and appetites augmented and more befitting creatures who are the 'masters of human fate' (NHR 3.4), towards whom, concomitantly, an array of ceremonies, rites and observances must be directed.[7] With its emphasis on a single deity, popular theism is a more refined version of these earlier polytheistic systems and, as Hume's thesis runs, a necessary development of them, as spiritualised objects of sense (inanimate objects of nature) are gradually denuded of their earthly stuff and the conception of intelligent invisible power becomes increasingly abstract. The same 'irrational and superstitious principles' are at work, Hume observes, manifest in theistic systems and that 'certain train of thinking' by which human beings move from deities modelled on themselves (a prince or supreme magistrate) to the pure abstraction of 'infinity itself' and the 'inexplicable mystery' of a single deity with an essence different in kind from human intelligence and beyond human comprehension (NHR 6.5). The ontogeny of popular theism recapitulates the phylogeny of earlier religious forms and retains within itself the trait of its primitive kin: it, too, involves a 'continued fear of a capricious and malevolent agent whom we seek to appease with ever inflated praises', as Falkenstein puts it nicely, and, being a 'development of a persistently capricious outlook', it is really in its heart and for all time 'demonic monotheism'.[8]

Religious Ideas as Artificial Fictions

While both polytheism and popular theism are false and share their origin in superstition, the fictions that appear in each are not the same. That the ideas of both *are* fictions seems uncontroversial and, given the nature of the putative objects to which such ideas ostensibly refer, they might even be taken to exemplify the concept's desiderata: whether the intelligent invisible powers of polytheists or the more abstract tenets of popular theism, they go beyond the evidence of sense and experience, are unverifiable, and transcend the human power of comprehension. The question is how the religious fictions of each should be categorised and understood. One possibility is that they are all artificial and, like all fictions of that kind, the result of a voluntary and deliberate act of the imagination to combine ideas and create new ones where no relation otherwise exists. Jennifer Herdt has proposed understanding Hume's view of popular theism along these lines, urging that religion be seen as analogous to literature in constituting a 'poetic reality', a 'system' that 'competes with the real, natural, this-worldly web of belief'. Herdt writes:

> In the *Natural History of Religion*, it becomes clear that Hume sees religious doctrine as a sort of 'poetical system'. Like poetry, religious doctrine forms an artificial union among ideas, using familiar terms in unfamiliar ways in order to make plausible incomprehensible or incoherent doctrines such as the immortality of the soul and the justice and loving kindness of a God who predestines people to everlasting torment and hell.[9]

Thus understood, popular theism competes directly with everyday life and, being contradicted by it, finds itself routinely subverted by the very reality it attempts to explain and supplant. As a result, popular theists are forced to make a choice between abandoning belief in a religious reality altogether or, as Herdt puts it, going to the 'extreme of adopting a voluntaristic attitude toward belief and responding to their current doubts by seeking to will themselves into believing religious doctrine'. This amounts to a form of 'self-deception', which, if carried through successfully, would mean intentionally acquiring and holding beliefs even though they conflict with others already held and justified unproblematically on the basis of experience. The artifice of theism is so extreme, and its juxtaposition to common life so glaring, that any profession of belief in its name is doomed to failure, for which reason one can interpret theism – or Hume's interpretation of it, at least – as an 'unsuccessful attempt at self-deception'.[10]

One problem with Herdt's proposal is that it effectively elides the difference between literary fictions and those of popular theism, and in so doing it shows why the latter cannot involve artificial fictions of the sort found in poetry. As we have seen, poetic fictions are rarely taken to refer to objects with real existence; they are ideas to which people only lend themselves, and any professed belief in them is properly classed as a matter of persuasion. The ideas of popular theism, by contrast, are taken by the faithful to refer to objects with real existence, a status quite different from the one conferred on the creations of poets. Correspondingly, such religious people are not merely persuaded temporarily by the objects to which the ideas refer – as the very same people are, no doubt, when reading a novel or watching a theatrical performance – but profess to hold beliefs about them with a 'serious conviction' that feels different from the 'fervours of poetry and eloquence' (to recall Hume's remarks on literature) and the merely phantom belief to which they give rise. That she ignores the artificiality of poetical fictions is perhaps the reason why Herdt misleadingly compares a poetic system to one of popular theism, when the former lacks a central feature that makes the latter religious, namely the demand that one take its fictions as real and *believe in* – not simply be persuaded by – the ideas that compose its system of belief. Without this demand, in fact, there would be no contradiction between religion and everyday life, and the need for voluntarism and self-deception would never arise.

In fact, Herdt's characterisation of religion as a poetical system of artificially created fictions captures the ideas of polytheism better than those of popular theism.[11] The origin of polytheistic fictions is of a piece with the origin of poetic fictions and the presence of persuasion over any sort of belief, and Hume, tellingly, draws on similar language to describe both types. The former might differ from the latter in being a psychological response to the 'disordered scene' (NHR 3.1) of human life but it, too, relies on the 'active fancy' and 'active imagination' (NHR 8.1 and 13.1) to conjure fabulous personages who have no more real existence than the 'winged horses, fiery dragons, and monstrous giants' of literary fables and romances. The 'embellishments of poets and orators' are one with the 'arts of priests and politicians' in the 'sublime topics' they embrace (EHU 12.25/SBN 162), and the same tendency for human beings to conceive the world in their own image and anthropomorphise nature explains both '*prosopopœia* in poetry' and the 'poetical figures and expressions' of polytheism. These 'gain not on the belief', moreover, but at once

> prove a certain tendency in the imagination, without which they could neither be beautiful nor natural. Nor is a river-god or a hamadryad always taken for a mere poetical or imaginary personage, but may sometimes enter the real creed of the ignorant vulgar; while each grove or field is represented as possessed of a particular *genius* or invisible power, which inhabits and protects it. (NHR 3.2)[12]

That same 'vigour of conception' that, as we saw in Chapter 4, poetry and eloquence receive from literary fictions also operates in the mind of polytheists, people who really only 'lend themselves' to the creations of the imagination. It is not a matter of false belief because it is not a case of belief at all, even if, as Hume acknowledges, the ideas in question have more force and vivacity than the fictions of poetry, strike the imagination with greater force, enter more deeply into the psychology of the individual in question, and thus endure longer than even the most engaging scenes of literature. This is a point to which we will return towards the end of this chapter.

Religious Ideas as Vulgar Fictions

While fictions of polytheism are appropriately categorised as artificial and the doxastic state they inspire called persuasion, this still leaves the ideas of popular theism, which – given that they involve some belief-like state – are better understood as a species of vulgar fiction that inspires natural belief. The first possibility in this regard is that they are first-order natural fictions, which arise without deliberation from the 'permanent, irresistible, and universal' principles of imagination, inspiring beliefs that are obstinate, intractable and unavoidable, similar to those met with in the form of vulgar fictions in metaphysics and the formation of property. The suggestion that Hume's approach to religious phenomena be understood along these lines is long-standing and has generated a good deal of lively debate in the literature. As we had occasion to remark in Chapter 1, the view is associated most closely with R. J. Butler and his thesis about belief in intelligent design, though others have proposed variations on the same theme.[13] Butler uses the fact that 'we commonly act in accordance with belief in design' to draw the conclusion that 'belief in design must be a natural rather than a rational belief'. Belief in such a God, that is, cannot be justified either on the basis of experience (a posteriori), since that would to infer more in the cause than is contained in the effect, or through reason (a priori), because whatever is conceived as existent can be conceived as non-existent without fear of contradiction. This leaves only the category of 'natural belief', Butler concludes, to explain an individual's belief in intelligent design.[14]

As we had occasion to emphasise in Chapter 1, in the *Natural History* Hume distinguishes clearly between an 'original or primary impression of nature' and 'principles' that are 'secondary', and this obviously casts doubt on the plausibility of Butler's thesis. Under the first, Hume includes self-love, sexual attraction, love of one's children, gratitude and resentment, all of which are marked by being universal, having specific objects and being pursued inflexibly across a range of social and historical circumstances. Under the latter, by contrast, he places religion, the rise and establishment of which is contingent on and 'may be easily perverted by various accidents and causes' or 'may, by an extraordinary concurrence of circumstances, be altogether prevented' (NHR Intro.1).[15] Hume also draws attention to the secondary character of religious belief in a well-known passage from a letter to Gilbert Elliot of Minto in March 1751; he there emphasises that our belief in matters of fact (from sense and experience) is a propensity of a different order than the one articulated by Cleanthes in the *Dialogues*, and that, in turn, from the one that generates the superstitions of polytheism and popular theism. He writes:

> I cou'd wish that Cleanthes' Argument [the argument from design in the *Dialogues*] could be so analys'd, as to be render'd quite formal & regular. The propensity of the Mind towards it, unless that Propensity were as strong & universal as that to believe in our Senses & Experience, will still, I am afraid, be esteem'd a suspicious Foundation ... We must endeavour to prove that this Propensity is somewhat different from our Inclination to find our own Figures in the Clouds, our Face in the Moon, our Passions & Sentiments even in inanimate Matter. Such an Inclination may, & ought to be controul'd, & can never be a legitimate Ground of Assent. (L 1.155)[16]

As Gaskin and subsequent commentators have emphasised, the problem with Butler's thesis as stated, then, is that belief in God – and by extension religious belief in general[17] – fails to satisfy the criteria governing what counts as 'natural belief'; it differs fundamentally from other natural fictions of vulgar reasoning without which 'human nature must immediately perish and go to ruin'. Religious beliefs might be non-rational but they do not arise from naive common sense, being acquired as part of exposure to a particular tradition; many people get on in the world quite well without them, for which reason religious beliefs hardly count as a precondition of action; and there is a reasonable alternative set of beliefs that one might adopt – atheism or simple agnosticism – which means that they are not universal. John Immerwahr thus expresses the quite reasonable position of many when he writes: 'I assume, without argument here, that it is also unlikely that Hume felt that religious beliefs were unavoidable "natural beliefs" such as our belief in the existence of external objects.'[18]

The second possibility, then – and the one that, on balance, best captures what Hume has to say about them – is that the ideas of popular theism are vulgar fictions that inspire belief-like states from a second-order propensity to believe in them. They are the result of the productive imagination combining ideas to create new ones, albeit maladies that can and should be corrected; they might even, to reiterate Hume's observation, be preventable altogether, even if some 'extraordinary concurrence of circumstances' is required for that to transpire.[19] While some commentators have argued forcefully against the suggestion that Hume takes religious belief to be natural in any sense, our discussion so far has shown that there is conceptual room for him to hold such a view. As we shall see below, it is also a strain of Hume's thinking that has been used to makes sense of Philo's professed deism at the end of the *Dialogues*.

Hume himself captures the thought that there is a 'natural' basis for religion in his suggestion that the propensity towards religious belief is 'almost universal' (NHR 4.1) and appears to be part of human nature.[20] He writes, for example, that there is a 'universal propensity to believe in invisible, intelligent power', and while not an 'original' (that is, primary) instinct, it remains 'at least a general attendant of human nature, [and] may be considered as a kind of mark or stamp, which the divine workman has set upon his work' (NHR 15.5). Hume does not think that this propensity always manifests itself – after all, it can be 'prevented' – or that, when it does, it is manifested in a uniform way; however, the 'doctrine of one supreme deity, the author of nature, is very ancient', he observes, 'has spread itself over great and populous nations, and among them has been embraced by all ranks and conditions of men' (NHR 6.1).

Hume's view that religious beliefs spring from a secondary propensity is also reflected at certain points in the *History*, where he expresses sympathy with figures who turned to religion for comfort and solace. He reports, for example, on Earpwold, seventh-century King of East Anglia, who was 'unable to resist those allurements [of religion], which have seduced the wisest of mankind' (H 1.39), and says of King Canute that, as he neared the end of his life, he 'began to cast his view towards that future existence, which it is so natural for the human mind, whether satiated by prosperity or disgusted with adversity, to make the object of its attention' (H 1.124). In a similar vein, Hume observes of Charles I that:

> While everything around him bore a hostile aspect; while friends, family, relations, whom he passionately loved, were placed at a distance, and unable to serve him; he reposed himself with confidence in the arms of that being, who penetrates and sustains all nature, and whose severities, if received with piety and resignation, he regarded as the surest pledges of unexhausted favour. (H 5.518)

Even the superstitious 'fooleries' that attend religious rituals, such as the reliquaries of the Catholics, Hume is willing to consider a regular expression of human nature, as they 'are to be found in all ages and nations, and even took place during the most refined periods of antiquity' (H 3.253). Hume seems to doubt that even Catholicism, that most superstitious of creeds, will disappear altogether and he suspects that if it did it would be replaced by doctrines equally 'absurd'. As he remarks at one point in the *Natural History*:

> Such are the doctrines of our brethren the CATHOLICS. But to these doctrines we are so accustomed, that we never wonder at them: Though, in a future age, it will probably become difficult to persuade some nations, that any human, two-legged creature could ever embrace such principles. And it is a thousand to one, but these nations themselves shall have something full as absurd in their own creed, to which they will give a most implicit and most religious assent. (NHR 12.5)

Hume has some hopes that, as he says in his discussion of miracles, his arguments will form an 'everlasting check to all kinds of superstitious delusion, and consequently, will be useful as long as the world endures. For so long, I presume, will accounts of miracles and prodigies be found in all history, sacred and profane' (EHU 10.2/SBN 110). According to Smith's report of Hume's last illness, this is a view he held until the very end.[21]

Hume might well find such beliefs non-rational, repugnant and even dangerous, but he appears to be under no illusion that sounder reasoning will eradicate superstition from the history of human kind; religious beliefs (polytheistic and theistic) have a natural basis and a natural history, and while their content may change, the beliefs have a tendency to reassert themselves in different forms over time. There might be good reason to doubt the degree of Hume's own religious convictions, but care and qualification are in order when it comes to announcing his outright hostility to religion, that he hoped for its eventual demise, or thought that the deeply held convictions that constitute faith and religious belief could be excised from their deep roots in human nature.[22]

Religious Belief and the Imagination

With religious ideas now sorted into artificial and vulgar fictions, the question that now presents itself is why religious ideas have such stamina and staying power and why the states they inspire endure as either persuasion (polytheism) or belief-like states (popular theism), even when they are exposed as fictions without basis in real existence or matter of fact. Hume does not explicitly raise and answer the question in quite these terms, but he does indicate three discernible ways in which the imagination can be called upon for an explanation: through the principle of easy transition that governs it; the enthusiasm it facilitates and encourages; and the capacity it exhibits for taking pleasure in being terrified. We can consider each in turn.

The Principle of Easy Transition

The first way in which the imagination asserts itself in the religious sphere is through the principle of easy transition and the desire to create a union or form a whole, from which it derives pleasure and avoids pain. The principle manifests itself, first, in the tendency of the imagination to be influenced more by what is large, superior, important, high and contiguous than by what is small, inferior, trivial, low and remote, according to the maxim that the greatest influence on the faculty follows from what is 'most taken notice of'. In the sphere of religion, this principle underlies the 'natural progress of thought' to which Hume attributes the development of theism from polytheism. The 'mind rises gradually, from inferior to superior', he writes. 'By abstracting from what is imperfect, it forms an idea of perfection: And slowly distinguishing the nobler parts of its own frame from the grosser, it learns to transfer only the former, much elevated and refined, to its divinity' (NHR 1.5). As a result, the mind leaves behind the particular, concrete beings

of polytheism and reaches the highest abstraction of divine intelligence and 'infinity itself'.

Second, the imagination is driven to form a union, a process in
which it is affected passively – moved by the hope and fear generated by unknown causes – and works actively in being 'equally
employed in forming ideas of those powers, on which we have so
entire a dependence'. Although these ideas are conceived only in
a 'general and confused manner', the imagination is driven by its
desire for completeness 'to form some particular and distinct idea
of them'. Hume observes of people that:

> The more they consider these causes themselves, and the uncertainty
> of their operation, the less satisfaction do they meet with in their
> researches; and, however unwilling, they must at last have abandoned
> so arduous an attempt, were it not for a propensity in human nature,
> which leads into a system, that gives them some satisfaction. (NHR
> 3.1)

The same principle is at work in Hume's observation that a philosophical bent of mind will find in the works of nature only a single
being rather than a multitude, because the 'conception of different authors . . . serves only to give perplexity to the imagination,
without bestowing any satisfaction on the understanding' (NHR
2.2).

Once the imagination has conjured ideas of intelligent invisible
powers, moreover – general and confused as they might be – it
then follows, third, its inclination to commit to a 'new relation'
by conferring a spatial location on qualities that do not otherwise
possess it, inventing an idea to reconcile contradictory and irreconcilable propositions that otherwise cause pain and bewilderment.
'[H]owever strong men's propensity to believe invisible, intelligent
power in nature', Hume writes, 'their propensity is equally strong
to rest their attention on sensible, visible objects; and in order to
reconcile these opposite inclinations, they are led to unite the invisible power with some visible object' (NHR 5.2). This propensity
also underlies the handy trick performed by believers in constant
need of making vivacious and perspicuous their otherwise faint
and confused ideas. A real object that resembles the remote object
of belief can always be employed to make the idea in question more
forceful, for which reason Roman Catholics employ mummeries,
from which 'they feel the good effect of those external motions,

and postures, and actions, in enlivening their devotion, and quickening their fervour, which otherwise would decay away, if directed entirely to distant and immaterial objects' (T 1.3.8.4/SBN 100). This is what Hume seems to have in mind when he observes that rendering a religious passion 'of continuance' requires that we embrace a 'method of affecting the senses and imagination', which includes 'some *historical*, as well as *philosophical* account of the divinity', a means of making lively and vivacious an idea that is otherwise too abstract and remote 'long [to] actuate the mind' (E 167).

The same tendency to 'shadow out' the objects of faith (T 1.3.8.4/SBN 100) – to embody what is immaterial in the form of images and sensible representations – also has profound consequences for how religion develops. We see this in human beings' tendency to derive qualities from themselves and confer them, initially, on the invisible powers taken to occupy objects of the natural world and then, as polytheism transmutes into popular theism, on the abstract concept of a single deity, terminating with divine intelligence and 'infinity itself'. As Hume observes in the first *Enquiry*, this idea of God 'as meaning an *infinitely intelligent, wise, and good Being*' is explicable as ideas of the operations of our mind augmented 'without limit' and conferred on an abstract invisible power (EHU 2.6/SBN 19). As Hume writes in the *Natural History*:

> There is a universal tendency among mankind to conceive all beings like themselves, and to transfer to every object, those qualities, with which they are familiarly acquainted, and of which they are intimately conscious. We find human faces in the moon, armies in the clouds; and by a natural propensity, if not corrected by experience and reflection, ascribe malice or good-will to every thing, that hurts or pleases us. (NHR 3.2)[23]

These latter aspects of the imagination – the desire to create a whole and the error of misplaced concreteness – are manifest in what Hume describes as the 'flux and reflux of polytheism and theism', the 'natural tendency' human beings display to 'rise from idolatry to theism, and to sink again from theism into idolatry' (NHR 8.1). This arises from the dual impulses of the imagination to move both downwards, where it gives physical form to invisible intelligence in nature and inanimate objects, and upwards, where it unifies disparate elements into an increasingly abstracted whole. Hume writes:

> By degrees, the active imagination of men, uneasy in the abstract conception of objects, about which it is incessantly employed, begins to render them more particular, and to clothe them in shapes more suitable to its natural comprehension. It represents them to be sensible, intelligent beings, like mankind; actuated by love and hatred, and flexible by gifts and entreaties, by prayers and sacrifices. Hence the origin of religion: And hence the origin of idolatry or polytheism. (NHR 8.1)

The idols of polytheism might arise from concerns over the vagaries of life, but they are not thereby abated, since the beings conjured are entrusted with the fate of humankind but given only limited power to complete their task; they soon appear inadequate to a people anxious and fearful in the face of an unknowable world. The people respond by piling 'exaggerated praises and compliments' on their creations and, 'elevating their deities to the utmost bounds of perfection, at last beget the attributes of unity and infinity, simplicity and spirituality' (NHR 8.2), the idea of a single being that renders the diversity of creation into a whole. This concept, however, is too abstract, and the first principle reasserts itself in the form of 'inferior mediators or subordinate agents, . . . demi-gods or middle beings' who 'partaking more of human nature' reinstate the original beings from whom a single abstract deity was derived; as conceptions of these beings in turn become 'grosser and more vulgar' the propensity for abstraction reasserts itself and the 'tide turns again towards theism'. For 'feeble apprehensions of men cannot be satisfied with conceiving their deity as a pure spirit and perfect intelligence', Hume writes, 'and yet their natural terrors keep them from imputing to him the least shadow of limitation and imperfection. They fluctuate between these opposite sentiments' (NHR 8.2). This process is an antinomy, the result of two competing and equally unassailable tendencies of the imagination that compete and, by turns, gain ascendancy and retreat, a movement that proceeds without end.

Enthusiasm

The second way in which the imagination explains the stamina and staying power of religious ideas is through enthusiasm. We have already seen that Hume explains the origin of religion – in its false forms, at least – in terms of superstition: the creation of fictional beings as a response to fear amid the otherwise mysterious vagaries of life. The accompanying corruption of religion is enthusiasm, which invites comparison to the way the fictions of poets engage and affect the imaginations of an audience. Enthusiasm rises from the forceful ideas that follow from the effects of elevation and the 'warm imagination' they occasion, a phenomenon that explains why religious ideas hold sway over their victims and endure with greater intensity than in the case of merely literary creations. Indeed, religion seems to require this movement. For 'religious motives, where they act at all, operate only by starts and bounds; and it is scarcely possible for them to become altogether habitual to the mind' (DNR 12.13), Hume observes, and, given that the religious motive is unfamiliar in everyday life and only 'acts by intervals on the temper, . . . [it] must be roused by continual efforts, in order to keep the pious zealot satisfied with his own conduct, and make him fulfil his devotional task' (DNR 12.17). Such efforts have their salutary effects only when from 'prosperous success, . . . from strong spirits, or from a bold and confident disposition . . . the imagination swells with great, but confused conceptions, to which no sublunary beauties or enjoyments can correspond' (E 74). Hume writes that, under the sway of enthusiasm,

> a full range [is] given to the fancy in the invisible regions or world of spirits, where the soul is at liberty to indulge itself in every imagination, which may best suit its present taste and disposition. Hence arise raptures, transports, and surprising flights of fancy; and confidence and presumption still encreasing, these raptures, being altogether unaccountable, and seeming quite beyond the reach of our ordinary faculties, are attributed to the immediate inspiration of that Divine Being, who is the object of devotion. (E 74)

Religious enthusiasm is a spectacular case of a lively imagination degenerating into madness; operations of the imagination overpower sound judgement and individuals, disordered in their powers and faculties, become incapable of distinguishing truth from falsehood. Hume compares the religious enthusiast to a 'fanatic madman', who, taken with 'frenzy', 'delivers himself over, blindly, and without reserve, to the supposed illapses of the spirit, and to inspiration from above' (E 74).

Like poets who manipulate their audience according to rules of art, priests also employ the power of language to enliven the ideas and raise the enthusiasm of their followers, although Hume is less sanguine about the motives of religious leaders whose aim is not to entertain or give pleasure but to exploit the natural weakness of human beings for their own ends. Testimony is an important and reliable source of knowledge, but (as already noted) it has the potential to pass over easily into credulity, 'a too easy faith in the testimony of others', an effect exploited in the case of religion where people are willing to accept from their leaders much more than daily experience and observation will support. 'The smallest spark may here kindle into the greatest flame', Hume observes, 'because the materials are always prepared for it. The *avidum genus auricularum*, the gazing populace, receive greedily, without examination, whatever soothes superstition, and promotes wonder' (EHU 10.30/SBN 126). The attraction of religion is strong, however, and as creators of literary fictions are carried away by their own 'fire and genius' (T 1.3.10.8/SBN 123), so the self-styled prophet is inspired by the thought of becoming 'so sublime a character' (EHU 10.29/SBN 125) and, having 'aided the ascent of reason by the wings of imagination', reaches the 'celestial regions' from which heights they claim privileged knowledge. These religious leaders conclude 'that a more perfect production than the present world would be more suitable to such perfect beings as the gods'; they quickly forget that they have no basis for doing so except 'what can be found in the present world' (EHU 11.16/SBN 138).

In general, Hume is critical of those who exploit tendencies of the imagination to give added force and vivacity to their doctrines, which, unlike the products of poets – harmless liars whose intention is only to please and entertain – are of serious and lasting consequence. The *History* is replete with instances where Hume takes great delight in exposing religious leaders who use every means at their disposal to subdue and mislead the ignorant, employing their doctrines as a 'veil' (H 1.324; 5.285) or 'mask' (H 1.315 and 333; 2.10) to hide their earthly ambition and hypocrisy (H 1.99; 2.117; 3.427). For 'ecclesiastical power . . . can always cover its operations under a cloak of sanctity' (H 2.4), Hume observes, concealing ambition, violence, bigotry, revenge and cruelty with 'the broad mantle of religion' and the 'duty' supposed to accompany it (H 1.152; 3.435; 5.31).[24]

Predictably, the cynical manipulation of the gazing populace

goes hand in hand with the inherent corruption of religious institutions, exemplified for Hume by the likes of Ethelwolf, who passed
in Rome 'a twelvemonth in exercises of devotion, and failed not
in that most essential part of devotion, liberality to the church of
Rome' (H 1.59), and John Mansel, chaplain to Henry II, who held
700 ecclesiastical livings and whose 'abuses became so evident as
to be palpable to the blindness of superstition itself' (H 2.24). On
occasion, Hume identifies such instances as the inevitable con-
comitant of doctrines founded on superstition and enthusiasm.
For 'where superstition has raised a church to such an exorbitant
height as that of Rome', he writes, 'persecution is less the result
of bigotry in the priests, than of necessary policy' (H 4.19), as
the 'very nature' of the Jesuits sent to oppose Elizabeth I was 'to
pervert learning . . . and to erect a regular system of casuistry,
by which prevarication, perjury, and every crime, when it served
their ghostly purposes, might be justified and defended' (H 4.188).
Aware of corruption and contradiction in their systems, moreover,
religious authorities are always capable of finding creative ways
to explain the failure of their doctrines and predictions. As Hume
writes of the Armada, defeated in 1588:

> The Spanish priests, who had so often blest this holy crusade . . . were
> somewhat at a loss to account for the victory gained over the Catholic
> monarch by excommunicated heretics and an execrable usurper: but
> they at last discovered, that all the calamities of the Spaniards had
> proceeded from their allowing the infidel Moors to live among them.
> (H 4.271)[25]

Pleasure in Agreeable Effects

Third, and finally, religious ideas enter so deeply into the minds
of professed believers because the imagination finds their effects
agreeable. The faculty takes pleasure not only when it forms a
whole but also in the particular passions ignited by religious ideas.
This is most obvious in flights of enthusiastic fancy into the celestial regions where the imagination indulges the raptures of divine
inspiration, but is also true of sentiments roused by ideas from the
darker realms of superstition. '[T]error is the primary principle of
religion', Hume writes, the 'passion which always predominates in
it, and admits but of short intervals of pleasure' (DNR 12.29). Of
short duration it might be, but no less than in the throes of painful

emotions from tragic scenes enacted in a theatre, 'in matters of religion men take a pleasure in being terrify'd', especially when preachers – popular for just this reason – excite the 'most dismal and gloomy passions' (T 1.3.9.15/SBN 115). This pleasure comes from the sense of mystery, novelty and wonder inspired by religious phenomena, and as literary representation converts what is painful into what is pleasant, so the disturbing sentiments that originate in hope and fear are spiritualised and rendered pleasing through idealised images of death, damnation and hellfire, even to the point (though Hume does not use the example specifically) where one can feel the passion of the crucifixion. The melancholic passions are redirected by the sentiments of beauty that arise from their representation in religious images, and the pain that would otherwise follow from them is converted into pleasure. Hume writes:

> In the common affairs of life, where we feel and are penetrated with the solidity of the subject, nothing can be more disagreeable than fear and terror; and 'tis only in dramatic performances and in religious discourses, that they ever give pleasure. In the latter cases the imagination reposes itself indolently on the idea; and the passion, being soften'd by the want of belief in the subject, has no more than the agreeable effect of enlivening the mind, and fixing the attention. (T 1.3.9.15/SBN 115)

In this sense, religious ideas transform and embellish experience, the result of the 'repining anxious disposition' of human beings. There is a 'secret chain . . . that holds us', Hume observes. 'We are terrified, not bribed to the continuance of our existence' (DNR 10.17), and more often than not the spirit of religion is imbued with sorrow rather than joy, its 'terrors' prevailing 'above its comforts' (DNR 12.25).

The psychological impact on believers is marked, arousing in them that 'whole train of monkish virtues' – celibacy, fasting, penance, mortification, self-denial, humility, silence, solitude – that make a man unfit for society and decrease his otherwise natural 'power of self-enjoyment' (EPM 9.3/SBN 270; see NHR 10.2). It can also have the inverse effect, and prevent individuals from doing what would otherwise naturally relieve them of pain, as in the case of the man who refuses to commit suicide in favour of prolonging 'a miserable existence, from a vain fear, lest he offend his maker, by using the power, with which that beneficent being has endowed him' (E 579); the natural course of suicide is ruled out by the artifice imposed by 'superstition and false religion' (E 578). In general, religious belief effectively 'disjoints the ordinary frame of the mind, and throws it into the utmost confusion', Hume observes; '. . . it is apt to make a considerable breach in the temper, and to produce that gloom and melancholy, so remarkable in all devout people' (DNR 12.30).

The Persistence of Religious Ideas

As we remarked at the beginning of the chapter, Hume considers religion a singular phenomenon, different in kind from other areas of philosophical inquiry. One of its distinguishing features is the fact that its fictions and the doxastic states they involve persist even when shown to contradict everyday experience. The fictions of polytheism are artificial and should inspire only temporary persuasion, and those of popular theism arise from a secondary propensity and should be correctable; in both cases, however, adherents appear convinced of the reality of the objects to which the ideas putatively refer: their power does not diminish as does that of fictional characters when one leaves the theatre (as one would expect in the case of polytheism); nor do the faithful give up (as one would expect in the case of popular theism) the ideas of God, miracles or the afterlife, even when the fictional status of the phenomena is articulated and the falsity of the related beliefs revealed. Religious fictions attain a force and vivacity such that the imagination is affected, filled, and assents to the existence of and belief in phenomena that it finds difficult to resist. Religion, to invoke Herdt, is really a case of *successful* self-deception.[26] Unsuccessful self-deception destroys the very belief it attempts to uphold because, in light of the obvious contradiction between religion and everyday life, people would quickly become aware of deceiving themselves and abandon their professed beliefs. In reality, this does not happen; on the contrary, religion proves itself an edifice that, despite the manifest contradictions between its web of belief and that of ordinary experience, remains remarkably stable. If anything, religious belief is strengthened through the ingenious ways discovered to reconcile doctrine with the world.

Hume *is* willing to entertain the possibility that in some instances – the 'eternal duration of their souls' being a case in point – people do realise the absurdity of the doctrines they profess and act from motives far removed from the religious ones they claim to hold. In general, an 'abstract, invisible object, like that which *natural* religion presents to us, cannot long actuate the mind, or be any moment in life' (E 167), and people are simply disingenuous because they do not 'really believe ... what they pretend to affirm', as Hume observes in the case of an afterlife; so 'faint' is the resemblance between this idea and experience that one can hardly be blamed for not really believing it with 'true and establish'd judgement'. A little observation soon reveals how actions are guided by concern for one's reputation in *this* world, and how quickly religious people depart from their own doctrines, quickly condemning immorality and cruelty against others whom, on the basis of their professed doctrines, they should 'condemn to eternal and infinite punishments' (T 1.3.9.13–14/SBN 113–15). That superstitious believers are obliged continually to keep their belief alive through sensible image and tangible representation surely confirms Hume's point about the inherent weakness of religious ideas.

On the other hand, we have seen how the principles of the imagination can account in some measure at least for the persistence of religious ideas: the principle of easy transition; its tendency to facilitate and encourage enthusiasm; and the pleasure it feels in being terrified. These are not sufficient to explain the power of religion entirely, however, something Hume himself appears to admit, both in accepting religious belief as 'natural' in some sense, and by recognising that ultimately faith is required for assenting to what is otherwise extraordinary, unaccountable and beyond the reach of our faculties, a 'fairy land' – as Hume describes the idea of a Supreme Being promulgated by occasionalism – where 'we have no reason to trust our common methods of argument, or to think that our usual analogies and probabilities have any authority' (EHU 7.24/SBN 72). Reason is both 'a sure method of exposing [our Holy religion] ... to a trial as it is, by no means, fitted to endure', Hume observes slyly, as that same faculty by itself is 'insufficient to convince us of its veracity' (EHU 10.40/SBN 130). He adds:

Whoever is moved by *Faith* to assent to it [Christianity], is conscious of a continued miracle in his own person, which subverts all the principles of his understanding; and gives him a determination to believe what is most contrary to custom and experience. (EHU 10.41/SBN 131)

Reason, to express Hume's thought otherwise, is insufficient to support religion, but it is equally impotent in undermining faith: the point at which justification ends and when religious ideas strike the imagination with sufficient force and vivacity to inspire, if not first-order natural belief, then a second-order variety that is difficult to dislodge.

True and False Religion

We have seen that superstitious religions are false, and that the imagination provides principles that explain why fictions arise, take hold and inspire beliefs that are difficult to correct. They are ultimately matters of faith rather than reason, which can neither support nor undermine them. There is, however, another form of religion that Hume describes as 'true', which, as its name suggests, contrasts with and excludes the features that make its opposite 'false': fictions, persuasion, belief-like states and the absence of justification through reason or from experience. Sometimes when Hume designates religion as 'true' (mostly in the *History*), he appears to describe what individuals at a given time and place *took* to be the correct form of religion,[27] but this is to be distinguished from his use of the epithet to describe a version of theism that appears variously in his writing under the guise of being 'pure', 'rational', 'speculative', or 'philosophical'.[28] As we saw in the previous chapter, Hume uses similar terminology in distinguishing 'true' or 'philosophical' history from its 'false' or 'fabulous' kin, and clarifying what he means by it in that context offers a clue to his use of the same in the sphere of religion. True history, to recall the earlier discussion, is based on evidence and involves the application of reason, both of which Hume takes as marks that distinguish true religion from its false counterpart.[29]

Religion and Evidence

In the case of history, evidence consists of testimony, written and oral, from which the historian aims to construct a true narrative of past events. History becomes false when diverted from this path either inadvertently (through the obscurity of testimony, genuine ignorance, or the intrinsically confusing nature of the events reported) or more deliberately (from prejudice, dogmatism and partiality). At bottom, however, historians presuppose, in the process of reconstruction, that there are facts of the matter, an original scene, albeit lost, lying at the heart of their memorial enterprise. In the strange land of religion, by contrast, where we lack the compass of 'common sense and experience' and encounter objects 'too large for our grasp', what counts as evidence is less clear. In the sphere of religion, moreover, the philosopher can reject a good number of the phenomena that compose it in favour of other, more plausible, explanations: the idea of God as a being infinitely intelligent, wise and good is explicable as ideas derived from of our own person augmented without limit; that of an immortal soul and the inference to a future state are confused ideas remote from common life; and belief in the occurrence of miracles shows that experience can never furnish sufficient grounds to warrant an inference that the laws of nature have been violated. On the contrary, experience teaches us that there is always an intervening cause to explain the miraculous event and it is never the case that the falsehood of the testimony on which it is based is 'more miraculous, than the fact, which it endeavours to establish' (EHU 10.13/SBN 116).

There remains, however, one area that Hume consistently admits as evidence for assenting to the existence of the object to which the idea in question refers, and that is a version of the design argument. This appears at various junctures in the *Natural History*, and is given, most famously, by Philo in the *Dialogues*: adumbrated earlier as concessions to Cleanthes (DNR 5.11–12 and 10.36) and reaching fruition in what is now widely referred to as Philo's 'about face' or 'reversal' in section 12, where he declares his 'veneration for true religion' and 'abhorrence of vulgar superstitions' (DNR 12.9).[30] In the culminating expression of his 'unfeigned sentiments' on the subject (DNR 12.9), he asks:

> If the whole natural theology . . . resolves itself into one simple, though somewhat ambiguous, at least undefined proposition, *that the cause or causes of order in the universe probably bear some remote analogy to human intelligence*: If this proposition be not capable of extension, variation, or more particular explication: If it affords no inference that affects human life, or can be the source of any action or forbearance: And if the analogy, imperfect as it is, can be carried no farther than to the human intelligence; and cannot be transferred, with any appearance of probability, to the other qualities of the mind: If this really be the case, what can the most inquisitive, contemplative, and religious man do more than give, plain, philosophical assent to the proposition,

as often as it occurs; and believe, that the arguments, on which it is established, exceed the objections, which lie against it? (DNR 12.33)

Philo's declaration is in the subjunctive mood and qualified at every turn; the proposition is 'ambiguous' and 'undefined'; the analogy in question is 'remote' and 'imperfect' and extends no further than 'human intelligence'; and it involves narrow 'philosophical assent' on the grounds that it is supported by arguments somewhat better than objections against it.[31] The extent – or lack thereof – of Philo's admission becomes clear when it is considered along with his earlier rejection of the first design argument in section 2. In his hortatory fashion, Cleanthes declares:

> Look around the world: Contemplate the whole and every part of it: You will find it to be nothing but one great machine, subdivided into an infinite number of lesser machines, which again admit of subdivisions, to a degree beyond what human senses and faculties can trace and explain. All these various machines, and even their most minute parts, are adjusted to each other with an accuracy, which ravishes into admiration all men, who have ever contemplated them. The curious adapting of means to ends, throughout all nature, resembles exactly, though it much exceeds, the productions of human contrivance; of human design, thought, wisdom, and intelligence. Since therefore the effects resemble each other, we are led to infer, by all the rules of analogy, that the causes also resemble; and that the author of nature is somewhat similar to the mind of man; though possessed of much larger faculties, proportioned to the grandeur of the work, which he has executed. By this argument *a posteriori*, and by this argument alone, do we prove at once the existence of a deity, and his similarity to human mind and intelligence. (DNR 2.5)

As various commentators have pointed out, Cleanthes' presentation takes the form of a 'regular' argument, that is, one involving rational inference from premises to conclusion, and its fate, whether it stands or falls, depends on satisfying criteria governing analogical reasoning ('all rules of analogy'): that analogues must be resembling and obtain among types rather than individuals, that from similar effects only similar causes can be inferred, and that what is projected in the cause must be proportional to the observed effect. This is where Philo aims his attack and shows, most fundamentally, that the differences between the universe and human productions (his example is a house) are 'vast' and the analogy therefore 'very weak' (DNR 2.7–8); that the inference to an intelligence as a source of order in the whole is arbitrary, since experience shows that ordered effects in the parts arise from non-intelligent sources as well (DNR 12.23); and that the beginning of the universe is a unique event rather than a 'species' of cause and therefore no sound basis on which to infer a designing God from the observed effect (DNR 12.24). Any designer that one infers, moreover, could possess only qualities proportional to our experience of them as evident in the observed universe; thus the 'supposition of farther attributes is mere hypothesis' (EHU 11.14/SBN 137). The picture that arises from Philo's 'proposition' in section 12 and what remains of the design argument in section 2 after his trenchant criticism is much the same: that from experience all one can infer is a very remote cause in the form of a being with limited attributes, along with only a 'general' (rather than particular) providence, namely, a chain of causes and effects set in motion by a deity and regulated by the universal laws of nature. As such, it does not appear that Philo's 'profession of faith' involves much of a 'reversal' at all.

There is good reason, then, to characterise Hume's position as falling short even of deism, properly called – the view that reason and observation of the natural world lead to a conclusion that there exists a single creator of the universe – and amounting instead only to a modest, weak, or, using Gaskin's phrase, 'attenuated deism', involving assent to an 'original source of order [that] could scarcely function even as the start for belief in a personal God exercising a moral jurisdiction, accessible to prayer, performing acts of intervention in his creation, and worthy of adoration'. Having nothing to do with morality or religion, and 'being utterly irrelevant to life and thought', as Yandell puts, believing the central claim 'leaves everything else the same as it was before one believed it'. Kemp Smith goes so far as to call it 'sheer negation', Hume having 'reduced the contents "God" and "religion" to a beggarly minimum'. [32] On the other hand, while this final position is modest, confined to those few individuals of a philosophical bent (DNR 12.32), not commonly found in the world (DNR 12.22), and 'religious' only in the specific sense delineated by Hume – 'belief of invisible, intelligent power' – it is justified by evidence, free of superstition and devoid of fictions. It might even be characterised, to use Garrett's words, as 'Hume's own true religion'.[33]

Religion and Reason

The second component of Hume's true religion is reason, the faculty responsible for making the inference from the evidence to the conclusion (however modest) of intelligent design. We have seen that, in historical writing, reason appears as the 'critical' response to testimony and reflects the demands of historical method to weigh conflicting reports in order to reconstruct, as accurately as possible, what actually happened. Reason involves inference from true premises to conclusions and belief based on probability, with the assumption that the truth is embedded ultimately in some matter of fact, albeit lost to a past from which it must be recovered. Hume appears to be employing (or assuming) the same concept of reason in his discussions of religion, certainly in a general sense when he evokes 'speculative curiosity, or the pure love of truth' as the means of making '*any* inference concerning invisible intelligent power' (NHR 2.5, emphasis added), but, in addition and often, when referring more specifically to theism, either in its popular form (where he talks about 'monotheism') or as philosophical theism. *All* forms of theism, that is, insofar as they are monotheistic, involve the admixture of reason that enables the mind to remove itself from fear and anxiety, abstract, weigh evidence, and draw a conclusion regarding intelligent design. Popular theism, however, is penetrated only *partially* by reason and thus remains superstitious even when it reaches 'infinity itself': it ascends to those regions 'by chance', coinciding with the 'principles of reason and true philosophy' when at bottom 'adulation and fears of the most vulgar superstition' remain the animating force (NHR 6.5). Philosophical theism, on the other hand, is penetrated *entirely* by the same and is therefore free of the corruptions dogging its superstitious kin; indeed, only 'some obvious and invincible argument' can *interrupt* the 'natural progress of thought' that leads to popular theism and, instead, 'might immediately lead the mind into the pure principles of theism' (NHR 1.5).

In this spirit, Hume writes in the *Natural History* that theism has a 'foundation in human reason', there being no 'rational inquirer' who 'after serious reflection' can 'suspend his belief a moment with regard to the primary principles of genuine Theism and Religion' (NHR Intro.1).[34] Hume writes in the same vein of the 'doctrine of one supreme Deity' being 'undoubtedly founded' on 'invincible reasons' (NHR 6.1); that the person of 'good understanding' cannot reject the idea of a 'sovereign author in the more obvious works of nature ... when once it is suggested to him' (NHR 15.1); and that the 'order and frame of the universe ... accurately examined' affords an 'argument' for the principles of theism (NHR 1.5). The same sense is invoked by Philo in the final section of the *Dialogues*, although here it refers to true religion, theism penetrated entirely by reason and so thoroughly as to be purged of the superstitious elements that beleaguer its popular counterpart: the inference that constitutes philosophical theism is proportioned to the evidence and gives assent only to a belief that is justified by the evidence. This is the doctrine Philo expresses when speaking of religion of the 'philosophical and rational kind' (DNR 12.13), and of the 'arguments' supporting the conclusion that the cause or causes of order in the universe probably bear remote analogy to human intelligence (DNR 12.33).

Taking note of Hume's language in the *Dialogues*, some commentators have attempted to find some way of accommodating a modified version of 'natural belief' within his notion of philosophical theism. Gaskin, for example, acknowledges that when Hume talks of a 'feeling for design' it certainly sounds natural,[35] and Penelhum claims that while Philo's position at the end of the *Dialogues* is '*un*like the natural beliefs in that ... it is not a belief that is arrived at without reasoning', it is a 'vestigial *rational* belief' or a 'reasonable belief' in the sense of having been 'brought about by reasoning' even if we have to 'stretch the concept [reasonable] to cover a case where the person himself cannot abandon the belief even though he recognises the inadequacy of the original reasons'.[36] We might 'think of belief in divinity not as a natural belief on the order of belief in self, world, and society', as Livingston writes in a similar vein, 'but as a virtually natural belief deeply embedded in participation in common life but more variable and more vulnerable to reflection'.[37]

One way to makes sense of this sort of 'virtually natural' belief is in terms of what Hume calls the '*sensitive*' rather than '*cogitative part of our nature*' (T 1.4.1.8/SBN 183). It is noticeable how, in discussions of both popular and philosophical theism, Hume replaces terms like 'understanding', 'reflection' and 'accurate examination' with language denoting passivity and aesthetic affect and suggesting, as Willem Lemmens observes, that having reached a 'certain degree of sophistication, the assent to the principle of design or a highest, intelligent cause as the origin of the order of

nature unfolds itself as a spontaneous, unavoidable conclusion'.[38]
Most striking in this context is Hume's use of terminology that
evokes the eighteenth-century discourse of the sublime: 'wonder'
and 'astonishment' are his favourite terms, the latter in particular
recalling Addison's *Spectator* essays on the 'Pleasures of the imagination' and Edmund Burke's treatment of sublimity as the highest
manifestation of 'delightful horror', with 'astonishment being' that
'state of the soul, in which all its motions are suspended'.[39] As
some commentators have observed, Hume associates philosophical
theism with beauty, a feeling or sentiment that, according to his discussion in the *Treatise*, corresponds to 'our sense of beauty', a 'calm
passion' (T 2.1.1.3/SBN 276) that is quite distinct from the 'violent'
ones – principally hope and fear – characteristic of polytheism
and popular theism.[40] We have observed before that Hume does
describe the imagination as 'sublime' – 'running, without controul,
into the most distant parts of space and time' (EHU 12.25/SBN
162) – but he is notably inattentive to prevailing distinctions that
others had drawn between it and beauty. Phenomenologically, if not
terminologically, however, the feeling he identifies with philosophical theism is the same as the one described by Addison and Burke
under the guise of astonishment: we are faced with something
beyond the grasp of our 'limited understanding' to comprehend or
our 'fond imagination' adequately to represent (EHU 11.23/SBN
142), and all we can do is submit to the aesthetic affect, the feeling
of calm, that we find rising within us.[41]

It is also worth emphasising the prominence of aesthetic language
in the amended version of the design argument that Cleanthes
advances in Part 3 of the *Dialogues*. The argument is framed so
as to overcome the objections to the first version that Philo had
attacked by appealing to the 'rules of analogy', which it achieves
by emphasising the psychological component of belief: Cleanthes
proposes that even when the rules are broken and only weak
analogies remain – between an articulate voice in the clouds and
a human voice (DNR 3.2), or between rational written books and
rational living books (DNR 3.4–5) – one moves irresistibly from
one's own 'feeling' to the 'idea of a contriver' that flows upon one
'immediately . . . with a force like that of sensation' (DNR 3.7). In
an attempt to drive the point home Cleanthes insists that:

> Some beauties in writing we may meet with, which seem contrary to
> rules, and which gain the affections, and animate the imagination,

in opposition to all the precepts of criticism, and to the authority of the established masters of art. And if the argument for theism be, as you pretend, contradictory to the principles of logic; its universal, its irresistible influence proves clearly, that there may be arguments of a like irregular nature. Whatever cavils may be urged, an orderly world, as well as a coherent, articulate speech, will still be received as an incontestable proof of design and intention. (DNR 3.8)

Unlike the earlier version, this argument is 'irregular' because, as Beryl Logan characterises the difference, it contravenes 'established rules of argumentation' and 'appeal[s] to affections that stimulate the imagination', so that one is 'compelled by a "feeling" to assent immediately and spontaneously to the conclusion'. Whether Philo's final assent to an intelligent designer in section 12 is, as Logan goes on to argue, an argument of this type is open to question, given that Hume appeals to the same instinctual sense of reason and employs aesthetic language when describing both popular and philosophical theism. Since Philo rejects the former but rejects the latter, the presence of an irregular argument cannot serve ultimately to distinguish one from the other.[42]

This being said, Hume does draw consistently on the same language and sense of reason that Cleanthe's irregular argument exploits. Commenting on theism generally, he writes, for example, of our 'contemplation of the works of nature' (NHR 2.4); of being 'acquainted with a first and Supreme Creator' (NHR 6.1); how the uniformity of the universe 'leads the mind to acknowledge one author' (NHR 2.2); and, echoing Addison, of the 'magnificent idea' of a supreme creator that is 'too big' for 'narrow conceptions, which can neither observe the beauty of the work, nor comprehend the grandeur of its author' (NHR 3.3). 'A purpose, an intention, a design is evident in every thing', Hume urges further, 'and when our comprehension is far enlarged as to contemplate the first rise of this visible system, we must adopt, with the strongest conviction, the idea of some intelligent cause or author' (NHR 15.1).

The same language is even more pronounced in the *Dialogues*, where Hume proposes the doctrine of philosophical theism, underlining his conviction that religious belief is a 'natural propensity' in the face of which any 'suspense of judgement' – that is, denial of design – is impossible (DNR 12.6). There is suddenly a 'new manner' of discourse, as William Lad Sessions observes, with Philo now a man of 'common sense' (DNR 12.2) who 'finds himself seized with an immediate sense of the natural world as somewhat like human contrivance and artifice, and ... [who] cannot help inferring that a "divine Being" somewhat like us is the world's original cause or Author, even if he cannot explain how or why such a Being acts'. [43] 'A purpose, an intention, a design, strikes everywhere even the most careless, the most stupid thinker' (DNR 12.2), Hume claims, and the 'comparison of the universe to a machine of human contrivance is so obvious and natural, and is justified by so many instances of order and design in nature, that it must immediately strike all unprejudiced apprehensions, and procure universal approbation' (DNR 12.5). The artifices of nature are so great, moreover, that 'no human imagination can compute their number, and no understanding estimate their cogency' (DNR 12.4), and it is 'wonderful variety' and 'striking appearances' (DNR 12.3) of design that impress Philo in his lengthy discourse on the artifice of the human body and the contrivances of nature. In the final analysis, the aesthetic impact of the evidence is sufficient to end debate and subvert reason in the traditional sense entirely: 'In many views of the universe, and of its parts, ... the beauty and fitness of final causes strike us with such irresistible force, that all objections appear ... mere cavils and sophisms' (DNR 10.36), Philo declares, and 'astonishment ... from the greatness of the object' shows that 'human reason' can find 'no solution more satisfactory with regard to so extraordinary and magnificent a question' (DNR 12.33).

The Antinomy of True and False Religion

We have seen how Hume identifies two competing tendencies within the psychology of human beings to conceive their deity as perfect, without limitation and pure, on the one hand, and imperfect, limited and possessing physical characteristics like themselves, on the other. Their apprehensions are too feeble to be satisfied with the former and their dispositions too fearful fully to embrace the latter; as a result, they 'fluctuate between these opposite sentiments' (NHR 8.2) in a flux and reflux of polytheism and popular theism. This is an antinomy, a contradiction without unassailable grounds for adopting one side or the other, which, although Hume articulates and diagnoses it, defies any permanent resolution. As Hume describes it, this movement is confined within the limits of false religion, a process internal to and set in motion by the imagination from principles that govern it. The faculty tends to be influenced by what is high and important and abstracts from what is imperfect to reach infinity, a totality from which it receives pleasure, only to fall back and rest on sensible, visible objects with which it unites invisible intelligent power.

The foregoing discussion of evidence and reason reveals a second, more fundamental antinomy, however: one that is neither the result of the imagination alone nor one that develops as a contradiction specific to false religion. It arises instead as a conflict between reason and imagination, and is manifest as an antinomy of true and false religion. On one side there is the almost universal propensity to belief in invisible intelligent powers, along with the 'train of thought' that leads from polytheism to popular theism and the principles of the imagination that give it momentum: the principle of easy transition, tendency to enthusiasm and the pleasure it takes in the gloomy passions aroused by religious ideas. On the other side stands reason, which can reflect upon and correct the superstitious forms that false religion takes and arrive, from a different origin, at true religion in the form of philosophical theism, which relies on evidence alone to reach the conclusion of intelligent design.

The doctrine of philosophical theism, moreover, being a species of religion, must involve 'belief of invisible intelligent power'; it depends, therefore, on the same principles that govern and explain *all* belief, namely, the imagination being affected in such a way that it confers force and vivacity on the ideas in question. The fundamental difference between philosophical theism and the superstitious religions of polytheism and popular theism is that they reach belief from different *origins* – reason rather than superstition – the very difference, as we observed at the beginning of the chapter, that distinguishes true from false religion. The philosophical theist is simply 'motivated to belief' from a different source, as Livingston characterises it, or, to translate the observation into the terms of the current inquiry, polytheism and popular theism involve persuasion by or natural belief in a fiction, while philosophical theism can boast justified belief in a non-fictional idea; in both cases belief itself still depends on the imagination.[44]

This phenomenology of belief is precisely why the antinomy of true and false religion arises. Being discovered by reason alone, the

God of the philosophical theist is necessarily abstract and remote, so much so that one might equally call it 'MIND or THOUGHT', as Philo happily admits (DNR 12.6), an idea comparable to that of a future state, which is 'far remov'd from our comprehension', so 'faint' and without resemblance to life actually lived that nobody really believes it with 'true and establish'd judgement'. Since 'belief is an act of the mind arising from custom', Hume writes in this context, "tis not strange the want of resemblance shou'd overthrow what custom has establish'd, and diminish the force of the idea, as much as that latter principle encreases it' (T 1.3.9.13/SBN 114). Even 'just' philosophy in general presents us with 'mild and moderate sentiments' (T 1.4.7.13/SBN 272). The same inconvenience besets the philosophical theist in particular, whose proposition *that the cause or causes of order in the universe probably bear some remote analogy to human intelligence*' – to recall the careful terms of Philo's 'reversal' – is ambiguous and undefined, the analogy remote and imperfect, and the assent philosophical and only slightly stronger than the objections against it. The result is but a weak belief in a faint idea. On the other side from philosophical theism stands superstitious religion with ideas that are fictions, and although these are artificial and possess only the power to persuade, they strike with such force and vivacity that they resist correction and persist, even when shown to be unjustified by any reference to matter of fact.

The antimony of true and false religion consists in the dialectic between these competing faculties and the systems of belief to which they give rise: imagination generates false religion, which is corrected by reason and replaced by the true religion of philosophical theism; the ideas of the latter are faint and its belief, though justified, is weak, and it is easily subverted by the imagination to which the ideas of superstitious religion are more appealing and into which they penetrate more deeply. Reason can again assert itself but with only temporary success; it is destined to be corrupted again in a process with no foreseeable end. In the final analysis, Hume does appear to consider religion a singular phenomenon that lacks conformity to the 'more ordinary' aspects of human existence – to echo Kemp Smith's comment – for although its fictions are either artificial ones that persuade or second-order natural ones that inspire natural beliefs, it has a strength that defies correction, and it persists along with the first-order fictions without which life would be impossible. Whether one approves of it or not, religious belief is part and parcel of human life, a fact for which we have the imagination to thank or, depending on one's inclinations, curse for all time.

Notes

1. The literature is extensive but, for a representative sample, see Shane Andre, 'Was Hume an Atheist?', *Hume Studies*, 19: 1 (1993), pp. 141–66; Holden, *Spectres of False Divinity*; John Immerwahr, 'Hume's Aesthetic Theism', *Hume Studies*, 22: 2 (1996), pp. 325–37; Livingston, *Hume's Philosophy of Common Life*, esp. pp. 172–86; James Noxon, 'Hume's Agnosticism', in V. C. Chappell (ed.), *Hume: A Collection of Critical Essays* (New York: Garden City, 1966), pp. 361–83; J. C. A. Gaskin, 'Hume's Attenuated Deism', *Archiv für Geschichte der Philosophie*, 65: 2 (1983), pp. 160–73; Willem Lemmens, '"Beyond the Calm Sunshine of the Mind": Hume on Religion and Morality', *Aufklärung und Kritik*, 37 (2011), pp. 214–40; and Richard H. Popkin, 'Editor's Introduction', in Richard H. Popkin (ed.), *David Hume: Dialogues Concerning Natural Religion and the Posthumous Essays* (Indianapolis: Hackett, 1980). That Hume is at best an 'attenuated deist', as characterised by Gaskin, appears to be the received wisdom now and there is indeed much that speaks in its favour.

2. See, for example, Andre C. Willis, *Toward a Humean True Religion: Genuine Theism, Moderate Hope, and Practical Morality* (University Park: Pennsylvania State University Press, 2015); William Lad Sessions, *Reading Hume's Dialogues: A Veneration for True Religion* (Bloomington: University of Indiana Press, 2002); David O'Connor, *Hume on Religion* (London: Routledge, 2001); Yandell, *Hume's 'Inexplicable Mystery'*; Stanley Tweyman, *Scepticism and Belief in Hume's Dialogues Concerning Natural Religion* (Dordrecht: Martinus Nijhoff, 1986); and Gaskin, *Hume's Philosophy of Religion*. None of these give the imagination much more than a passing remark. The notable exception is Logan's under-appreciated *A Religion Without Talking*, esp. Ch. 2.

3. Norman Kemp Smith, 'Introduction', in Norman Kemp Smith (ed.), *Hume's Dialogues Concerning Natural Religion*, 2nd edn (London: Thomas Nelson & Sons, [1935] 1947), p.1.

4. Lorne Falkenstein, 'Hume on "Genuine", "True", and "Rational" Religion', *Eighteenth-Century Thought*, 4 (2009), pp. 171–201, esp. 185–7. The quote is from p. 186.

5. See Holden, *Spectres of False Divinity*, who observes that Hume's characterisation of 'God' as an 'original cause or organising principle of the ordered universe' (p. 7) makes the idea 'relative' rather than 'positive': 'it picks out a referent by way of its relational place rather than . . . by specifying its intrinsic character' (p. 5).

6. See O'Connor, *Hume on Religion*, pp. 15–16, who refers to the same as 'standard theism', which he distinguishes from the 'limited theism' that he takes Hume to articulate in parts 2 and 11 of the *Dialogues*: the deity of 'limited theism' has all the attributes of standard theism but his 'goodness, power, and knowledge are less than perfect or infinite' (p. 15). Both are different again from 'philosophical theism', the final position adopted by Philo in Part 12. The difference between standard and limited theism is not pertinent to the current discussion, and I shall use 'popular theism' in the sense stated as one of the two forms of false religion that Hume identifies.

7. This *Natural History* account of the origin of polytheism echoes Hume's earlier treatment of 'two corruptions of true religion' in the essay 'Of Superstition and Enthusiasm' (E 73–9): 'Weakness, fear, melancholy, together with ignorance, are . . . the causes of SUPERSTITION', Hume writes there, and 'Hope, pride, presumption, a warm imagination, together with ignorance, are . . . the true sources of ENTHUSIASM' (p. 74). The essay appeared in *Essays Moral and Political* of 1741, and the *Natural History* was likely drafted and even completed between 1749 and 1752; see editor's introduction in Tom L. Beauchamp (ed.), *A Dissertation on the Passions; The Natural History of Religion: A Critical Edition* (Oxford: Clarendon Press Press, 2007), pp. xx–xxvii. Lorne Falkenstein, 'Hume's Project in the Natural History of Religion', *Religious Studies*, 39: 1 (2003), pp. 1–21, emphasises that the corruption of enthusiasm, very different in character to superstition, 'finds no echo in the [*Natural History*]' (p. 6); given that both polytheism and popular theism are reduced to the same corruption, Falkenstein concludes, '"The natural history of religion" is really just a natural history of superstition' (p. 7). The notion of religious enthusiasm does find an echo in the *Dialogues*, however. See DNR 1.7, 12.16 and 12.21.

8. Falkenstein, 'Hume's Project in the Natural History of Religion', p. 7. For an earlier discussion of the same point, see Martin Bell, 'Hume on Superstition', in D. Z. Phillips and Timothy Tessin (eds), *Religion and Hume's Legacy* (New York: St Martin's Press, 1999), esp. pp. 159–62. Cf. Herdt, *Religion and Faction*, pp. 171–2, who

emphasises that polytheism differs from popular theism in not being *irrational* because 'not *contradicted* by any experiences available to primitive peoples'; it is thus reasonable (as far as adherents to the world view are concerned) that followers would attempt to influence deities through rites that define their religion even if the beliefs are without justification. In general, Herdt's focus on the voluntaristic character of religious belief leads her to *distinguish* popular theism from polytheism, when, in light of their superstitious origins and falsehood, they are fundamentally the same.

9. Herdt, *Religion and Faction*, pp. 179 and 114.

10. See Herdt, *Religion and Faction*, pp. 178–9. See also P. J. E. Kail, 'Understanding Hume's Natural History of Religion', *Philosophical Quarterly*, 57: 227 (2007), pp. 190–211, who makes a similar point by adopting a phrase of David Pears and speaking of religious belief as 'motivated irrationality' (p. 199).

11. The cases do not coincide unambiguously, especially if one empha- sises the difference Hume draws between the 'two species of false religion' in 'Of Superstition and Enthusiasm' where it is religious *enthusiasts* with their 'warm imagination' and 'raptures, transports, and surprising flights of fancy' into which they are led that comes closer to the 'fervours' of poetry (E 73–4). Hume also thinks (as we shall see later in the chapter) that the same characteristics of enthu- siasm that explain the appeal of literary creations are applicable to religion as well, and might account for their tendency to persuade in more than a temporary way and inspire beliefs that resist correction. That being said, polytheistic and poetic fictions share more than enough features to identify them as conceptual kin.

12. See David M. Holley, 'The Role of Anthropomorphism in Hume's Critique of Theism', *International Journal for Philosophy of Religion*, 51: 2 (2002), pp. 83–99, who emphasises that Hume con- siders human beings to have a natural tendency towards 'anthropo- morphic projection'; the further religious systems are removed from polytheism the more unintelligible the idea of the deity becomes. Holden, *Spectres of False Divinity*, suggests that Hume is articulating the idea that for 'most of us at least, the human need to fix emotions on concrete sensible objects is simply irresistible' (p. 82).

13. See above p. 52n 70, and Logan, *A Religion without Talking*, esp. Chs. 5 and 6; Tweyman, *Scepticism and Belief in Hume's Dialogues Concerning Natural Religion*, pp. 133–46; Terence Penelhum, 'Hume's Skepticism and the *Dialogues*', in David Fate Norton, Nicolas Capaldi, and Wade L. Robeson (eds), *McGill Hume Studies*

(San Diego: Austin Hill, 1979), pp. 253–78; Nelson Pike, 'Hume on the Argument from Design', in Nelson Pike (ed.), *Hume: Dialogues Concerning Natural Religion* (Indianapolis: Bobbs-Merrill, 1970), esp. pp. 225–35; and Charles W. Hendel, *Studies in the Philosophy of David Hume* (1925; reprint Indianapolis: Bobbs-Merrill, 1963), pp. 267–309. See also nn. 17–18 below.

14. Butler, 'Natural Belief and the Enigma of David Hume', p. 88.

15. See in this context, Christopher J. Wheatley, 'Polemical Aspects of Hume's Natural History of Religion', *Eighteenth-Century Studies*, 19: 4 (1986), pp. 502–14, who argues that 'one is inclined to think that the list of consequences from primary propensities can be explained from the same list that cause [sic] polytheism' so that, especially given the ambiguity of what Hume means by 'universal', it is 'hard to tell the difference between primary and secondary propensities by their results' (pp. 506 and 507). While the specific components of Hume's list of original impressions might be questioned, he is on firm ground suggesting that religion is not universal in the same way as other more fundamental instincts that appear to manifest themselves without exception.

16. See J. C. A. Gaskin, 'God, Hume, and Natural Belief', *Philosophy*, 49: 189 (1974), pp. 281–94, who, commenting on the passage, observes that 'the most straightforward reading of the conditional "unless that propensity were as strong and universal as that to believe in our Senses and Experience" would suggest that Hume thinks the condition is not satisfied' (p. 289).

17. Butler's primary concern is the existence of God, but, as Gaskin argues, there is no reason why the claim cannot be extended to religious ideas in general. Butler's thesis goes to a broader point about making 'Hume's theory of belief and his account of religious belief into a connected whole'. If Butler is correct, Gaskin observes, then 'something will have been established which is both of enormous importance in understanding Hume's philosophy of religion as a whole, and of enormous general importance in justifying what could be used as a basis for theistic religion'. See Gaskin, *Hume's Philosophy of Religion*, pp. 120–1.

18. Immerwahr, 'Hume's Aesthetic Theism', p. 327. See also Gaskin, *Hume's Philosophy of Religion*, Chs. 6 and 7, and Terence Penelhum, *Hume: An Introduction to his Philosophical System* (West Lafayette: Purdue University Press, 1992), p. 187. O'Connor, *Hume on Religion*, pp. 86–93, provides a useful summary of the cases for and against religious beliefs being classed as natural.

19. See Terence Penelhum, *God and Skepticism. A Study in Skepticism and Fideism* (Dordrecht: Reidel Publishing Company, 1987), who observes that Hume's 'account of the *origins* of religious beliefs has to be one which does not present them as benign natural provisions that make human life possible, but shows them to be pathological hindrances to it' (p. 132).

20. This point has been made forcefully by Livingston in particular. See *Hume's Philosophy of Common Life*, pp. 172–4, and *Philosophical Melancholy and Delirium*, pp. 61–7. Especially in the *History*, Hume also identifies various ways in which religion has exerted a positive and even civilising influence on the development of various social and political institutions. For a discussion of this aspect of Hume's view, see Timothy M. Costelloe, '"In every civilized community": Hume on Belief and the Demise of Religion', *International Journal for Philosophy of Religion*, 55: 3 (2004), pp. 171–85.

21. Smith reports how Hume – reading Lucian's *Dialogues of the Dead* on his deathbed – joked that he could not find among the excuses there cited one that might delay him from boarding Charon's boat. 'He then diverted himself', Smith writes, 'with inventing several jocular excuses ... "If I live a few years longer, I may have the satisfaction of seeing the downfall of some of the prevailing systems of superstition." But Charon would then lose all temper and decency. "You loitering rogue, that will not happen these many hundred years. Do you fancy I will grant you a lease for so long a term?"' (L2: 451).

22. See in this context the discussions in Mark Webb, 'The Argument of the *Natural History*', *Hume Studies*, 17: 2 (1991), esp. p. 141; Adam Potkay, 'Hume's "Supplement to Gulliver": The Medieval Volumes of *The History of England*', *Eighteenth-Century Life*, 25: 2 (2001), pp. 32–46; Bongie, *David Hume*, pp. 15–35; and Schneewind, *The Invention of Autonomy*, pp. 374–6. Schneewind does not regard Hume as providing a 'calculus of reform' in the case of religion, but does conclude that his 'theory could ... easily be turned in that direction; and his attack on the monkish virtues points the way' (p. 377). Cf. Siebert, *The Moral Animus of David Hume*, esp. pp. 95, 111 and 113, and 'Hume on Idolatry and Incarnation', *Journal of the History of Ideas*, 45: 3 (1984), pp. 379–96; and Costelloe, '"In every civilized community"'.

23. The role Hume gives imagination in the rise of polytheism – especially the importance of personification and association by resemblance – has been emphasised by Bell, 'Hume on Superstition', pp. 163–5.

24. See also Hume's comments on the spread of Christianity among the Saxons (H 1.56); on Papal authority (H 1.264–5); the charge of pretended witchcraft against Henry VI (H 2.420); and the manipulation of Joan of Arc by French commanders (H 2.399).

25. In the passages excised from the *History*, Hume expresses the view that on the eve of the Reformation the Church had become an institution on the verge of enlightenment, a state of affairs undone eventually by the Protestant Reformation. I owe this observation to Adam Potkay.

26. Cf. Holden, *Spectres of False Divinity*, who writes that, in Hume's view, 'believers tend to hide the true character of their feelings from themselves through a species of wishful thinking or self-deceit that in his [Hume's] judgement permeates religious belief and practice' (p. 82). Holden also emphasises Hume's observation that the passions of religious people are not really directed to a transcendental cause at all: these are either cases of misinterpreted feelings about mundane matters of everyday life or they are actually directed towards 'readily visualised and comprehensible substitutes, either fictitious or real: anthropomorphic demigods, finite angels, and saints – or even statues, paintings, and the sensible forms of ritual and ceremony' (p. 75). This compensates for the fact that, according to Hume, 'we lack the sort of rich mental imagery of the original cause required to focus our conative and affective attitudes towards' (p. 67).

27. I owe this observation to Don Garrett, 'What's True About Hume's "True Religion"?', *Journal of Scottish Philosophy*, 10: 2 (2012), pp. 199–220, esp. 199–200.

28. I should note that in what follows I deliberately omit using the term 'genuine theism' or 'pure theism' as synonyms for 'true religion', although one finds it in the literature. See, for example, Lemmens, 'Beyond the Calm Sunshine of the Mind', p. 232; Livingston, *Hume's Philosophy of Common Life*, p. 174; and Immerwahr, 'Hume's Aesthetic Theism', p. 325. The meaning Hume assigns the term is difficult to interpret unambiguously, which is a source of interpretive difficulty, and omitting it makes no material difference in the present context anyway. Hume uses the phrase in the *Natural History* (NHR Intro. 1, 4.1, 7.3, 15.4), but only in the *Dialogues* (DNR 12.24), in words spoken by Cleanthes, does he offer any definition. For the difficulties endemic to clarifying the concept, see Falkenstein, 'Hume on "Genuine", "True", and "Rational" Religion', who uses this passage in the *Dialogues* to distinguish 'genuine theism . . . in a nor-

mative sense' from 'theism' as a synonym for 'pure monotheism' (in a non-normative sense), and Garrett, 'What's True About Hume's "True Religion"?', esp. pp. 205–8, who brings out some textual and interpretive difficulties involved in Falkenstein's thesis.

29. Cf. Willis, *Toward a Humean True Religion*, who suggests that Hume's use of 'true' is 'not a reference to epistemic status, for the "truth" is well beyond the reach of the human mind'; he proposes that 'Hume had more of a pragmatic notion of "true"' that involves moderating our beliefs and behaviour for the 'effective functioning of the individual and society' (p. 7; see also pp. 40–2). There is little evidence (and Willis provides none) that Hume either connected such ends with religion or that his use of 'true' was intended to convey such a view.

30. The characterisation of Philo's final position as a 'reversal' appears to begin with Noxon, 'Hume's Agnosticism', p. 367, who writes that one of the 'difficulties involved in identifying Hume . . . is the complete reversal of standpoint made by Philo in the twelfth and final dialogue.' Those who read Hume as a total sceptic, thorough-going naturalist or as a straightforward atheist are inclined to read him as insincere and/or ironic, an interpretation with a history going back to Kemp Smith. The literature is extensive but see, for example, on the former (that he is insincere), the 'Editor's Introduction', in Henry D. Aiken (ed.), *Dialogues Concerning Natural Religion by David Hume* (New York: Hafner, 1948); James Fieser, 'Hume's Concealed Attack on Religion and his Early Critics', *Journal of Philosophical Research*, 20 (1995), pp. 431–49; Falkenstein, 'Hume's Project in the Natural History of Religion', and 'Hume on "Genuine", "True", and "Rational" Religion'; and Wheatley, 'Polemical Aspects of Hume's Natural History of Religion'; for the latter (that he is ironic), see Popkin, 'Introduction'; Kemp Smith, 'Introduction', esp. pp. 45–75; Price, *The Ironic Hume*, esp. pp. 130–3 and 138–40; and Scott Davis, 'Irony and Argument in *Dialogues*, 12', *Religious Studies*, 27: 2 (1991), pp. 239–57.

31. Philo's earlier concession to Cleanthes is, if anything, even weaker: somebody following the 'hypothesis' of design 'is able, perhaps, to assert, or conjecture, that the universe, sometime, arose from something like design' with anything further being the 'utmost licence of fancy and hypothesis' (DNR 5.12).

32. Gaskin, *Hume's Philosophy of Religion*, p. 221; Yandell, *Hume's 'Inexplicable Mystery'*, p. 44; and Kemp Smith, 'Introduction', p. 25. With different degrees of emphasis, this has become the widely

accepted way of understanding Philo's, and by extension Hume's, position. See, most recently, Sessions, *Reading Hume's Dialogues*, Ch. 15; O'Connor, *Hume on Religion*, Ch. 10; and Garrett, 'What's True About Hume's "True Religion"?' Cf. Aiken, 'Editor's Introduction' in *Dialogues Concerning Natural Religion*, p. viii, who refers to Hume's position as an 'attenuated version of theism' and one that is 'hard to take very seriously'.

33. Garrett, 'What's True About Hume's "True Religion"?', p. 219. See also his comment that 'Philo's proposition affirms only a minimum degree of probability for a remote analogy', but '[a]s a correct judgement, it may properly be epistemically 'venerated' – that is, normatively, honoured and respected – as true' (p. 218). Cf. Holden, *Spectres of False Divinity*, who argues that Hume professes a 'modest sort of natural theology' that does not violate his mitigated scepticism but is opposed to any version of 'core natural theology', namely, the 'programme of employing natural reason to work our way to species-specific knowledge of the intrinsic character of the original cause' (pp. 27 and 28).

34. Here, I take it, Hume is contrasting 'genuine theism' with 'true religion', and thus referring to the role of reason in founding the monotheism characteristic of Christianity. See n. 28 above.

35. Gaskin, *Hume's Philosophy of Religion*, p. 129. Gaskin rejects the possibility on the grounds that such a belief is 'not universal' and 'not a precondition for practical life'.

36. Terence Penelhum, 'Natural Belief and Religious Belief in Hume's Philosophy', *Philosophical Quarterly*, 33: 131 (1983), p. 171. Penelhum's observation is a modified version of his earlier and somewhat stronger claims in *Hume* (London: Hutchinson, 1975) that 'true religion is a conviction of the omnipresence of natural order, a vague deistic belief in the probably existence of an individual intelligence (or perhaps several intelligences) at the back of it all' (p. 195), and in 'Hume's Skepticism and the *Dialogues*' (1979) that 'perception of design in nature is a prephilosophical interpretation of it – a natural belief that is not established by argument but that, for that very reason, is not eliminated when arguments in its favour are refuted' (p. 274).

37. Livingston, *Philosophical Melancholy and Delirium*, pp. 65. See also Siebert, 'Hume on Idolatry and Incarnation', p. 394, who remarks how 'Hume seems to recognise that man needs to invest objects with significance, that he is a contriver of symbols, a Vates or Maker. The recognition of this fact in the NHR [*Natural History of Religion*],

as it probably is in most of Hume's philosophy, is grudging and somewhat disapproving. But it exists nonetheless.'

38. Lemmens, '"Beyond the Calm Sunshine of the Mind"', p. 233.

39. 'The passion caused by the great and sublime in *nature*', Burke writes, 'when those causes operate most powerfully, is Astonishment; and astonishment is that state of the soul, in which all its motions are suspended, with some degree of horror.' Edmund Burke, *A Philosophical Enquiry into the Sublime and Beautiful*, ed. James T. Boulton (London: Routledge & Kegan Paul, [1757] 1958), p. 57. In the *Spectator*, Addison had observed earlier how 'Our imagination loves to be filled with an Object, or to graspe at any thing that is too big for its Capacity. We are flung into a pleasing Astonishment at such unbounded Views, and feel a delightful Stillness and Amazement in the Soul at the Apprehension of them' (No. 412, 540). For an extended discussion, see Costelloe, *The British Aesthetic Tradition*, Ch. 2.

40. This comparison is made by Immerwahr, 'Hume's Aesthetic Theism', pp. 330–1, and, more recently, Lemmens, '"Beyond the Calm Sunshine of the Mind"', p. 233, both of whom attempt to connect it to Hume's 'moral critique' of religion.

41. The identification of Hume's religious feeling with the *calm* passion of beauty reflects the eighteenth-century tradition of associating 'beauty' with gentle qualities, calm passions and pleasing effects (the imagination is amused by playing with the object) and reserving the sublime (or grand) for irregular qualities, violent passions and pain (the capacity of the imagination is surpassed). Hume clearly connects philosophical theism with the same calm feeling that Addison and Burke denote with astonishment, even though they subsume it into the category of sublimity or grandeur and not, as Hume does, into that of beauty. For the development of these and related concepts in the course of the eighteenth century and beyond, see Costelloe, *The British Aesthetic Tradition*, esp. Part 1.

42. See Logan, *A Religion Without Talking*, Ch. 5. The quote is from p.97.

43. Sessions, *Reading Hume's Dialogues*, p. 186. Sessions emphasises (pp. 183–4) that this is a 'new manner' of discourse between Philo and Cleanthes that can commence only with the departure of Demea, after which they are free to converse as old friends in an open conversation; there is no reason, then, Sessions concludes, to complicate the otherwise 'straightforward reading' that Philo is being sincere and honest in confessing his true feelings on the matters under discussion.

See also Hendel, *Studies in the Philosophy of David Hume*, p. 358, who concludes his discussion of the *Dialogues* by remarking that 'We might even say . . . that Hume chooses the principles of theism, in preference to those of naturalism. . . . There is no reason to doubt that this was the sincere expression of Hume's final opinion.'

44. See Donald Livingston, 'Hume's Conception of True Religion', in Anthony Flew, Donald Livingston, George I. Mavrodes and David Fate Norton (eds), *Hume's Philosophy of Religion: The Sixth James Montgomery Hester Seminar* (Winston-Salem: Wake Forest University Press, 1986), pp. 33–73, who remarks that the 'philosophical theist is motivated to belief not by fear but by wonder and an appreciation of the lawlikeness of the universe' (p. 43). A similar point is made by Immerwahr, 'Hume's Aesthetic Theism', pp. 329–30, although he claims that 'pure theism is based on an emotion', which (unlike Livingston's formulation and the distinction drawn above) obscures the singular feature of philosophical theism, namely, that it is based on reason; *belief* in the doctrine attained, by contrast, is due to the effect the ideas so raised have on the imagination.

7

Philosophy

We have seen in the foregoing chapters how Hume appeals consistently and across a variety of subjects to the concept of the imagination, which, though not delineated systematically, he takes to be composed of principles that are wide-ranging in scope and profound in effect. In this final chapter, we turn our attention to the role Hume takes the imagination to play in philosophy, the very activity through which the nature and effects of that faculty are made perspicuous. Philosophy, we should not be surprised to learn, itself depends on and is in certain respects governed by the same principles of imagination that it discovers. Central to Hume's approach is the distinction he draws between its 'true' and 'false' forms, epithets already applied in the context of history and religion. There are important differences in the way they operate in each case but, in general terms, they denote doctrines and beliefs that, on the side of the 'true', emerge from taking a disinterested attitude towards evidence and drawing conclusions that stay within the limits of experience; the same are 'false' when these criteria are not met. True or 'philosophical' history describes a narrative that preserves past events in their original form, due position and temporal sequence, achieved by historians when they take a critical approach to the testimony they encounter. True religion or 'philosophical theism' describes a modest or attenuated deism that involves assent to the experience of design and infers an original source of order that arises naturally from contemplating phenomena beyond our grasp. History is false, by contrast, when corrupted by prejudice of one sort or another, and the same is manifest in the religious sphere when superstition terminates in the corrupt forms of polytheism and popular theism.

As some commentators have rightly emphasised, in the course of applying 'true' and 'false' to the particular case of philosophy,

Hume articulates a sort of proto-Hegelian dialectic, casting himself as a player in his own drama of doubt and self-critique. Philosophy aims at human self-understanding but when it finds itself governed by principles 'inconsistent with human nature' – as Livingston understands Hume's insight – 'it must take account of this discovery and reform itself' if it is to continue and complete its task.[1] At the very least, as Ainslie has argued more recently, Hume shows that, while philosophy is *'optional*, appropriate only for those who are so inclined' and hardly necessary for us to 'reason and sense as successfully as we can', for those who pursue it, understanding the enterprise and the curiosity that drives it is inseparable from engaging in the activity itself.[2] Hume himself describes this dialectical movement as:

> a graduation of three opinions, that rise above each other, according as the persons, who form them, acquire new degrees of reason and knowledge. These opinions are that of the vulgar, that of a false philosophy, and that of the true; where we shall find upon enquiry, that the true philosophy approaches nearer to the sentiments of the vulgar, than to those of a mistaken knowledge. (T 1.4.3.9/SBN 223)

This appears as a natural history of philosophy, a process that, when pursued, leads from pre-reflective immersion in everyday life to genuine philosophical understanding, albeit mediated by a stage that, due to the corruption it involves, is (to quote Ainslie) *'epistemologically* inferior'.[3]

We can understand and gain some insight into this movement by shifting focus from its dialectical form to the role played in it by the imagination. At the lowest 'gradation', and prior to reflection, the faculty provides for the vulgar fictions and natural beliefs (such as distinct and continued existence, personal identity or rules governing property) that go unnoticed yet make life possible; in the middle, one finds artificial fictions, which form the doctrines that philosophers invent when they follow the principles of imagination beyond their natural home; and at the highest, these mistakes are corrected through further reflection by moderating and neutralising the effects of imagination in the form of true philosophy. Philosophers then return to the same 'common and careless' way of thinking that the vulgar achieved instinctively and maintain through habit and custom (T 1.4.3.9/SBN 223). Focusing on the imagination also reveals a further aspect of Hume's dialectic of true and false philosophy, which the metaphors of painter and anatomist help bring out. Both figures represent practitioners of true philosophy, and are in certain respects analogous to what we have seen to constitute the same in history and religion; they rely on evidence and reason, and draw inferences from observation and experience. When either engages in 'hypothetical reasoning', however, their respective philosophies become false: they generate fictions and are persuaded to take their creations as real. At the same time, philosophers do not share the luxury of historians who can guarantee the veracity of their claims by reconstructing a causal chain linking one event with another to terminate in some matter of fact; the movement of the philosophical mind is towards the ultimate springs and principles that lie beyond possible experience. Hume laments the state of his science and hopes to improve matters with his experimental philosophy, but the presence of the imagination, as he portrays it, casts doubt on his chances and undermines his hopes for success. This might not be Hume's explicit message, but it emerges nevertheless that, as in the case of popular theism, there is a tendency among those who practise it for the fictions to endure, even though they can and should be corrected. As with true and false religion, so with true and false philosophy, there is a conflict between reason and imagination that resolves into an antinomy that is persistent and ineradicable, and through it the imagination has the last word.

The Painter and the Anatomist

Hume draws a distinction between philosophical painters, who represent the world in carefully chosen colours designed to inspire certain forms of conduct, and philosophical anatomists who, like their counterparts in the natural sciences, undertake the accurate dissection of human nature.[4] As Hume writes in a well-known letter to Hutcheson:

> There are different ways of examining the Mind as well as the Body. One may consider it either as an Anatomist or as a Painter; either to discover its most secret Springs & Principles or to describe the Grace & Beauty of its Actions. (L1:32)

As Immerwahr has characterised it, Hume envisages 'two kinds of philosophy', each having its distinct purposes, techniques and justifications; the anatomist describes human nature in 'abstruse' terms in order to assist the practical moralist, while the painter aims to arouse sentiments of virtue in an 'easy' style in order 'to make people virtuous'.[5] These constitute such different, even mutually exclusive, enterprises with respect to their primary goals – one explanatory, the other normative – that Hume finds it difficult to conceive them 'united in the same Work': after all, to reveal the minute parts of the body the anatomist must remove the external layer through which airs and graces make their appearance, and the painter can render it beautiful only by 'cloathing the Parts again with Skin & Flesh' (L1:33).[6]

This does not mean that the two enterprises are unrelated, however, and Hume considers each able to succour, help and offer advice to the other. Neither in the letter to Hutcheson nor on the other occasions where the metaphor appears (EHU 1.8/SBN 9–10 and T 3.3.3.6/SBN 605) does Hume make clear precisely how a 'Metaphysician may be helpful to a Moralist' (L1:33), but he has much to say about the dependence of a moralist on a metaphysician: painters can depict the grace and beauty of a body only if they know about its 'inward structure' – the 'positions of the muscles, the fabric of the bones, and the use and figure of every part or organ' – as, the parallel runs, a moralist can only 'inspire us with different sentiments' if he or she has 'an accurate knowledge of the internal fabric, the operations of the understanding, the workings of the passions, and the various species of sentiment which discriminate vice and virtue'. The success of the 'practical' moralist thus presupposes that the work of the anatomist has to some degree been completed, and for this reason Hume emphasises the 'subserviency' of the 'accurate and abstract philosophy' to the 'easy and humane' (EHU 1.8/SBN 9).

Despite the mutual support that anatomy and painting give each other, however, fundamental differences remain. The former takes a disinterested view of experience, while the latter gives added force and vivacity to our ideas by staining them a particular hue, and, through a kind of artifice, raises what might otherwise remain unattractive and obscure to the point of belief and conviction. The painter exploits the fact that human beings are persuaded less by the truth or falsehood of matters of fact than by the *way* in which characters and actions are represented to the imagination. If the imagination has a role to play in philosophical practice, then, it would seem to do so under the rubric of the philosophical painter who recognises that ''tis necessary the objects shou'd be set more at a distance, and be more cover'd up from sight, to make them engaging to the eye and imagination' (T 3.3.6.6/SBN 621).[7] In Hume's view, to recall a passage quoted in an earlier chapter, all poetry is a 'species of painting', and one would expect philosophical painters to have much in common with their poetic counterparts.

In certain respects, this expectation appears to be borne out. First, philosophical painting transforms ordinary experience and at once embellishes it, highlighting certain details while casting others into shadow; through the philosophical lens what is in reality ugly, repellent or mundane appears beautiful, appealing or in some way fascinating. As literary art creates a poetic reality consisting of scenes and images, which an audience is enticed to enter and take as real, so the philosophical painter creates what can be thought of as a moral reality, populated by models and images that promise the pleasure of virtue while avoiding the pain of vice. In order to achieve this – to adopt and modify Land's phrase – the philosopher aims at *philosophical* imitation' and, rather than simply describing what is given in experience, represents and embellishes it in such a way that the brilliance of virtue and good character shines out and eclipses the darkness of vice and poor character. The practical moralist effectively covers the details of deformity and transforms human nature into a thing of beauty, just as the poet draws the graces and ornaments of *la belle nature* over the insipid details presented by the copyist.

For this reason, investigations pursued in the 'easy and obvious manner', as Hume writes, are

> best fitted to please the imagination and engage the affections. They [philosophers] select the most striking observations and instances from common life; place opposite characters in a proper contrast; and alluring us into the paths of virtue by the views of glory and happiness, direct our steps in those paths by the soundest precepts and most illustrious examples. (EHU 1.1/SBN 5–6)

As he puts it in the second *Enquiry*, the practical moralist employs the flowers of rhetoric in order 'to recommend generosity and benevolence' and 'paint, in their true colours, all the genuine charms of ... [the] social virtues' (EPM 2.5/SBN 177). This is exemplified most clearly in philosophers of the ancient schools who, in their treatment of human nature, have

> shown more of a delicacy of sentiment, a just sense of morals, or
> a greatness of soul, than a depth of reasoning and reflection. They
> content themselves with representing the common sense of mankind in
> the strongest lights, and with the best turn of thought and expression,
> without following out steadily a chain of propositions, or forming the
> several truths into a regular science. (T Abstract 1/SBN 645)

Such 'proper representations' of the world are possible only because
the landscape of human action is purified of its vicious elements
and thereby transformed into an object of aesthetic appreciation.
Like the poet, the practical moralist creates an alternative world,
adorned and rendered beautiful by the power of language.

Second, in transforming and embellishing experience, the philosopher at once creates ideas that are agreeable and bring pleasure. The philosopher engages the receptive capacity of an audience
whose members, due to the effect of sympathy, cannot remain
indifferent to the images of virtue and vice that confront them.
Philosophy thus represents but does not reproduce the original
sentiment, which through this representation becomes a source of
pleasure rather than pain. Here the psychological mechanism of
conversion that Hume develops in his discussions of sympathy and
tragedy operates so that scenes of moral life that would otherwise
be painful are fashioned in such a way to bring pleasure. This
mechanism is aptly demonstrated in Hume's comparison – already
noted in Chapter 4 – between the '*philosophical* fiction of the *state
of nature*' and the '*poetical fiction* of the *golden age*'. The difference between them is that while the latter 'is represented as the
most charming and most peaceable condition, which can possibly
be imagined', the former 'is painted out as a state of mutual war
and violence, attended with the most extreme necessity' (EPM
3.15/SBN 189). Even here, the reader does not feel the pain of such
a life through having original sentiments reproduced, but finds
them represented and converted into a source of pleasure.

Third, in order to arouse agreeable ideas, philosophical painters
practise skills and employ techniques deliberately to bring about
a particular response in the audience; transforming human nature
into a thing of beauty, philosophers aim explicitly to arouse a
corresponding pleasure in the reader. They describe the grace and
beauty of conduct and character in order to bring about 'the
correction of our manners, and extirpation of our vices' (EHU
5.1/SBN 40), as Hume puts it, and endeavour 'to make us *feel*

the difference between vice and virtue; they excite and regulate our sentiments; and ... bend our hearts to the love of probity and true honour' (EHU 1.1/SBN 6). By drawing the reader nearer to the objects under investigation, philosophy pursued in the easy and obvious manner throws a stronger light upon them and delineates 'more distinctly those minute circumstances, which ... serve mightily to enliven the imagery, and gratify the fancy' (EHU 3.11). Success will be proportionate to the intensity with which the appropriate passion is raised in writer and audience and the corresponding belief it inspires.

If the pursuit of the philosophical painter resembles that of the literary artist, the work of the anatomist seems to be of a different order. While the painter looks outward and represents the world on the canvas of the mind, the anatomist is taken by the 'spirit of accuracy' and carries 'his attention to the inward structure of the human body' (EHU 1. 8/SBN 10). Hume writes that, for this reason:

The anatomist ought never to emulate the painter; nor in his accurate dissections and portraitures of the smaller parts of the human body, pretend to give his figures any graceful and engaging attitude or expression. There is even something hideous, or at least minute in the views of things, which he presents. (T 3.3.6.6/SBN 621)

This anatomical philosophy appears to hold no place for the 'eloquence and copious expression of the world' portrayed by the painter; the anatomist seeks an exact depiction of experience, 'reserve[ing] the flowers of rhetoric for subjects which are more adapted to them' (EHU 7.30/SBN 79). As such, Hume warns at the end of the *Treatise*, practical morality 'require[s] a work apart, very different from the genius of the present' (T 3.3.6.6/SBN 620). For this reason, philosophical anatomy appears closer to the craft of the historian than to the art of the poet. As the historian searches the body of history for connections among events that together form the tissue of a true narrative, so the philosophical anatomist is beholden to facts, and relies not primarily on imaginative representation that inevitably subverts the course of a disinterested dissection, but on the power of memory to copy accurately the details of human life.

As we saw in Chapter 5, however, historians are not freed from the imagination by pleading favour for some peculiarity of their enterprise. On the contrary, the nature of the enterprise itself condemns them to adopt its principles. The temporal remoteness of events and the interpreted nature of testimony oblige historians to reinvigorate the past and represent it in such a way as to add force and vivacity to the ideas they express in their narrative. The historian's craft is thus guided by considerations similar to those governing literary creativity and philosophical painting. The philosophical anatomist is not in the same position as the historian in having to revive a lost past life; neither is his main business that of entertainment, as for the poet; nor, like the painter, is it to inspire virtue. The principal goal of anatomy is to convince an audience, however, and have them believe that its inquiries are true, a task impossible to achieve without the imagination. All belief depends upon a strong and vigorous imagination, on the part of both the writer who elicits ideas and the audience in whom the ideas are aroused, and the philosophical anatomist must employ the same skills and techniques to present the ideas and inspire belief. He transforms the world by representing it in a particular way, effectively creating through his own genius a philosophical reality, within which readers might be convinced that the propositions of his proposed system are true.

There is no better example of philosophical anatomy in pursuit of this end than Hume himself, who, in all his writing, not only indulged the 'ruling passion' of his life – 'love of literary fame' (E xl) – but in the course of doing so deliberately employed a wide range of devices and techniques to draw an audience into a world of his own making, to enliven ideas of the doctrines presented, and have them 'prevail upon the fancy' and thus enter with facility and deeply into the minds of his readers, an endeavour in which he had a good deal of success. Hume saw 'philosophical discourse as a set of rhetorical gestures', as John Richetti puts it in an appropriately poetic way; 'he dramatises thought and restores it to its status as largely another sort of speaking'.[8] The *Treatise* alone is a literary tour de force that exploits almost every conceivable trope to move readers and convince them of the truth of its content: allegory, fable, drama, comedy, tragedy, paradox, parody, personification, soliloquy, vignette, irony; even the innocent deceit of 'transparent pseudoinference', the self-styled 'fiction of amateurism' and the 'pose of spontaneity' combine, Richetti observes, in a 'stance that makes Hume's world remarkably like a literary universe in its mixture of falsity and necessity and its exploration of fictionality'. In a final irony, Hume even manages to depict the 'fantastic epistemological world' of his own philosophical imagination as something 'normal and natural'.[9]

One only has to consider some of the striking images Hume employs to see how inseparable is his philosophical message from the literary medium of its presentation, and the degree to which they work themselves unnoticed into the fabric of his narrative. In some cases, one might think of these images as primarily a means of carrying the doctrine under discussion, but more often than not sign and signified are so inseparable that an attempt to distinguish one from the other would be to risk annihilation of both. Hume draws, to give but a sample, from science (force, vivacity and liveliness), painting (practical moralist, portraiture, colouring, tincture, gilding and staining), medicine (anatomy and animal spirits), and health and sickness (sympathy is a contagion and fictions are a malady). He draws on military enterprise in the *Treatise* and first *Enquiry* to depict the 'poor condition of the sciences' (T Intro.2/SBN xiv) and convey hope of 'success in our philosophical researches' (T. Intro.6/SBN xvi; see EHU 1.12/SBN 12), and on robbers lurking in tangled woods to depict the dangerous cowardice of dogma and superstition (EHU 1.11/SBN 11). The mind, moreover, is a 'kind of theatre' (T 1.4.6.4/SBN 253) with a 'mental geography' (EHU 1.13/SBN 13) and the propensity to 'spread itself' on external objects (T 1.3.14.25/SBN 167); the momentum of imagination is captured by galley and oars, and its purview through the image of planetary space; and the psychology of the philosopher dramatised as a scale of health and sickness, a balance moving ineluctably between successive states of 'melancholy and delirium' (T 1.4.7.9/SBN 269). Most dramatic of all, perhaps, is the picture Hume paints of himself – the philosopher – embarking alone and lonely in his 'leaky weather-beaten vessel', beset on all sides by doubt and uncertainty, on to those 'immense depths of philosophy' (T 1.4.7.1/SBN 263). This image is central to Hume's treatment of philosophy and the imagination, and we shall return to it below.

Philosophy, Fictions and Belief

We have observed how the philosophical painter and the anatomist are comparable to the poet and the historian, respectively; the painter sets out deliberately to show readers the proper direction for normative conduct, while the anatomist seeks an accurate explanation of human nature. For this reason, anatomists might appear to escape the pull of imagination, but they, too, must raise conviction in readers about the truth of their narrative, and this is only possible, in turn, if they employ their own imagination to effect the same in an audience. The enterprise of both painter and anatomist, moreover, count as what Hume calls 'true' because, like their counterparts in the spheres of history and religion, they confine themselves to evidence and reason: for the philosopher, this is given in the form of experience and observation of common life, and reflection on it. The moral reality of the philosophical painter likewise, though it requires the imagination, differs markedly from the creations of the poet, because it can be traced to real existence in the form of the internal impressions of pleasure and pain that underlie approbation and disapprobation based on agreeableness and utility. The ideas of the philosophical painter reflect moral reality and recommend the right and the good as a matter of practical concern. The involvement of the imagination per se is no barrier to true philosophy but an integral part of it; only when the imagination holds sway so as to produce fictions does the philosophical enterprise become corrupted and false.[10]

In the course of their inquiries, in fact, philosophers of both the painterly and anatomical variety face the constant threat of their enquiries turning in this direction. As in the case of historical investigation, Hume does not rule out the possibility that some philosophical mistakes are 'natural and almost unavoidable'; even the most attentive philosopher may find it 'difficult to abstain from some sally of panegyric, as often occur in discourse or reasoning' (EPM 2.5/SBN 177), and there is always a risk that the 'generosity, or baseness of our temper, our meekness or cruelty, our courage or pusillanimity, influence the fictions of the imagination with the most unbounded liberty, and discover themselves in the most glaring colours' (T 1.4.3.1/SBN 219). Honest, or at least pardonable, oversights based on tendencies of this sort, however, are to be distinguished from systematic errors that result from departing experience and producing fictions of one sort or another. For the painter and the anatomist, this spectre of false philosophy might have different manifestations, but it can be traced to the same origin: philosophy becomes false and produces fictions when it grows speculative and works by 'imposing conjectures and hypotheses on the world' (T Intro.9/SBN xviii). Hume seems to have settled on this view before the composition and publication of the *Treatise*.[11]

For the anatomist, more specifically, this is manifest in the doc-trines of substance and accidents, occult qualities, faculties, sym-pathies, antipathies and the like, which Hume associates with 'the ancient philosophy' and its proclivity to trade in the sort of fictions we met with in Chapter 2, where the imagination either confuses ideas to create a new one or invents one to reconcile contradic-tory and irreconcilable propositions that otherwise cause pain and bewilderment. For the painter, on the other hand, fictions appear when the practical moralist abandons the experimental method of discovering what pleases and displeases, and, rather than recom-mending conduct on the basis of moral principles drawn from a survey of what is praised and blamed, instead founds an ethical system on some supposition that strikes and warms the imagina-tion. Such 'imprudent management' finds expression in those who distil from human conduct an 'abstract theory of morals' that 'excludes all sentiment, and pretends to found every thing on reason' (EPM 3.34n12/SBN 197n1), Hume remarks, or in others who deduce morals speculatively from self-love or private interest rather than utility and agreeableness that observation shows to be their real basis (EPM Appx.2.5/297–8). These purported explana-tions are a subterfuge or distortion, theories imposed on the world and maintained despite evidence to the contrary. The unprejudiced philosophical eye discovers that the institutions of property and civil law are founded on interest rather than reason, and the fact that human beings 'frequently bestow praise on virtuous actions, performed in very distant ages and remote countries' or on people, even enemies, who do not have our interests in mind, undermines any theory that reduces morals to self-interest alone (EPM 5.7/SBN 215).[12] In a similar way, the 'monkish virtues' urged by austere religious moralists are shown to be in reality pernicious, serving only to 'stupefy the understanding and harden the heart, obscure the fancy and sour the temper' and doing nothing to advance an individual as a 'valuable member of society' (EPM 9.3/SBN 270).

The question that presents itself now – as it also did in the case of religion – is how these fictions of false philosophy arise and why they persist even when they are exposed as theories, speculative ideas that are open to reflection and correction. Hume's answer to these questions can be found in the same principles of the imagina-tion we have been emphasising throughout, which in the case of philosophy consist primarily of the principle of easy transition and the effects of superstition and enthusiasm.

First, the faculty always seeks an easy transition among its ideas in order to achieve the satisfaction that comes only when it has completed a union or discovered a whole. Under its sway, the philosopher seeks 'ultimate springs and principles' that animate and explain the universe, even though these are 'totally shut up from human curiosity and enquiry'.[13] The philosopher is comparable to the natural scientist, who can frame 'general causes' through reasoning by analogy, experience and observation, but never reach 'causes of these general causes' (EHU 4.12/SBN 30). Philosophy, likewise, can employ the same methods to reach general conclusions, which, it discovers, constitutes the limits of penetration; for this reason, as natural philosophy 'only staves off our ignorance a little longer', so the 'most perfect philosophy of the moral or metaphysical kind serves only to discover larger portions of [it]' (EHU 4.12/SBN 31). The discovery of this gap between the knowledge it desires and the human capacity to realise it constitutes an interruption in the movement of the imagination, a source of pain from which it seeks relief by following its momentum towards a totality that can never be attained within the confines of experience. As a result, the imagination forms a system from which it derives pleasure, even though it is hypothetical and more than the evidence can justify. Philosophical fictions thus have much in common with those of religion, one reason, perhaps, why Hume takes the latter to be 'nothing but a species' of the former in its pretensions to 'carry us beyond the usual course of experience' (EHU 11.27/SBN 146). False philosophers, moreover, never stand content with a partial explanation of the whole or a full explanation of a part, but (as already noted) broaden their extravagant theories to embrace existence in its entirety by taking hold of a 'favourite principle' and reducing everything to it (E 159).

Second, Hume often presents the false philosopher as somebody under the sway of superstition or enthusiasm, both of which, to recall earlier discussions, arise from ignorance, along with weakness, fear and melancholy in the case of the former, and hope, pride, presumption and a warm imagination in the case of the latter. Superstition is characterised by ceremonies and observances in response to credulity, and enthusiasm with raptures, transports and flights of fancy. On occasion, Hume appears to suggest that the fictions of the philosopher are too abstruse and far removed from common life to have an influence of this sort. There can be 'no enthusiasm among philosophers', he writes at one point in the first *Enquiry*, because 'their doctrines are not very alluring to the people' (EHU 11.29/SBN 147). In addition, philosophical ideas seem comparable to religious fictions such as a future state, declared belief in which is undermined by the practical concerns of daily life that closer examination reveals as the actual source of a person's conduct. Philosophical ideas might have great force and vivacity while they occupy the mind but, as Hume writes,

> When we leave our closet and engage in the common affairs of life, its [abstruse reasoning's] conclusions seem to vanish, like the phantoms of the night on the appearance of the morning; and 'tis difficult for us to retain even that conviction, which we had attain'd with difficulty. (T 3.1.1.1/SBN 455)

Similarly, Hume expresses doubts about philosophy being properly superstitious, especially when compared to religion; the latter is 'much more bold in its systems and hypotheses' than the former, he observes, and 'opens a world of its own . . . with scenes, and beings, and objects, which are altogether new'. While philosophy assigns 'new causes and principles' to the phenomena it studies, at least these 'appear in the visible world' rather than populating a reality projected beyond possible experience. Even when philosophy is 'false and extravagant', moreover, its opinions are 'merely the objects of a cold and general speculation'; unlike the fictions of polytheism and popular theism, which rouse violent passions, these 'seldom go as far as to interrupt the course of our natural propensities' (T 1.4.7.13/SBN 272). This is one reason, presumably, why Hume concludes that 'errors in religion are dangerous; those in philosophy only ridiculous' (T 1.4.7.13/SBN 272).

At the same time, Hume clearly considers philosophy to be susceptible to both forms of corruption. 'Very refin'd reflections have little or no influence upon us;' he remarks, 'and yet we do not, and cannot establish it for a rule, that they ought not to have any influence' (T 1.4.7.7/SBN 268). Hume also identifies the 'warm imagination' with the tendency of philosophers to embrace hypotheses 'merely for being specious and agreeable' (T 1.4.7.14/SBN 272), and he observes how they 'paint out' ideas to themselves, which 'either resolves all into a false idea, or returns in a circle' (T 1.4.4.10/SBN 229). After all, to quote the passage again, the imagination is 'naturally sublime' and, easily delighted with what is 'remote and extraordinary', runs 'without controul, into the most distant parts of space and time' (EHU 12.25/SBN 162). '*Philosophical devotion* . . . like the enthusiasm of a poet, is the transitory effect of high spirits, great leisure, a fine genius, and a habit of study and contemplation' (L 167). As poets are carried by their 'fire and genius' into the creations of their own making and religious prophets ascend into the 'celestial regions' of divine inspiration, so philosophers fall under the influence of their own spell and succumb to the 'intemperate desire' to seek out 'obscure and uncertain relations'. Hume observes that:

> The passion for philosophy, like that of religion, seems liable to this inconvenience, that, though it aims at the correction of our manners, and extirpation of our vices, it may only serve, by imprudent management, to foster a predominant inclination, and push the mind, with more determined resolution, towards that side, which already *draws* too much, by the biass and propensity of the natural temper. (EHU 5.1/SBN 40)

As Hume says of himself, philosophers, when warmed by their inquiries, are 'ready to reject all belief and reasoning, and can look up one opinion even as more probable or likely than another' (T 1.4.7.8/SBN 268–9). They are subject to becoming dogmatic, moreover, and would rather accept 'contradictions and absurdities' (T 2.2.6.2/SBN 366) than change or abandon a system once it has been created. Even doctrines that are abstruse and absurd become the objects of professed belief when the idea strikes the imagination of the philosopher with sufficient force and vivacity. Not only do the poetical and superstitious figures of religion 'sometimes enter the real creed of the ignorant vulgar', to recall a passage cited in Chapter 6, but 'philosophers cannot entirely exempt themselves from this natural frailty', having, as we know, 'ascribed to inanimate matter the horror of a *vacuum*, sympathies, antipathies, and other affections of human nature' (NHR 3.2).

Hume also thinks that there is something about the pursuit of philosophy itself and those stained with its 'tincture' that makes it susceptible to the pull of superstition and enthusiasm. Philosophy is by its nature a solitary activity that puts one spatially, socially and psychologically beyond the normal rounds of common life. The philosopher is 'closeted', 'secluded', 'monstrous', 'striving against the current of nature', as Hume variously describes it. His brain is 'tortured' by 'subtilities and sophistries' (T 1.4.7.10/SBN 270), drawn perversely to find pleasure in places where others would fear to tread; even the 'movements of his heart are not forwarded by correspondent movements in his fellow-creatures' (EPM 5.18/SBN 220). Isolated and in a world of one's own making, the presence of the imagination is almost tangible; there, one is more easily fooled by tricks of the fancy, seduced more profoundly by the pleasures it offers. As Hume observes:

> Whatever has the air of a paradox, and is contrary to the first and most unprejudic'd notions of mankind is often greedily embrac'd by philosophers, as showing the superiority of their science, which cou'd discover opinions so remote from vulgar conception. On the other hand, any thing propos'd to us, which causes surprize and admiration, gives such a satisfaction to the mind, that it indulges itself in those agreeable emotions, and will never be perswaded that its pleasure is entirely without foundation. From these dispositions in philosophers and their disciples arises that mutual complaisance betwixt them; while the former furnish such plenty of strange and unaccountable opinions, and the latter so readily believe them. (T 1.2.1.1/SBN 26)

Since philosophy in its very heart is unnatural and asocial, it is but a small step for practitioners to 'depart from the maxims of common reason' and 'affect *artificial* lives' in which 'no one can answer for what will please and displease'. Consider the 'extravagant philosophy' of Diogenes the Cynic, or Pascal, whose thought was directed by the 'most ridiculous superstitions' (EPM Dialogue 54/SBN 342). 'They are in a different element from the rest of mankind', Hume urges, 'and the natural principles of their mind play not with the same regularity, as if left to themselves, free from the illusions of religious superstition or philosophical enthusiasm' (EPM Dialogue 57/SBN 343).

The Antinomy of Philosophy

At this point we have hit upon the central tension between philosophy and the imagination. Whether of the painterly or anatomical variety, like historian and poet, philosophers rely on the imagination to bring about their effects, to employ and engage the imagination and exploit its principles to convince readers of their doctrines. At the same time, philosophy is susceptible – again, like those other enterprises – to the principles of the imagination that can lead it away from reason and experience and towards speculative systems and the fictions that compose them. The conclusions of true philosophy do not satisfy the imagination's desire for completion and, consisting of faint ideas that do not enter deeply into the imagination, they are soon subverted by the false. The fictions of false philosophy are indeed artificial and only persuade, but they tend to persist nevertheless; the imagination shows its Janus-faced character again, being at once the origin of curiosity among those with the disposition to pursue philosophy, the secret of their success in inspiring belief in an audience, and the source of the temptation that leads them to adopt strange and unaccountable opinions.

This dynamic is reflected in the well-known 'dilemma' Hume raises in his Conclusion to Book 1 of the *Treatise*, where he battles single-handed with the forces of 'radical' or 'total' scepticism, the threat that both his philosophical opinions and everyday beliefs are ungrounded and unjustifiable. The threat comes in the form of a conflict, or 'tension', as Karánn Durland has recently characterised it, between his 'doubts and his commitments to philosophy and common life'. Hume offers 'no clear account' of how to handle this tension, Durland argues, although 'many strategies for defusing it seem available to him'.[14] Interpreters have seized on these and rescued him by suggesting variously that he does nothing, restricts his doubts but speaks with a single voice, or commands multiple voices that he adopts at different times (the 'No-Hume', 'Single-Hume' and 'Several-Humes' strategies, respectively).[15] Durland finds reasons to reject each strategy in turn and concludes that the 'nature of the depth of the conflict' makes it unlikely that any 'satisfying resolution' will be found.[16]

Hume himself at least appears less pessimistic than Durland's conclusion allows. In the Introduction to the *Treatise*, he laments the 'imperfect conditions of the sciences' and the fact that philosophers are led not by reason but by

> eloquence; and no man needs ever despair of gaining proselytes to the most extravagant hypothesis, who has art enough to represent it in any favourable colours. The victory is not gain'd by the men at arms, who manage the pike and the sword; but by the trumpeters, drummers, and musicians of the army. (T Intro.2/SBN xiv)

To this sad state of affairs, Hume optimistically juxtaposes his own approach and its aim to 'propose a compleat system of the sciences, built on a foundation almost entirely new, and the only one upon which they can stand with any security' (T Intro.6/SBN xvi). In the Conclusion to Book 1, he follows this up with a confident declaration that the subversive tendency of the imagination can be (indeed, has been) overcome. He observes:

> While a warm imagination is allow'd to enter into philosophy, and hypotheses embrac'd merely for being specious and agreeable, we can never have any steady principles, nor any sentiments, which will suit with common practice and experience. But were these hypotheses once remov'd, we might hope to establish a system or set of opinions, which if not true (for that, perhaps, is too much to be hop'd for) might at least be satisfactory to the human mind, and might stand the test of the most critical examination. Nor shou'd we despair of attaining this end, because of the many chimerical systems, which have successfully arisen and decay'd away among men, wou'd we consider the shortness of that period, wherein these questions have been the subjects of enquiry and reasoning. (T 1.4.7.14/SBN 272–3)

To what extent is Hume's assessment accurate or, to put the question another way, how far is his confidence in having overcome the subversive tendencies of the imagination justified?

My suggestion is that Hume's view of the imagination effectively sets up an antimony, a conflict engaged by two irreconcilable forces where unassailable principles on both sides prevent a decisive victory of one over the other. Hume might sound confident about cooling the warmed imagination, but the very principles of that faculty upon which he draws throughout casts a shadow over his optimism, and one that he sometimes appears to acknowledge. As Hume articulates it, the initial dilemma is generated by two conclusions to which the imagination leads. On the one side, it is the foundation upon which all thought and intelligibility depend: the faculty is both affected passively by the force and vivacity of the ideas it confronts, and actively provides the connecting principle that relates them in orderly and predicable ways. Without its principles, we could not conjoin past events through experience, expect the future to resemble the past, attribute existence to objects of sense, have a conception of ourselves, admit anything beyond present impressions, or be sure that images of memory were 'true pictures of past impressions'. 'The memory, senses, and understanding are, therefore', Hume concludes, 'all of them founded on the imagination, or the vivacity of our ideas', a 'trivial' quality, moreover – common and everyday – and 'so little founded on reason' (T 1.4.7.3/SBN 265). On the other side, the same faculty leads to errors and operations of the mind that contradict each other, as, for example, in concluding that colour, sound, taste and smell all have (from the senses) and do not have (reasoning from cause and effect) an independent existence.

Recourse to the inferential faculty of reason is no antidote, given that it subverts itself and destroys belief; the search for ultimate principles terminates with the force and vivacity of ideas and thus the imagination itself (T 1.4.7.5/SBN 266). The question, as Hume then poses it, is whether one should follow 'every trivial suggestion of the fancy' into 'errors, absurdities, and obscurities', or adhere instead to the 'general and more establish's properties' of that faculty in the form of understanding. The former is hardly palatable, given the errors to which it leads, but the latter, again, subverts itself and returns one to the total scepticism Hume is trying to escape. The choice, as he finally presents it, is either to embrace the imagination and its absurdities or reject the imagination in favour of the understanding, knowing full well that it inevitably subverts itself: the choice is between a 'false reason and none at all' (T 1.4.7.7/SBN 268).

This contradiction is reminiscent of the case of superstitious religion, where competing tendencies of the imagination produce a 'flux and reflux' of polytheism and popular theism. The present case, however, is different in two important ways. First, rather than identifying competing tendencies of the imagination, Hume really isolates a single feature of the faculty – its 'trivial' quality in the shape of force and vivacity – and shows how it produces different results: errors, absurdities and obscurities on the one hand and the subversion of reason on the other. These are contradictory conclusions, both of which refer ultimately to the imagination, but there are no competing principles and therefore no antinomy is set in motion. Second, these conclusions are of a wholly philosophical nature, a world apart from that of daily life. The 'deficiency in our ideas is not . . . perceiv'd in common life', as Hume points out in the course of his discussion, nor does our ignorance of any ultimate principle hinder the natural course of our instinct to conjoin cause and effect (T 1.4.7.6/SBN 267); the threat of 'embrac[ing] a manifest contradiction' is faced by the philosopher alone (T 1.4.7.4/SBN 266). Whereas religion is a system that (to invoke Herdt's phrase again) '*competes* with the real, natural, this-worldly web of belief' (emphasis added), philosophy offers an alternative that leaves common life untouched. This is another reason, one assumes, why Hume thinks, as already noted, that errors in religion are 'dangerous', while those in philosophy 'only ridiculous' (T 1.4.7.13/SBN 272).

The fact that philosophy and common life are not competitors opens the way for one obvious and immediate resolution of the tension: quit the artifice of the former and return to the course of nature that governs in the latter. Where reason cannot dispel the clouds of 'deepest darkness' to which its abstruse labours have led, 'nature herself suffices', as Hume observes; chimeras conjured by the warmed imagination are dissipated by absorption in 'some avocation, and lively impression of [the] senses' (T 1.4.7.9/ SBN 269): dining, backgammon, the company of friends, in the face of which the refined speculations of philosophy 'appear so cold, and strain'd, and ridiculous' (T 1.4.7.9/SBN 269). The dilemma faced by the radical sceptic, the choice between 'false reason and none at all', is abrogated by denying the bent of mind that gives it life. The empire of philosophy falls.

For those, like Hume, touched with a tincture of philosophy, however, this solution is of limited value, and philosophy regains her crown as soon as those so disposed return to the closet and pursue the very activity that gave rise to the dilemma in the first place. Hume himself might drink and dine with friends to dispel his 'deepest darkness', but from the curiosity, ambition and weakness that 'spring' from his disposition, he is 'naturally *inclin'd*' to return to his chamber and then enter again into those disputes that are the source of his disquiet. Yet 'should I endeavour to banish [these sentiments]', he declares, 'by attaching myself to any other business or diversion, I *feel* I should be a loser in point of pleasure; and this is the origin of my philosophy' (T 1.4.7.12/SBN 271). He feels drawn, compelled even, and is certainly willing to be 'led into such inquiries' even though they are 'without the sphere of common life' (T 1.4.7.13/SBN 271). Once this eventuality is admitted, a conflict quickly follows, one between reason and imagination and similar in kind to the antinomy that we identified in the sphere of religion. The difference, again, is that it is not a function of the (almost) universal human propensity to believe in invisible intelligent powers, but follows from the rarer inclination of those few to be drawn into a particular mode of reflection and way of life: it takes the form of an antinomy between true and false philosophy.[17]

In the case of religion, to recall, the tendency towards invisible powers produces superstitious religion (false religion), which is corrected by philosophical theism (true religion), against which the imagination reasserts itself in terms of false religion. In a similar way, imagination gives rise to false philosophy, which is corrected by reason and replaced by true philosophy that stays within the limits of experience; the ideas of the latter are faint, however, and its belief, though justified, weak, and it is easily subverted by the imagination to which the ideas of false philosophy are more appealing and into which they penetrate more deeply. Reason can again assert itself, but with only temporary success, destined to be corrupted again in a process with no foreseeable end. Without ceasing to do philosophy altogether, this dilemma appears irresolvable.

One immediate response would be simply to urge vigilance on the part of philosophers that they stay within the confines of experience and temper their hubris with humility and what Hume captures under the aegis of 'mitigated scepticism', a 'moderate and fallibilistic attitude to one's own beliefs', as Holden describes it, that 'urges us to refrain from speculating in those particular domains that are beyond the reach of our faculties'.[18] One could leave the 'more sublime topics' to poets and priests and avoid 'distant and high inquiries', limiting oneself instead to 'such subjects as fall under daily practice and experience' (EHU 12.25/SBN 162). One might then rest content, albeit with revised expectations and imperfect conclusions. Philosophy would be 'happy', as Hume puts it,

> if she be thence sensible of her temerity, when she pries into these sublime mysteries; and leaving a scene so full of obscurities and perplexities, return, with suitable modesty, to her true and proper province, the examination of common life; where she will find difficulties enow to employ her enquiries, without launching into so boundless an ocean of doubt, uncertainty, and contradiction!' (EHU 8.36/SBN 103)

After all, the objects of philosophical inquiry and the results it yields are removed from our natural affections and tend not to disorder the mind permanently. This presumably is the thought that allows Hume to sail happily, or at least relatively untroubled, into Books 2 and 3 of the *Treatise*.

The problem, however, is that the fictions of philosophy, like those of religion, have a tendency to persist. Philosophical conviction develops from the same origin as other beliefs and those with greater force and vivacity will carry the day, not from following a chain of reasoning to its conclusion but because the ideas in question strike the imagination in a certain *manner*. As already noted, this is one reason Hume cites for the 'imperfect conditions of the sciences' in his own day. The ideas of true philosophy are faint and weak, and do not satisfy the imagination's impulse to form a union or complete a whole; philosophers do not rest content with the recommendations of the practical moralist, nor are they satisfied with the mitigated scepticism of the anatomist. They are driven, at the urging of the imagination, to push on to the ultimate springs and principles, a course of action that leads them to embrace errors, absurdities and obscurities, which, as the history of the discipline shows, have become perennial features of the philosophical canon. Practitioners are enamoured with and return over and over again to the same 'problems', and whatever ostensibly new theory or 'view' is canvassed for their solution, they remain for a subsequent generation of philosophers to rediscover, reformulate and attempt to solve.

Hume's suggestion, and surely an appropriate place to conclude the present study, is that imagination will always win the day, with reason and understanding being, as we saw at the outset, ultimately features of the representational faculty of imagination and reducible to that same trivial quality of the force and vivacity of ideas: it is taste, disposition and the pleasure of satisfying the imagination that ultimately leads philosopher and audience alike to adopt one view rather than another. "Tis not solely in poetry and music, we must follow our taste and sentiment', Hume remarks, 'but likewise in philosophy'. He continues:

> When I am convinc'd of any principle, 'tis only an idea, which *strikes more strongly upon me*. When I give the preference to one set of arguments above another, I do nothing but decide from my feeling

concerning the superiority of their influence. Objects have no discoverable connexion together; nor is it from any principle but custom operating upon the imagination, that we can draw any inference from the appearance of one to the existence of the other. (T 1.3.8.12/SBN 103, emphasis added)

That philosophical disputes are resolved ultimately through the principles of the imagination is a disturbing thought to those taught that reason and argument are the *sine qua non* of philosophical inquiry, itself at bottom a species of faith in the power of the human mind, to which, thanks to the imagination, they give a preference. Reflection on philosophy shows that not only the phenomena studied but also the explanations of the phenomena are often creations that compensate for the inability of philosophers to reach the ultimate springs and principles they seek. Given, as we have seen throughout, that so many fundamental beliefs and institutions follow from the imagination and its principles, this discovery should come as no surprise; neither should it disturb nor disappoint. Perhaps we should, instead, rest content with what we can know and be grateful that we possess a faculty that, despite its tendency to error and fiction, makes life – in all its booming, buzzing confusion – possible.

Notes

1. See Livingston, *Philosophical Melancholy and Delirium*, Ch. 2. The quotation is from p. 19.
2. See Ainslie, *Hume's True Scepticism*, esp. pp. 152–62 and Ch. 7. The quotations are from pp. 219 and 244, respectively.
3. See Ainslie, *Hume's True Scepticism*: '*developmentally*, one progresses from vulgar opinion, through false philosophy, to true philosophy. But, *epistemologically*, false philosophy is inferior to the vulgar consciousness, while true philosophy improves on both' (p. 154).
4. Hume sometimes uses 'anatomy' in a literal sense to characterise the work of 'natural' as opposed to the 'moral' philosophers. See, for example, T 1.1.3.1/SBN 8–9 and 2.1.8.7/SBN 301–2.
5. See John Immerwahr, 'The Anatomist and the Painter: The Continuity of Hume's Treatise and Essays', *Hume Studies*, 17: 1 (1991), pp. 1–14. The quotes are taken from pp. 5–6. Immerwahr

goes on to argue that the *Treatise* contains Hume's anatomy while the *Essays* represent the work of the painter since they are not intended to 'dissect politics and morality but ... encourage morals and political virtue' (pp. 6–7). Cf. Adam Potkay, *The Passion for Happiness: Samuel Johnson and David Hume* (Ithaca: Cornell University Press, 2000), who sees anatomy and painting combined in both the *Enquiries* and the *History*: 'Hume recognizes that anatomy by itself will never appeal widely, and he thought it would not appeal for long; Hume sought to write in such a way as to attract a "general" audience, hoping both to gratify a passion for fame and to serve an enlightened age' (p. 21).

6. Cf. Robert Shaver, 'Hume's Moral Theory?', *History of Philosophy Quarterly*, 12: 3 (1995), who argues that Hume's 'anatomist/painter distinction does not divide the factual from the normative'; it is not, he says, a 'distinction ... between the normative and the descriptive, but between the engaging and the "accurate"' (p. 319). See also Korsgaard, *The Sources of Normativity*, who endorses the schema of explanation and normativity, even though she finds Hume's distinction itself 'odd' because 'Neither the anatomist nor the painter seems to be interested in the *justification* of morality's claims. The theoretical philosopher is concerned only with providing a true explanation of the origin of moral concepts. The practical philosopher is a preacher or Mandevillian politician. His task is to get people to behave themselves in socially useful ways. ... So we have explanation on the one hand and persuasion on the other' (p. 52).

7. See Siebert, *The Moral Animus of David Hume*, p. 32, who remarks that 'used well, however, nothing can equal the power for moral education wielded by ... dramatizers of human emotion'.

8. Richetti, *Philosophical Writing*, pp. 245–6. Richetti also notes the 'necessity of rhetorical effect for rendering the discovery philosophy makes about itself' (p. 245).

9. See Richetti, *Philosophical Writing*, esp. p.183ff. The quotations are taken from pp. 40, 187 and 224–5. For discussion of Hume's ubiquitous use of irony in particular, see Price, *The Ironic Hume*; Nicholas Phillipson, 'Hume as Moralist: A Social Historian's Perspective', in *Philosophers of the Enlightenment, Royal Institute of Philosophy Lectures* vol. 12, 1977–8 (Atlantic Highlands, NJ: Humanities Press, 1979), pp. 140–61; and Potkay, *The Fate of Eloquence in the Age of Hume, passim.*

10. Cf. Owen, *Hume's Reason*, who, of Hume's preference for philosophy over superstition, reason over bigotry and scepticism over dogmatism, writes: 'It is the same as his, and our, preference for virtue over vice. In each case the former is more pleasant and useful to ourselves and others. Although engaged in "accurate and abstruse" philosophy, this reasoner is aware of the limitations of human reason and conscious of its benefits to society. Hume's wise philosopher is a sceptical reasoner and a virtuous person' (p. 222).

11. Hume writes in the famous 'letter to a physician' – probably Dr George Cheyne – of March or April 1734: 'I found that the Moral philosophy transmitted to us by Antiquity, labor'd under the same Inconvenience that has been found in their natural Philosophy, of being entirely Hypothetical, & depending more upon Invention than Experience. Every one consulted his Fancy in erecting Schemes of Virtue & Happiness, without regarding human Nature, upon which every moral Conclusion must depend' (L1:16). For a discussion of the letter's composition and consideration of its intended recipient, see John P. Wright, 'George Cheyne, Chevalier Ramsay, and Hume's Letter to a Physician', *Hume Studies*, 29: 1 (2003), pp. 125–41.

12. Hume adds to this the observation that 'It is but a weak subterfuge, when pressed by these facts and arguments, to say, that we transport ourselves, by the force of imagination, into distant ages and countries, and consider the advantage, which we should have reaped from these characters, had we been contemporaries, and had any commerce with the persons. It is not conceivable, how a *real* sentiment or passion can ever arise from a known *imaginary* interest; especially when our *real* interest is still kept in view, and is often acknowledged to be entirely distinct from the imaginary, and even sometimes opposite to it' (EPM 5.13/SBN 217).

13. See Livingston, *Philosophical Melancholy and Delirium*, p. 18, who calls this the 'principle of ultimacy', that 'one who philosophizes is trying to understand things as they are ultimately'. This is the first of three principles that Livingston takes to define the 'philosophical act.' The other two are 'autonomy' (philosophy is a 'radically free and self-justifying inquiry') and 'dominion' ('philosophical systems that are different are contrary').

14. See Karánn Durland, 'Extreme Skepticism and Commitment in the *Treatise*', *Hume Studies*, 37: 1 (2011), pp. 65–98. The quotes are from p. 66. Cf. Garrett, *Cognition and Commitment*, who suggests that whether 'Hume's positive "system of the sciences" [can]

properly withstand his own skeptical arguments and conclusions . . . [is] perhaps the most fundamental question in the interpretation of his [Hume's] entire philosophy' (p. 206).

15. Durland's schema is neither clean nor exhaustive, but it is useful for parsing the various interpretive solutions on offer in the literature. A 'No-Hume' solution (a group of one it seems) – as Durland presents it – is to be found in J. H. Randall, Jr, 'David Hume: Radical Empiricist and Pragmatist', in S. Hook and M. R. Konvitz (eds), *Freedom and Experience: Essays Presented to Horace M. Kallen* (Ithaca: Cornell University Press, 1947), pp. 289–312. 'Single-Hume' strategies (by far the largest group) include Garrett, *Cognition and Commitment*; Paul Russell, *The Riddle of Hume's Treatise: Skepticism, Naturalism, and Irreligion* (Oxford: Oxford University Press, 2008); Kenneth Winkler, 'Hume's Inductive Skepticism', in Margaret Atherton (ed.), *The Empiricists: Critical Essays on Locke, Berkeley, and Hume* (Lanham, MD: Rowman & Littlefield, 1999), pp. 183–212; and Donald C. Ainslie, 'Hume's Scepticism and Ancient Scepticisms', in Jon Miller and Brad Inwood (eds), *Hellenistic and Early Modern Philosophy* (Cambridge: Cambridge University Press, 2003), pp. 251–73. 'Several-Humes' strategies (a fairly small group) are represented by Robert J. Fogelin, *Hume's Skeptical Crisis: A Textual Study* (Oxford: Oxford University Press, 2009), and Graciela de Pierris, 'Hume's Pyrrhonian Skepticism and the Belief in Causal Laws', *Journal of the History of Philosophy*, 39: 3 (2001), pp. 351–83.

16. Durland, 'Extreme Skepticism and Commitment in the *Treatise*', pp. 66 and 90. Cf. Ainslie, *Hume's True Scepticism*, Ch. 7, who divides the interpretations of the Conclusion into 'sceptical' (despondency about our cognitive condition), 'naturalist' (we do not believe sceptical challenges and return to our previous confidence in reason and the senses), 'dialectical' (Hume is not speaking in his own voice), and (Ainslie's own), 'philosophical' (that Hume is really interested in how philosophy fits into everyday life).

17. For a somewhat different view of the 'dialectic between true and false philosophy', see Livingston, *Philosophical Melancholy and Delirium*, esp. Ch. 2. As noted above, Livingston presents the dialectic as a process of 'reform' whereby, through engaging in the activity, one comes to understand that philosophy is 'inconsistent with *its* own nature' because the principles that govern it do not 'cohere with others of our nature.' Hume's 'true philosophers', then, are those who have 'passed through this disturbing circle of

self-understanding' while 'false philosophers' are those who have not and thus represent a 'failure of philosophical self-knowledge' (p. 19).

18. Holden, *Spectres of False Divinity*, p. 22.

Bibliography

Addison, Joseph and Richard Steele [1711] (1965), *The Spectator*, ed. Donald F. Bond, 5 vols, Oxford: Clarendon Press.

Aiken, Henry. D. (1948), 'Introduction', in *Dialogues Concerning Natural Religion by David Hume*, ed. Henry D. Aiken, New York: Hafner.

Ainslie, Donald C. (2003), 'Hume's Scepticism and Ancient Scepticisms', in Jon Miller and Brad Inwood (eds), *Hellenistic and Early Modern Philosophy*, Cambridge: Cambridge University Press, pp. 251–73.

Ainslie, Donald C. (2005), 'Sympathy and the Unity of Hume's Idea of the Self', in Joyce Jenkins, Jennifer Whiting, and Christopher Williams (eds), *Persons and Passions: Essays in Honor of Annette Baier*, Notre Dame: University of Notre Dame Press, pp. 143–72.

Ainslie, Donald C. (2015), *Hume's True Scepticism*, Oxford: Oxford University Press.

Alison, Archibald (1790), *Essays on the Nature and Principles of Taste*, Dublin: Byrne, Moore, Grueber, McAllister, Jones & White.

Allison, Henry E. (2008), *Custom and Reason in Hume: A Kantian Reading of the First Book of the Treatise*, Oxford: Oxford University Press.

Altmann, R. W. (1980), 'Hume on Sympathy', *Southern Journal of Philosophy*, 18: 2, pp. 123–36.

Andre, Shane (1993), 'Was Hume an Atheist?', *Hume Studies* 19: 1, pp. 141–66.

Anscombe, G. E. M. (1973), 'Hume and Julius Caesar', *Analysis* 34: 1, reprinted in *The Collected Philosophical Papers of G. E. M. Anscombe* (1981), 3 vols, Minneapolis: University of Minnesota Press, 1: pp. 86–92.

Árdal, Páll S. (1966), *Passion and Value in Hume's Treatise*, Edinburgh: Edinburgh University Press.

Arnold, Scott N. (1983), 'Hume's Skepticism about Inductive Inference', *Journal of the History of Philosophy*, 21: pp. 31–55.

Baier, Annette C. (1991), *A Progress of Sentiments: Reflections on Hume's Treatise*, Cambridge, MA: Harvard University Press.

Baier, Annette C. (1997), *The Commons of the Mind*, Chicago: Open Court.

Baillie, James (2000), *Hume on Morality*, London: Routledge.

Banwart, Mary (1994), *Hume's Imagination*, New York: Peter Lang.

Baxter, Donald L. M. (1998), 'Hume's Labyrinth concerning the Idea of Personal Identity', *Hume Studies*, 24: 2, pp. 203–34.

Baxter, Donald L. M. (2008), *Hume's Difficulty: Time and Identity in the* Treatise, New York: Routledge.

Bell, Martin (1999), 'Hume on Superstition', in D. Z. Phillips and Timothy Tessin (eds), *Religion and Hume's Legacy*, New York: St. Martin's Press, pp. 153–70.

Berkeley, George [1710] (1998), *A Treatise Concerning the Principles of Human Knowledge*, ed. Jonathan Dancy, Oxford: Oxford University Press.

Blackburn, Simon (1993), 'Hume on the Mezzanine Level', *Hume Studies,* 19: 2, pp. 273–88.

Beckwith, Francis J. (1989), *David Hume's Argument Against Miracles*, Lanham, MD: University Press of America.

Bongie, Laurence L. [1965] (2000), *David Hume: Prophet of the Counter-Revolution*, 2nd edn, Indianapolis: Liberty Fund.

Box, M. A. (1990), *The Suasive Art of David Hume*, Princeton: Princeton University Press.

Brann, Eva T. H. (1991), *The World of the Imagination: Sum and Substance*, Savage, MD: Rowman & Littlefield.

Bricke, John (1996), *Mind and Morality: An Examination of Hume's Moral Psychology*, Oxford: Clarendon Press.

Brunius, Teddy (1952), *David Hume on Criticism*, Figura 2, Studies edited by the Institute of Art History, University of Uppsala, Stockholm: Almquist & Wiksell.

Bullough, Edward (1912), 'Psychical Distance', *British Journal of Psychology*, 5, pp. 87–117.

Bundy, Murray Wright (1927), *The Theory of Imagination in Classical and Medieval Thought* (*University of Illinois Studies in Language and Literature*), Urbana: University of Illinois Press, vol. 12, nos. 2–3, May-August.

Burke, Edmund [1757] (1958), *A Philosophical Enquiry into the Sublime and Beautiful*, ed. James T. Boulton, London: Routledge & Kegan Paul.

Butler, R. J. (1960), 'Natural Belief and the Enigma of David Hume', *Archiv für Geschichte der Philosophie*, 42: 1, pp. 73–100.

Butterfield, Herbert (1951), *History and Human Relations*, London: Collins.

Campbell, George [1762] (1766), *A Dissertation on Miracles: Containing an Examination of the Principles Advanced by David Hume, Esq.; in An Essay on Miracles*, 2nd edn, Edinburgh: Kincaid & Bell.

Castro, Juan Samuel Santos (2017), 'Hume and Conjectural History', *Journal of Scottish Philosophy*, 15: 2, pp. 157–74.

Charles, Sébastien (2009), 'Fictions in Berkeley: From Epistemology to Morality', *Berkeley Studies*, 20, pp. 13–21.

Coady, C. A. J. (1973), 'Testimony and Observation', *American Philosophical Quarterly*, 108: 2, pp. 149–55.

Coady, C. A. J. (1992), *Testimony: A Philosophical Study*, Oxford: Clarendon Press.

Cohon, Rachel (1997), 'The Common Point of View in Hume's Ethics', *Philosophy and Phenomenological Research*, 57: 4, pp. 827–50.

Cohon, Rachel (2008), *Hume's Morality: Feeling and Fabrication*, Oxford: Oxford University Press.

Cohen, Ralph (1976), 'The Rationale of Hume's Literary Inquiries', in Kenneth R. Merrill and Robert W. Shahan (eds), *David Hume: Many-sided Genius*, Norman: University of Oklahoma Press, pp. 97–115.

Coleman, Dorothy (1984), 'Hume's Dialectic', *Hume Studies*, 10: 2 pp. 139–55.

Coleridge, Samuel Taylor [1817] (1983), *Biographia Literaria or Biographical Sketches of My Literary Life and Opinions*, in James Engell and W. Jackson Bate (eds), *The Collected Works of Samuel Taylor Coleridge*, 16 vols, Princeton: Princeton University Press, vol. 7 (two parts).

Collier, Mark (2010), 'Hume's Theory of Moral Imagination', *History of Philosophy Quarterly* 27: 3, pp. 255–73.

Collingwood, R. G. (1938), *The Principles of Art*, Oxford: Clarendon Press.

Collingwood, R. G. [1946] (1993), *The Idea of History*, rev. edn, Oxford: Oxford University Press.

Cooper, Anthony Ashley, Third Earl of Shaftesbury [1711] (2001), *Characteristicks of Men, Manners, Opinions, Times*, 3 vols, Indianapolis: Liberty Fund.

Costa, Michael (1990), 'Hume, Strict Identity, and Time's Vacuum', *Hume Studies* 16: 1, pp. 1–16.

Costelloe, Timothy M. (2004a), 'Beauty, Morals, and Hume's Conception of Character', *History of Philosophy Quarterly*, 21: 4, pp. 397–415.

Costelloe, Timothy M. (2004b), 'Hume's Aesthetics: The Literature and Directions for Future Research', *Hume Studies,* 30: 1, pp. 87–126.

Costelloe, Timothy M. (2004c), '"In every civilized community": Hume on Belief and the Demise of Religion', *International Journal for Philosophy of Religion,* 55: 3, pp. 171–85.

Costelloe, Timothy M. (2007a), *Aesthetics and Morals in the Philosophy of David Hume,* London: Routledge

Costelloe, Timothy M. (2007b), 'Hume's Phenomenology of the Imagination', *Journal of Scottish Philosophy,* 5: 1, pp. 31–45.

Costelloe, Timothy M. (2012), 'Hume as Historian', in Alan Bailey and Dan O'Brien (eds), *The Continuum Companion to Hume,* London and New York: Continuum Publishing, pp. 364–76.

Costelloe, Timothy M. (2013a), *The British Aesthetic Tradition: From Shaftesbury to Wittgenstein,* Cambridge: Cambridge University Press.

Costelloe, Timothy M. (2013b), 'Fact and Fiction: Memory and Imagination in Hume's Approach to History and Literature', in Mark G. Spencer (ed.), *David Hume: Historical Thinker, Historical Writer,* University Park: The Pennsylvania State University Press, pp. 181–99.

Cottrell, Jonathan (2016), 'A Puzzle about Fictions in the *Treatise*', *Journal of the History of Philosophy,* 54: 1, pp. 47–73.

Dadlez, Eva (2011), 'Ideal Presence: How Kames Solved the Problem of Fiction and Emotion', *Journal of Scottish Philosophy,* 9: 1, pp. 115–33.

Damrosch, Leopold (1989), *Fictions of Reality in the Age of Hume and Johnson,* Madison: University of Wisconsin Press.

Daniel, S. C. (1988), 'The Nature and Function of Imagination in Hume and Kant', *Indian Philosophical Quarterly,* 15: 1, pp. 85–97.

Darwall, Stephen (1995), *The British Moralists and the Internal 'Ought': 1640–1740,* Cambridge: Cambridge University Press.

Davis, Scott (1991), 'Irony and Argument in *Dialogues,* 12', *Religious Studies,* 27: 2, pp. 239–57.

de Pierris, Graciela (2001), 'Hume's Pyrrhonian Skepticism and the Belief in Causal Laws', *Journal of the History of Philosophy,* 39: 3, pp. 351–83.

Descartes, René (1964–74), *Ouvres de Descartes,* C. Adam and P. Tannery (eds), new edn, 11 vols, Paris: J. Vrin.

Descartes, René (1984), *The Philosophical Writings of Descartes,* 2 vols, trans. John Cottingham, Robert Stoothoff and Dugald Murdoch, Cambridge: Cambridge University Press.

Dickie, George (1974), *Art and The Aesthetic. An Institutional Analysis,* Ithaca: Cornell University Press.

Dickie, George (1996), *The Century of Taste: The Philosophical Odyssey of Taste in the Eighteenth Century*, Oxford: Oxford University Press.

Driver, Julia (2004), 'Pleasure as the Standard of Virtue in Hume's Moral Philosophy', *Pacific Philosophical Quarterly*, 85: 2, pp. 173–94.

Dryden, John (1962), *On Dramatic Poesy and Other Critical Essays*, ed. George Watson, London: Dent & Dutton.

Duff, William (1767), *An Essay on Original Genius; and Its Various Modes of Exertion in Philosophy and the Fine Arts, Particularly in Poetry*, London: Edward & Charles Dilly.

Durland, Karánn (2011), 'Extreme Skepticism and Commitment in the *Treatise*', *Hume Studies*, 37: 1, pp. 65–98.

Echelbarger, Charles (1997), 'Hume and the Logicians', in Patricia E. Easton (ed.), *Logic and the Workings of the Mind: The Logic of Ideas and Faulty Psychology in Early Modern Philosophy*, North American Kant Society Studies in Philosophy, vol. 5, Atascadero, CA: Ridgeview Publishing Company.

Engell, James (1981), *The Creative Imagination: Enlightenment to Romanticism*, Cambridge, MA: Harvard University Press.

Evnine, Simon (1993), 'Hume, Conjectural History, and the Uniformity of Human Nature', *Journal of the History of Philosophy*, 31: 4, pp. 589–606.

Falkenstein, Lorne (1997), 'Hume on Manner of Disposition and the Ideas of Space and Time', *Archiv für Geschichte der Philosophie*, 79: 2, pp. 179–201.

Falkenstein, Lorne (2003), 'Hume's Project in the Natural History of Religion', *Religious Studies*, 39: 1, pp. 1–21.

Falkenstein, Lorne (2009), 'Hume on "Genuine", "True", and "Rational" Religion', *Eighteenth-Century Thought*, 4, pp. 171–201.

Farr, James (1978), 'Hume, Hermeneutics, and History: A "Sympathetic" Account', *History and Theory*, 17: 3, pp. 285–310.

Faulkner, Paul (1998), 'David Hume's Reductionist Epistemology of Testimony', *Pacific Philosophical Quarterly*, 79: 4, pp. 302–13.

Fieser, James (1995), 'Hume's Concealed Attack on Religion and his Early Critics', *Journal of Philosophical Research*, 20, pp. 431–49.

Fleischacker, Samuel (2012), 'Sympathy in Hume and Smith: A Contrast, Critique, and Reconstruction', in Christel Fricke and Dagfinn Føllesdal (eds), *Intersubjectivity and Objectivity in Adam Smith and Edmund Husserl*, Frankfurt: Ontos, pp. 273–312.

Flew, Anthony (1961), *Hume's Philosophy of Belief: A Study of His First 'Inquiry'*, New York: Humanities Press.

Fodor, Jerry A. (2003), *Hume Variations*, Oxford: Oxford University Press.

Fogelin, Robert J. (2009), *Hume's Skeptical Crisis: A Textual Study*, Oxford: Oxford University Press.

Forbes, Duncan (1970), 'Introduction', in Duncan Forbes (ed.), *David Hume, The History of Great Britain: The Reigns of James I and Charles I*, Harmondsworth: Penguin.

Forbes, Duncan (1975), *Hume's Philosophical Politics*, Cambridge: Cambridge University Press.

Forster, Stephen Paul (1989), 'Different Religions and the Difference they Make: Hume on the Political Effects of Religious Ideology', *Modern Schoolman*, 66: 4, pp. 253–74.

Fóti, Véronique M. (1986), 'The Cartesian Imagination', *Philosophy and Phenomenological Research*, 46: 4, pp. 631–42.

Frasca-Spada, Marina (1990), 'Some Features of Hume's Conception of Space', *Studies in History and Philosophy of Science*, 21: 3, pp. 371–411.

Frasca-Spada, Marina (2003), 'Belief and Animal Spirits in Hume's *Treatise*', *Eighteenth-Century Thought*, I, pp. 151–69.

Frykholm, Erin (2016), 'Narrative and History in Hume's Moral Epistemology', *Journal of Scottish Philosophy*, 14: 1, pp. 21–50.

Furlong, E. J. (1961), *Imagination*, London: Allen & Unwin.

Garrett, Don (1997), *Cognition and Commitment in Hume's Philosophy*, Oxford: Oxford University Press.

Garrett, Don (2003), 'The Literary Arts in Hume's Science of the Fancy', *Kriterion*, 44: 108, pp. 161–79.

Garrett, Don (2006), 'Hume's Naturalistic Theory of Representation', *Synthese*, 152: 3, pp. 301–19.

Garrett, Don (2012), 'What's True About Hume's "True Religion"?', *Journal of Scottish Philosophy*, 10: 2, pp. 199–220.

Garrett, Don (2015), *Hume*, London: Routledge.

Gaskin, J. C. A. (1974), 'God, Hume, and Natural Belief', *Philosophy* 49: 189, pp. 281–94.

Gaskin, J. C. A. (1983), 'Hume's Attenuated Deism', *Archiv für Geschichte der Philosophie*, 65: 2, pp. 160–73.

Gaskin, J. C. A. [1978] (1988), *Hume's Philosophy of Religion*, 2nd edn, London: Palgrave Macmillan.

Gerard, Alexander [1759] (1780), *An Essay on Taste. To Which Is Now Added Part Fourth, Of the Standard of Taste; with Observations Concerning the Imitative Nature of Poetry*, 3rd edn, Edinburgh: J. Bell & W. Creech; London: T. Cadell.

Gerard, Alexander (1774), *An Essay on Genius*, London: W. Strahan; Edinburgh: W. Creech.

Gilbert, Katherine Everett and Helmut Kuhn [1939] (1972), *A History of Esthetics*, 2nd edn, rev., Westport, CT: Greenwood Publishers.

Goldman, Alvin I. (2002), *Pathways to Knowledge: Public and Private*, Oxford: Oxford University Press.

Gore, Willard Clarke (1902), *The Imagination in Spinoza and Hume: A Comparative Study in the Light of Some Recent Contributions to Psychology*, *University of Chicago Contributions to Philosophy*, 2: 4, Chicago: The University of Chicago Press.

Gracyk, Theodore A. (1994), 'Rethinking Hume's Standard of Taste', *Journal of Aesthetics and Art Criticism*, 52: 2, pp. 169–82.

Gurstein, Rochelle (2000), 'Taste and the "Conversible World" in the Eighteenth Century', *Journal of the History of Ideas*, 61: 2, pp. 203–21.

Guyer, Paul (1993), 'The Standard of Taste and the "Most Ardent Desire of Society"', in Ted Cohen, Paul Guyer and Hilary Putman (eds), *Pursuits of Reason: Essays in Honor of Stanley Cavell*, Lubbock: Texas Tech University Press, pp. 37–66.

Guyer, Paul (2014a), *A History of Modern Aesthetics*, vol. 1, *The Eighteenth Century*, Cambridge: Cambridge University Press.

Guyer, Paul (2014b), *A History of Modern Aesthetics*, vol. 2, *The Nineteenth Century*, Cambridge: Cambridge University Press.

Halberstadt, William H. (1971), 'A Problem in Hume's Aesthetics', *Journal of Aesthetics and Art Criticism*, 30: 2, pp. 209–14.

Hall, Roland (1989), 'Some Uses of Imagination in the British Empiricists: A Preliminary Investigation of Locke, as Contrasted with Hume', *The Locke Newsletter: An Annual Journal of Locke Research*, 20, pp. 47–62.

Hardin, Russell (2007), *David Hume: Moral and Political Theorist*, Oxford: Oxford University Press.

Harris, James A. (2015), *Hume: An Intellectual Biography*, Cambridge: Cambridge University Press.

Harrison, Jonathan (1976), *Hume's Moral Epistemology*, Oxford: Clarendon Press.

Harrison, Jonathan (1981), *Hume's Theory of Justice*, Oxford: Clarendon Press.

Hatfield, Gary (1998), 'The Cognitive Faculties', in Daniel Garber and Michael Ayers (eds), *The Cambridge History of Seventeenth-Century Philosophy*, 2 vols, Cambridge: Cambridge University Press, 2, pp. 953–1002.

Hendel, Charles W. [1925] (1963), *Studies in the Philosophy of David Hume*, 2nd edn, Indianapolis: Bobbs Merrill.

Herdt, Jennifer A. (1997), *Religion and Faction in Hume's Moral Philosophy*, Cambridge: Cambridge University Press.

Hobbes, Thomas [1651] (1991), *Leviathan, or the Matter, Forme, and Power of a Common-wealth Ecclesiasticall and Civill*, ed. Richard Tuck, Cambridge: Cambridge University Press.

Holden, Thomas (2010), *Spectres of False Divinity: Hume's Moral Atheism*, Oxford: Oxford University Press.

Holley, David M. (2002), 'The Role of Anthropomorphism in Hume's Critique of Theism', *International Journal for Philosophy of Religion*, 51: 2, pp. 83–99.

Home, Henry, Lord Kames [1785; 1st edn 1762] (2005), *Elements of Criticism: The Sixth Edition. With the Author's Last Corrections and Additions*, 2 vols, Indianapolis: Liberty Fund.

Horace (1926), *Satires, Epistles, and Art of Poetry*, trans. H. Rushton Fairclough, Loeb Classical Library, Cambridge, MA: Harvard University Press.

Hume, David (1969), *The Letters of David Hume*, ed. J. Y. T. Greig, 2 vols, Oxford: Oxford University Press.

Hume, David [1888] (1974), *Enquiries Concerning Human Understanding and Concerning the Principles of Morals, Reprinted from the 1777 edition with Introduction and Analytical Index by L.A. Selby-Bigge*, Oxford: Clarendon Press.

Hume, David [1888] (1978), *A Treatise of Human Nature*, ed. with an analytic index by L. A. Selby-Bigge, 2nd edn, rev. with variant readings by P. H. Nidditch, Oxford: Oxford University Press.

Hume, David (1983), *The History of England, From the Invasion of Julius Caesar to the Revolution in 1688*, based on the 1778 edition with the author's last corrections and improvements, ed. William B. Todd, 6 vols, Indianapolis: Liberty Fund.

Hume, David (1985), *Essays: Moral, Political, and Literary*, ed. Eugene F. Miller, Indianapolis: Liberty Fund.

Hume, David [1751] (1998), *An Enquiry Concerning the Principles of Morals*, ed. Tom L. Beauchamp, Oxford: Oxford University Press.

Hume, David [1748] (1999), *An Enquiry Concerning Human Understanding*, ed. Tom L. Beauchamp, Oxford: Oxford University Press.

Hume, David [1738] (2001), *A Treatise of Human Nature*, ed. David Fate Norton and Mary Norton, Oxford: Oxford University Press.

Hume, David [1779] (2007a), *Dialogues Concerning Natural Religion and Other Writings on Religion*, ed. Dorothy Coleman, Cambridge: Cambridge University Press.

Hume, David [1757] (2007b), *A Dissertation on the Passions; The Natural History of Religion*, ed. Tom L. Beauchamp, Oxford: Clarendon Press.

Hutcheson, Francis [1726] (2004), *An Inquiry into the Original of Our Ideas of Beauty and Virtue in Two Treatises*, 2nd edn, Indianapolis: Liberty Fund.

Immerwahr, John (1991), 'The Anatomist and the Painter: The Continuity of Hume's Treatise and Essays', *Hume Studies*, 17: 1, pp. 1–14.

Immerwahr, John (1996), 'Hume's Aesthetic Theism', *Hume Studies, 22*: 2, pp. 325–37.

James, D. G. (1949), *The Life of Reason: Hobbes, Locke, Bolingbroke*, London: Longmans.

Johnson, Oliver (1987), '"Lively" Memory and "Past" Memory', *Hume Studies, 13*: 2, pp. 343–59.

Jones, Peter (1976), 'Hume's Aesthetics Reassessed', *Philosophical Quarterly*, 26, pp. 48–62.

Jones, Peter (1982), *Hume's Sentiments: Their Ciceronian and French Context*, Edinburgh: Edinburgh University Press.

Jones, Peter (1993), 'Hume's Literary and Aesthetic Theory', in David Fate Norton (ed.), *The Cambridge Companion to Hume*, Cambridge: Cambridge University Press, pp. 255–80.

Kail, P. J. E. (2007a), *Projection and Realism in Hume's Philosophy*, Oxford: Oxford University Press.

Kail, P. J. E. (2007b), 'Understanding Hume's Natural History of Religion', *Philosophical Quarterly*, 57: 227, pp. 190–211.

Kant, Immanuel (1902), *Kritik der reinen Vernunft. Kants gesammelte Schriften, herausgegeben von der Deutschen* (formerly *Königlich Preussischen) Akademie der Wissenschaften*, 29 vols, Berlin: Walter de Gruyter [and predecessors], vols 3 and 4.

Kearney, Richard (1988), *The Wake of Imagination: Ideas of Creativity in Western Culture*, London: Hutchinson.

Keats, John (1970), *The Poetical and Other Writings of John Keats, Hampstead Edition*, ed. H. Buxton Forman, rev. Maurice Buxton Forman, 8 vols, New York: Phaeton Press.

Kemp Smith, Norman (1905a), 'The Naturalism of David Hume (I)', *Mind*, 14: 54, pp. 149–73.

Kemp Smith, Norman (1905b), 'The Naturalism of David Hume (II)', *Mind*, 14: 55, pp. 335–47.

Kemp Smith, Norman (1941), *The Philosophy of David Hume*, London: Macmillan.

Kemp Smith, Norman [1935] (1947), 'Introduction', in *Hume's Dialogues Concerning Natural Religion*, ed. Norman Kemp Smith, 2nd edn, London: Thomas Nelson & Sons.

Kivy, Peter (1983), 'Hume's Neighbour's Wife: An Essay on the Evolution of Hume's Aesthetics', *British Journal of Aesthetics*, 23: 3, pp. 195–208.

Kivy, Peter [1976] (2003), *The Seventh Sense: Francis Hutcheson and Eighteenth-Century British Aesthetics*, 2nd edn, rev., Oxford: Clarendon Press.

Korsgaard, Christine M. (1996), *The Sources of Normativity*, Cambridge: Cambridge University Press.

Korsgaard, Christine M. (1999), 'The General Point of View: Love and Moral Approval in Hume's Ethics', *Hume Studies*, 25: 1 and 2, pp. 3–51.

Korsmeyer, Carolyn W. (1976), 'Hume and the Foundations of Taste', *Journal of Aesthetics and Art Criticism*, 35: 2, pp. 201–15.

Kuehn, Manfred (1983), 'Hume's Antinomies', *Hume Studies*, 9: 1, pp. 25–45.

Kydd, Rachel M. (1946), *Reason and Conduct in Hume's Treatise*, Oxford: Oxford University Press.

Lackey, Jennifer and Ernest Sosa (eds) (2006), *The Epistemology of Testimony*, Oxford: Oxford University Press.

Laird, John (1932), *Hume's Philosophy of Human Nature*, London: Methuen.

Land, Stephen K. (1974), *From Signs to Propositions: The Concept of Form in Eighteenth-Century Semantic Theory*, London: Longman.

Lemmens, Willem (2011), '"Beyond the Calm Sunshine of the Mind": Hume on Religion and Morality', *Aufklärung und Kritik*, 37, pp. 214–40.

Livingston, Donald W. (1974–5), 'Anscombe, Hume and Julius Caesar', *Analysis*, 35: 1, pp. 13–19.

Livingston, Donald W. (1984), *Hume's Philosophy of Common Life*, Chicago: Chicago University Press.

Livingston, Donald W. (1986), 'Hume's Conception of True Religion', in Anthony Flew, Donald Livingston, George I. Mavrodes, and David Fate Norton (eds), *Hume's Philosophy of Religion: The Sixth James Montgomery Hester Seminar*, Winston-Salem: Wake Forest University Press, pp. 33–73.

Livingston, Donald W. (1998), *Philosophical Melancholy and Delirium: Hume's Pathology of Philosophy*, Chicago: Chicago University Press.

Locke, John [1689] (1975), *An Essay Concerning Human Understanding*, ed. P. H. Nidditch, Oxford: Oxford University Press.

Loeb, Louis E. (2002), *Stability and Justification in Hume's 'Treatise'*, Oxford: Oxford University Press.

Logan, Beryl (1993), *A Religion Without Talking: Religious Belief and Natural Belief in Hume's Philosophy of Religion*, Dordrecht: Nijhoff.

Long, Douglas (1998), 'Hume's "Imagination" Revisited', *Lumen; Selected Proceedings from the Canadian Society for Eighteenth-Century Studies*, 17, pp. 127–49.

Long, Douglas (2013), 'Hume's Historiographical Imagination', in Mark G. Spencer (ed.), *David Hume: Historical Thinker, Historical Writer*, University Park: The Pennsylvania State University Press, pp. 201–24.

Mackie, J. L. (1980), *Hume's Moral Theory*, London: Routledge & Kegan Paul.

Malebranche, Nicolas (1958–84), *Oeuvres complètes de Malebranche*, ed. A. Robinet, 20 vols, Paris: J. Vrin.

McArthur, Neil (2007), *David Hume's Political Theory: Law, Commerce, and the Constitution of Government*, Toronto: University of Toronto Press.

McGinn, Colin (2004), *Mindsight: Image, Dream, Meaning*, Cambridge, MA: Harvard University Press.

McRae, Robert (1980), 'The Import of Hume's Theory of Time', *Hume Studies*, 6: 2, pp. 119–32.

Mercer, Phillip (1972), *Sympathy and Ethics: A Study of the Relationship between Sympathy and Morality with Special Reference to Hume's 'Treatise'*, Oxford: Clarendon Press.

Miller, David (1981), *Philosophy and Ideology in Hume's Political Thought*, Oxford: Clarendon Press.

Morrow, Glenn R. (1923), 'The Significance of the Doctrine of Sympathy in Hume and Adam Smith', *Philosophical Review*, 32: 1, pp. 60–78.

Moses, Gregory (1989), 'David Hume as Philosophical Historian', *Australian Journal of Politics and History*, 35: 1, pp. 80–91.

Mossner, Ernest Campbell [1954] (1980), *The Life of David Hume*, 2nd edn, Oxford: Oxford University Press.

Mossner, Ernest Campbell (1967), 'Hume's "Of Criticism"', in Howard Anderson and John S. Shea (eds), *Studies in Criticism and Aesthetics, 1660–1800: Essays in Honor of Samuel Holt Monk*, Minneapolis: University of Minnesota Press, pp. 232–48.

Mothersill, Mary (1989), 'Hume and the Paradox of Taste', in George Dickie, Richard Scalfani and Ronald Roblin (eds), *Aesthetics: A Critical Anthology*, 2nd edn, New York: St. Martin's Press, pp. 269–86.

Neill, Alex (1992), 'Yanal and Others on Hume and Tragedy', *Journal of Aesthetics and Art Criticism*, 50: 2, pp. 151–4.

Neill, Alex (1999), 'Hume's Singular Phænomenon', *British Journal of Aesthetics*, 39: 2, pp. 112–25.

Nietzsche, Friedrich [1876] (1997), *Untimely Meditations*, trans. R. J. Hollingdale, Cambridge: Cambridge University Press.

Noonan, Harold W. (1999), *Hume On Knowledge*, New York: Routledge.

Norton, David Fate (1965), 'History and Philosophy in Hume's Thought', in David Fate Norton and Richard Popkin (eds), *David Hume: Philosophical Historian*, New York: Bobbs-Merrill.

Noxon, James (1961), 'Hume's Opinion of Critics', *Journal of Aesthetics and Art Criticism*, 20: 2, pp. 157–62.

Noxon, James (1966), 'Hume's Agnosticism', in V. C. Chappell (ed.), *Hume: A Collection of Critical Essays*, New York: Garden City, pp. 361–83.

Oakeshotte, Michael [1962] (1991), *Rationalism in Politics and Other Essays*, new and expanded edn, Indianapolis: Liberty Fund.

O'Connor, David (2001), *Hume on Religion*, London: Routledge.

Okie, Laird (1985), 'Ideology and Partiality in David Hume's *History of England*', *Hume Studies*, 11: 1, pp. 1–32.

Oldfield, Adrian (1981), 'Moral Judgments in History', *History and Theory*, 20: 3, pp. 260–77.

Osborne, Harold (1979), 'Some Theories of Aesthetic Judgment', *Journal of Aesthetics and Art Criticism*, 38: 2, pp. 135–44.

Owen, David (1999), *Hume's Reason*, Oxford: Oxford University Press.

Packer, Mark (1989), 'Dissolving the Paradox of Tragedy', *Journal of Aesthetics and Art Criticism*, 47: 3, pp. 211–19.

Passmore, J. A. (1952), *Hume's Intentions*, Cambridge: Cambridge University Press.

Paton, Margaret (1973), 'Hume on Tragedy', *British Journal of Aesthetics*, 13: 2, pp. 121–32.

Pears, David (1990), *Hume's System: An Examination of the First Book of his 'Treatise'*, Oxford: Oxford University Press.

Penelhum, Terence (1979), 'Hume's Skepticism and the *Dialogues*', in David Fate Norton, Nicolas Capaldi and Wade L. Robeson (eds), *McGill Hume Studies*, San Diego: Austin Hill, pp. 253–78.

Penelhum, Terence (1983), 'Natural Belief and Religious Belief in Hume's Philosophy', *Philosophical Quarterly*, 33: 131, pp. 166–81.

Penelhum, Terence (1987), *God and Skepticism: A Study in Skepticism and Fideism*, Dordrecht: Reidel Publishing Company.

Penelhum, Terence (1992), *Hume: An Introduction to his Philosophical System*, West Lafayette: Purdue University Press.

Phillipson, Nicholas (1979), 'Hume as Moralist: A Social Historian's Perspective', *Philosophers of the Enlightenment, Royal Institute of Philosophy Lectures*, vol. 12, 1977–8, Atlantic Highlands, NJ: Humanities Press, pp. 140–61.

Pike, Nelson (1970), 'Hume on the Argument from Design', in Nelson Pike (ed.), *Hume: Dialogues Concerning Natural Religion*, Indianapolis: Bobbs-Merrill.

Pitson, A. E. (1996), 'Sympathy and Other Selves', *Hume Studies*, 22: 2, pp. 255–72.

Pitson, A. E. (2002), *Hume's Philosophy of the Self*, London: Routledge.

Pitson, Tony (2006), 'George Campbell's Critique of Hume on Testimony', *Journal of Scottish Philosophy*, 4: 1, pp. 1–15.

Plato (1997), *The Complete Works of Plato*, ed. John M. Cooper, Indianapolis: Hackett.

Popkin, Richard H. (1976), 'David Hume: Philosophical Versus Prophetic Historian', in Kenneth R. Merill and Robert W. Shahan (eds), *David Hume: Many-sided Genius*, Norman: University of Oklahoma Press, pp. 83–95.

Popkin, Richard H. (1980), 'Editor's Introduction', in Richard H. Popkin (ed.), *David Hume, Dialogues Concerning Natural Religion and the Posthumous Essays*, Indianapolis: Hackett.

Postema, Gerald J. (2005), '"Cemented with Diseased Qualities": Sympathy and Comparison in Hume's Moral Psychology', *Hume Studies*, 31: 2, pp. 249–98.

Potkay, Adam (1994), *The Fate of Eloquence in the Age of Hume*, Ithaca: Cornell University Press.

Potkay, Adam (2000), *The Passion for Happiness: Samuel Johnson and David Hume*, Ithaca: Cornell University Press.

Potkay, Adam (2001), 'Hume's "Supplement to Gulliver": the medieval volumes of *The History of England*', *Eighteenth-Century Life*, 25: 2, pp. 32–46.

Price, H. H. (1940), *Hume's Theory of the External World*, Oxford: Clarendon Press.

Price, John Vladimir (1965), *The Ironic Hume*, Austin: University of Texas Press.

Radcliffe, Elizabeth S. (1994), 'Hume on Motivating Sentiments, the General Point of View, and the Inculcation of "Morality"', *Hume Studies*, 20: 1, pp. 37–58.

Railton, Peter (1998), 'Aesthetic Value, Moral Value, and the Ambitions of Naturalism', in Jerrold Levinson (ed.), *Aesthetics and Ethics: Essays at the Intersection*, Cambridge: Cambridge University Press, pp. 59–105.

Randall, J. H., Jr (1947), 'David Hume: Radical Empiricist and

Pragmatist', in S. Hook and M. R. Konvitz (eds), *Freedom and Experience: Essays Presented to Horace M. Kallen*, Ithaca: Cornell University Press, pp. 289–312.

Reid, Thomas [1764] (1997), *An Inquiry into the Human Mind on the Principles of Common Sense*, ed. Derek R. Brookes, Edinburgh: Edinburgh University Press.

Reynolds, Sir Joshua [1797] (1997), *Discourses on Art*, ed. Robert R. Wark, New Haven: Yale University Press.

Richetti, John J. (1983), *Philosophical Writing: Locke, Berkeley, Hume*, Cambridge, MA: Harvard University Press.

Root, Michael (2001), 'Hume on the Virtues of Testimony', *American Philosophical Quarterly*, 38: 1 pp. 19–35.

Roth, Robert J. (1991), 'David Hume on Religion in England', *Thought: A Journal of Philosophy*, 66, pp. 51–64.

Ruskin, John (1903–12), *The Complete Works of John Ruskin (Library Edition)*, ed. E. T. Cook and Alexander Wedderburn, 39 vols, London: George Allen.

Russell, Paul (2008), *The Riddle of Hume's Treatise: Skepticism, Naturalism, and Irreligion*, New York: Oxford University Press.

Sabl, Andrew (2012), *Hume's Politics. Coordination and Crisis in the 'History of England'*, Princeton: Princeton University Press.

Sayre-McCord, Geoffrey (1994), 'On Why Hume's "General Point of View" Isn't Ideal – and Shouldn't Be', *Social Philosophy and Policy*, 11: 1, pp. 202–28.

Schmidt, Claudia M. (2013), 'David Hume as a Philosopher of History', in Mark G. Spencer (ed.), *David Hume: Historical Thinker, Historical Writer*, University Park: The Pennsylvania State University Press, pp. 161–79.

Schmitt, Frederick F. (1987), 'Justification, Sociality, and Autonomy', *Synthese*, 73: 1, pp. 43–85.

Schneewind, J. B. (1998), *The Invention of Autonomy: A History of Modern Moral Philosophy*, Cambridge: Cambridge University Press.

Sepper, Dennis L. (1996), *Descartes' Imagination: Proportion, Images, and the Activity of Thinking*, Berkeley: University of California Press.

Sessions, William Lad (2002), *Reading Hume's Dialogues: A Veneration for True Religion*, Bloomington: University of Indiana Press.

Shaver, Robert (1995), 'Hume's Moral Theory?', *History of Philosophy Quarterly*, 12: 3, pp. 317–31.

Shelley, James (1998), 'Hume and the Nature of Taste', *Journal of Aesthetics and Art Criticism*, 56: 1, pp. 29–38.

Shiner, Roger A. (1996), 'Hume and the Causal Theory of Taste', *Journal of Aesthetics and Art Criticism,* 54: 3, pp. 237–49.

Siebert, Donald T. (1984), 'Hume on Idolatry and Incarnation', *Journal of the History of Ideas,* 45: 3, pp. 379–96.

Siebert, Donald T. (1989), 'The Sentimental Sublime in Hume's *History of England*', *Review of English Studies, New Series,* 40: 159, pp. 352–72.

Siebert, Donald T. (1990), *The Moral Animus of David Hume,* Newark: University of Delaware Press.

Skinner, Andrew S. (1974), 'Adam Smith, Science and the Role of Imagionation', in William B. Todd (ed.), *Hume and the Enlightenment: Essays Presented to Ernest Campbell Mossner,* Edinburgh: Edinburgh University Press.

Smith, Adam [1759] (1976), *The Theory of Moral Sentiments,* ed. D. D. Raphael and A. L. Macfie, *The Glasgow Edition of the Works and Correspondence of Adam Smith,* 7 vols, Oxford: Oxford University Press, vol 1.

Sokolowski, Robert (1968), 'Fiction and Illusion in David Hume's Philosophy', *The Modern Schoolman,* 45: 3, pp. 189–225.

Spinoza, Baruch (1985), *The Collected Works of Spinoza,* ed. and trans. Edwin Curley, Princeton: Princeton University Press.

Stewart, Carole (1976), 'The Moral Point of View', *Philosophy,* 51: 196, pp. 177–87.

Stewart, Dugald (1854–60), *The Collected Works of Dugald Stewart,* ed. Sir William Hamilton, 11 vols, Edinburgh: Thomas Constable & Co.

Stewart, John B. (1963), *The Moral and Political Philosophy of David Hume,* New York: Columbia University Press.

Stewart, John B. (1992), *Opinion and Reform in Hume's Political Philosophy,* Princeton: Princeton University Press.

Strawson, Galen (2011), *The Evident Connexion: Hume on Personal Identity,* Oxford: Oxford University Press.

Strawson, Galen [1989] (2014), *The Secret Connexion: Causation, Realism, and David Hume,* 2nd edn, Oxford: Oxford University Press.

Strawson, P. F. (1970), 'Imagination and Perception', in Lawrence Foster and J. W. Swanson (eds), *Experience and Theory,* Cambridge, MA: MIT Press, pp. 31–54.

Streminger, Gerhard (1980), 'Hume's Theory of Imagination', *Hume Studies,* 6: 2, pp. 91–118.

Stroud, Barry (1977), *Hume,* London: Routledge.

Stroud, Barry (1991), 'Hume's Scepticism: Natural Instincts and Philosophical Reflection', *Philosophical Topics,* 19: 1, pp. 271–91;

reprinted in Barry Stroud (2011), *Philosophers Past and Present*, Oxford: Oxford University Press, pp. 144–66.

Stroud, Barry (1993), '"Guilding and Staining" the World with "Sentiments" and "Phantoms"', *Hume Studies*, 19: 2, pp. 253–72.

Sugg, Redding S., Jr (1957), 'Hume's Search for the Key with the Leather Thong', *Journal of Aesthetics and Art Criticism*, 16: 1, pp. 96–102.

Susato, Ryu (2015), *Hume's Sceptical Enlightenment*, Edinburgh: Edinburgh University Press.

Taylor, Jacqueline A. (2002), 'Hume on the Standard of Virtue', *Journal of Ethics*, 6: 1, pp. 43–62.

Taylor, Jacqueline A. (2015), *Reflecting Subjects: Passion, Sympathy, and Society in Hume's Philosophy*, Oxford: Oxford University Press.

Taylor, William (1813), '*Imagination, Fancy*', in William Taylor, *British Synonyms Discriminated*, London: W. Pople.

Thiel, Udo (2011), *The Early Modern Subject: Self-consciousness and Personal Identity from Descartes to Hume*, Oxford: Oxford University Press.

Townsend, Dabney (2001), *Hume's Aesthetic Theory: Taste and Sentiment*, London: Routledge.

Traiger, Saul (1987), 'Impressions, Ideas, and Fictions', *Hume Studies*, 13: 2, pp. 381–99.

Traiger, Saul (1993), 'Humean Testimony', *Pacific Philosophical Quarterly*, 74: 2, pp. 135–49.

Traiger, Saul (2008), 'Hume on Memory and Imagination', in Elizabeth S. Radcliffe (ed.), *A Companion to Hume*, Oxford: Blackwell, pp. 58–71.

Traiger, Saul (2010), 'Experience and Testimony in Hume's Philosophy', *Episteme*, 7: 1, pp. 42–57.

Tweyman, Stanley (1986), *Scepticism and Belief in Hume's Dialogues Concerning Natural Religion*, Dordrecht: Martinus Nijhoff.

Van Cleve, James (2006), 'Reid on the Credit of Human Testimony', in Jennifer Lackey and Ernest Sosa (eds), *The Epistemology of Testimony*, Oxford: Oxford University Press, pp. 50–74.

Van Inwagen, Peter, and Meghan Sullivan (2015), 'Metaphysics', *The Stanford Encyclopedia of Philosophy* (Spring 2015 edition), ed. Edward N. Zalta, http://plato.stanford.edu/archives/spr2015/entries/metaphysics/ (last accessed 30 July 2017).

Warnock, Mary (1976), *Imagination*, Berkeley: University of California Press.

Waxman, Wayne (1992), 'Hume's Quandary Concerning Personal Identity', *Hume Studies*, 18: 2, pp. 233–54.

Waxman, Wayne (1994), *Hume's Theory of Consciousness*, Cambridge: Cambridge University Press.

Webb, Mark (1991), 'The Argument of the *Natural History*', *Hume Studies*, 17: 2, pp. 141–59.

Webb, Mark Owen (1993), 'Why I Know About as Much as You: A Reply to Hardwig', *Journal of Philosophy*, 90: 5, pp. 260–70.

Welbourne, Michael (1981), 'The Community of Knowledge', *Philosophical Quarterly*, 31: 125, pp. 302–14.

Welbourne, Michael (2001), *Knowledge*, Montreal: McGill-Queen's University Press.

Welbourne, Michael (2002), 'Is Hume Really a Reductivist?', *Studies in History and Philosophy of Science*, 33: 2, pp. 407–23.

Welburn, Andrew J. (1989), *The Truth of Imagination*, New York: St Martin's Press.

Wertz, S. K. (1994), 'Collingwood's Understanding of Hume', *Hume Studies*, 20: 2, pp. 261–87.

Wertz, S. K. (1996), 'Moral Judgments in History: Hume's Position', *Hume Studies*, 22: 2, pp. 339–67.

Wexler, Victor G. (1976–7), 'David Hume's Discovery of a New Scene of Historical Thought', *Eighteenth-Century Studies*, 10: 2, pp. 185–202.

Wexler, Victor G. (1979), *David Hume and the 'History of England'*, Philadelphia: The American Philosophical Society.

Wheatley, Christopher J. (1986), 'Polemical Aspects of Hume's Natural History of Religion', *Eighteenth-Century Studies*, 19: 4, pp. 502–14.

Whelan, Frederick G. (1985), *Order and Artifice in Hume's Political Philosophy*, Princeton: Princeton University Press.

White, Alan R. (1990), *The Language of Imagination*, Oxford: Basil Blackwell.

Wieand, Jeffrey (1984), 'Hume's Two Standards of Taste', *Philosophical Quarterly*, 34: 135, pp. 129–42.

Wiener, Philip P. (1974), 'Kant and Hume on Reason and Experience in Ethics', in William B. Todd (ed.), *Hume and the Enlightenment: Essays Presented to Ernest Campbell Mossner*, Edinburgh: Edinburgh University Press.

Wilbanks, Jan (1968), *Hume's Theory of Imagination*, The Hague: Martinus Nijhoff.

Willis, Andre C. (2015), *Toward a Humean True Religion: Genuine Theism, Moderate Hope, and Practical Morality*, University Park: Pennsylvania State University Press.

Wilson, Fred (2010), 'Hume and the Role of Testimony in Knowledge', *Episteme*, 7: 1, pp. 58–78.

Winkler, Kenneth (1999), 'Hume's Inductive Skepticism', in Margaret Atherton (ed.), *The Empiricists: Critical Essays on Locke, Berkeley, and Hume*, Lanham, MD: Rowman & Littlefield, pp. 183–212.

Winters, Barbara (1979), 'Hume on Reason', *Hume Studies*, 5: 1, pp. 20–35.

Wordsworth, William (1974), 'Preface to the Edition of 1815', in W. J. B. Owen and Jane Washington Smyser (eds), *The Prose Works of William Wordsworth*, 3 vols, Oxford: Clarendon Press, vol. 3, pp. 26–39.

Wright, John P. (1983), *The Sceptical Realism of David Hume*, Minneapolis: University of Minnesota Press.

Wright, John P. (2003), 'George Cheyne, Chevalier Ramsay, and Hume's Letter to a Physician', *Hume Studies*, 29: 1, pp. 125–41.

Wright, Sarah (2011), 'Hume on Testimony: A Virtue-Theoretic Defense', *History of Philosophy Quarterly*, 28: 3, pp. 247–65.

Yandell, Keith E. (1990), *Hume's 'Inexplicable Mystery': His Views on Religion*, Philadelphia: Temple University Press.

Zangwill, Nick (1994), 'Hume, Taste, and Teleology', *Philosophical Papers*, 23: 1, pp. 1–18.

Index

EU representative:
Easy Access System Europe
Mustamäe tee 50, 10621 Tallinn, Estonia
Gpsr.requests@easproject.com

www.ingramcontent.com/pod-product-compliance
Lightning Source LLC
Chambersburg PA
CBHW050628280326
41932CB00015B/2566